Ōoku

 THE INNER CHAMBERS

by **Fumi Yoshinaga**

VOL. **5**

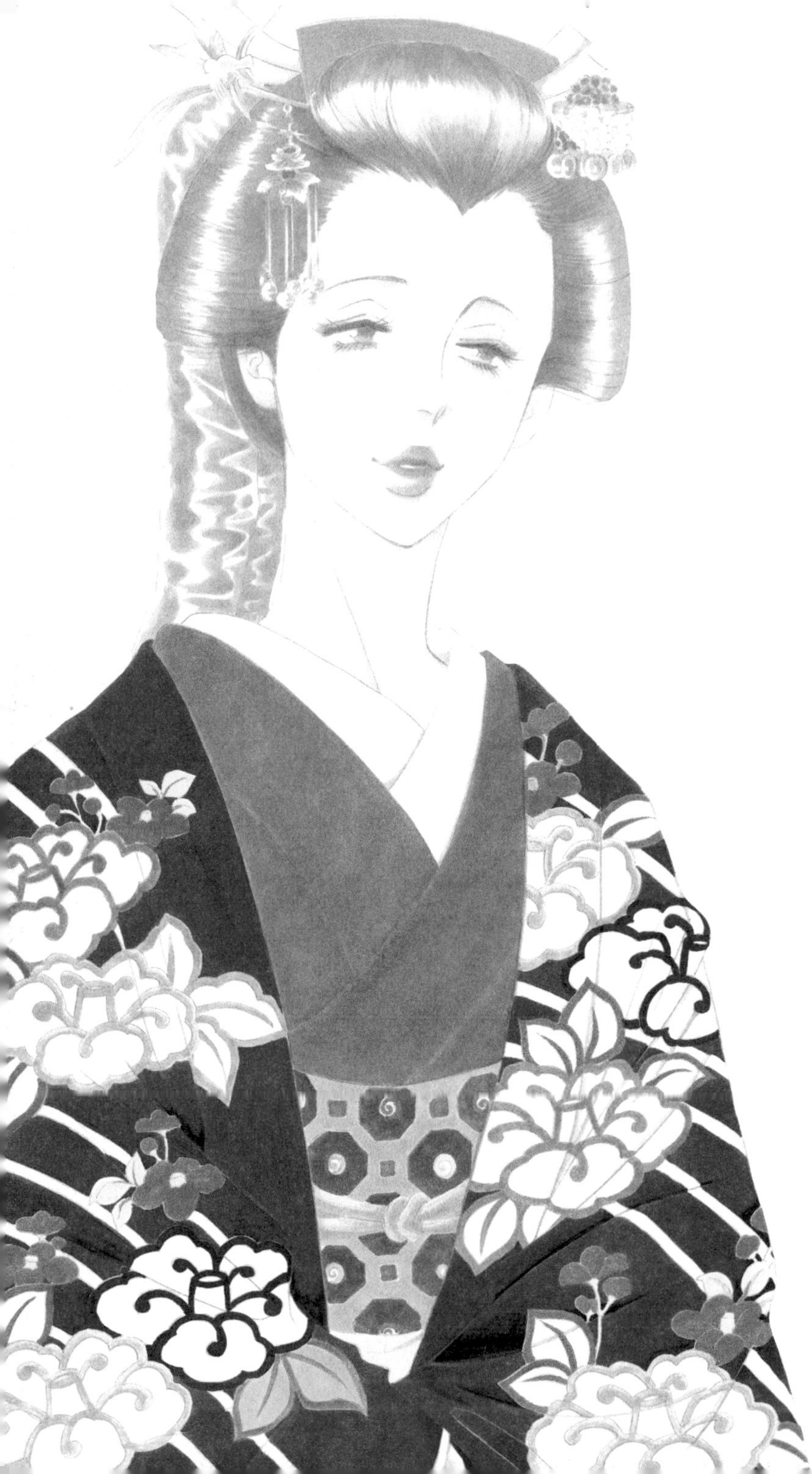

TABLE *of* CONTENTS

Ōoku

THE INNER CHAMBERS

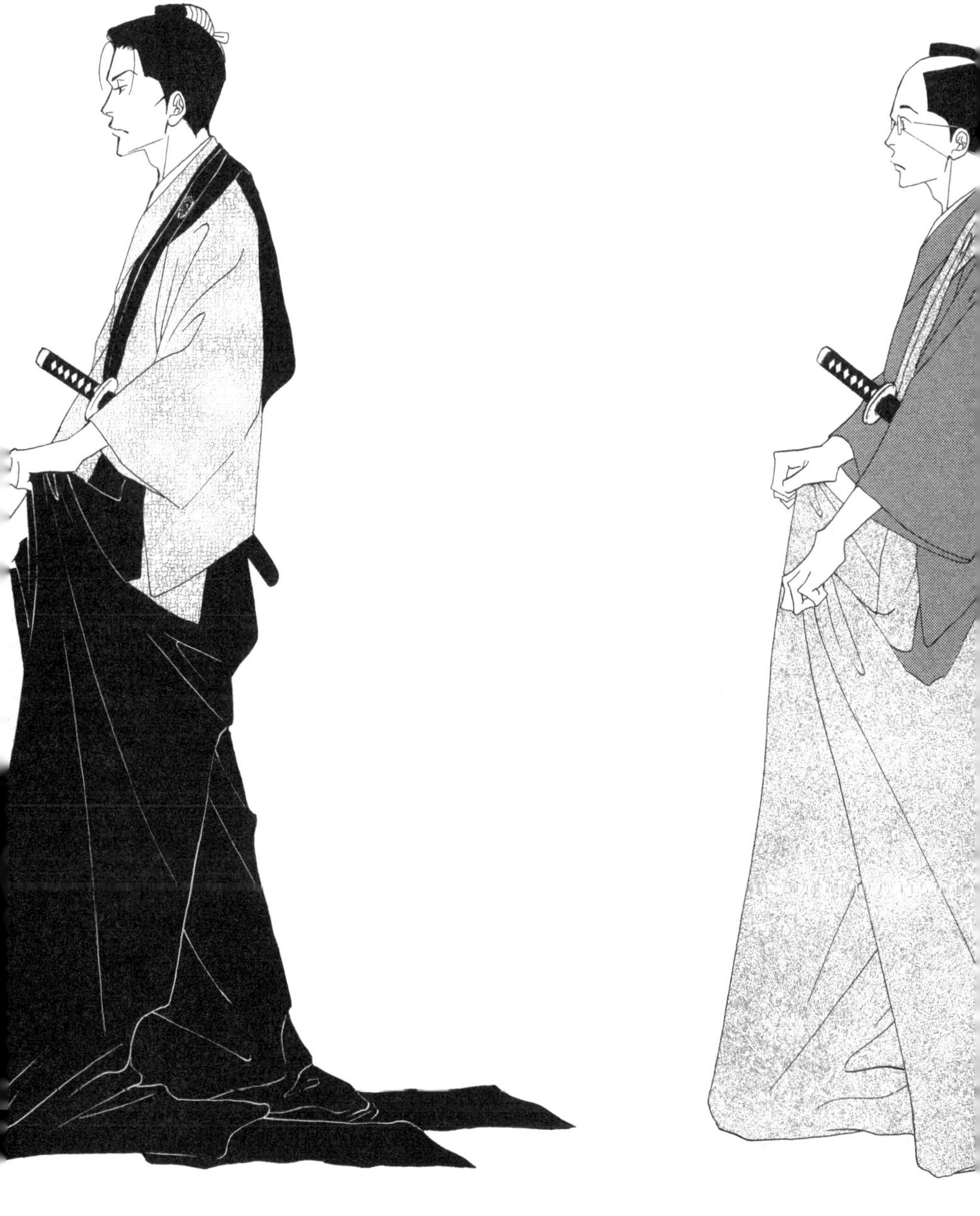

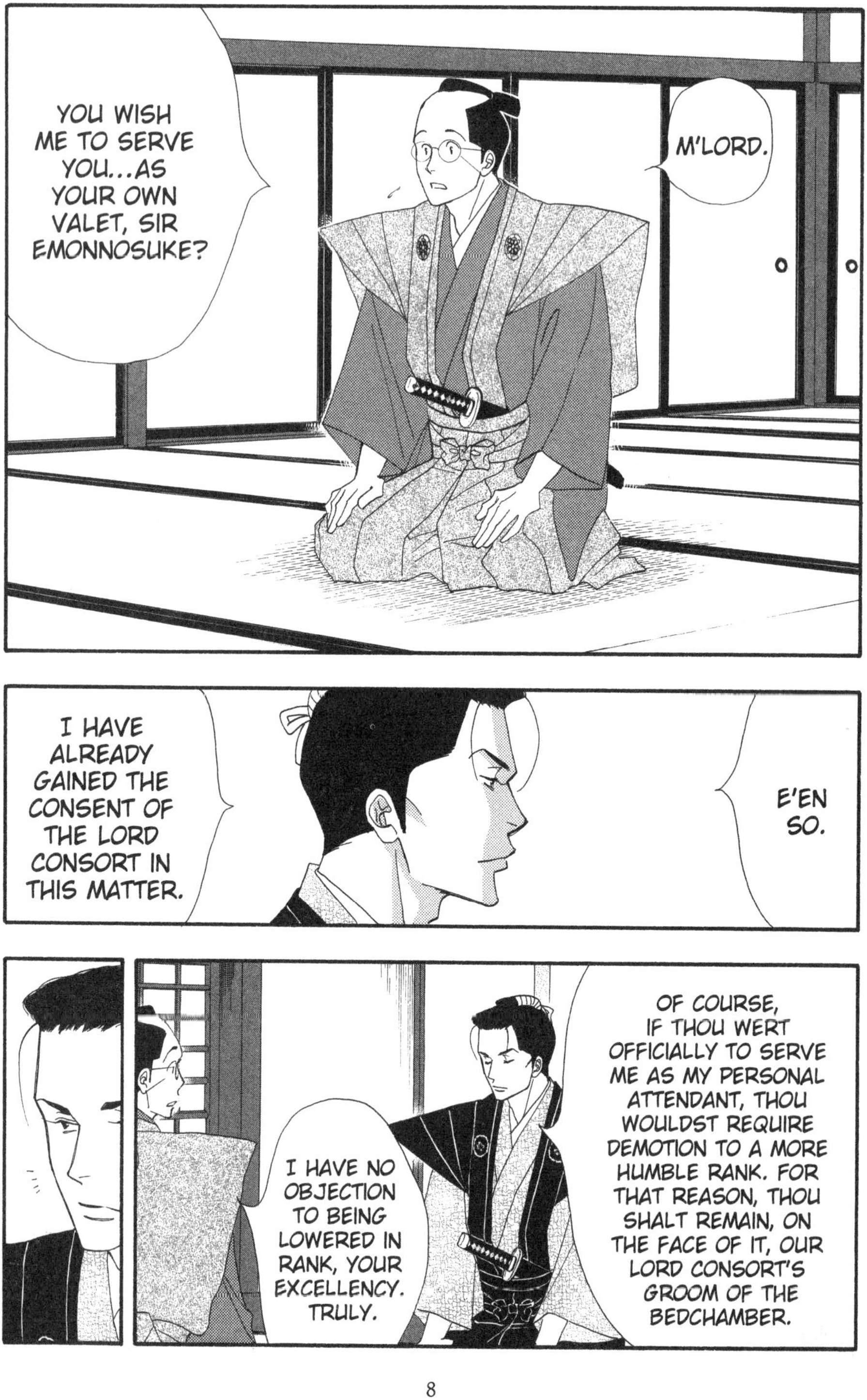
M'LORD.
YOU WISH ME TO SERVE YOU...AS YOUR OWN VALET, SIR EMONNOSUKE?
E'EN SO.
I HAVE ALREADY GAINED THE CONSENT OF THE LORD CONSORT IN THIS MATTER.
OF COURSE, IF THOU WERT OFFICIALLY TO SERVE ME AS MY PERSONAL ATTENDANT, THOU WOULDST REQUIRE DEMOTION TO A MORE HUMBLE RANK. FOR THAT REASON, THOU SHALT REMAIN, ON THE FACE OF IT, OUR LORD CONSORT'S GROOM OF THE BEDCHAMBER.
I HAVE NO OBJECTION TO BEING LOWERED IN RANK, YOUR EXCELLENCY. TRULY.

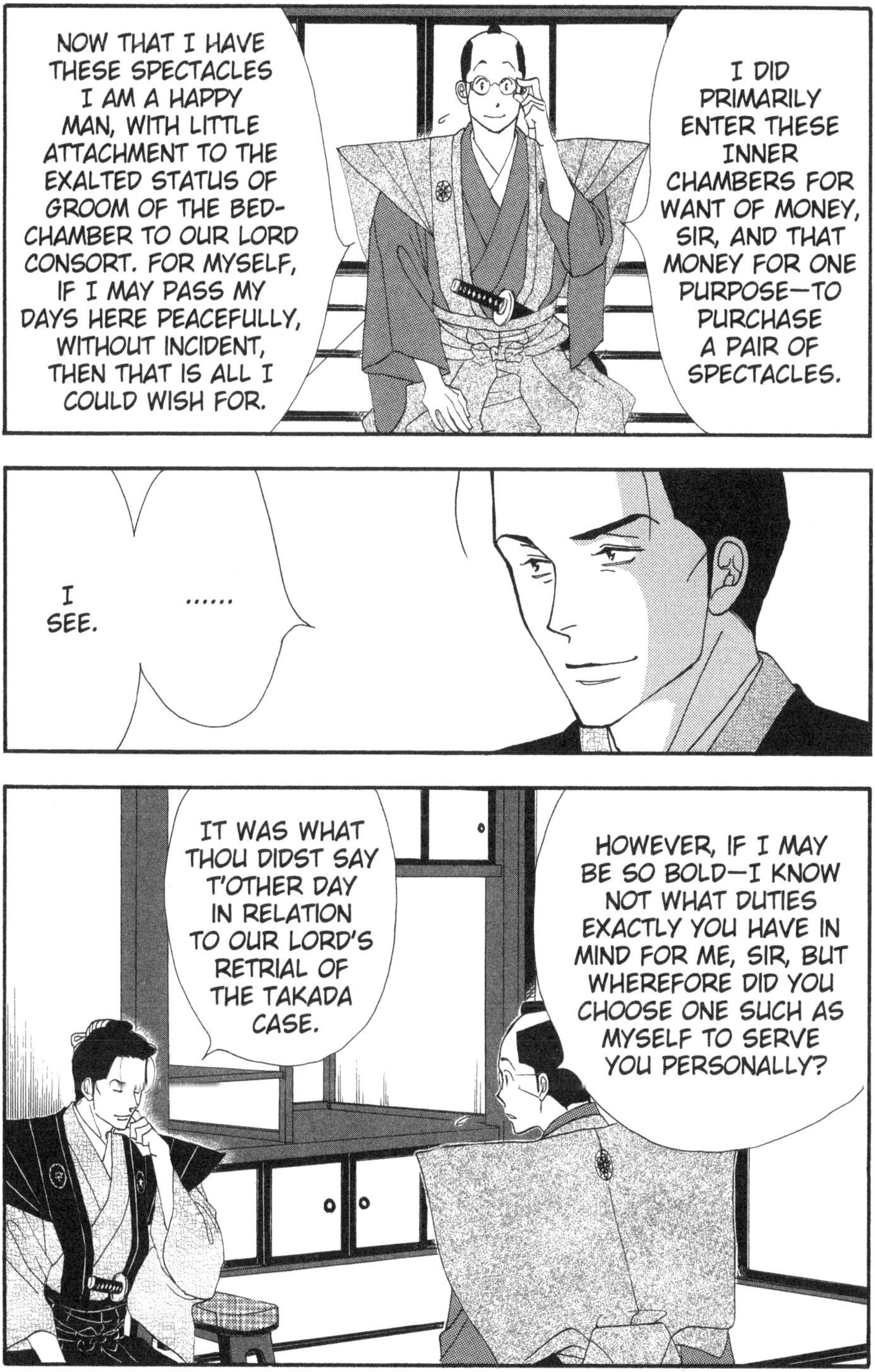
I DID PRIMARILY ENTER THESE INNER CHAMBERS FOR WANT OF MONEY, SIR, AND THAT MONEY FOR ONE PURPOSE—TO PURCHASE A PAIR OF SPECTACLES.
NOW THAT I HAVE THESE SPECTACLES I AM A HAPPY MAN, WITH LITTLE ATTACHMENT TO THE EXALTED STATUS OF GROOM OF THE BED-CHAMBER TO OUR LORD CONSORT. FOR MYSELF, IF I MAY PASS MY DAYS HERE PEACEFULLY, WITHOUT INCIDENT, THEN THAT IS ALL I COULD WISH FOR.
......
I SEE.
HOWEVER, IF I MAY BE SO BOLD—I KNOW NOT WHAT DUTIES EXACTLY YOU HAVE IN MIND FOR ME, SIR, BUT WHEREFORE DID YOU CHOOSE ONE SUCH AS MYSELF TO SERVE YOU PERSONALLY?
IT WAS WHAT THOU DIDST SAY T'OTHER DAY IN RELATION TO OUR LORD'S RETRIAL OF THE TAKADA CASE.

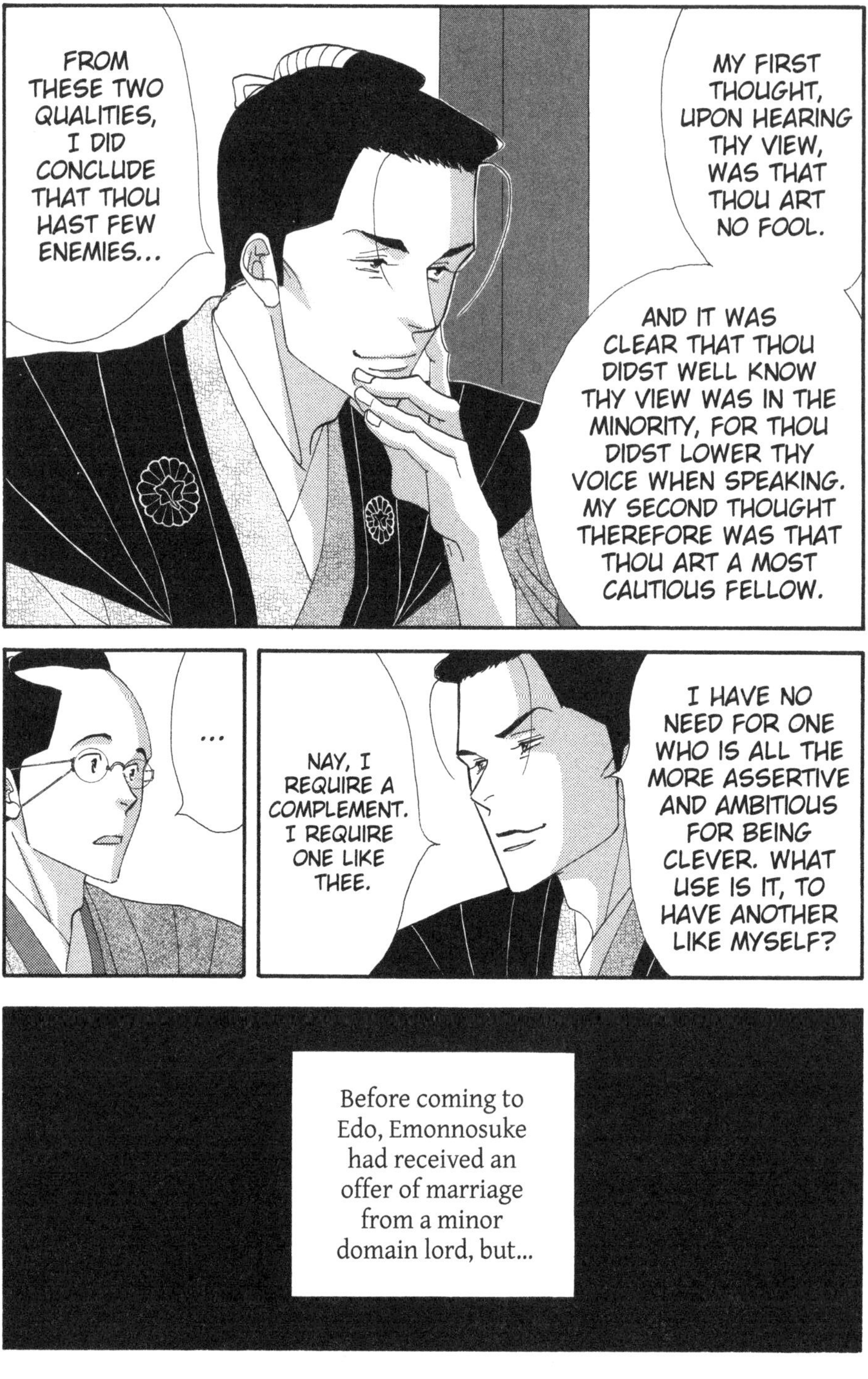
MY FIRST THOUGHT, UPON HEARING THY VIEW, WAS THAT THOU ART NO FOOL.
AND IT WAS CLEAR THAT THOU DIDST WELL KNOW THY VIEW WAS IN THE MINORITY, FOR THOU DIDST LOWER THY VOICE WHEN SPEAKING. MY SECOND THOUGHT THEREFORE WAS THAT THOU ART A MOST CAUTIOUS FELLOW.
FROM THESE TWO QUALITIES, I DID CONCLUDE THAT THOU HAST FEW ENEMIES...
I HAVE NO NEED FOR ONE WHO IS ALL THE MORE ASSERTIVE AND AMBITIOUS FOR BEING CLEVER. WHAT USE IS IT, TO HAVE ANOTHER LIKE MYSELF?
NAY, I REQUIRE A COMPLEMENT. I REQUIRE ONE LIKE THEE.
...
Before coming to Edo, Emonnosuke had received an offer of marriage from a minor domain lord, but...

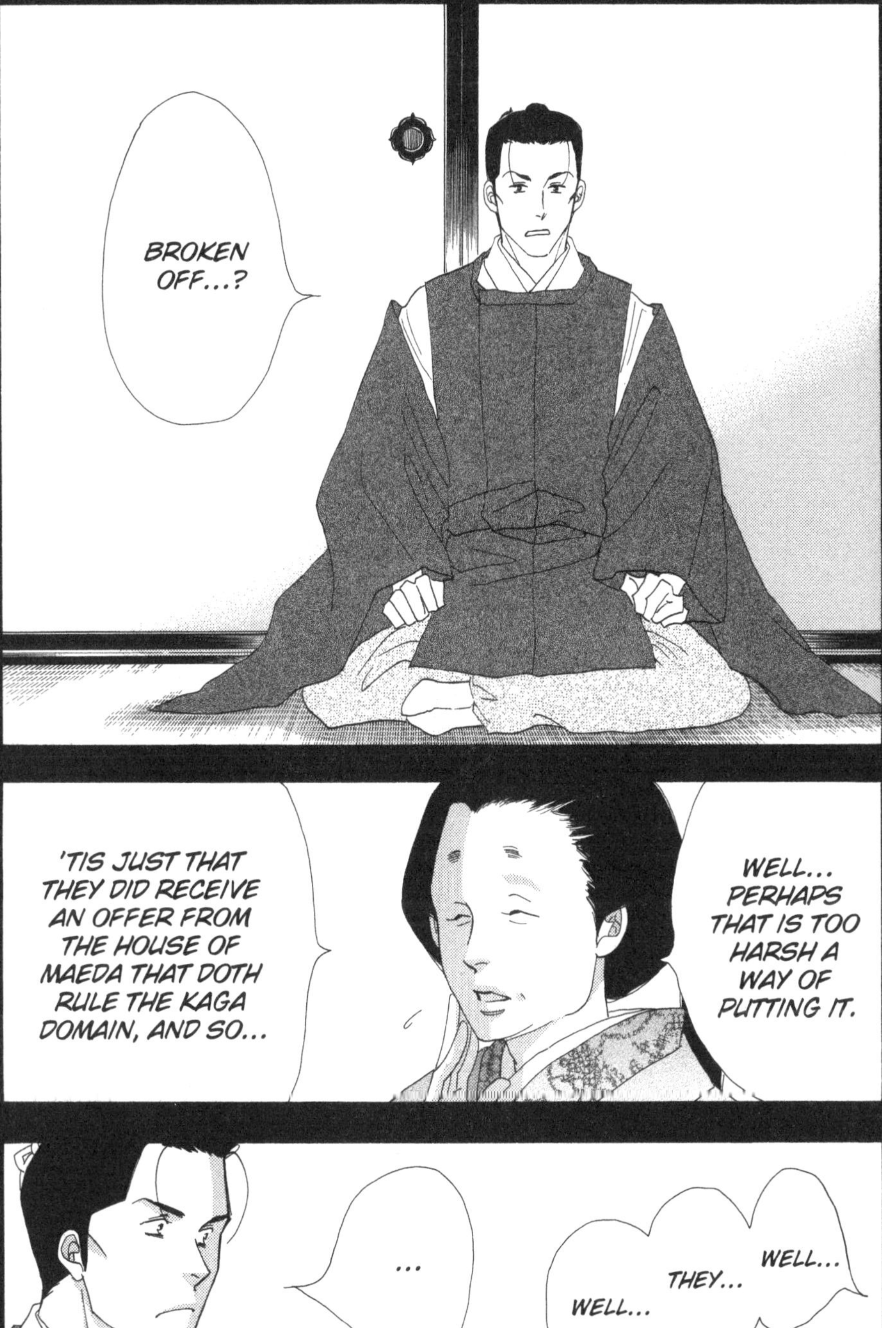
BROKEN OFF...?
WELL... PERHAPS THAT IS TOO HARSH A WAY OF PUTTING IT.
'TIS JUST THAT THEY DID RECEIVE AN OFFER FROM THE HOUSE OF MAEDA THAT DOTH RULE THE KAGA DOMAIN, AND SO...
WELL... THEY... WELL...
...

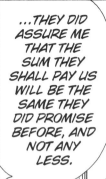

I SEE.
'TIS LITTLE MATTER. WE OUGHT TO BE GRATEFUL THAT THEY ARE WILLING TO PAY SUCH A HIGH DOWRY FOR ONE SO ADVANCED IN AGE AS MYSELF. SO WHAT IF I AM NOT THE LORD'S CONSORT, BUT ONLY A CONCUBINE? 'TIS OF LITTLE CONSEQUENCE.
A-AYE, VERILY 'TIS SO. INDEED, TSUGU-HITO...
...THEY DID ASSURE ME THAT THE SUM THEY SHALL PAY US WILL BE THE SAME THEY DID PROMISE BEFORE, AND NOT ANY LESS.
I CAN ONLY SAY, 'TIS A GREAT COMFORT THAT THIS BE SO...

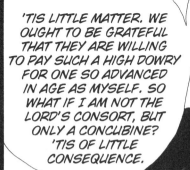

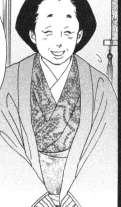

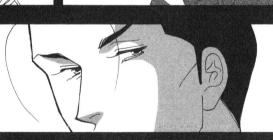

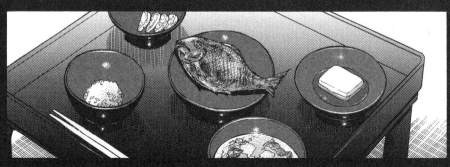

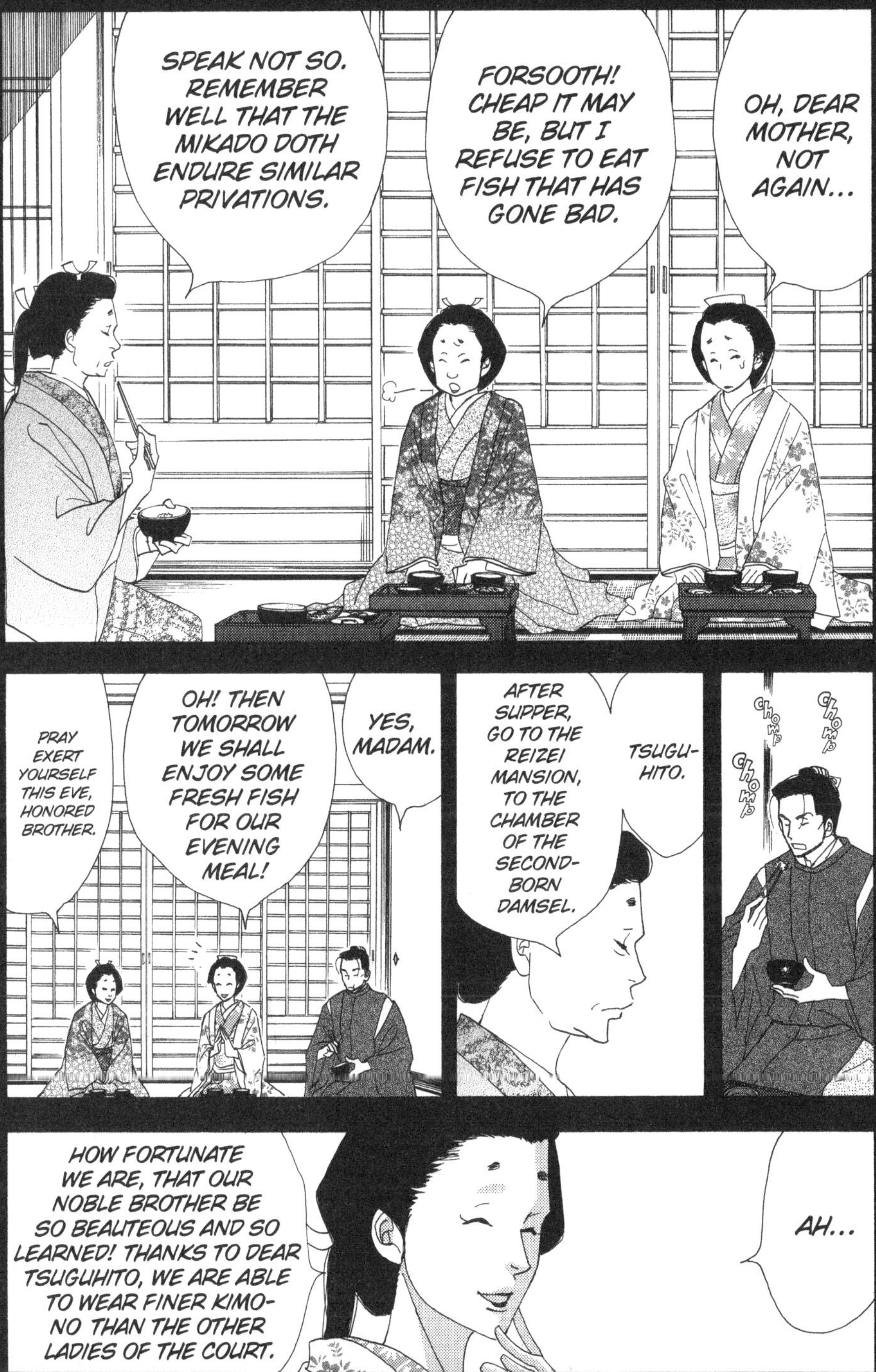
OH, DEAR MOTHER, NOT AGAIN...
FORSOOTH! CHEAP IT MAY BE, BUT I REFUSE TO EAT FISH THAT HAS GONE BAD.
SPEAK NOT SO. REMEMBER WELL THAT THE MIKADO DOTH ENDURE SIMILAR PRIVATIONS.
CHOMP CHOMP CHOMP
TSUGU-HITO.
AFTER SUPPER, GO TO THE REIZEI MANSION, TO THE CHAMBER OF THE SECOND-BORN DAMSEL.
YES, MADAM.
OH! THEN TOMORROW WE SHALL ENJOY SOME FRESH FISH FOR OUR EVENING MEAL!
PRAY EXERT YOURSELF THIS EVE, HONORED BROTHER.
AH...
HOW FORTUNATE WE ARE, THAT OUR NOBLE BROTHER BE SO BEAUTEOUS AND SO LEARNED! THANKS TO DEAR TSUGUHITO, WE ARE ABLE TO WEAR FINER KIMO-NO THAN THE OTHER LADIES OF THE COURT.

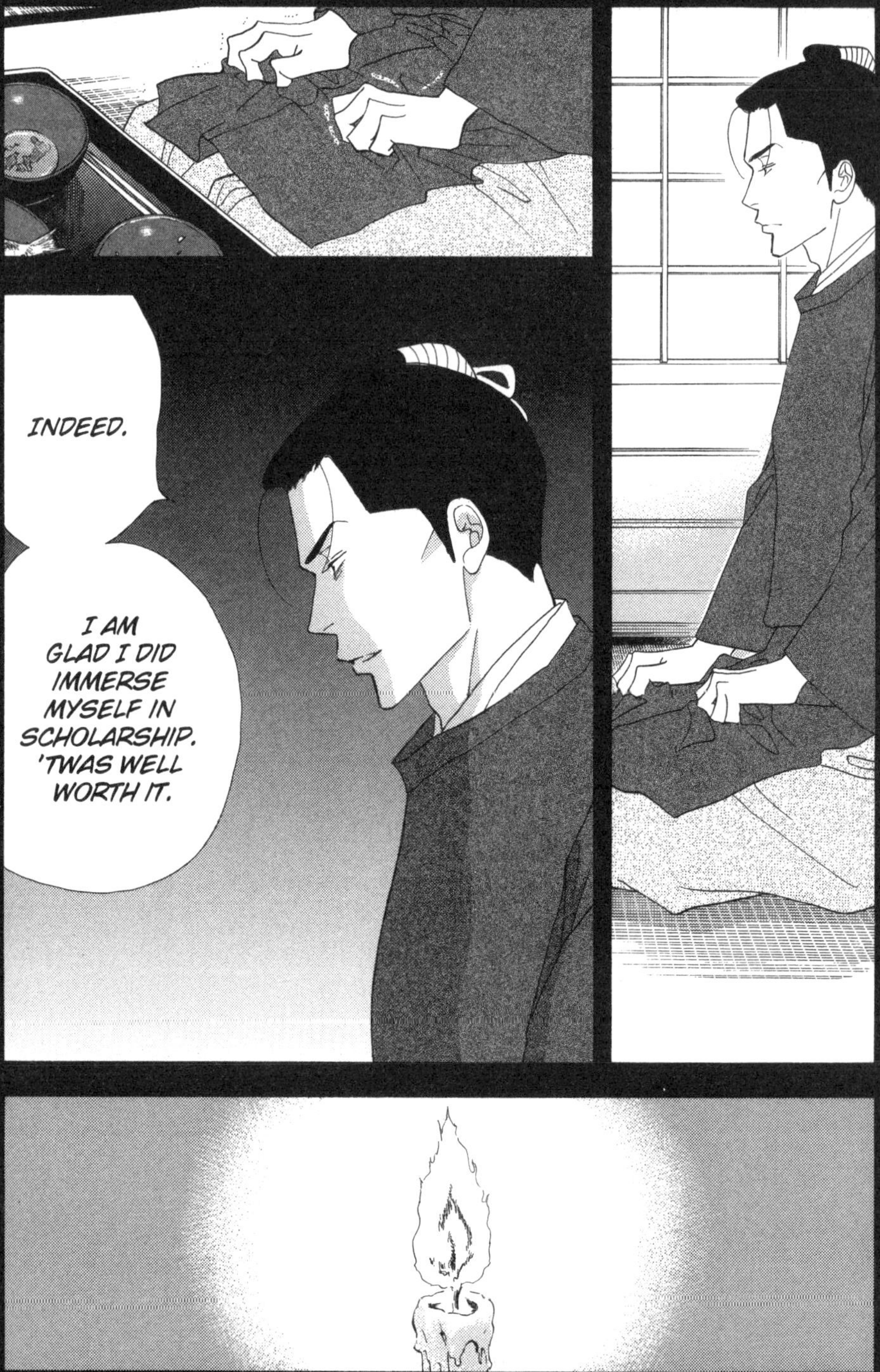
INDEED.
I AM GLAD I DID IMMERSE MYSELF IN SCHOLARSHIP. 'TWAS WELL WORTH IT.

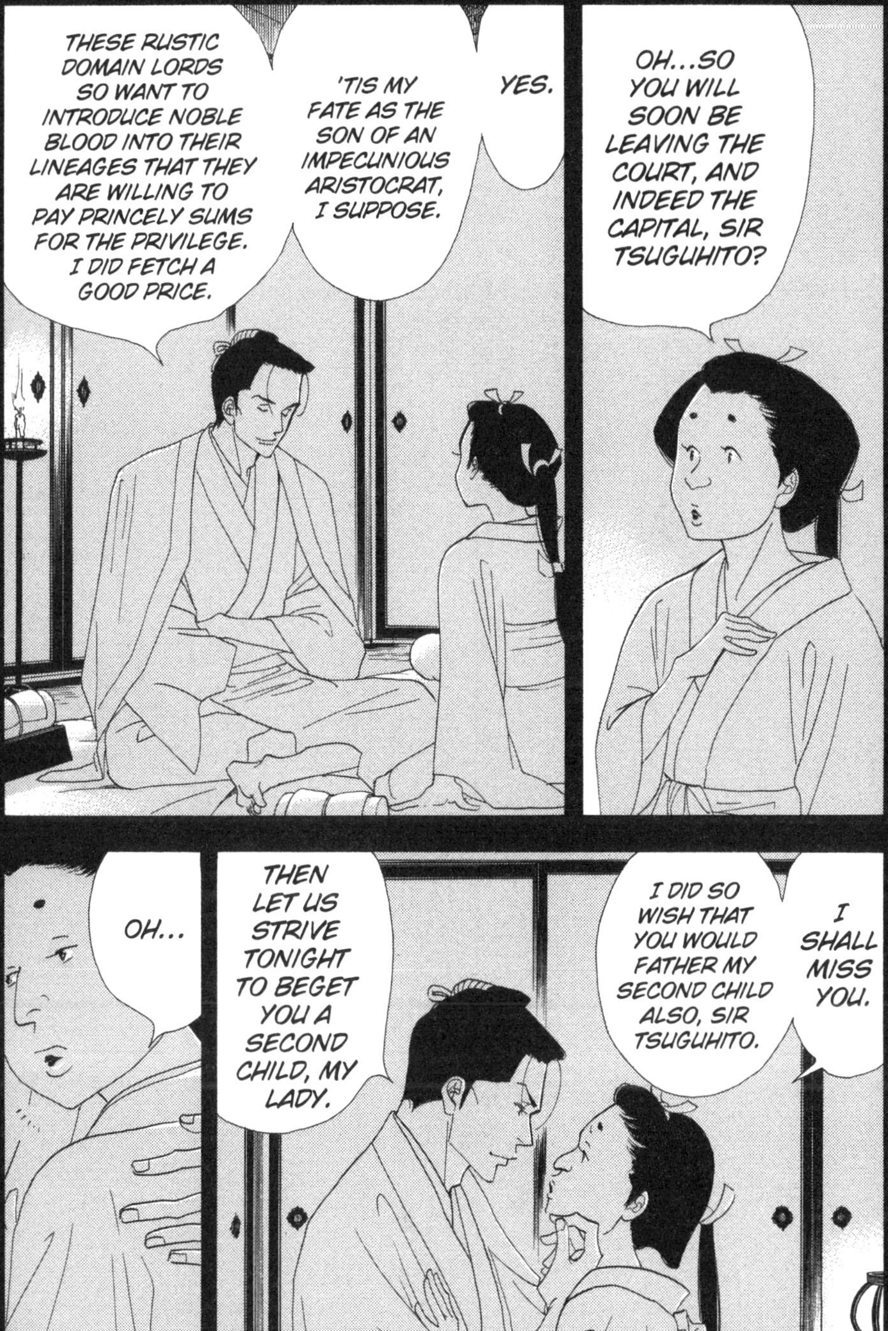
OH...SO YOU WILL SOON BE LEAVING THE COURT, AND INDEED THE CAPITAL, SIR TSUGUHITO?
YES.
'TIS MY FATE AS THE SON OF AN IMPECUNIOUS ARISTOCRAT, I SUPPOSE.
THESE RUSTIC DOMAIN LORDS SO WANT TO INTRODUCE NOBLE BLOOD INTO THEIR LINEAGES THAT THEY ARE WILLING TO PAY PRINCELY SUMS FOR THE PRIVILEGE. I DID FETCH A GOOD PRICE.
I SHALL MISS YOU.
I DID SO WISH THAT YOU WOULD FATHER MY SECOND CHILD ALSO, SIR TSUGUHITO.
THEN LET US STRIVE TONIGHT TO BEGET YOU A SECOND CHILD, MY LADY.
OH...

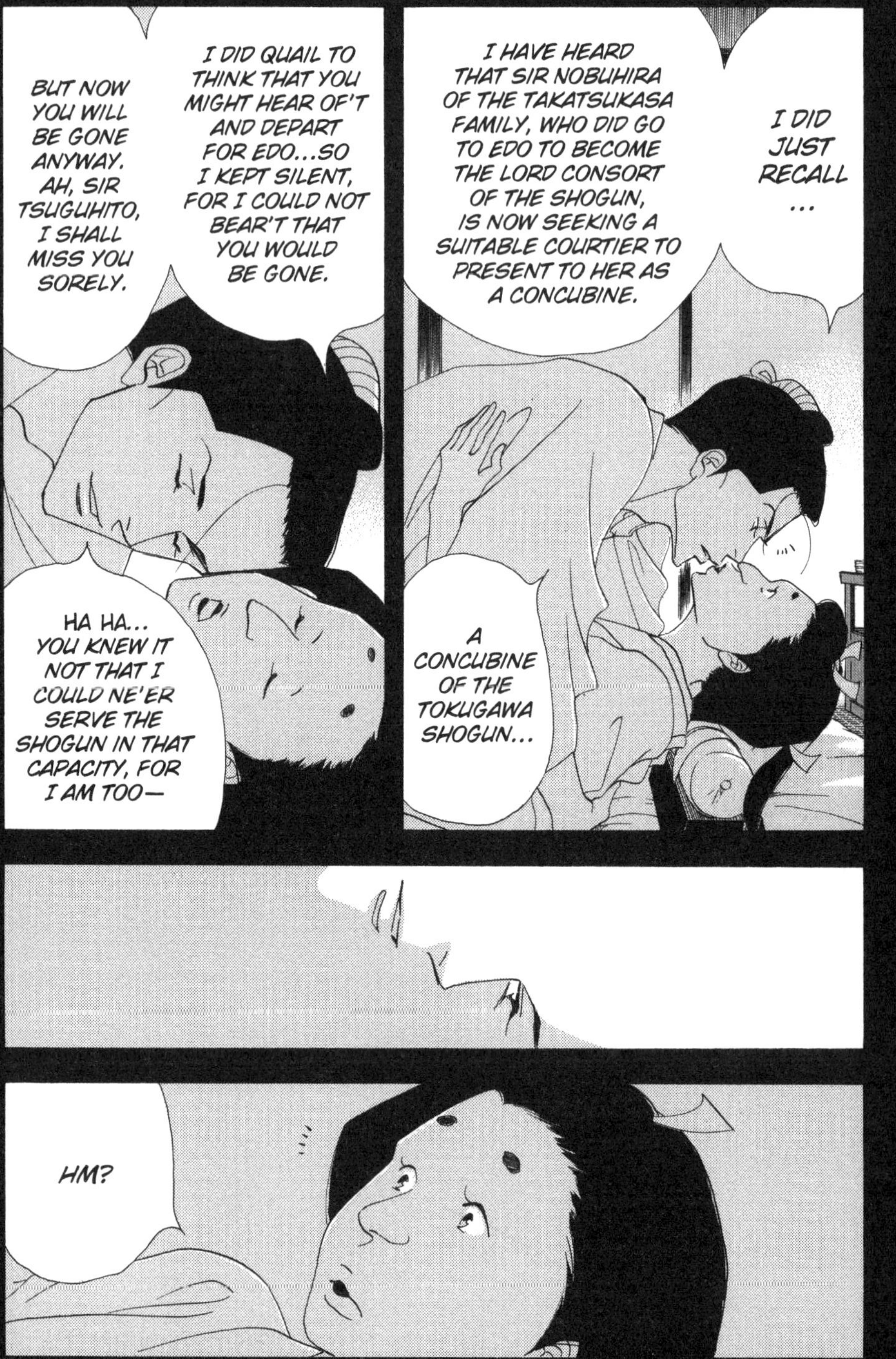
I DID JUST RECALL...
I HAVE HEARD THAT SIR NOBUHIRA OF THE TAKATSUKASA FAMILY, WHO DID GO TO EDO TO BECOME THE LORD CONSORT OF THE SHOGUN, IS NOW SEEKING A SUITABLE COURTIER TO PRESENT TO HER AS A CONCUBINE.
A CONCUBINE OF THE TOKUGAWA SHOGUN...
I DID QUAIL TO THINK THAT YOU MIGHT HEAR OF'T AND DEPART FOR EDO...SO I KEPT SILENT, FOR I COULD NOT BEAR'T THAT YOU WOULD BE GONE.
BUT NOW YOU WILL BE GONE ANYWAY. AH, SIR TSUGUHITO, I SHALL MISS YOU SORELY.
HA HA... YOU KNEW IT NOT THAT I COULD NE'ER SERVE THE SHOGUN IN THAT CAPACITY, FOR I AM TOO—
HM?

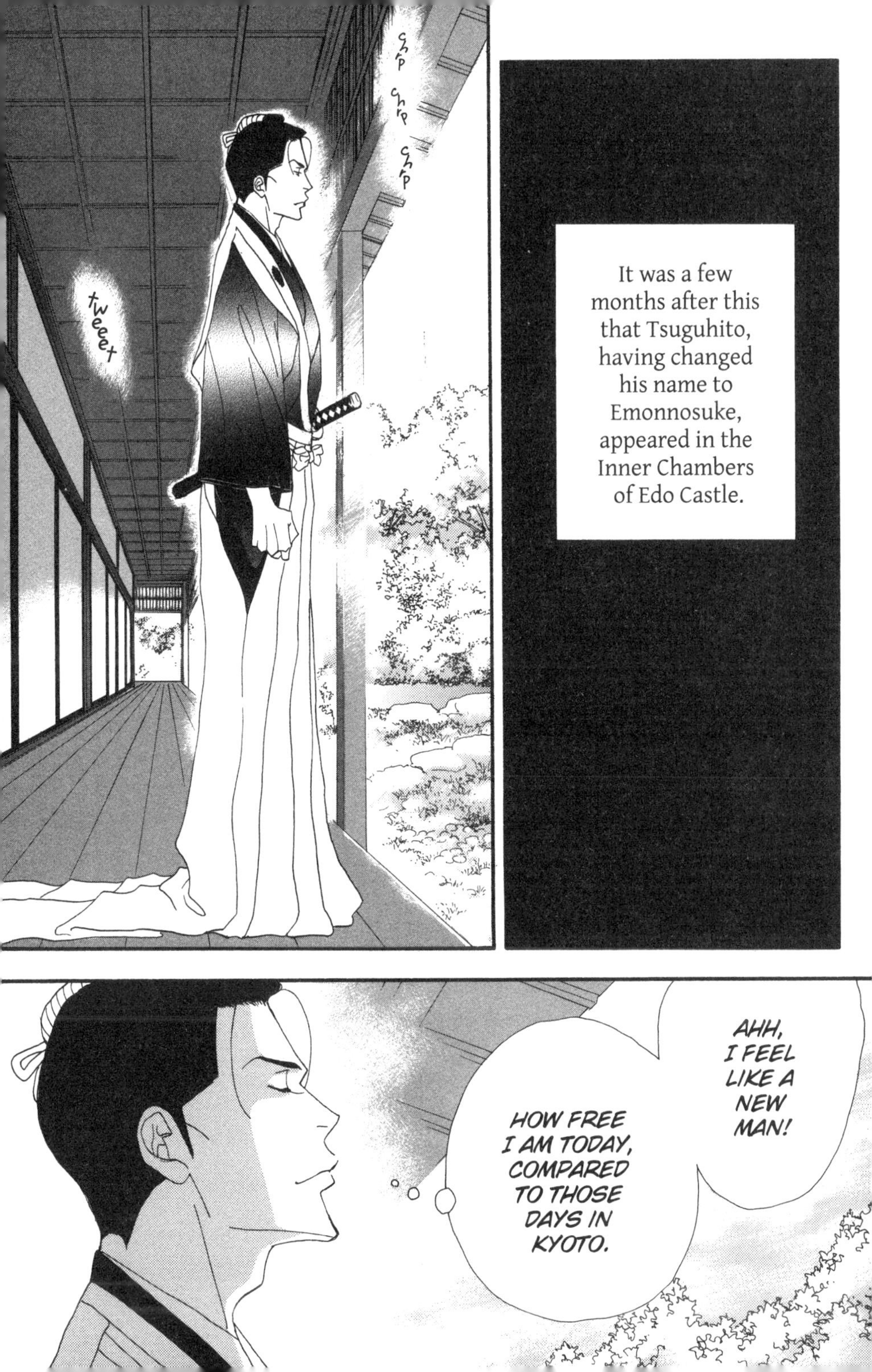
It was a few months after this that Tsuguhito, having changed his name to Emonnosuke, appeared in the Inner Chambers of Edo Castle.
chrp
chrp
chrp
tweeet
AHH, I FEEL LIKE A NEW MAN!
HOW FREE I AM TODAY, COMPARED TO THOSE DAYS IN KYOTO.

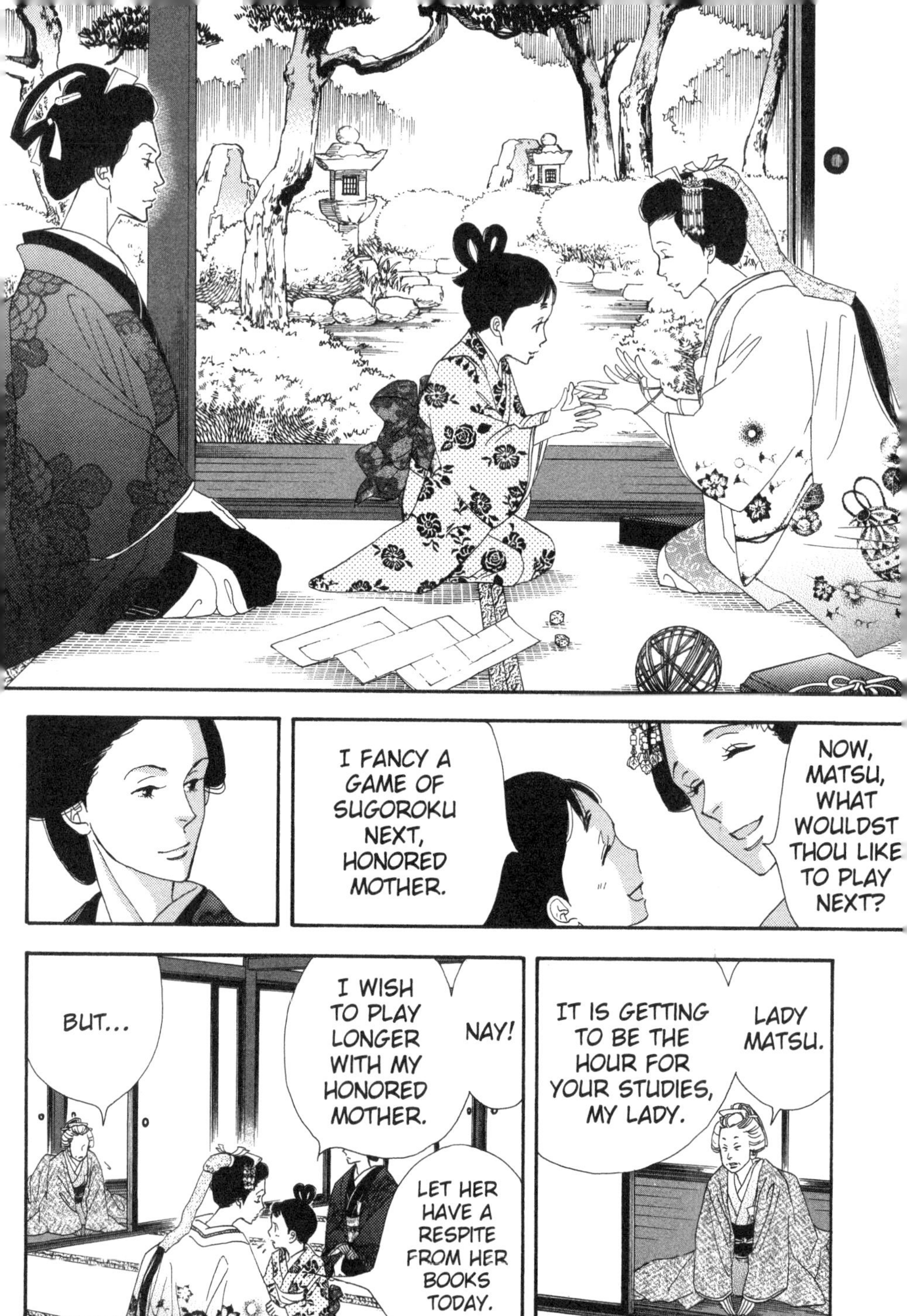
NOW, MATSU, WHAT WOULDST THOU LIKE TO PLAY NEXT?
I FANCY A GAME OF SUGOROKU NEXT, HONORED MOTHER.
LADY MATSU.
IT IS GETTING TO BE THE HOUR FOR YOUR STUDIES, MY LADY.
NAY!
I WISH TO PLAY LONGER WITH MY HONORED MOTHER.
LET HER HAVE A RESPITE FROM HER BOOKS TODAY.
BUT...

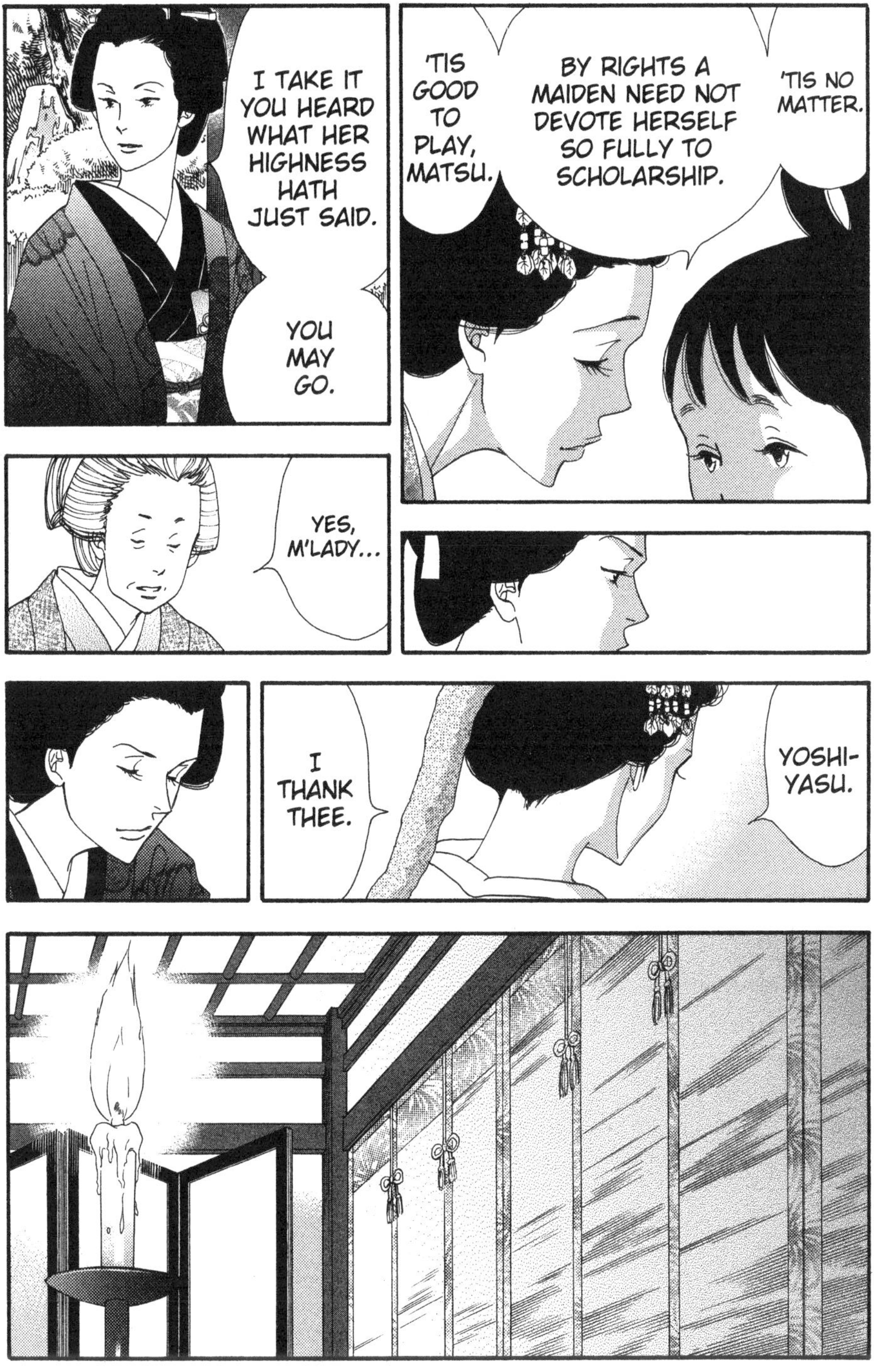
'TIS NO MATTER.
BY RIGHTS A MAIDEN NEED NOT DEVOTE HERSELF SO FULLY TO SCHOLARSHIP.
'TIS GOOD TO PLAY, MATSU.
I TAKE IT YOU HEARD WHAT HER HIGHNESS HATH JUST SAID.
YOU MAY GO.
YES, M'LADY...
YOSHI-YASU.
I THANK THEE.

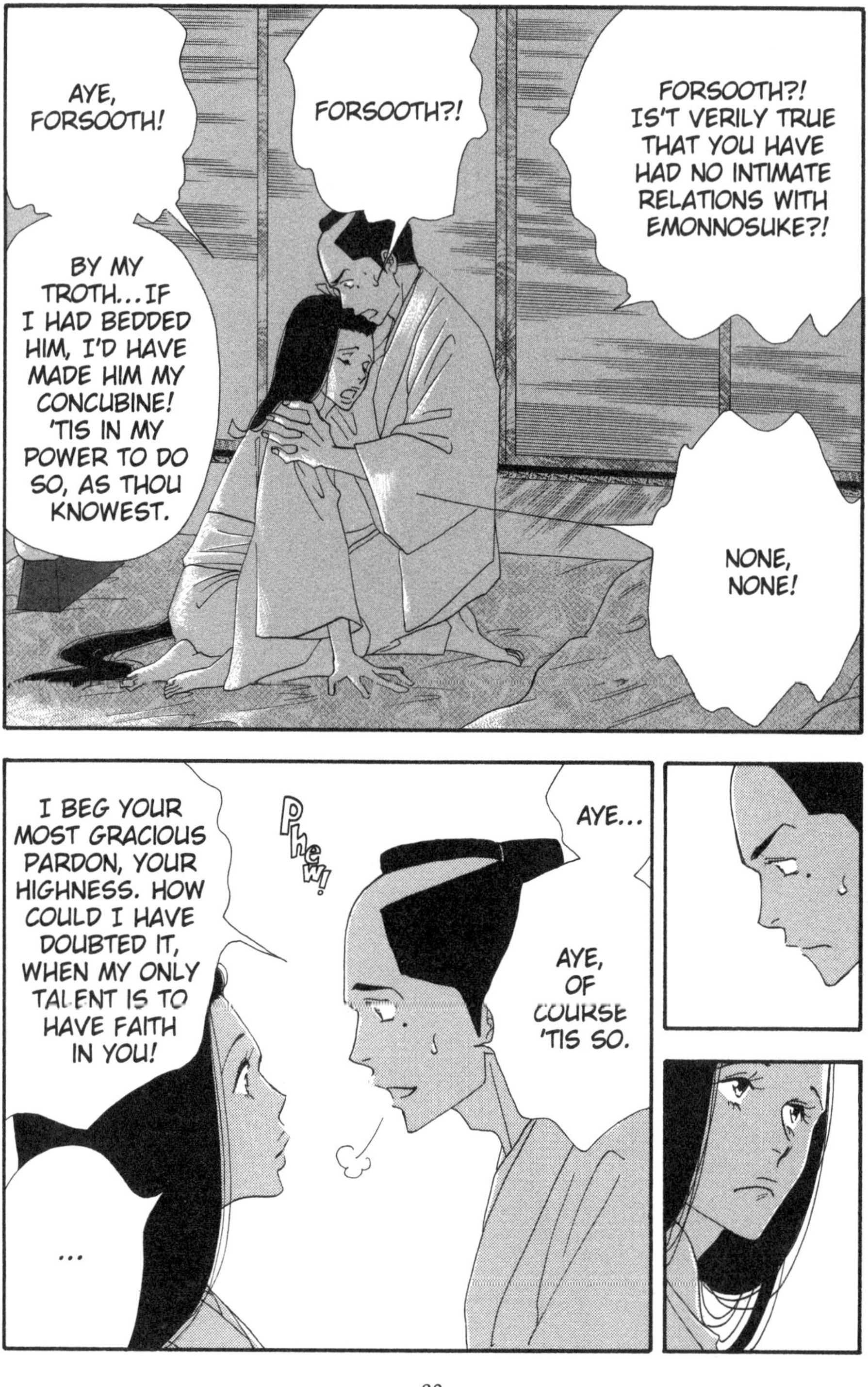
FORSOOTH?! IS'T VERILY TRUE THAT YOU HAVE HAD NO INTIMATE RELATIONS WITH EMONNOSUKE?!
NONE, NONE!
FORSOOTH?!
AYE, FORSOOTH!
BY MY TROTH...IF I HAD BEDDED HIM, I'D HAVE MADE HIM MY CONCUBINE! 'TIS IN MY POWER TO DO SO, AS THOU KNOWEST.
AYE...
AYE, OF COURSE 'TIS SO.
Phew!
I BEG YOUR MOST GRACIOUS PARDON, YOUR HIGHNESS. HOW COULD I HAVE DOUBTED IT, WHEN MY ONLY TALENT IS TO HAVE FAITH IN YOU!
...

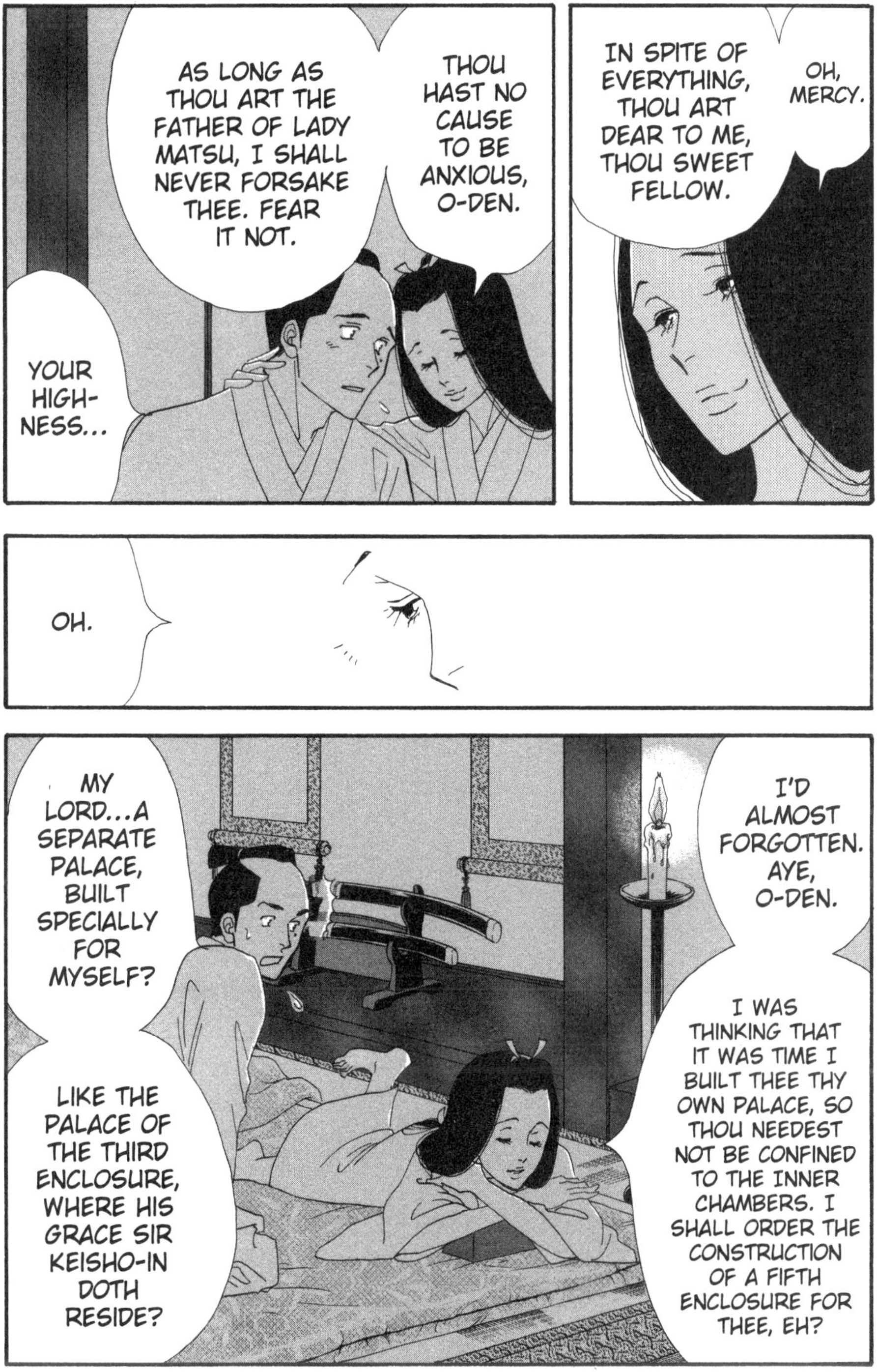
OH, MERCY.
IN SPITE OF EVERYTHING, THOU ART DEAR TO ME, THOU SWEET FELLOW.
THOU HAST NO CAUSE TO BE ANXIOUS, O-DEN.
AS LONG AS THOU ART THE FATHER OF LADY MATSU, I SHALL NEVER FORSAKE THEE. FEAR IT NOT.
YOUR HIGHNESS...
OH.
I'D ALMOST FORGOTTEN. AYE, O-DEN.
I WAS THINKING THAT IT WAS TIME I BUILT THEE THY OWN PALACE, SO THOU NEEDEST NOT BE CONFINED TO THE INNER CHAMBERS. I SHALL ORDER THE CONSTRUCTION OF A FIFTH ENCLOSURE FOR THEE, EH?
MY LORD...A SEPARATE PALACE, BUILT SPECIALLY FOR MYSELF?
LIKE THE PALACE OF THE THIRD ENCLOSURE, WHERE HIS GRACE SIR KEISHO-IN DOTH RESIDE?

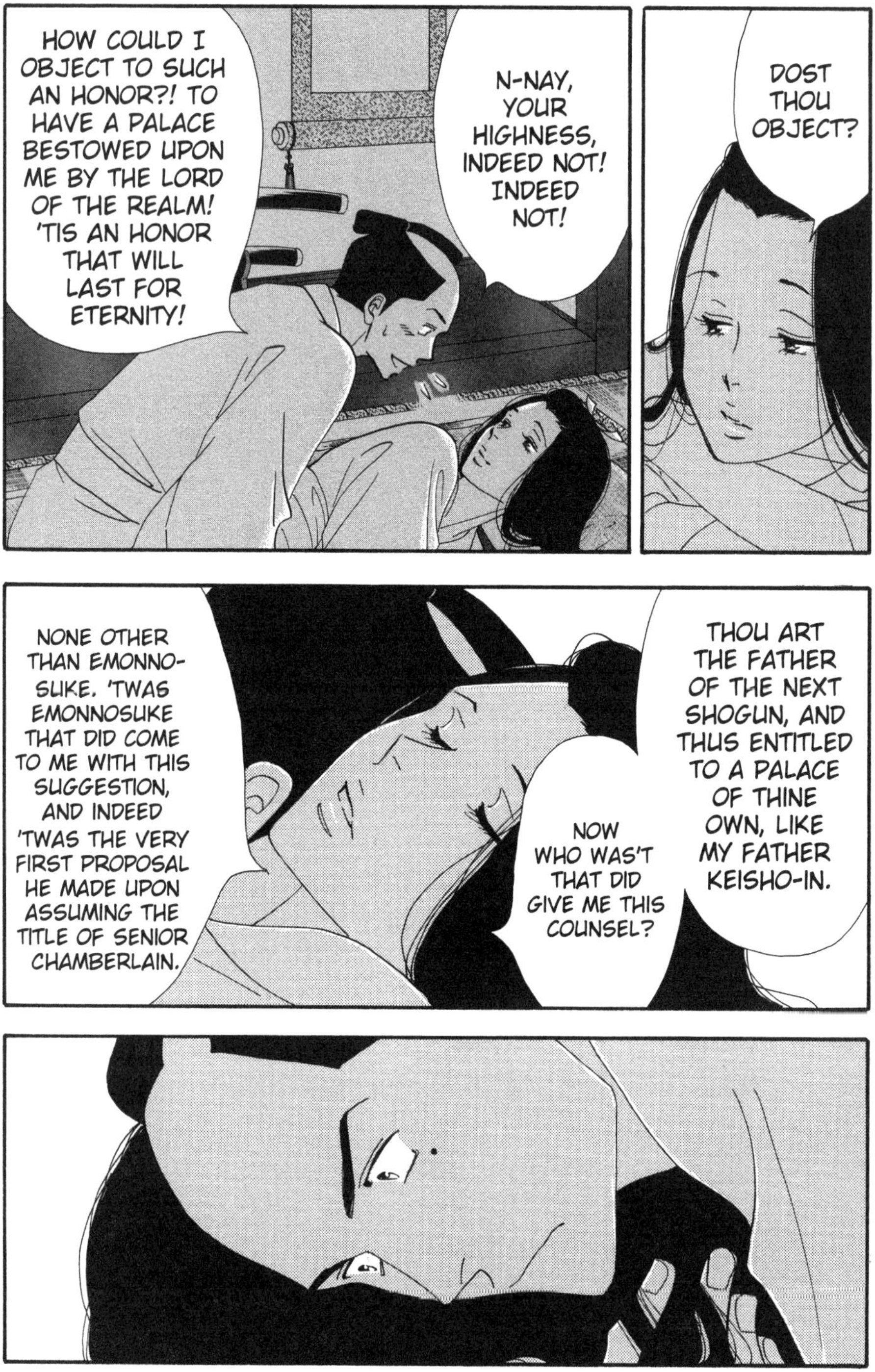
DOST THOU OBJECT?
N-NAY, YOUR HIGHNESS, INDEED NOT! INDEED NOT!
HOW COULD I OBJECT TO SUCH AN HONOR?! TO HAVE A PALACE BESTOWED UPON ME BY THE LORD OF THE REALM! 'TIS AN HONOR THAT WILL LAST FOR ETERNITY!
THOU ART THE FATHER OF THE NEXT SHOGUN, AND THUS ENTITLED TO A PALACE OF THINE OWN, LIKE MY FATHER KEISHO-IN.
NOW WHO WAS'T THAT DID GIVE ME THIS COUNSEL?
NONE OTHER THAN EMONNO-SUKE. 'TWAS EMONNOSUKE THAT DID COME TO ME WITH THIS SUGGESTION, AND INDEED 'TWAS THE VERY FIRST PROPOSAL HE MADE UPON ASSUMING THE TITLE OF SENIOR CHAMBERLAIN.

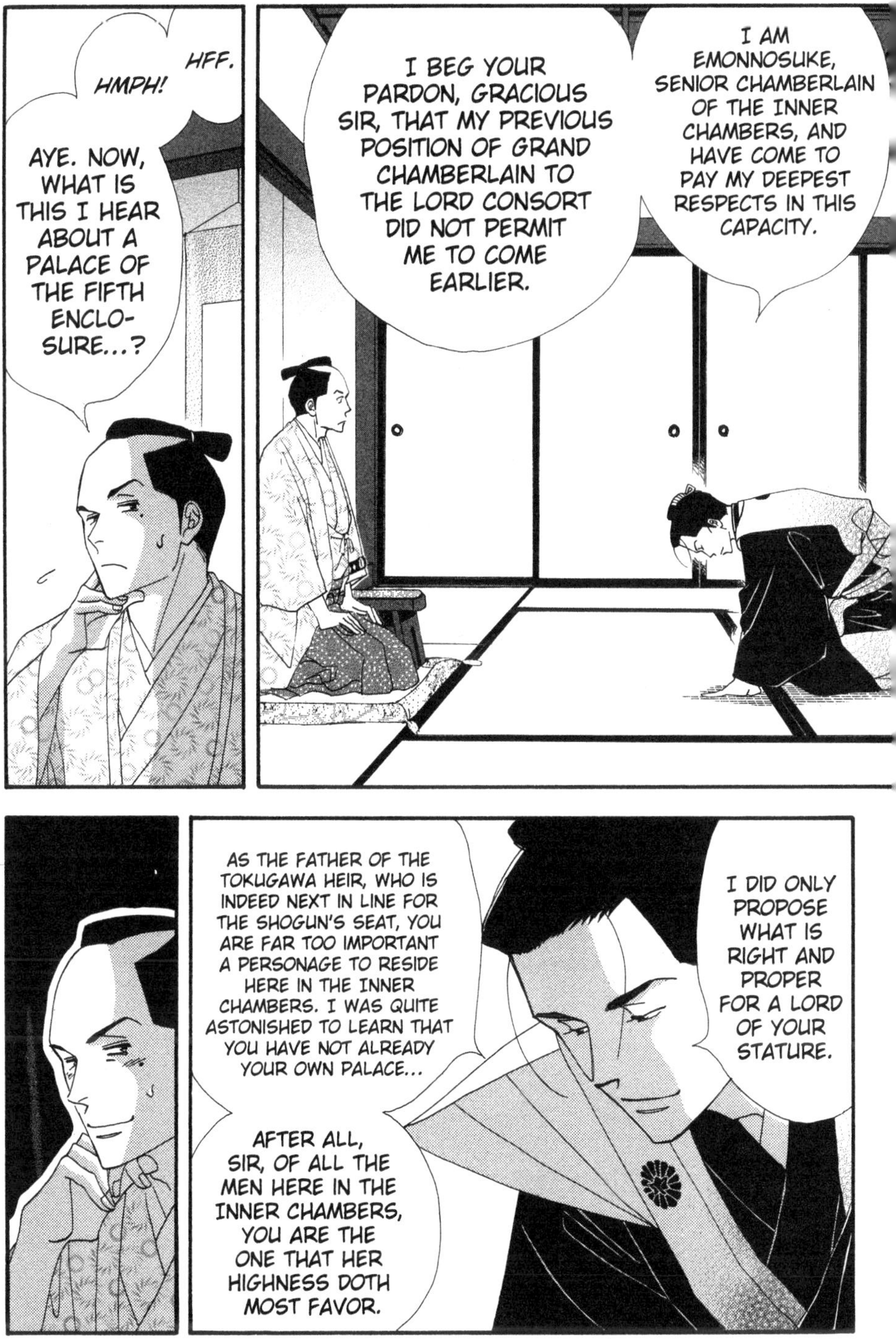
I AM EMONNOSUKE, SENIOR CHAMBERLAIN OF THE INNER CHAMBERS, AND HAVE COME TO PAY MY DEEPEST RESPECTS IN THIS CAPACITY.
I BEG YOUR PARDON, GRACIOUS SIR, THAT MY PREVIOUS POSITION OF GRAND CHAMBERLAIN TO THE LORD CONSORT DID NOT PERMIT ME TO COME EARLIER.
HFF.
HMPH!
AYE. NOW, WHAT IS THIS I HEAR ABOUT A PALACE OF THE FIFTH ENCLO-SURE...?
I DID ONLY PROPOSE WHAT IS RIGHT AND PROPER FOR A LORD OF YOUR STATURE.
AS THE FATHER OF THE TOKUGAWA HEIR, WHO IS INDEED NEXT IN LINE FOR THE SHOGUN'S SEAT, YOU ARE FAR TOO IMPORTANT A PERSONAGE TO RESIDE HERE IN THE INNER CHAMBERS. I WAS QUITE ASTONISHED TO LEARN THAT YOU HAVE NOT ALREADY YOUR OWN PALACE...
AFTER ALL, SIR, OF ALL THE MEN HERE IN THE INNER CHAMBERS, YOU ARE THE ONE THAT HER HIGHNESS DOTH MOST FAVOR.

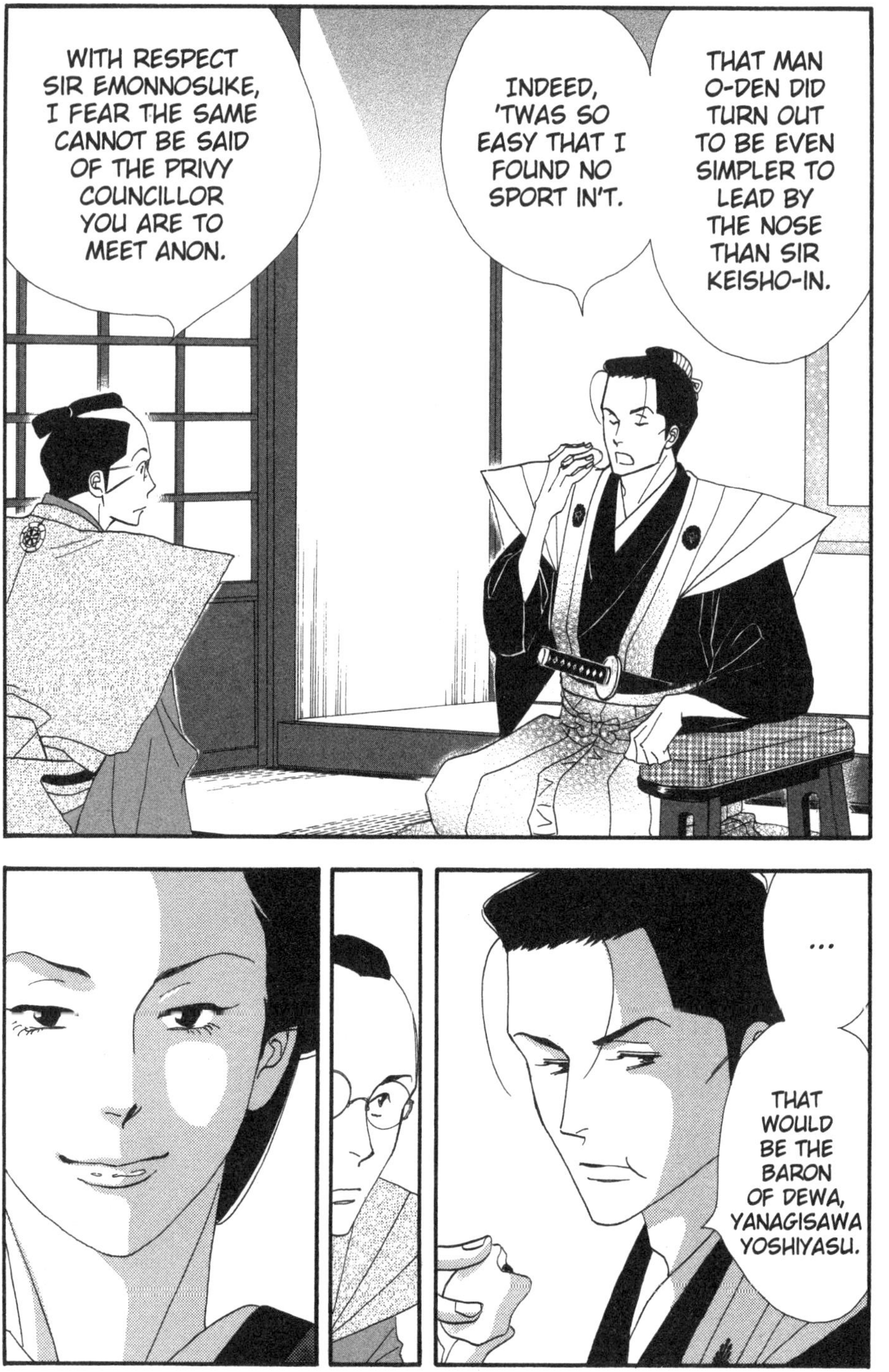
THAT MAN O-DEN DID TURN OUT TO BE EVEN SIMPLER TO LEAD BY THE NOSE THAN SIR KEISHO-IN.
INDEED, 'TWAS SO EASY THAT I FOUND NO SPORT IN'T.
WITH RESPECT SIR EMONNOSUKE, I FEAR THE SAME CANNOT BE SAID OF THE PRIVY COUNCILLOR YOU ARE TO MEET ANON.
...
THAT WOULD BE THE BARON OF DEWA, YANAGISAWA YOSHIYASU.

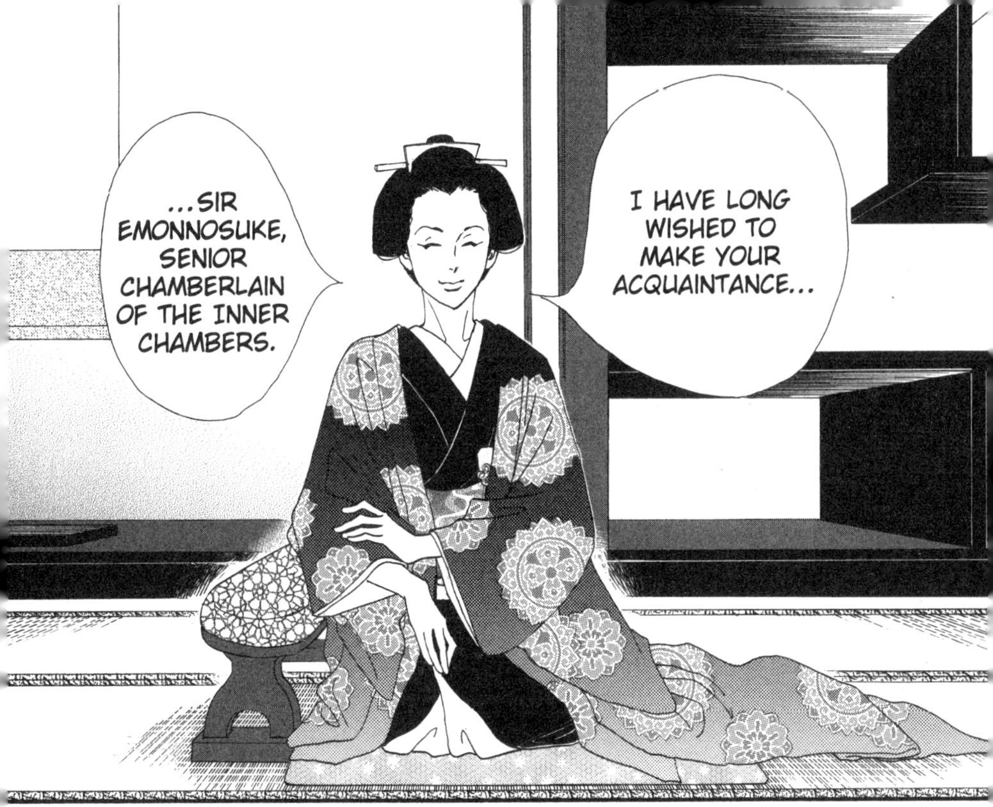
I HAVE LONG WISHED TO MAKE YOUR ACQUAINTANCE...
...SIR EMONNOSUKE, SENIOR CHAMBERLAIN OF THE INNER CHAMBERS.

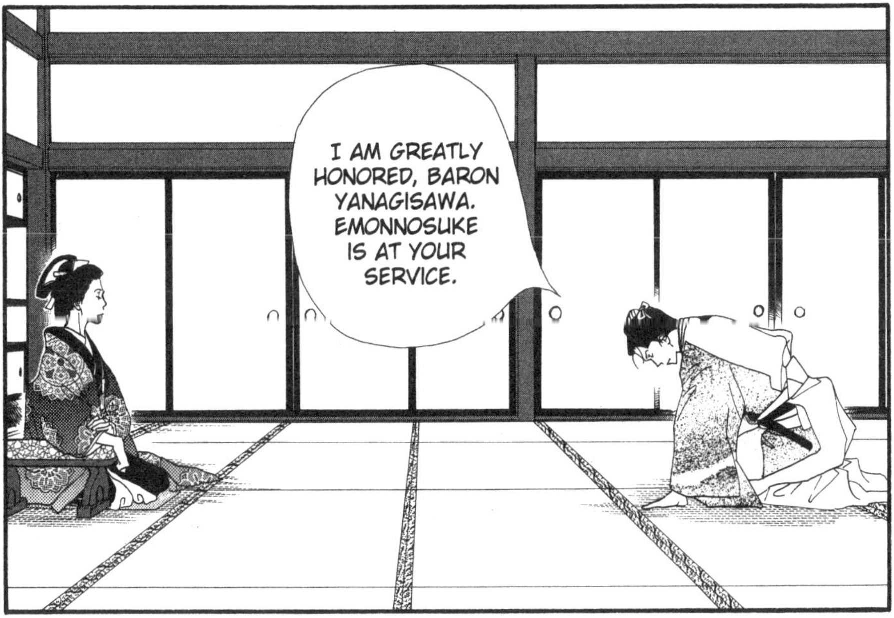
I AM GREATLY HONORED, BARON YANAGISAWA. EMONNOSUKE IS AT YOUR SERVICE.

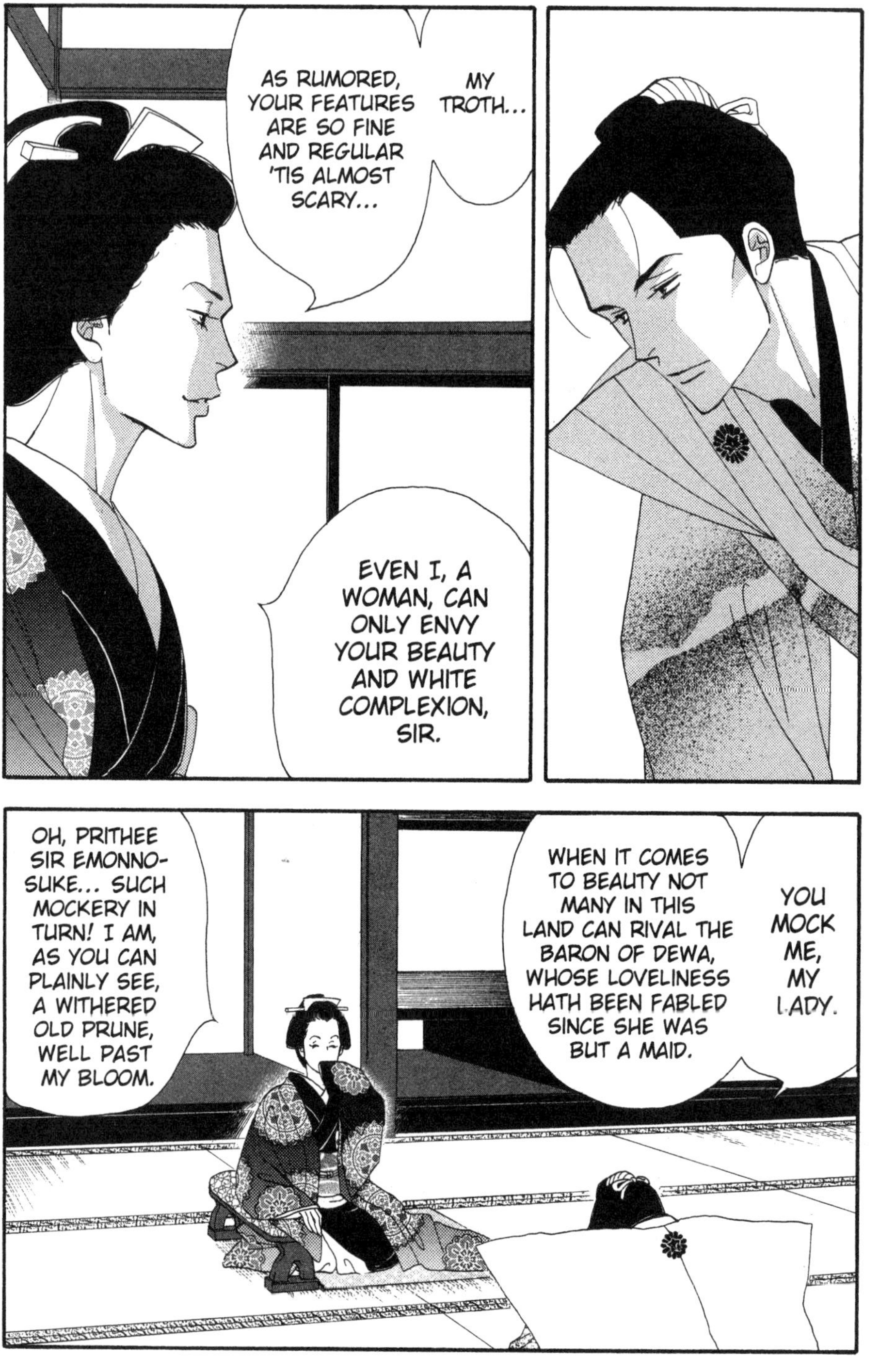
MY TROTH...
AS RUMORED, YOUR FEATURES ARE SO FINE AND REGULAR 'TIS ALMOST SCARY...
EVEN I, A WOMAN, CAN ONLY ENVY YOUR BEAUTY AND WHITE COMPLEXION, SIR.
YOU MOCK ME, MY LADY.
WHEN IT COMES TO BEAUTY NOT MANY IN THIS LAND CAN RIVAL THE BARON OF DEWA, WHOSE LOVELINESS HATH BEEN FABLED SINCE SHE WAS BUT A MAID.
OH, PRITHEE SIR EMONNO-SUKE... SUCH MOCKERY IN TURN! I AM, AS YOU CAN PLAINLY SEE, A WITHERED OLD PRUNE, WELL PAST MY BLOOM.

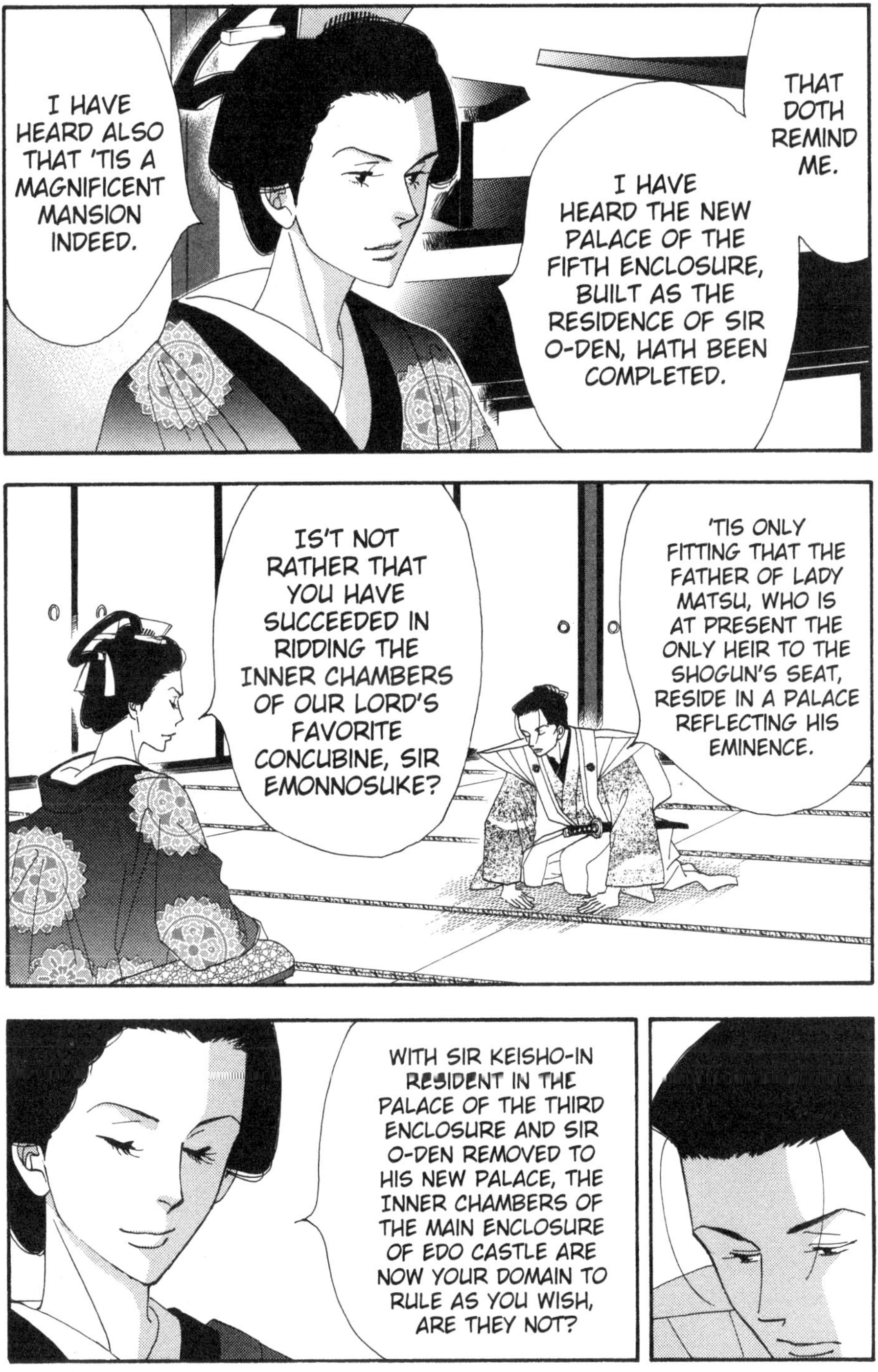
THAT DOTH REMIND ME.
I HAVE HEARD THE NEW PALACE OF THE FIFTH ENCLOSURE, BUILT AS THE RESIDENCE OF SIR O-DEN, HATH BEEN COMPLETED.
I HAVE HEARD ALSO THAT 'TIS A MAGNIFICENT MANSION INDEED.
'TIS ONLY FITTING THAT THE FATHER OF LADY MATSU, WHO IS AT PRESENT THE ONLY HEIR TO THE SHOGUN'S SEAT, RESIDE IN A PALACE REFLECTING HIS EMINENCE.
IS'T NOT RATHER THAT YOU HAVE SUCCEEDED IN RIDDING THE INNER CHAMBERS OF OUR LORD'S FAVORITE CONCUBINE, SIR EMONNOSUKE?
WITH SIR KEISHO-IN RESIDENT IN THE PALACE OF THE THIRD ENCLOSURE AND SIR O-DEN REMOVED TO HIS NEW PALACE, THE INNER CHAMBERS OF THE MAIN ENCLOSURE OF EDO CASTLE ARE NOW YOUR DOMAIN TO RULE AS YOU WISH, ARE THEY NOT?

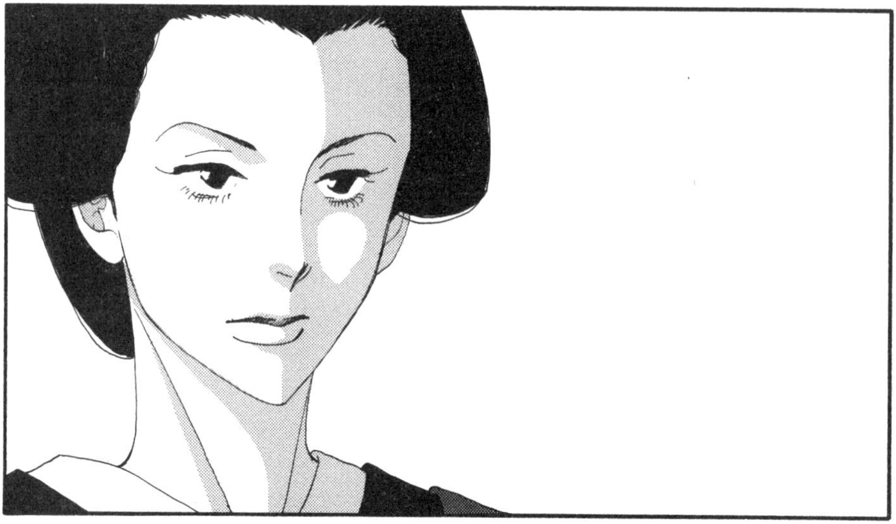
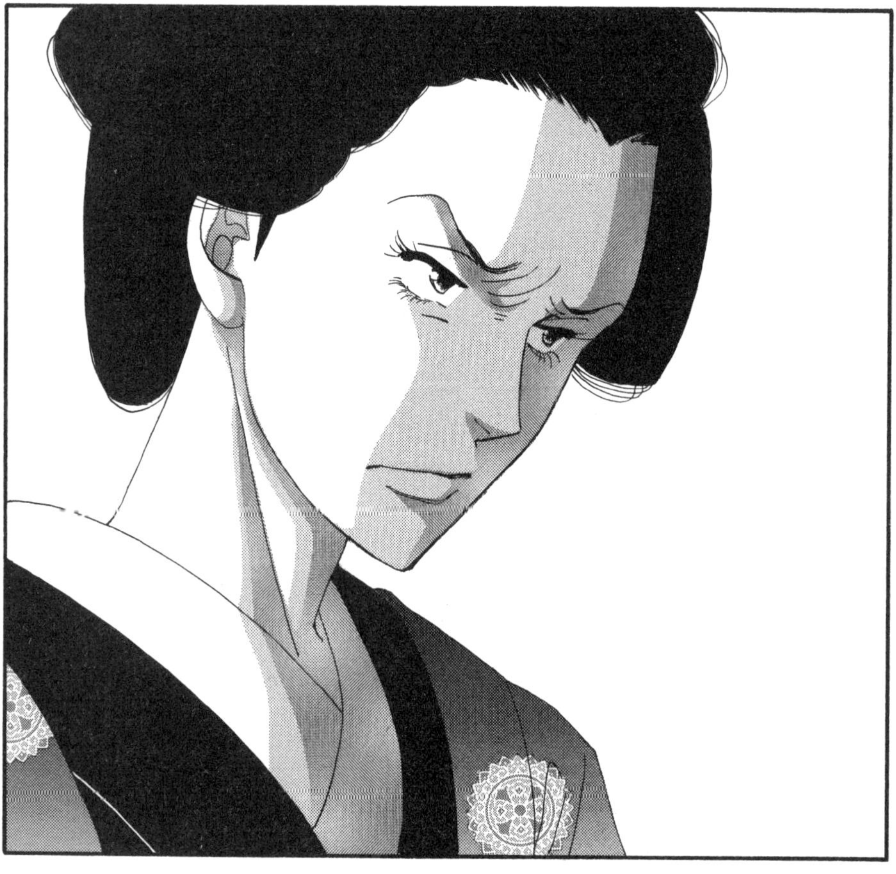

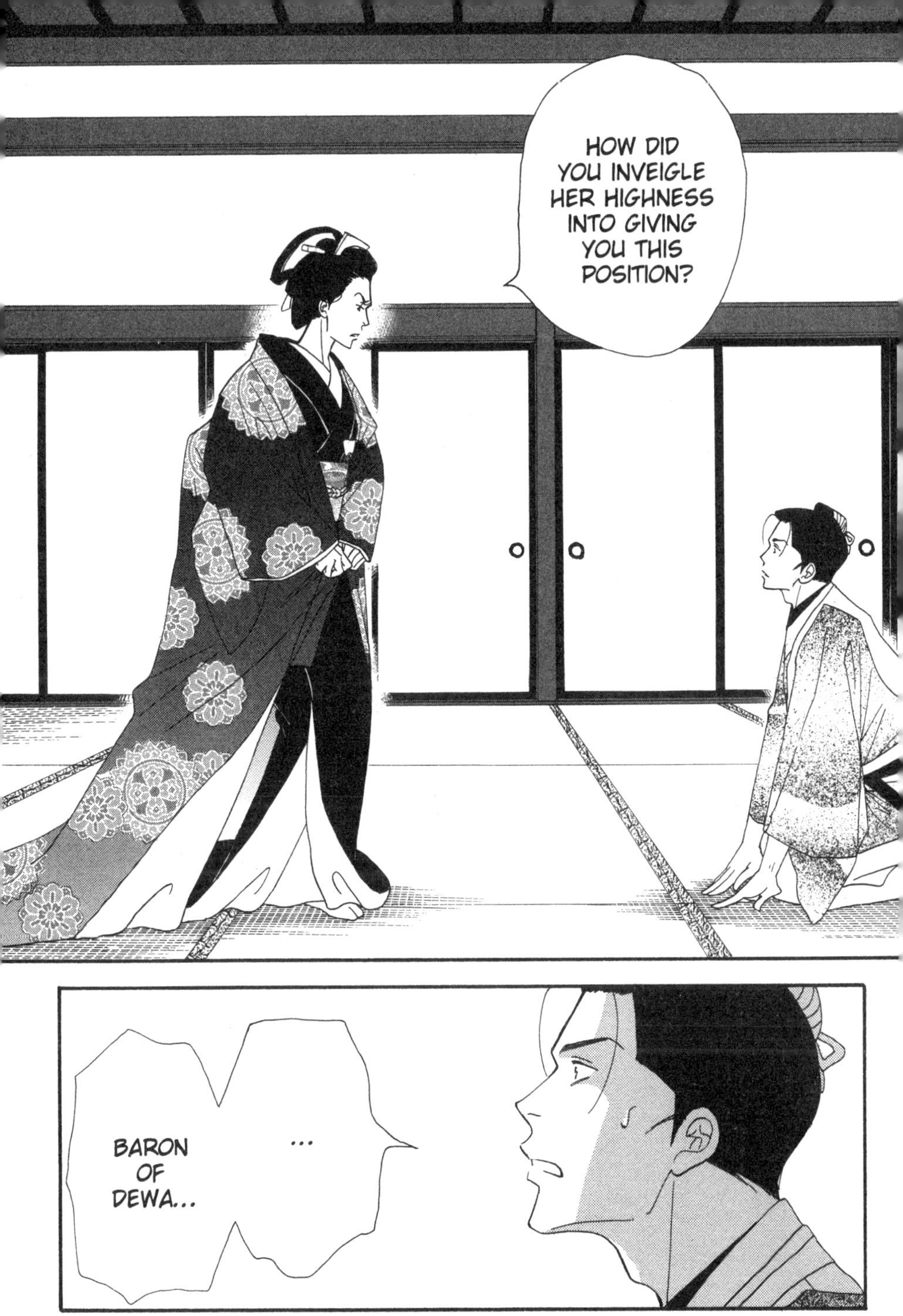
HOW DID YOU INVEIGLE HER HIGHNESS INTO GIVING YOU THIS POSITION?
...
BARON OF DEWA...

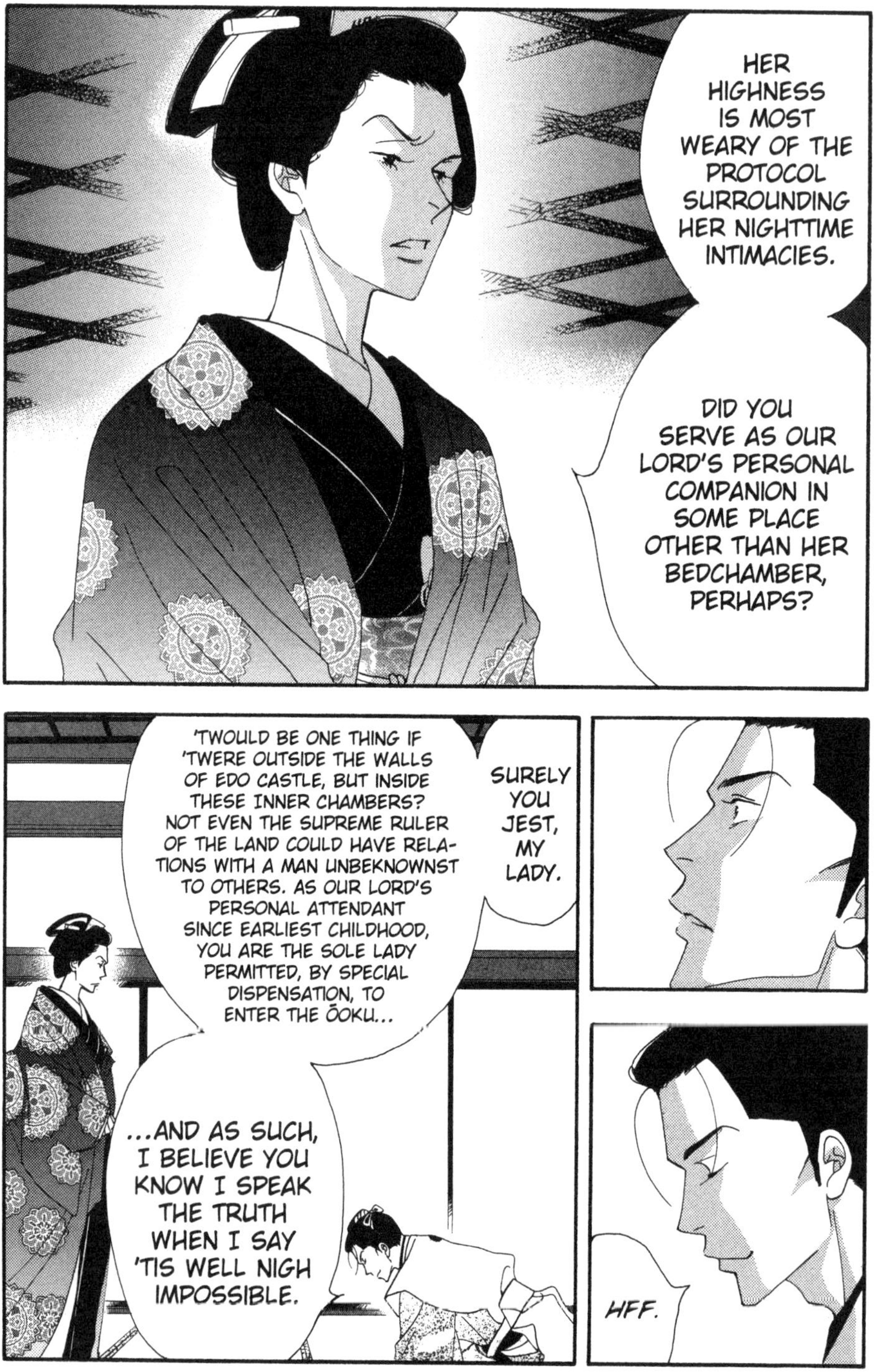
HER HIGHNESS IS MOST WEARY OF THE PROTOCOL SURROUNDING HER NIGHTTIME INTIMACIES.
DID YOU SERVE AS OUR LORD'S PERSONAL COMPANION IN SOME PLACE OTHER THAN HER BEDCHAMBER, PERHAPS?
HFF.
SURELY YOU JEST, MY LADY.
'TWOULD BE ONE THING IF 'TWERE OUTSIDE THE WALLS OF EDO CASTLE, BUT INSIDE THESE INNER CHAMBERS? NOT EVEN THE SUPREME RULER OF THE LAND COULD HAVE RELATIONS WITH A MAN UNBEKNOWNST TO OTHERS. AS OUR LORD'S PERSONAL ATTENDANT SINCE EARLIEST CHILDHOOD, YOU ARE THE SOLE LADY PERMITTED, BY SPECIAL DISPENSATION, TO ENTER THE ŌOKU...
...AND AS SUCH, I BELIEVE YOU KNOW I SPEAK THE TRUTH WHEN I SAY 'TIS WELL NIGH IMPOSSIBLE.

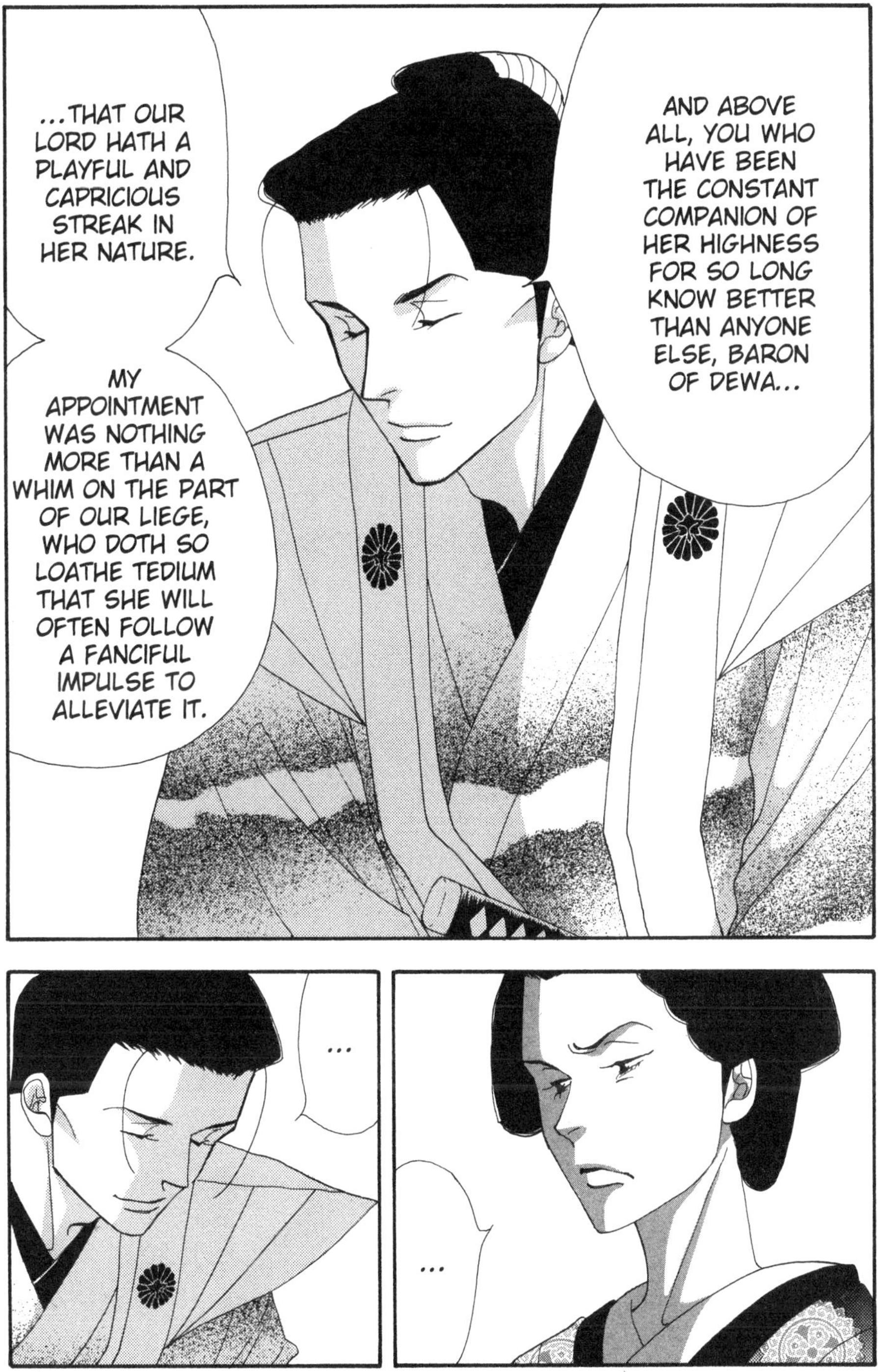
AND ABOVE ALL, YOU WHO HAVE BEEN THE CONSTANT COMPANION OF HER HIGHNESS FOR SO LONG KNOW BETTER THAN ANYONE ELSE, BARON OF DEWA...
...THAT OUR LORD HATH A PLAYFUL AND CAPRICIOUS STREAK IN HER NATURE.
MY APPOINTMENT WAS NOTHING MORE THAN A WHIM ON THE PART OF OUR LIEGE, WHO DOTH SO LOATHE TEDIUM THAT SHE WILL OFTEN FOLLOW A FANCIFUL IMPULSE TO ALLEVIATE IT.
...
...

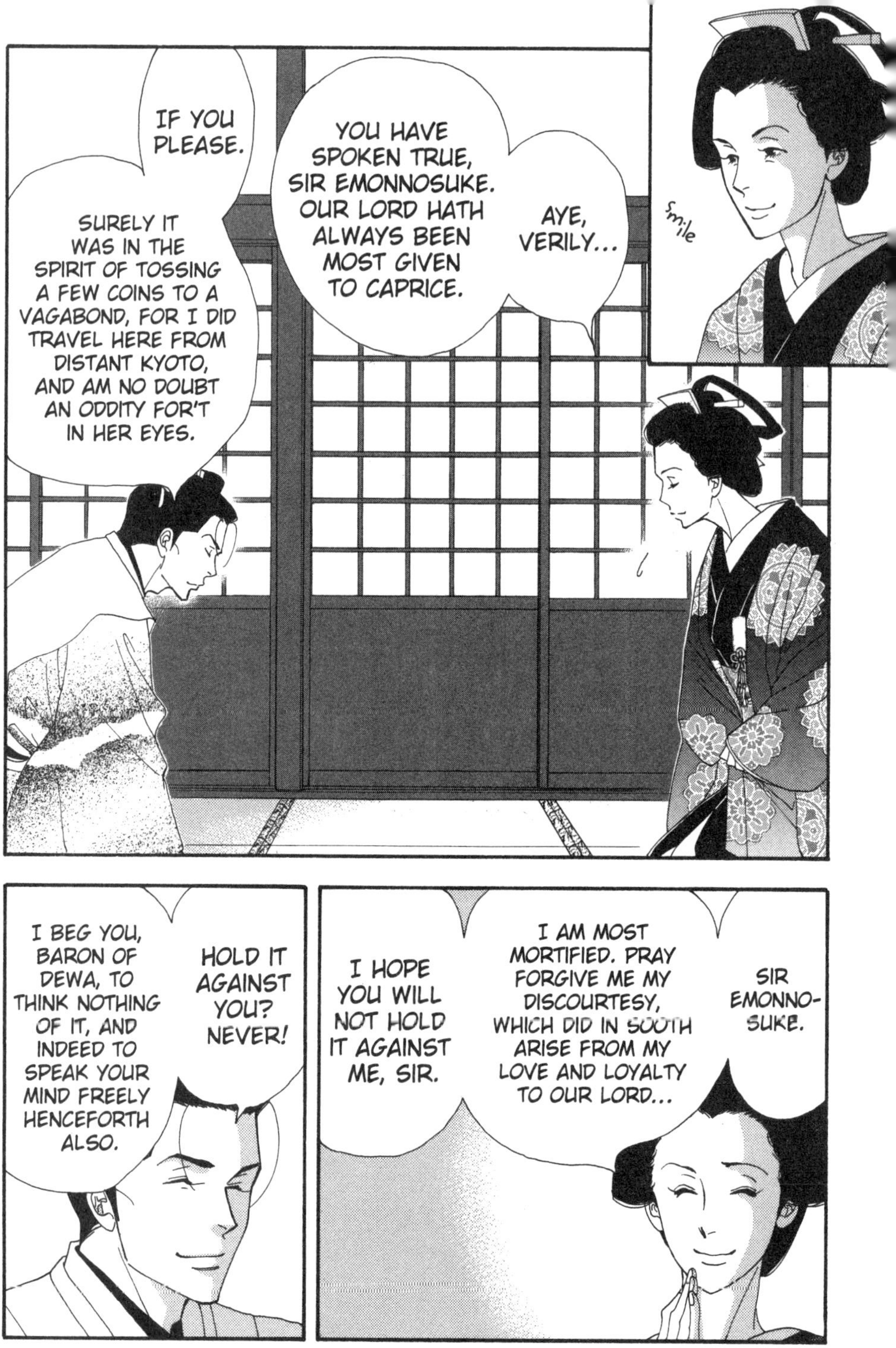
smile
AYE, VERILY...
YOU HAVE SPOKEN TRUE, SIR EMONNOSUKE. OUR LORD HATH ALWAYS BEEN MOST GIVEN TO CAPRICE.
IF YOU PLEASE.
SURELY IT WAS IN THE SPIRIT OF TOSSING A FEW COINS TO A VAGABOND, FOR I DID TRAVEL HERE FROM DISTANT KYOTO, AND AM NO DOUBT AN ODDITY FOR'T IN HER EYES.
SIR EMONNOSUKE.
I AM MOST MORTIFIED. PRAY FORGIVE ME MY DISCOURTESY, WHICH DID IN SOOTH ARISE FROM MY LOVE AND LOYALTY TO OUR LORD...
I HOPE YOU WILL NOT HOLD IT AGAINST ME, SIR.
HOLD IT AGAINST YOU? NEVER!
I BEG YOU, BARON OF DEWA, TO THINK NOTHING OF IT, AND INDEED TO SPEAK YOUR MIND FREELY HENCEFORTH ALSO.

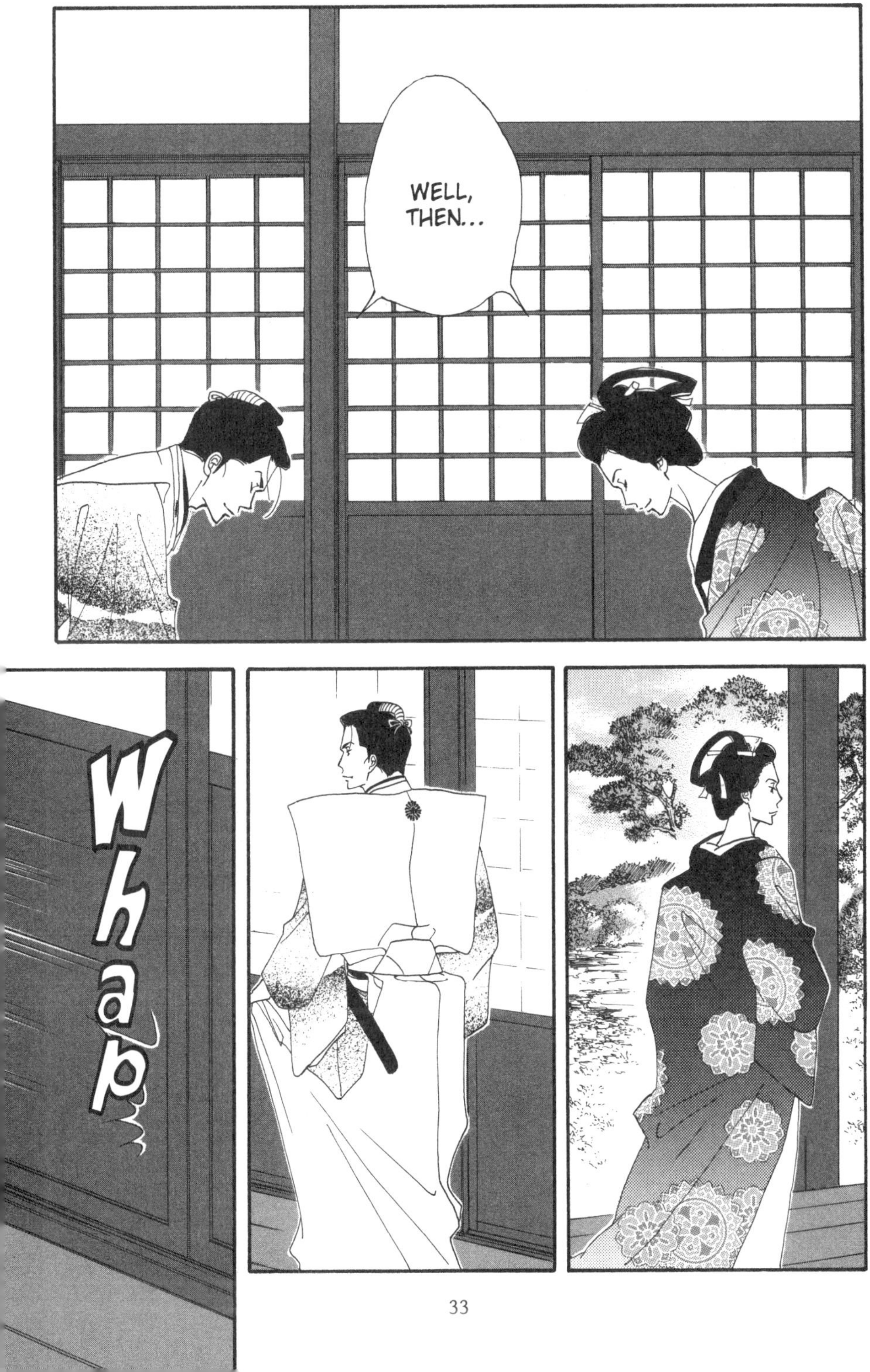
WELL, THEN...
Whap

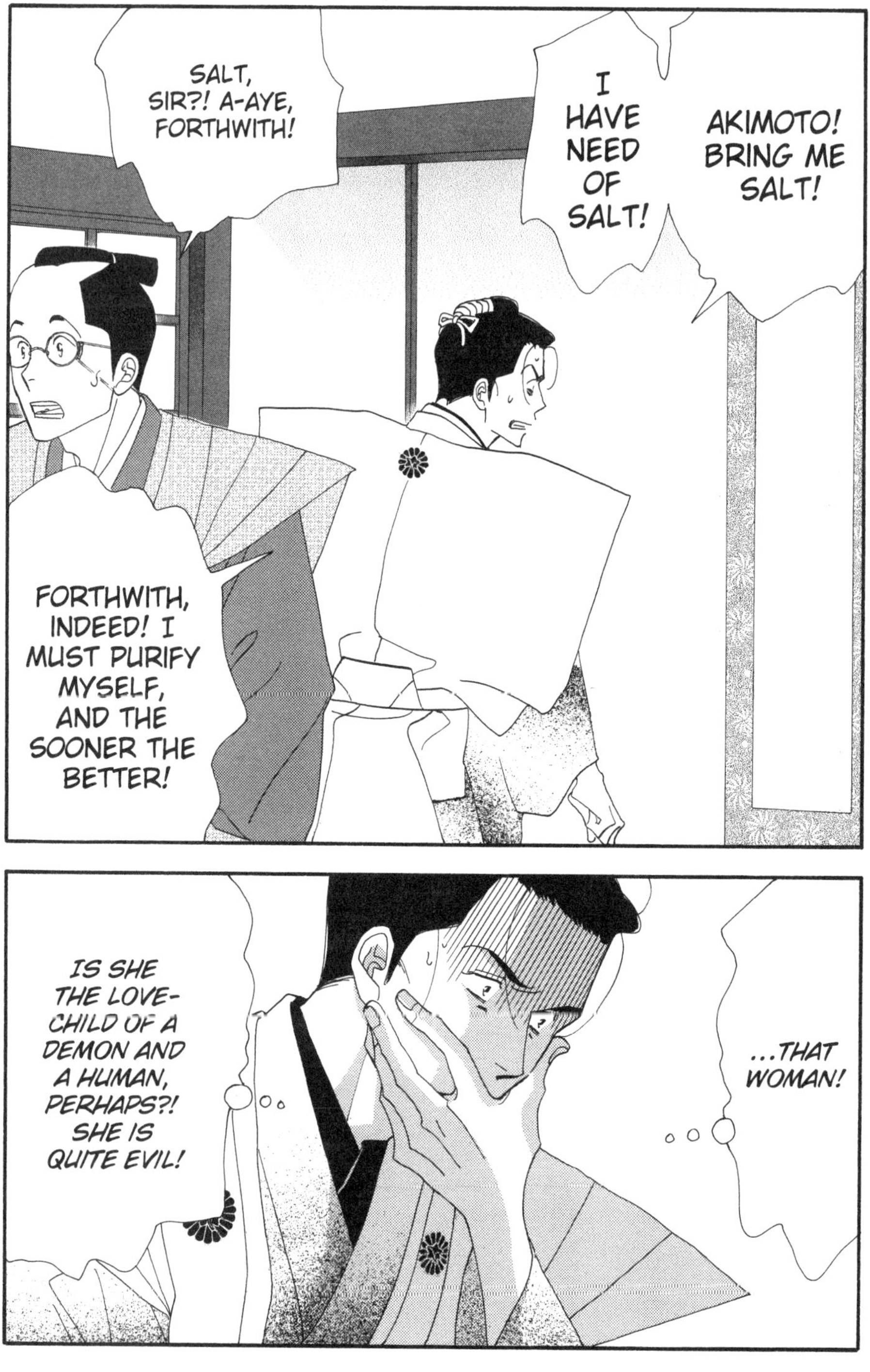
AKIMOTO! BRING ME SALT!
I HAVE NEED OF SALT!
SALT, SIR?! A-AYE, FORTHWITH!
FORTHWITH, INDEED! I MUST PURIFY MYSELF, AND THE SOONER THE BETTER!
...THAT WOMAN!
IS SHE THE LOVE-CHILD OF A DEMON AND A HUMAN, PERHAPS?! SHE IS QUITE EVIL!

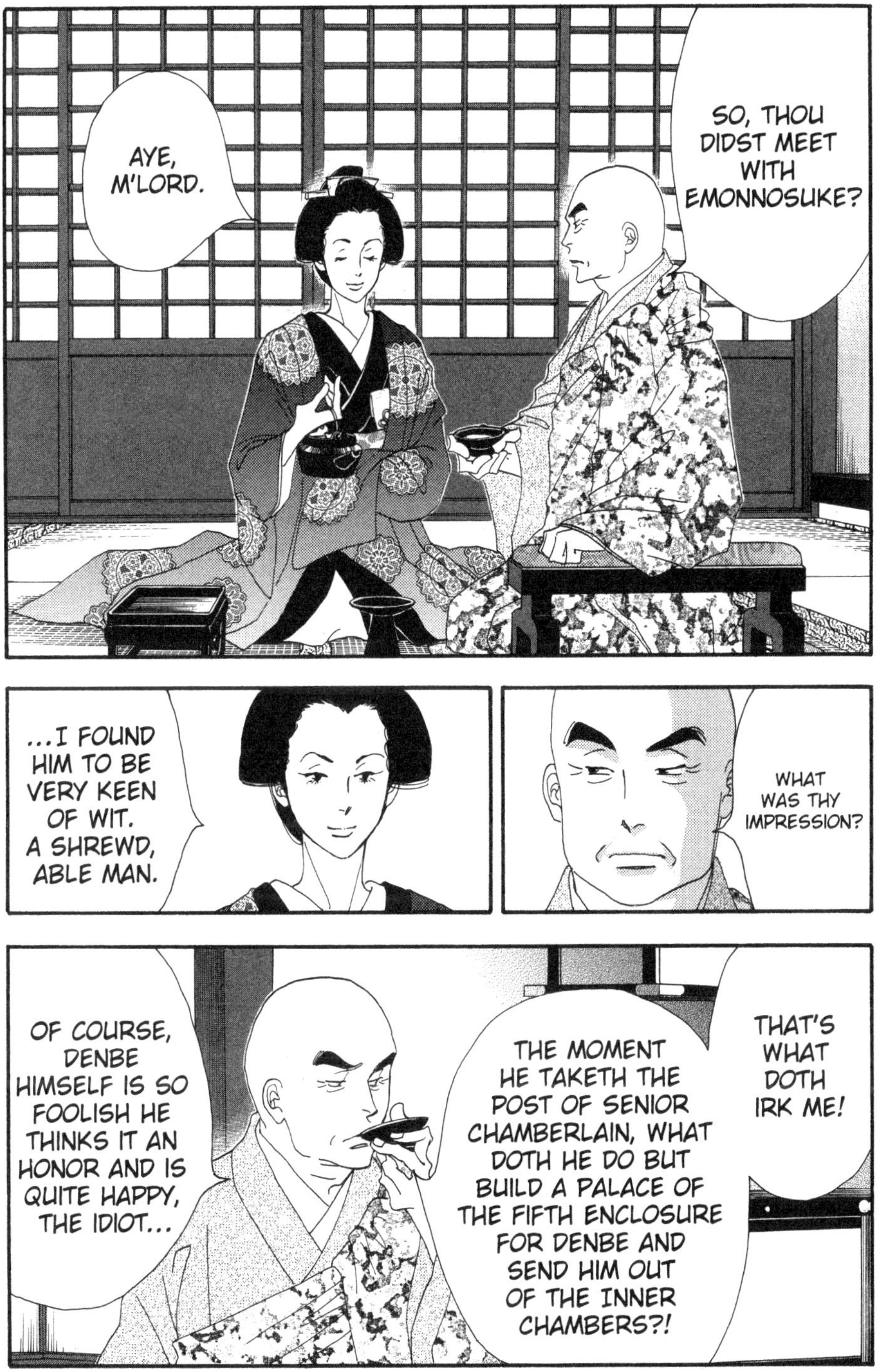
SO, THOU DIDST MEET WITH EMONNOSUKE?
AYE, M'LORD.
WHAT WAS THY IMPRESSION?
...I FOUND HIM TO BE VERY KEEN OF WIT. A SHREWD, ABLE MAN.
THAT'S WHAT DOTH IRK ME!
THE MOMENT HE TAKETH THE POST OF SENIOR CHAMBERLAIN, WHAT DOTH HE DO BUT BUILD A PALACE OF THE FIFTH ENCLOSURE FOR DENBE AND SEND HIM OUT OF THE INNER CHAMBERS?!
OF COURSE, DENBE HIMSELF IS SO FOOLISH HE THINKS IT AN HONOR AND IS QUITE HAPPY, THE IDIOT...

BUT IT SEEMS TO ME THAT YOU, SIR KEISHO-IN, ALREADY HAVE AN IDEA HOW TO COUNTER THE UPSTART.

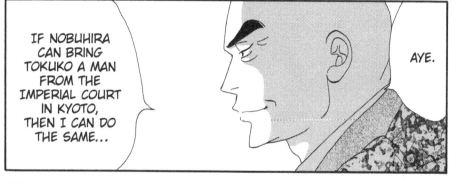

IF NOBUHIRA CAN BRING TOKUKO A MAN FROM THE IMPERIAL COURT IN KYOTO, THEN I CAN DO THE SAME...

AYE.

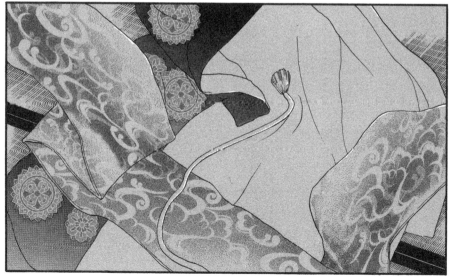

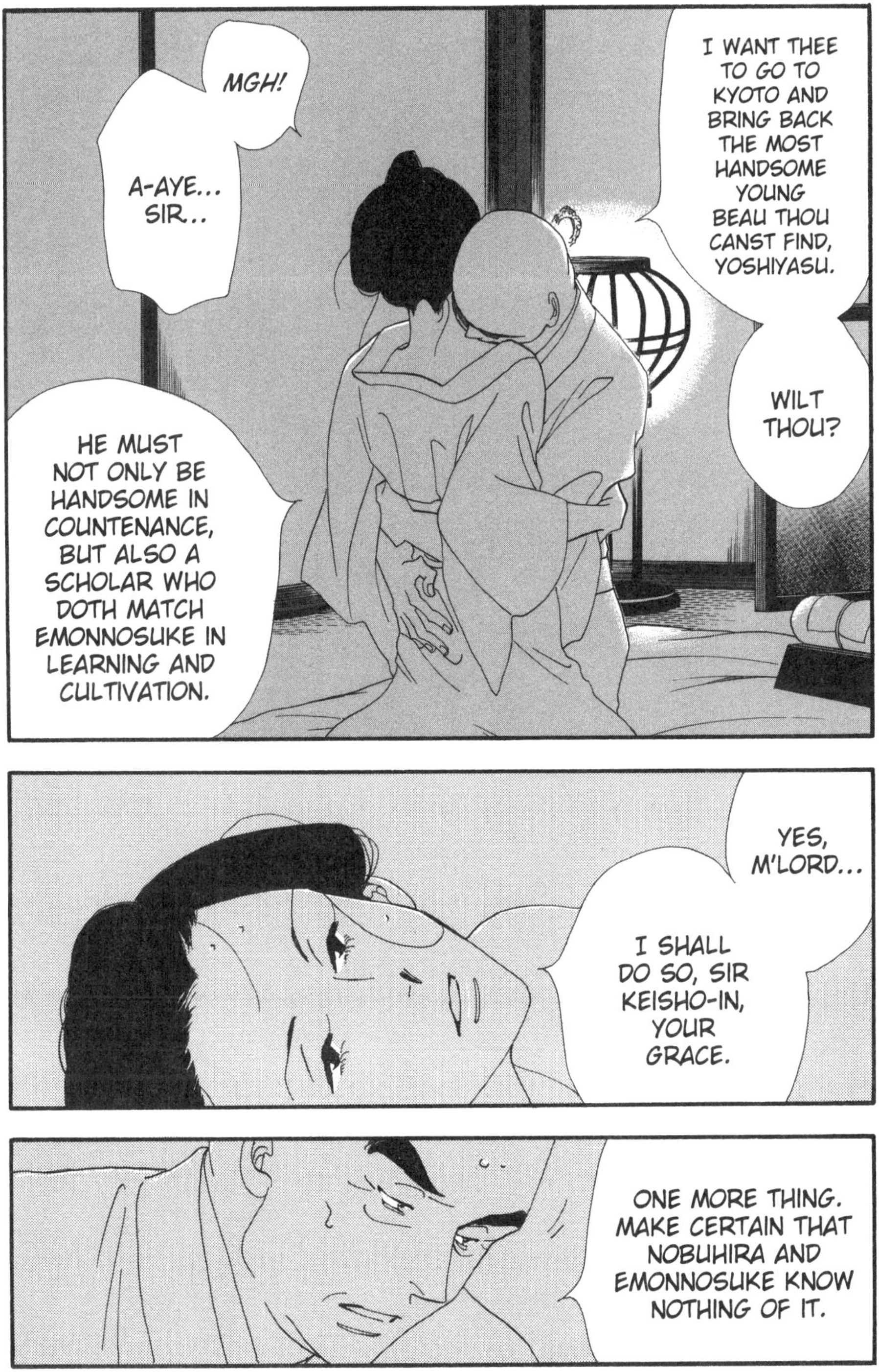
I WANT THEE TO GO TO KYOTO AND BRING BACK THE MOST HANDSOME YOUNG BEAU THOU CANST FIND, YOSHIYASU.
MGH!
A-AYE... SIR...
WILT THOU?
HE MUST NOT ONLY BE HANDSOME IN COUNTENANCE, BUT ALSO A SCHOLAR WHO DOTH MATCH EMONNOSUKE IN LEARNING AND CULTIVATION.
YES, M'LORD...
I SHALL DO SO, SIR KEISHO-IN, YOUR GRACE.
ONE MORE THING. MAKE CERTAIN THAT NOBUHIRA AND EMONNOSUKE KNOW NOTHING OF IT.

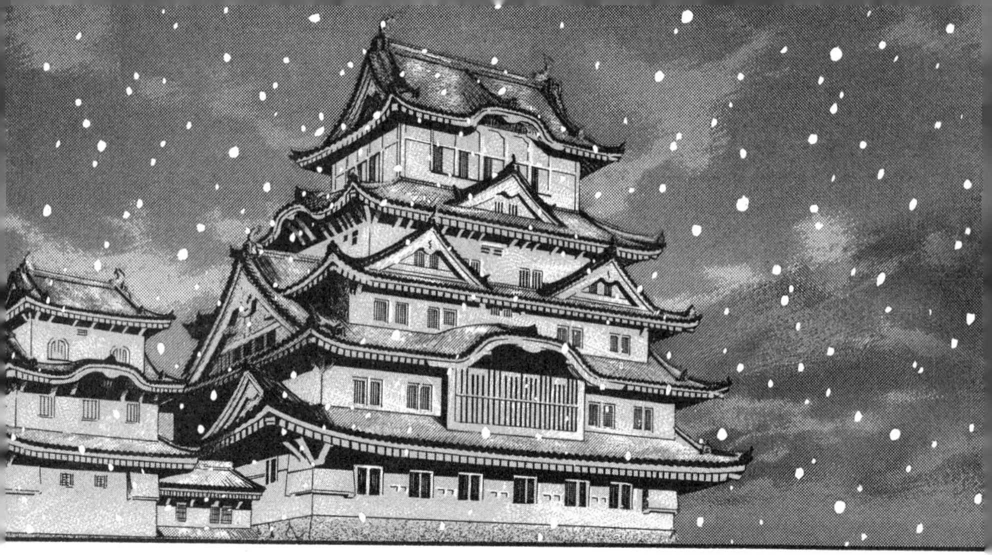

It was on a snowy spring day that the man Yoshiyasu found, Ōsuke, arrived at Edo Castle.

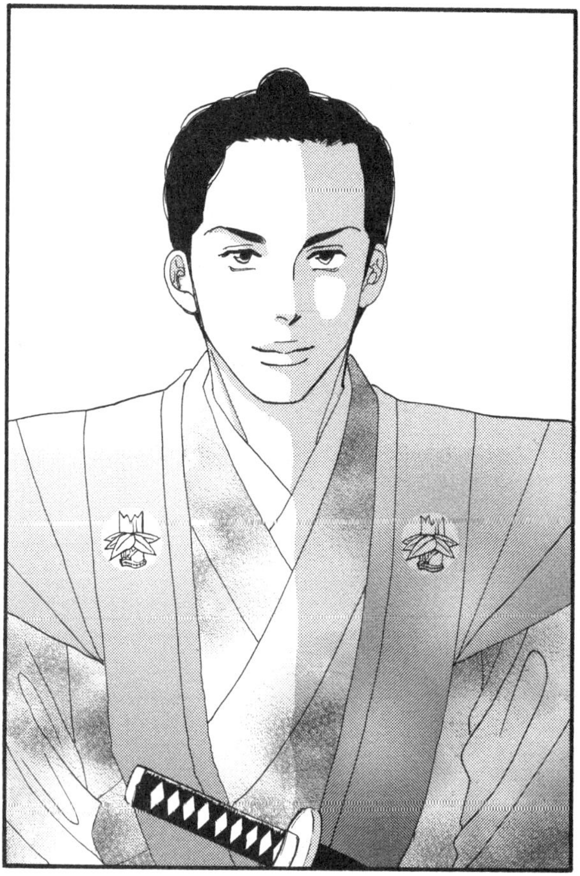

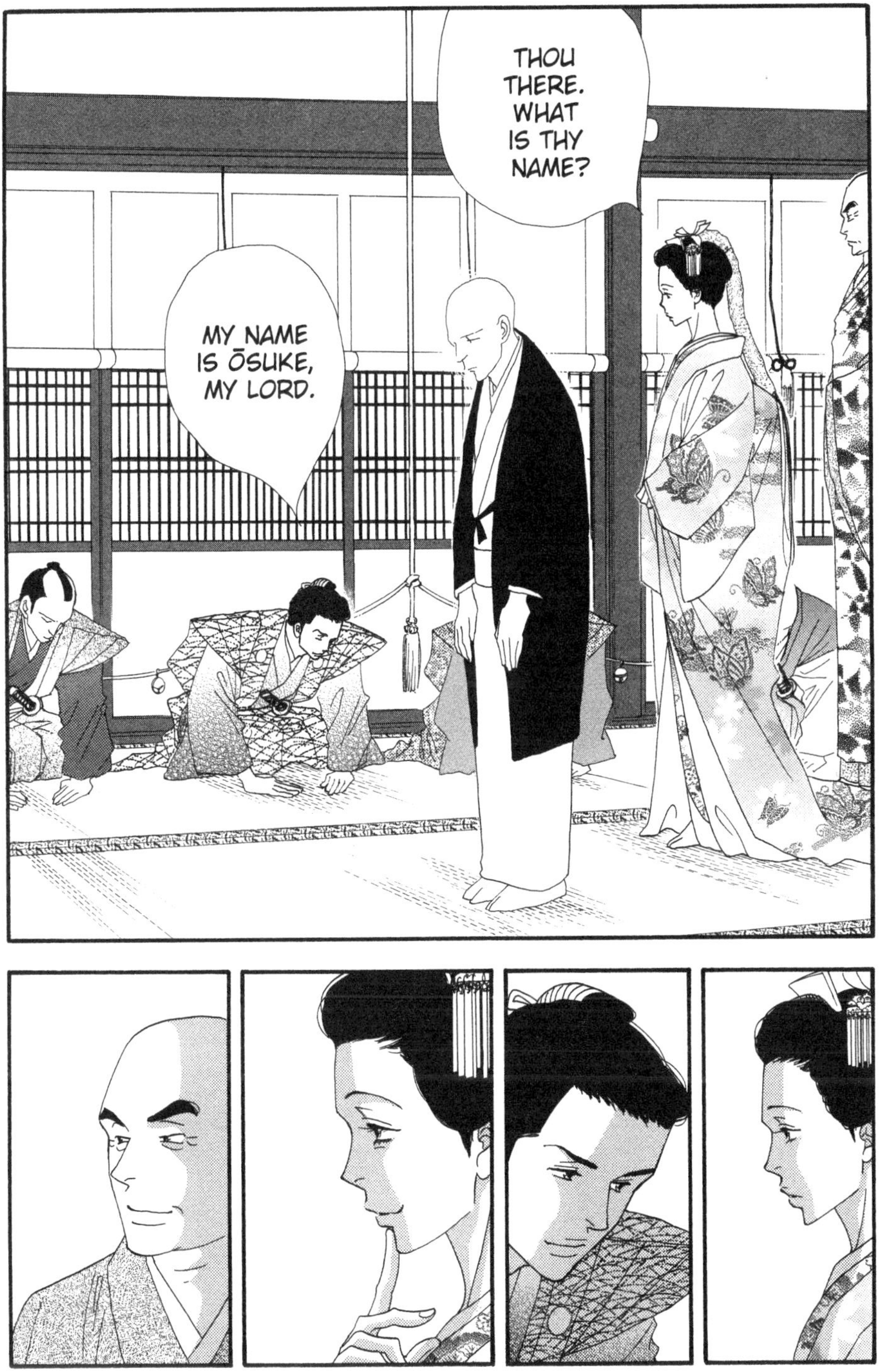
THOU THERE. WHAT IS THY NAME?
MY NAME IS ŌSUKE, MY LORD.

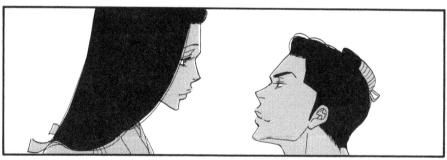

Tsunayoshi
made
Ōsuke her
concubine
at once.

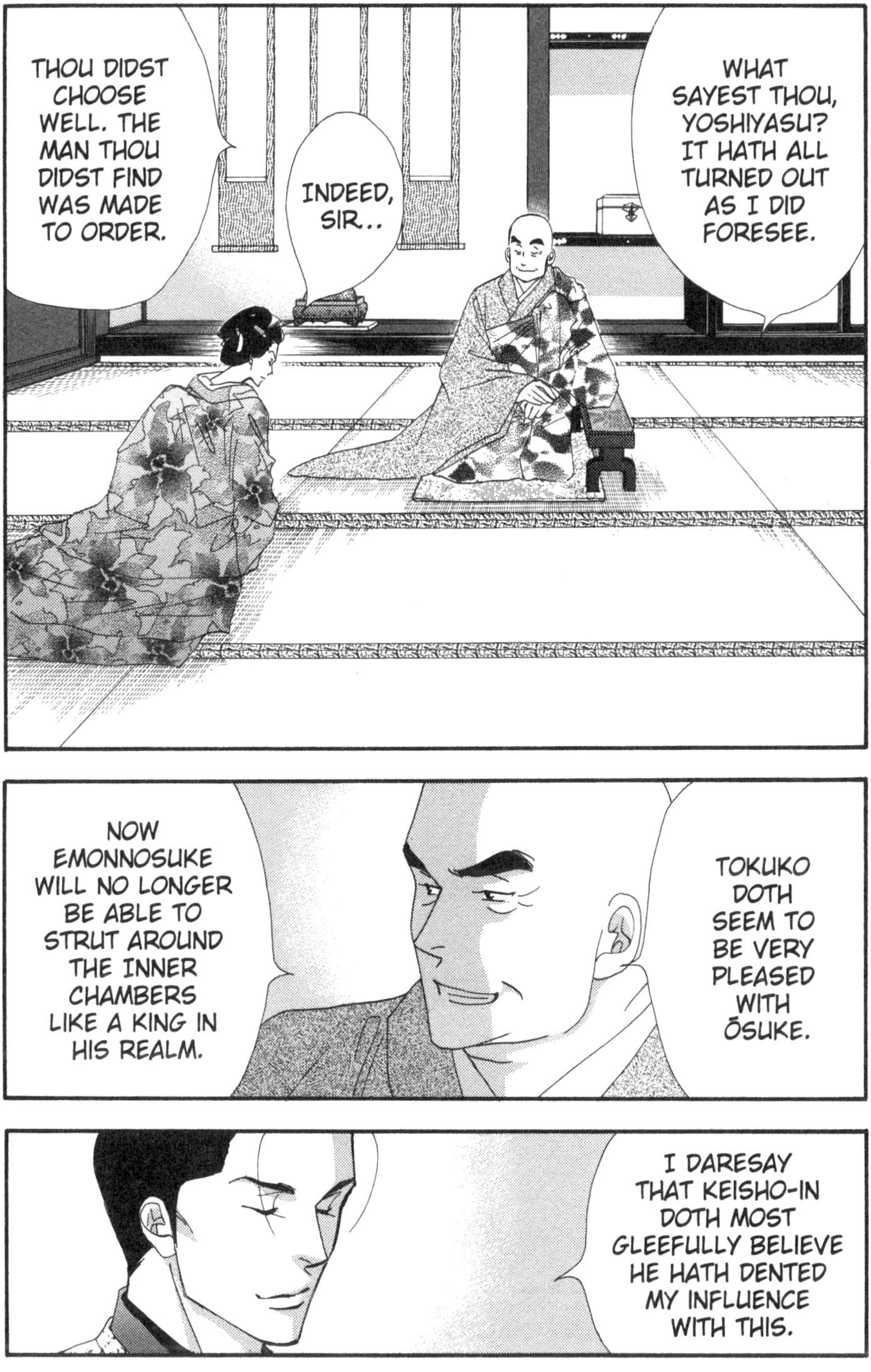
WHAT SAYEST THOU, YOSHIYASU? IT HATH ALL TURNED OUT AS I DID FORESEE.
INDEED, SIR...
THOU DIDST CHOOSE WELL. THE MAN THOU DIDST FIND WAS MADE TO ORDER.
TOKUKO DOTH SEEM TO BE VERY PLEASED WITH ŌSUKE.
NOW EMONNOSUKE WILL NO LONGER BE ABLE TO STRUT AROUND THE INNER CHAMBERS LIKE A KING IN HIS REALM.
I DARESAY THAT KEISHO-IN DOTH MOST GLEEFULLY BELIEVE HE HATH DENTED MY INFLUENCE WITH THIS.

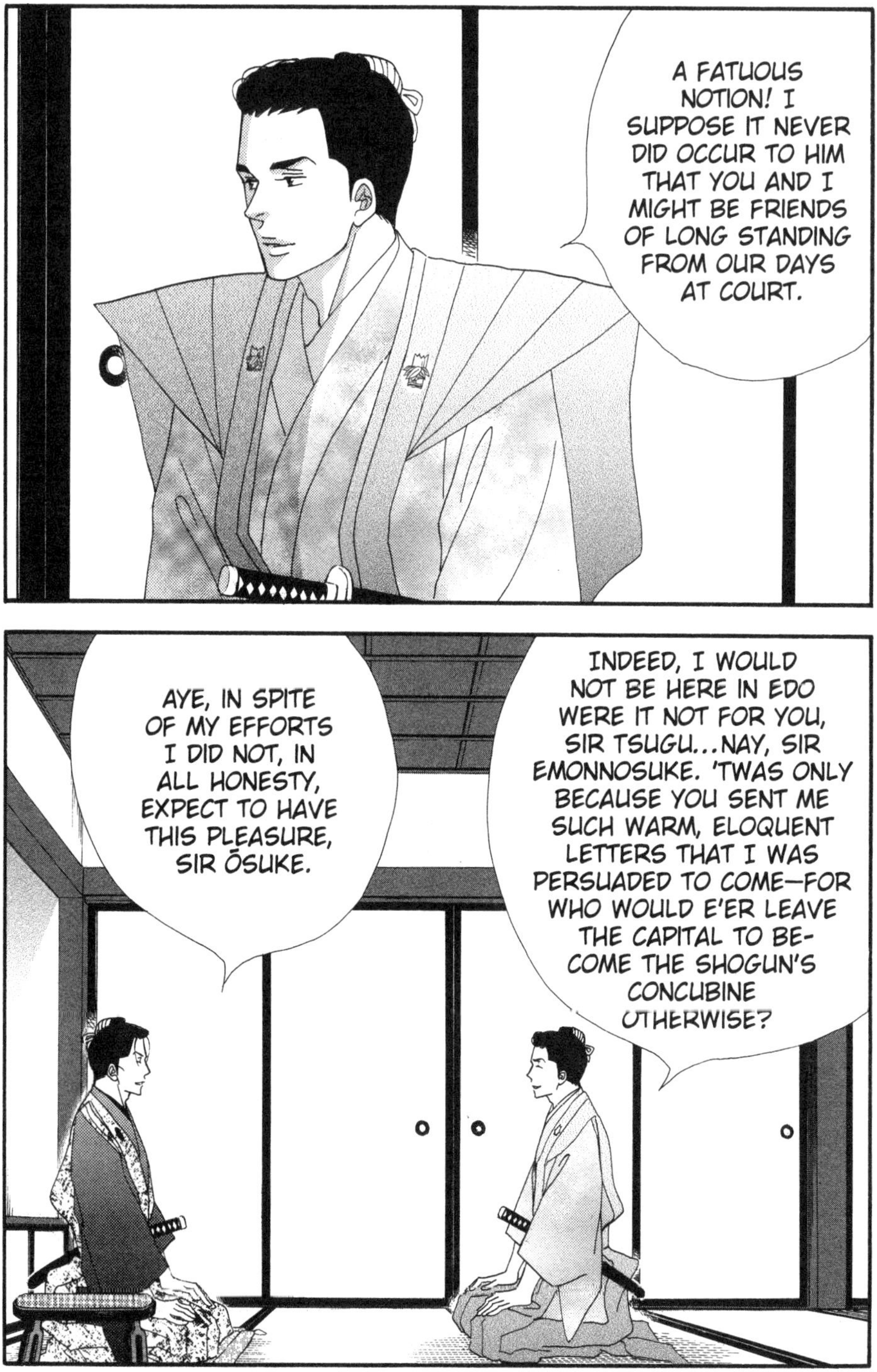
A FATUOUS NOTION! I SUPPOSE IT NEVER DID OCCUR TO HIM THAT YOU AND I MIGHT BE FRIENDS OF LONG STANDING FROM OUR DAYS AT COURT.
INDEED, I WOULD NOT BE HERE IN EDO WERE IT NOT FOR YOU, SIR TSUGU...NAY, SIR EMONNOSUKE. 'TWAS ONLY BECAUSE YOU SENT ME SUCH WARM, ELOQUENT LETTERS THAT I WAS PERSUADED TO COME—FOR WHO WOULD E'ER LEAVE THE CAPITAL TO BE-COME THE SHOGUN'S CONCUBINE OTHERWISE?
AYE, IN SPITE OF MY EFFORTS I DID NOT, IN ALL HONESTY, EXPECT TO HAVE THIS PLEASURE, SIR ŌSUKE.

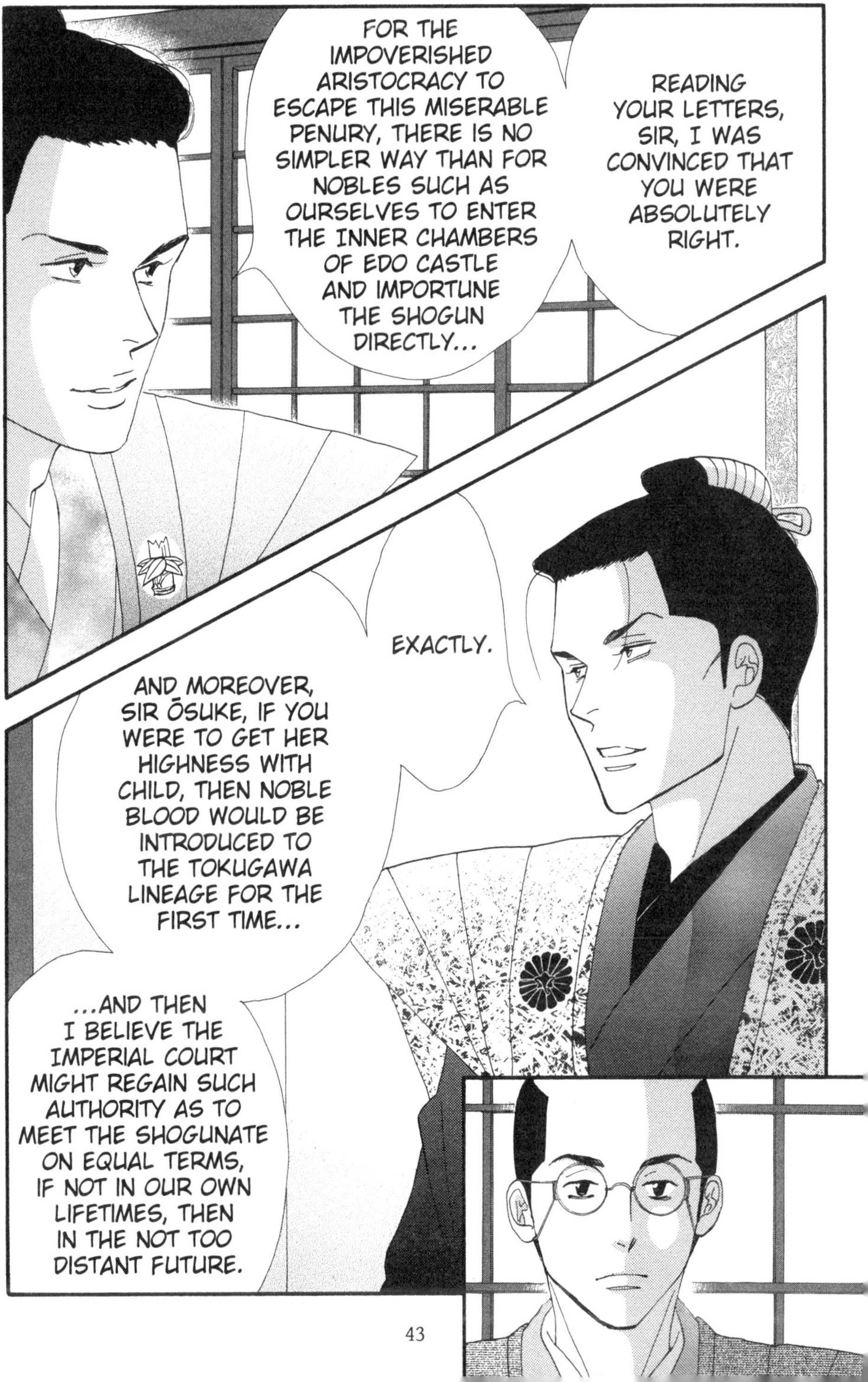
READING YOUR LETTERS, SIR, I WAS CONVINCED THAT YOU WERE ABSOLUTELY RIGHT.
FOR THE IMPOVERISHED ARISTOCRACY TO ESCAPE THIS MISERABLE PENURY, THERE IS NO SIMPLER WAY THAN FOR NOBLES SUCH AS OURSELVES TO ENTER THE INNER CHAMBERS OF EDO CASTLE AND IMPORTUNE THE SHOGUN DIRECTLY...
EXACTLY.
AND MOREOVER, SIR ŌSUKE, IF YOU WERE TO GET HER HIGHNESS WITH CHILD, THEN NOBLE BLOOD WOULD BE INTRODUCED TO THE TOKUGAWA LINEAGE FOR THE FIRST TIME...
...AND THEN I BELIEVE THE IMPERIAL COURT MIGHT REGAIN SUCH AUTHORITY AS TO MEET THE SHOGUNATE ON EQUAL TERMS, IF NOT IN OUR OWN LIFETIMES, THEN IN THE NOT TOO DISTANT FUTURE.

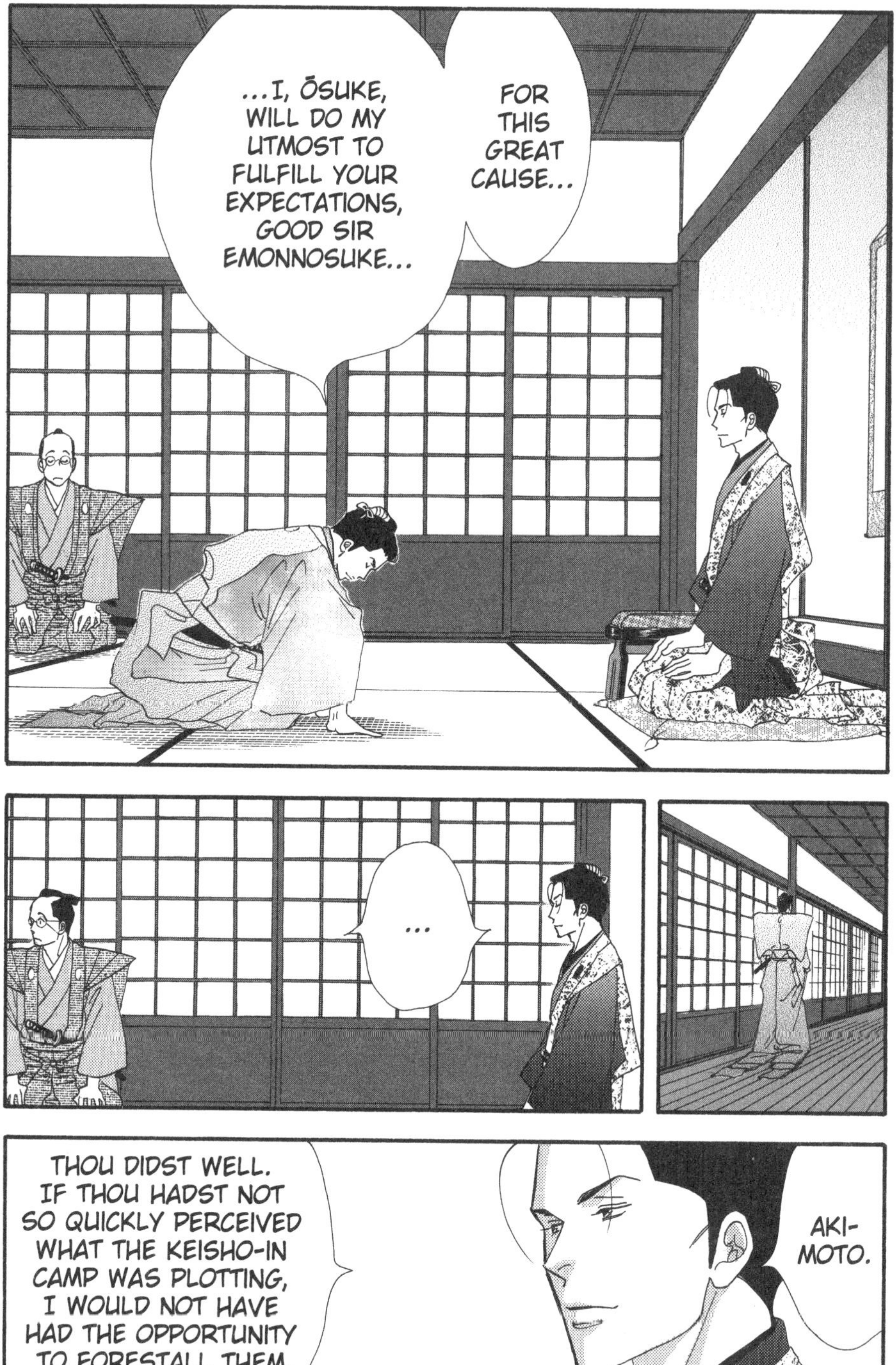
FOR THIS GREAT CAUSE...
...I, ŌSUKE, WILL DO MY UTMOST TO FULFILL YOUR EXPECTATIONS, GOOD SIR EMONNOSUKE...
...
AKI-MOTO.
THOU DIDST WELL. IF THOU HADST NOT SO QUICKLY PERCEIVED WHAT THE KEISHO-IN CAMP WAS PLOTTING, I WOULD NOT HAVE HAD THE OPPORTUNITY TO FORESTALL THEM.

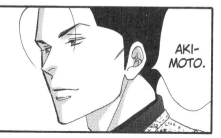

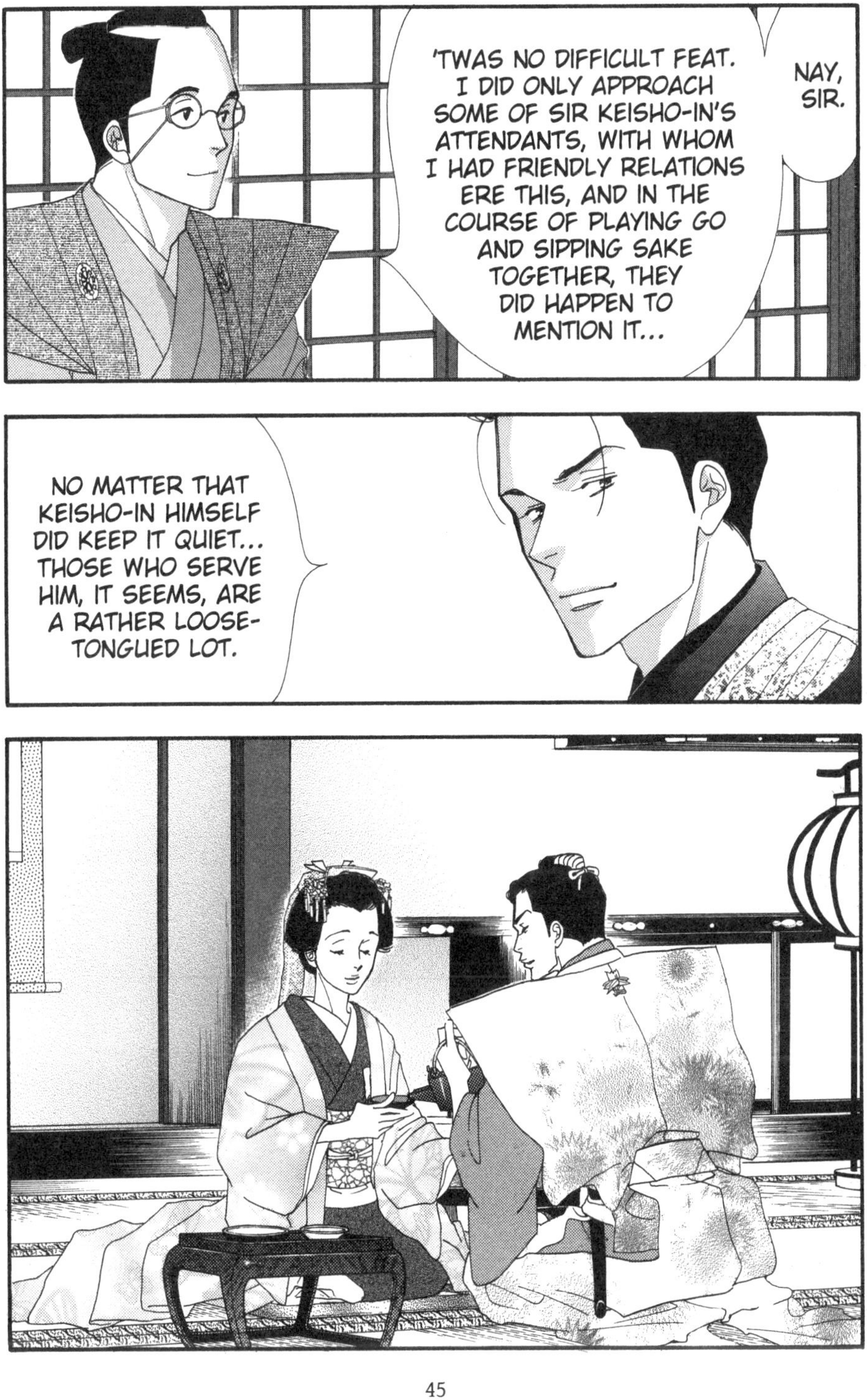
NAY, SIR.
'TWAS NO DIFFICULT FEAT. I DID ONLY APPROACH SOME OF SIR KEISHO-IN'S ATTENDANTS, WITH WHOM I HAD FRIENDLY RELATIONS ERE THIS, AND IN THE COURSE OF PLAYING GO AND SIPPING SAKE TOGETHER, THEY DID HAPPEN TO MENTION IT...
NO MATTER THAT KEISHO-IN HIMSELF DID KEEP IT QUIET... THOSE WHO SERVE HIM, IT SEEMS, ARE A RATHER LOOSE-TONGUED LOT.

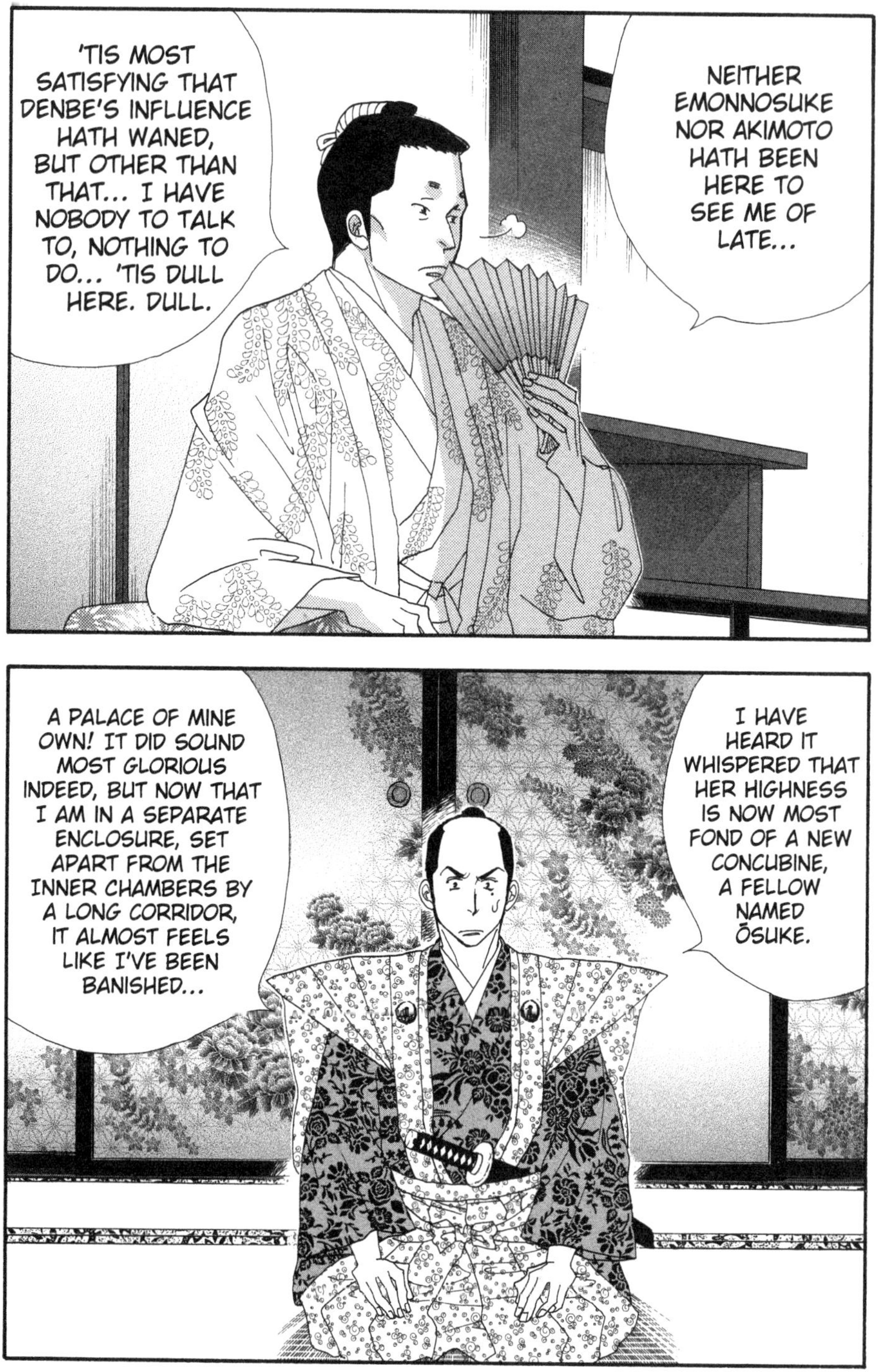
NEITHER EMONNOSUKE NOR AKIMOTO HATH BEEN HERE TO SEE ME OF LATE...
'TIS MOST SATISFYING THAT DENBE'S INFLUENCE HATH WANED, BUT OTHER THAN THAT... I HAVE NOBODY TO TALK TO, NOTHING TO DO... 'TIS DULL HERE. DULL.
I HAVE HEARD IT WHISPERED THAT HER HIGHNESS IS NOW MOST FOND OF A NEW CONCUBINE, A FELLOW NAMED ŌSUKE.
A PALACE OF MINE OWN! IT DID SOUND MOST GLORIOUS INDEED, BUT NOW THAT I AM IN A SEPARATE ENCLOSURE, SET APART FROM THE INNER CHAMBERS BY A LONG CORRIDOR, IT ALMOST FEELS LIKE I'VE BEEN BANISHED...

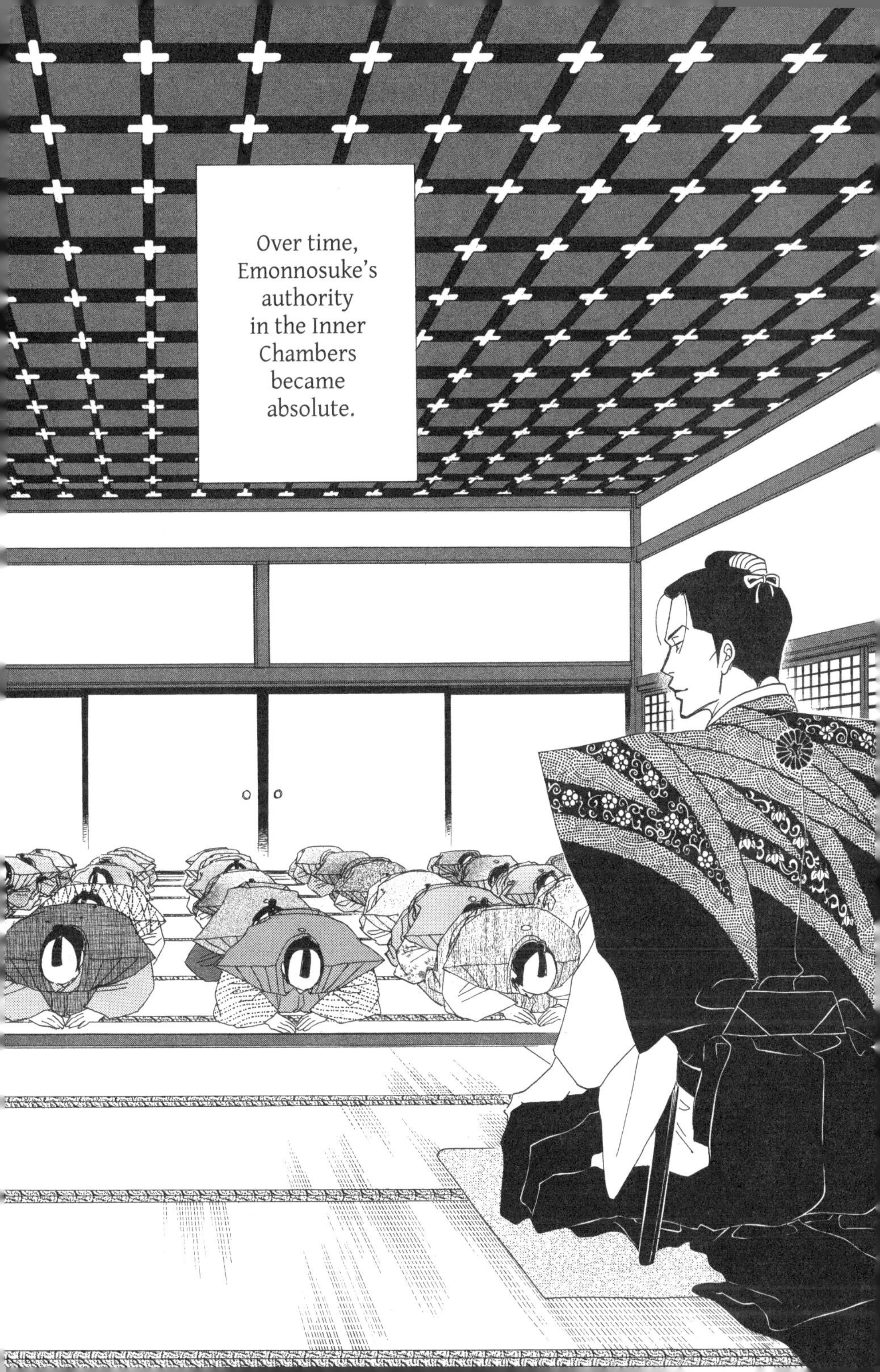
Over time, Emonnosuke's authority in the Inner Chambers became absolute.

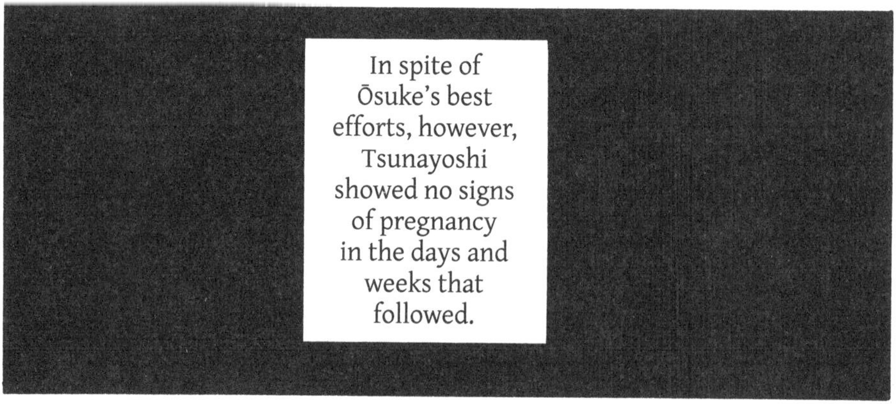
In spite of Ōsuke's best efforts, however, Tsunayoshi showed no signs of pregnancy in the days and weeks that followed.

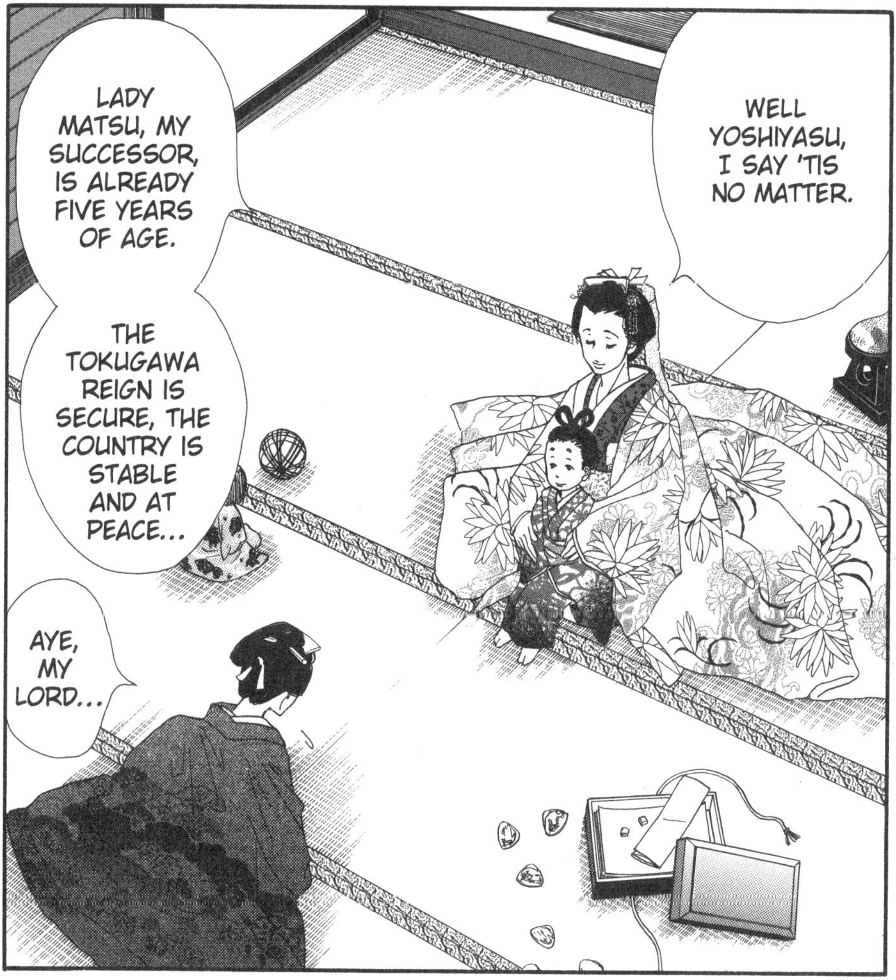
WELL YOSHIYASU, I SAY 'TIS NO MATTER.
LADY MATSU, MY SUCCESSOR, IS ALREADY FIVE YEARS OF AGE.
THE TOKUGAWA REIGN IS SECURE, THE COUNTRY IS STABLE AND AT PEACE...
AYE, MY LORD...

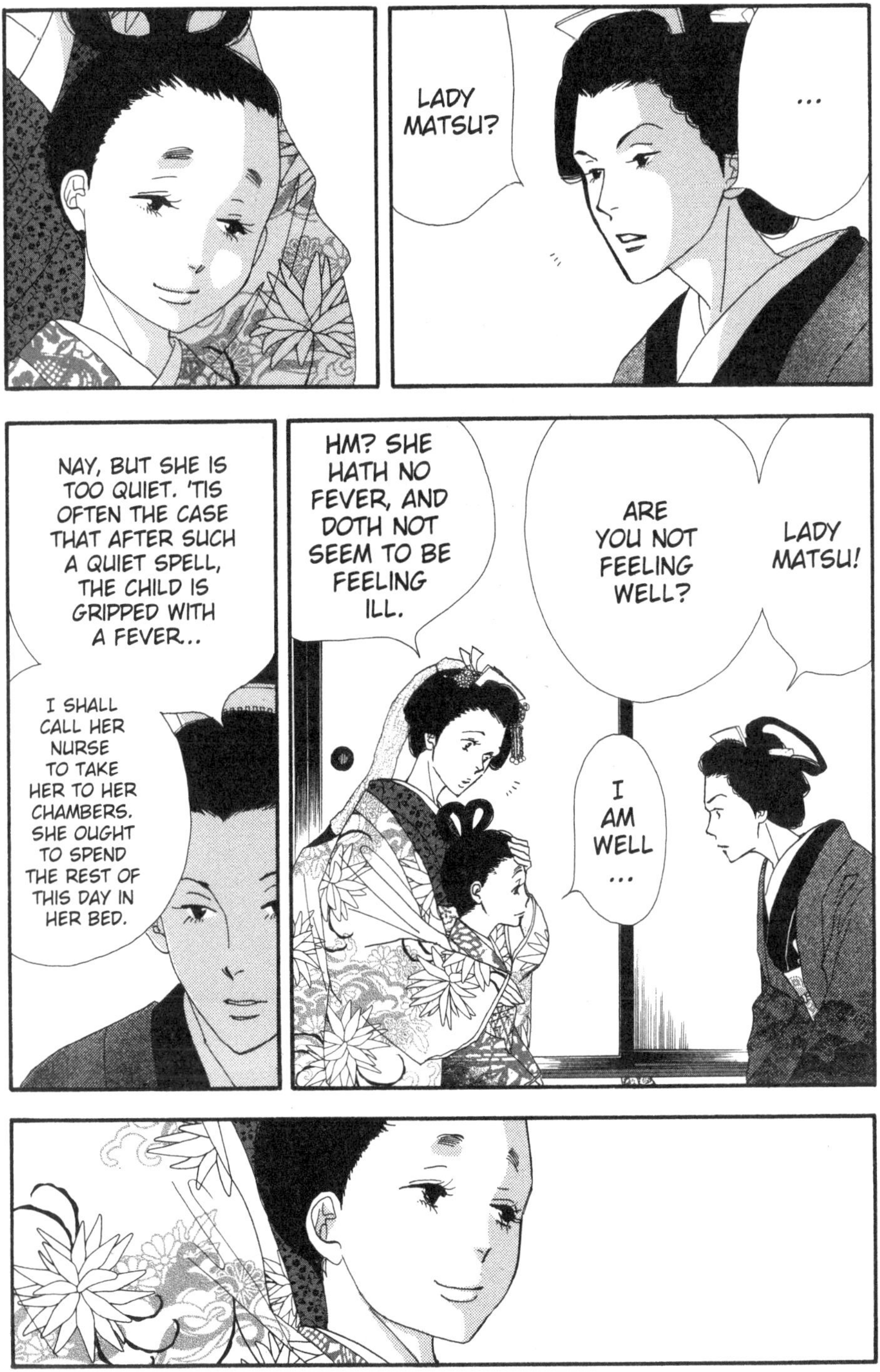
...
LADY MATSU?
LADY MATSU!
ARE YOU NOT FEELING WELL?
HM? SHE HATH NO FEVER, AND DOTH NOT SEEM TO BE FEELING ILL.
I AM WELL ...
NAY, BUT SHE IS TOO QUIET. 'TIS OFTEN THE CASE THAT AFTER SUCH A QUIET SPELL, THE CHILD IS GRIPPED WITH A FEVER...
I SHALL CALL HER NURSE TO TAKE HER TO HER CHAMBERS. SHE OUGHT TO SPEND THE REST OF THIS DAY IN HER BED.

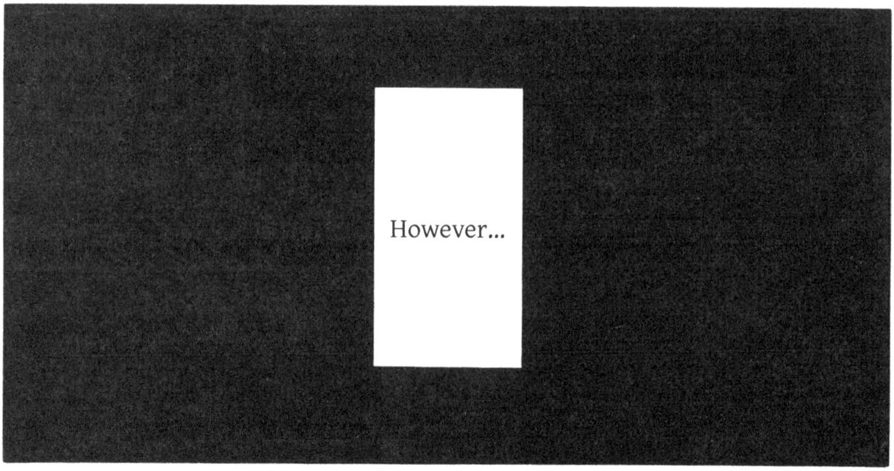
However...

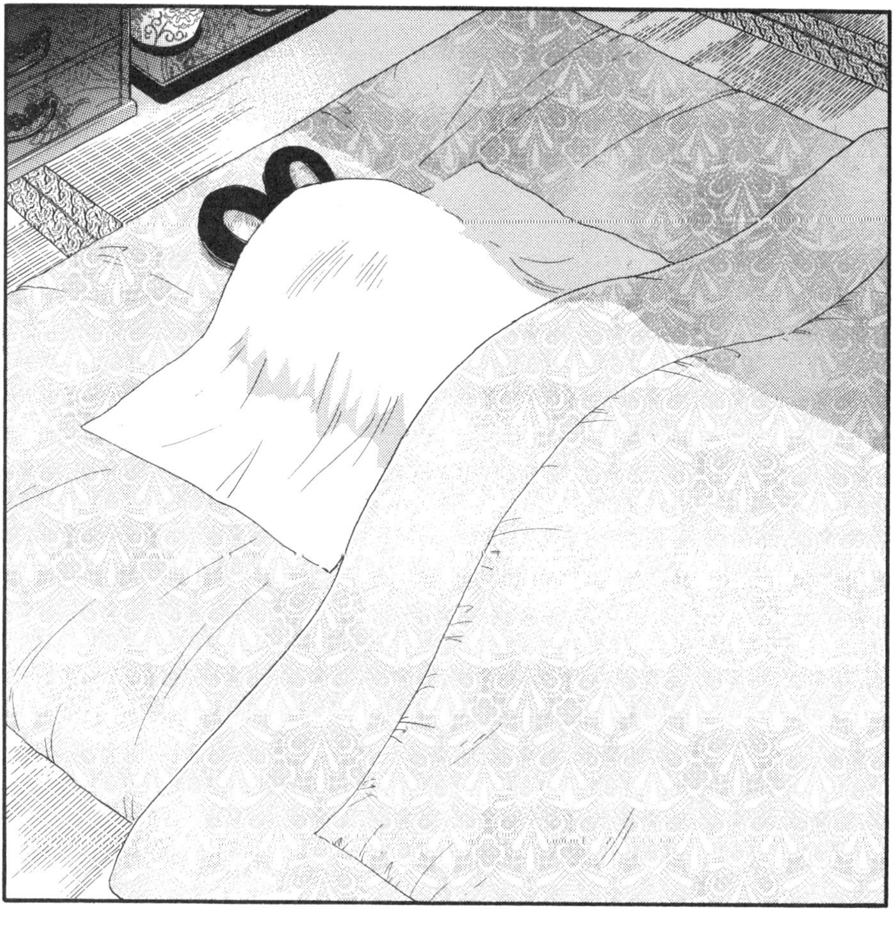

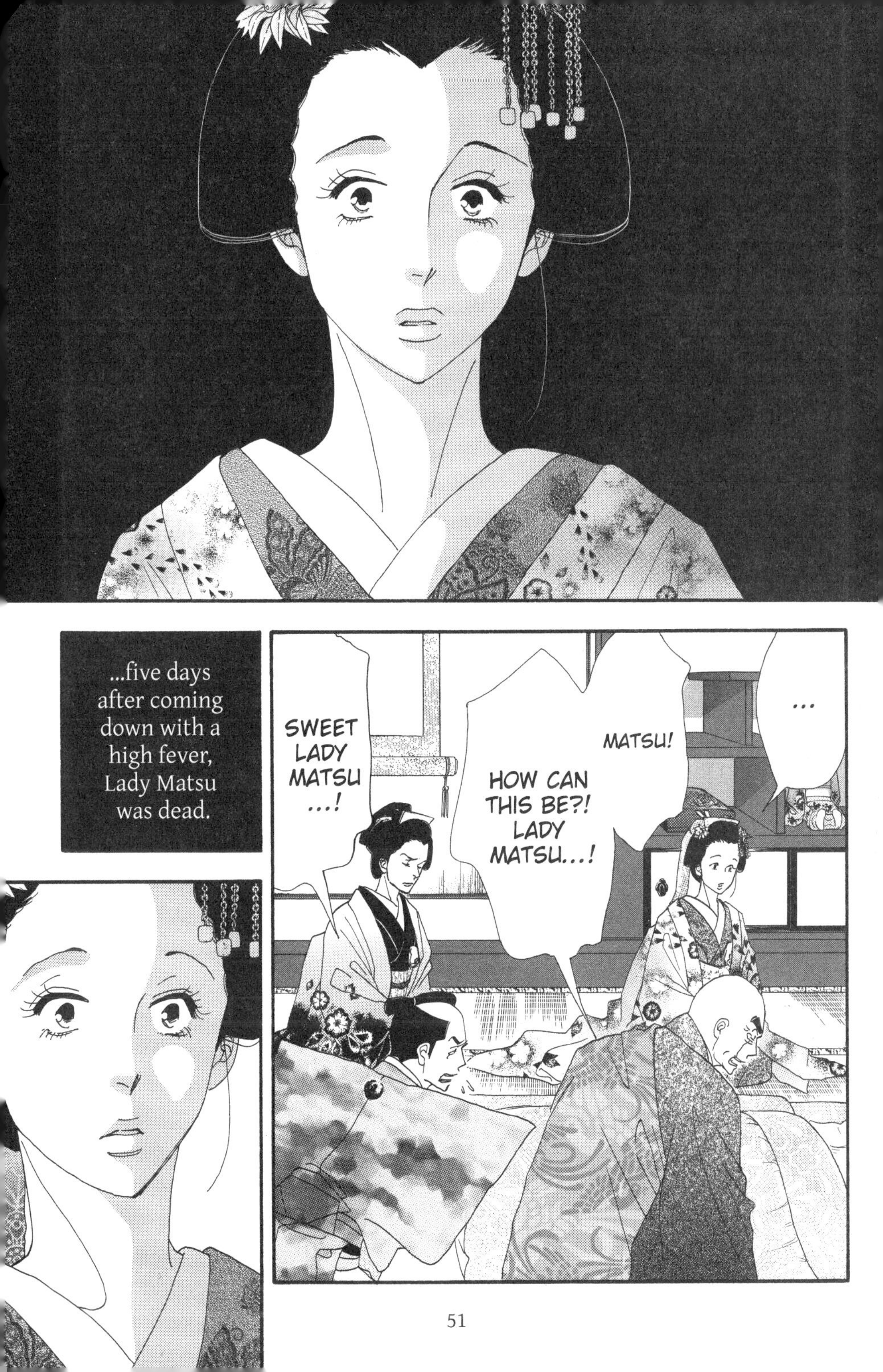
...
MATSU!
HOW CAN THIS BE?! LADY MATSU...!
SWEET LADY MATSU...!
...five days after coming down with a high fever, Lady Matsu was dead.

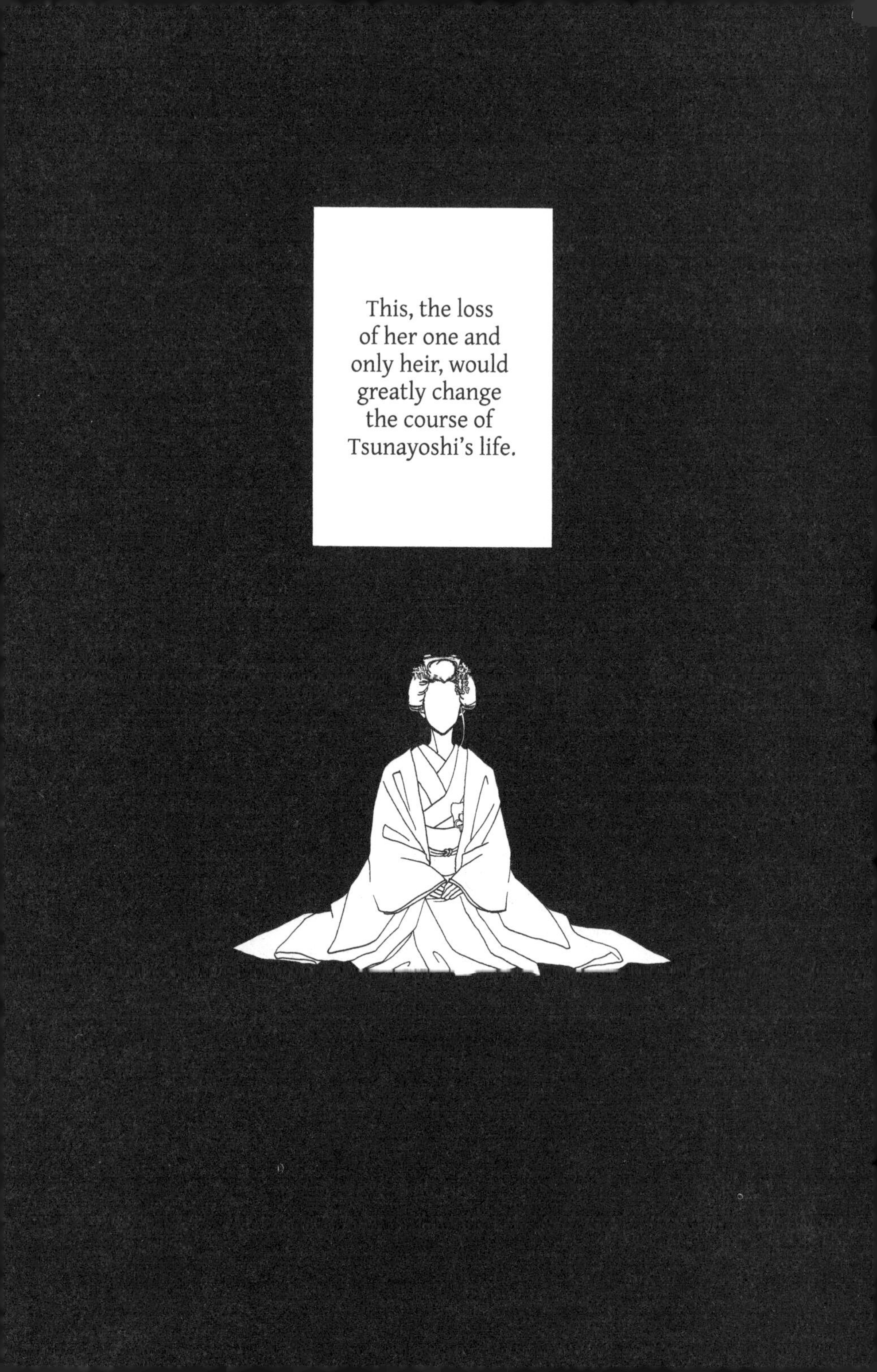
This, the loss of her one and only heir, would greatly change the course of Tsunayoshi's life.

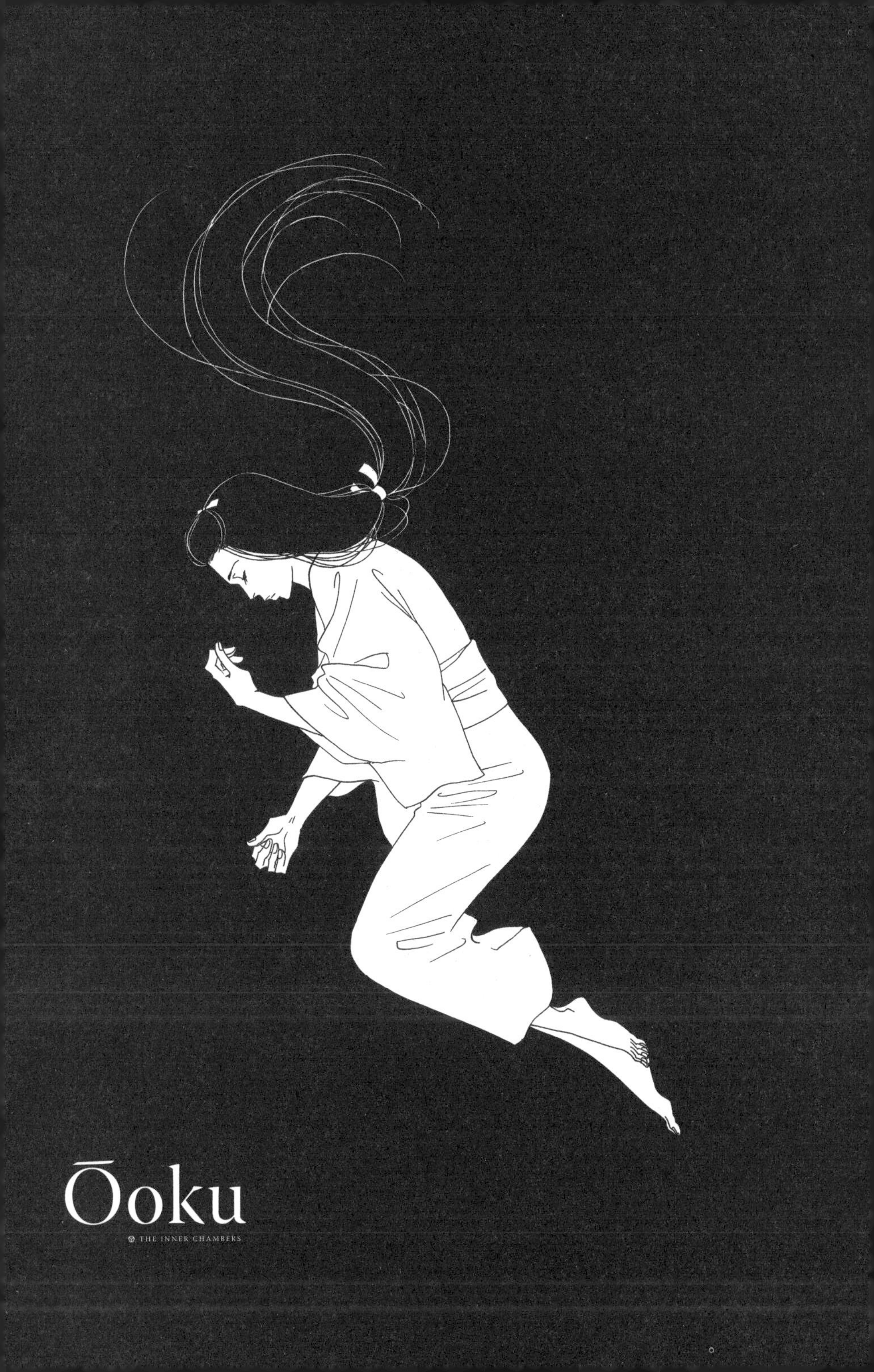
Ōoku
THE INNER CHAMBERS

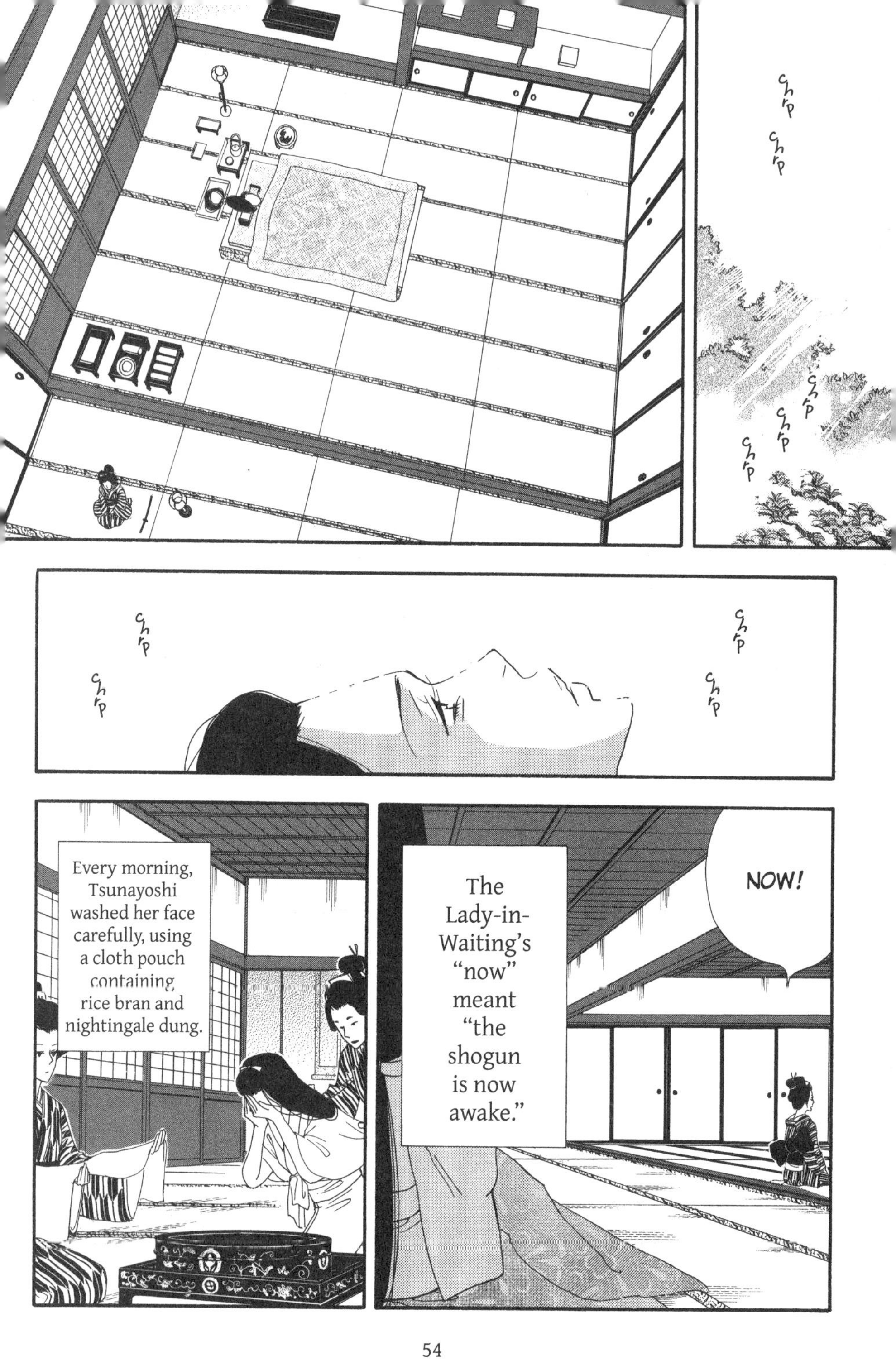
chrp
chrp
chrp
chrp
chrp
chrp
chrp
chrp
chrp
NOW!
The Lady-in-Waiting's "now" meant "the shogun is now awake."
Every morning, Tsunayoshi washed her face carefully, using a cloth pouch containing rice bran and nightingale dung.

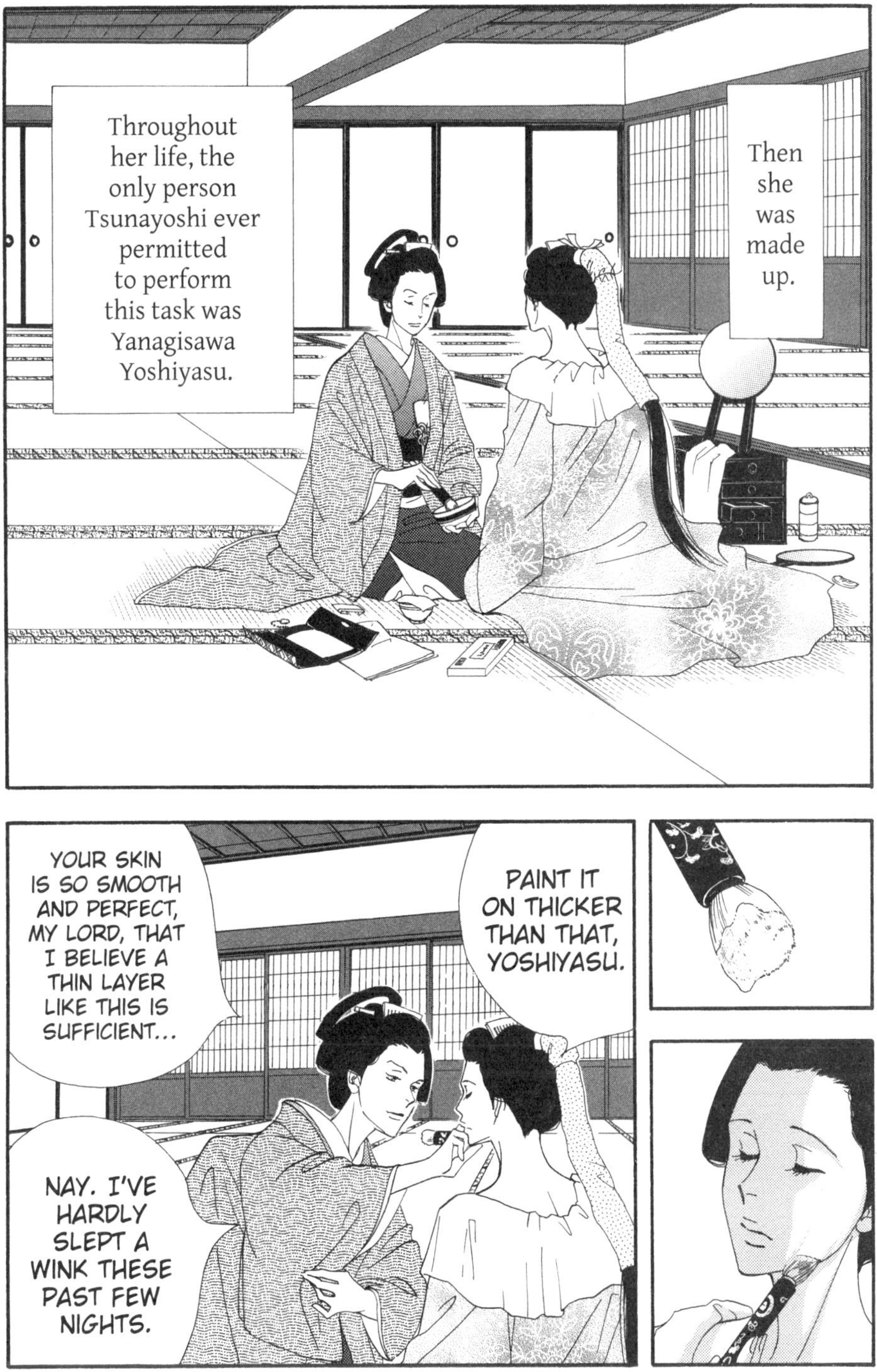
Then she was made up.
Throughout her life, the only person Tsunayoshi ever permitted to perform this task was Yanagisawa Yoshiyasu.
PAINT IT ON THICKER THAN THAT, YOSHIYASU.
YOUR SKIN IS SO SMOOTH AND PERFECT, MY LORD, THAT I BELIEVE A THIN LAYER LIKE THIS IS SUFFICIENT...
NAY. I'VE HARDLY SLEPT A WINK THESE PAST FEW NIGHTS.

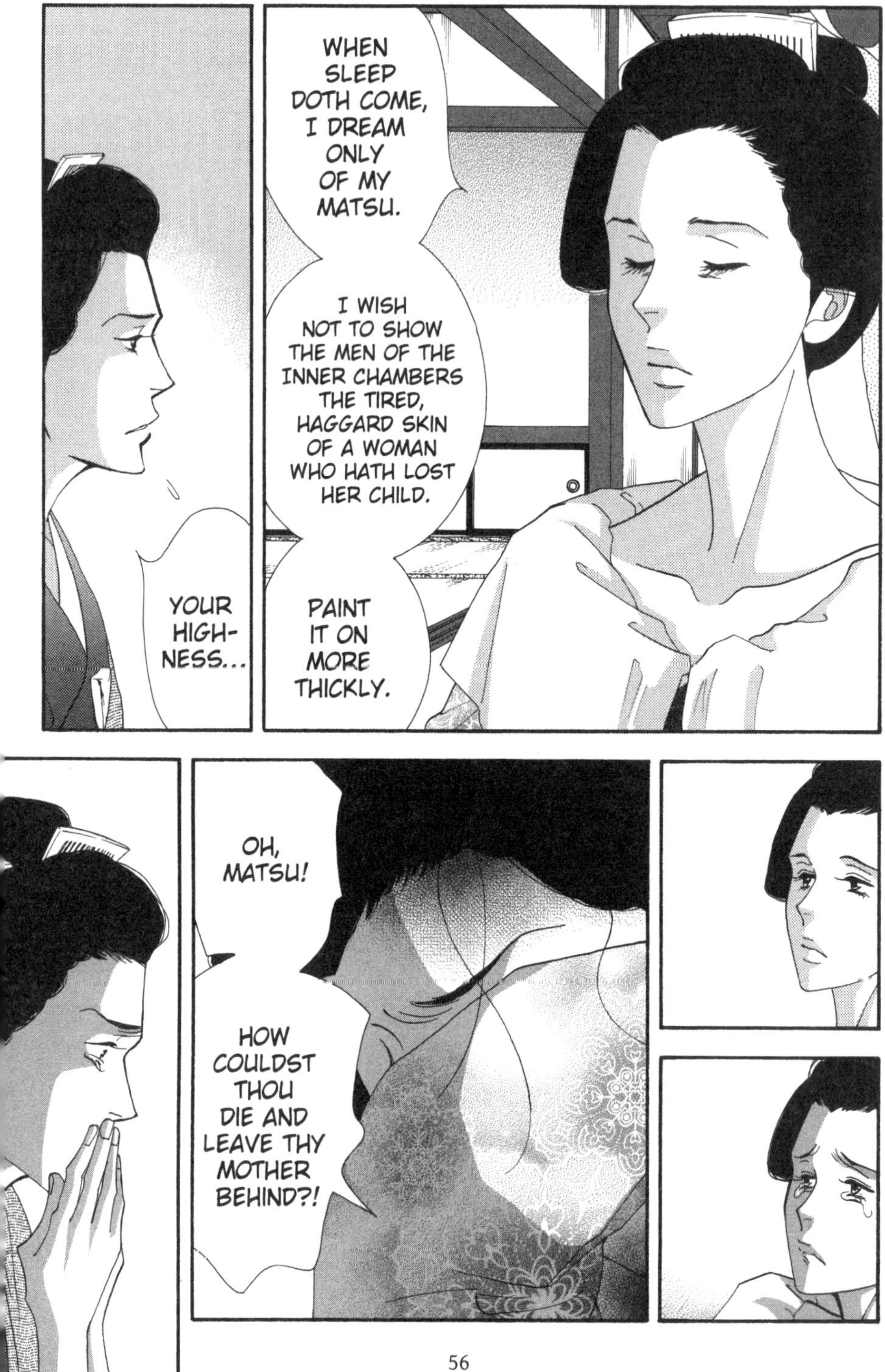
WHEN SLEEP DOTH COME, I DREAM ONLY OF MY MATSU.
I WISH NOT TO SHOW THE MEN OF THE INNER CHAMBERS THE TIRED, HAGGARD SKIN OF A WOMAN WHO HATH LOST HER CHILD.
PAINT IT ON MORE THICKLY.
YOUR HIGH-NESS...
OH, MATSU!
HOW COULDST THOU DIE AND LEAVE THY MOTHER BEHIND?!

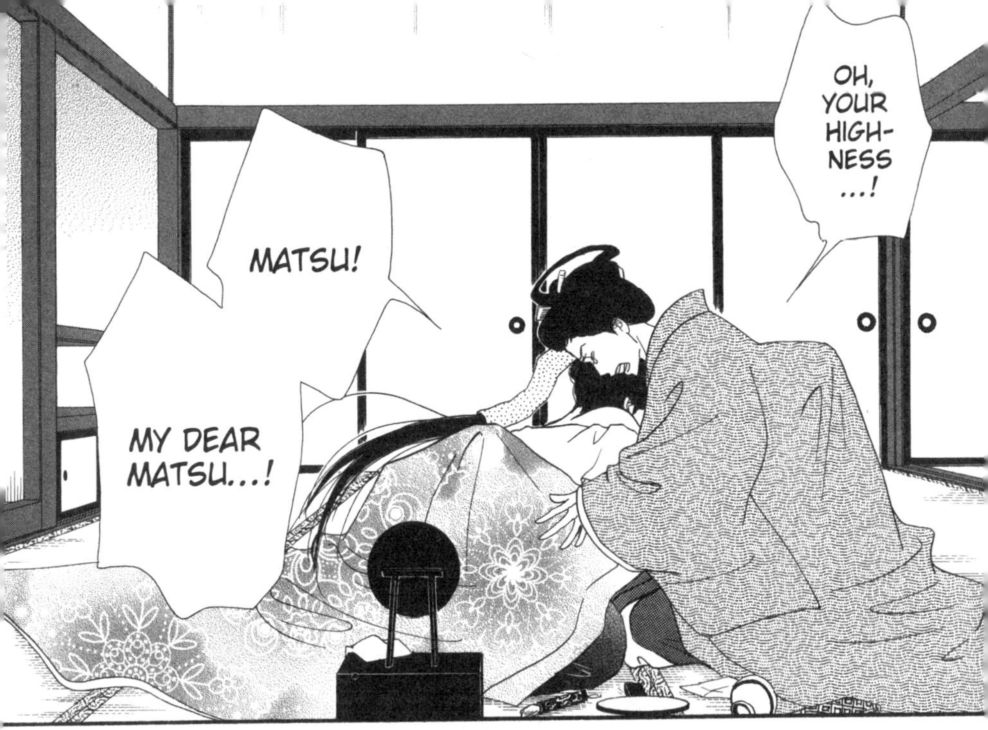
OH, YOUR HIGH-NESS...!
MATSU!
MY DEAR MATSU...!

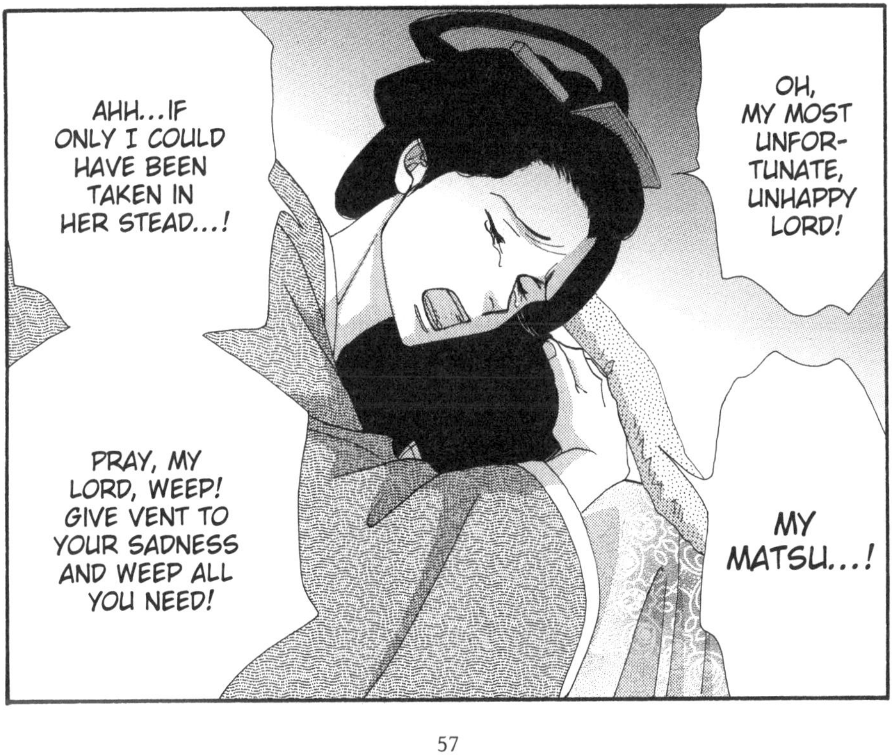
OH, MY MOST UNFOR-TUNATE, UNHAPPY LORD!
AHH...IF ONLY I COULD HAVE BEEN TAKEN IN HER STEAD...!
MY MATSU...!
PRAY, MY LORD, WEEP! GIVE VENT TO YOUR SADNESS AND WEEP ALL YOU NEED!

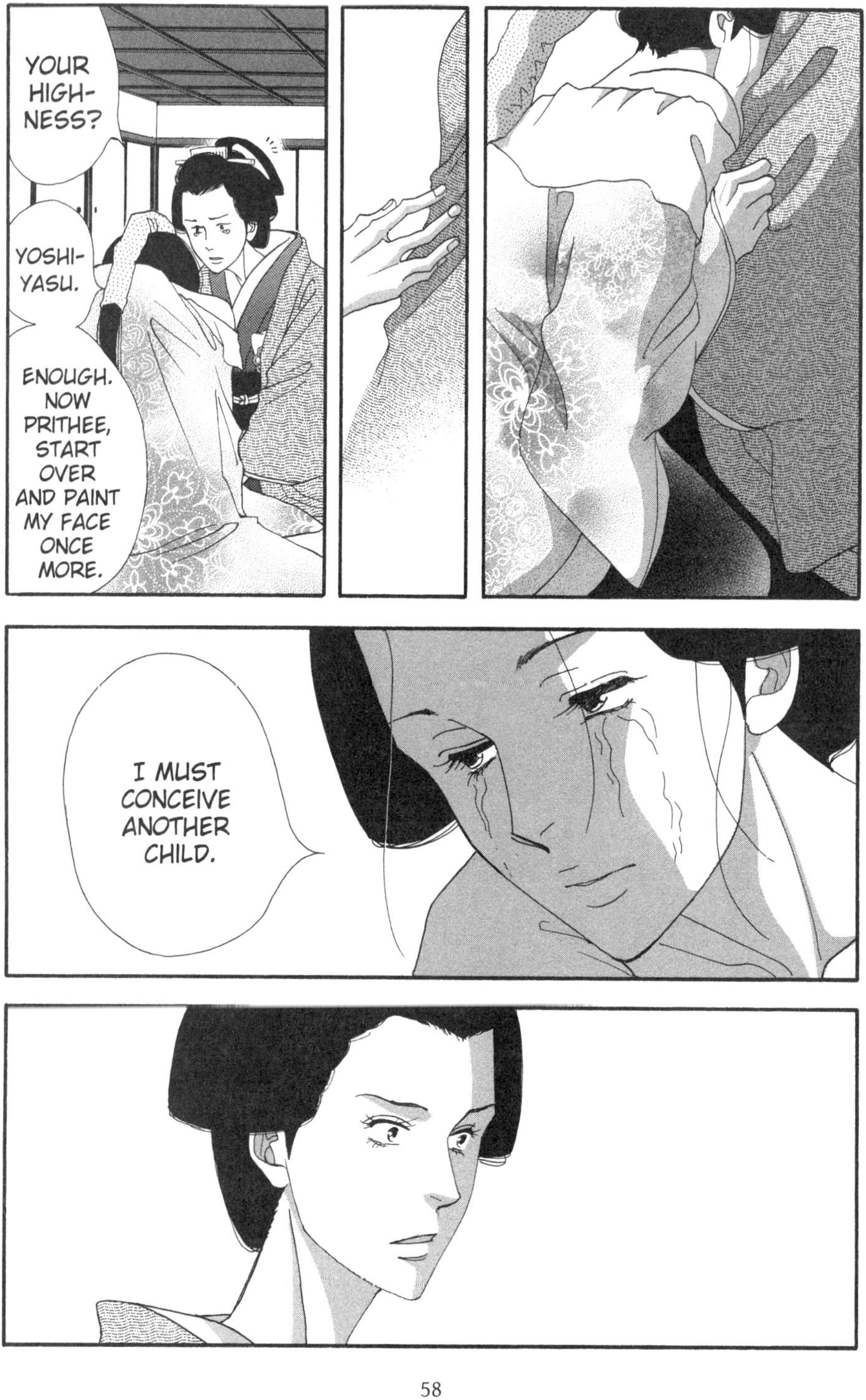
YOUR HIGH-NESS?
YOSHI-YASU.
ENOUGH. NOW PRITHEE, START OVER AND PAINT MY FACE ONCE MORE.
I MUST CONCEIVE ANOTHER CHILD.

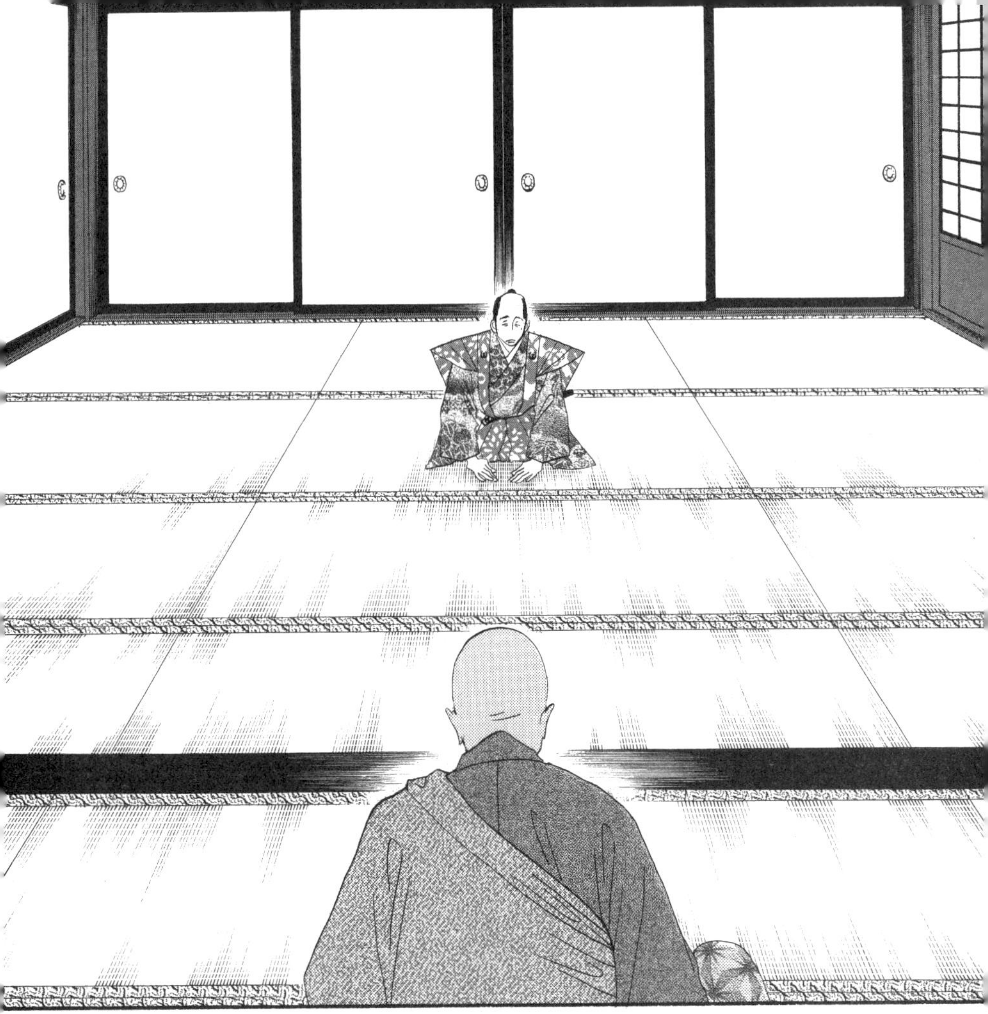

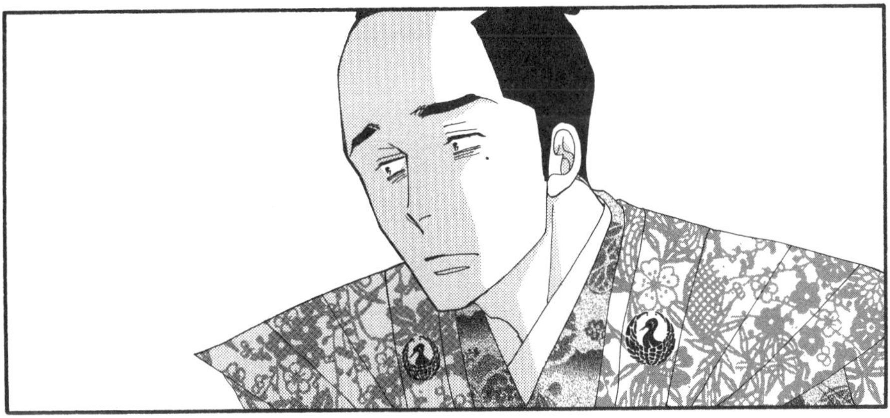

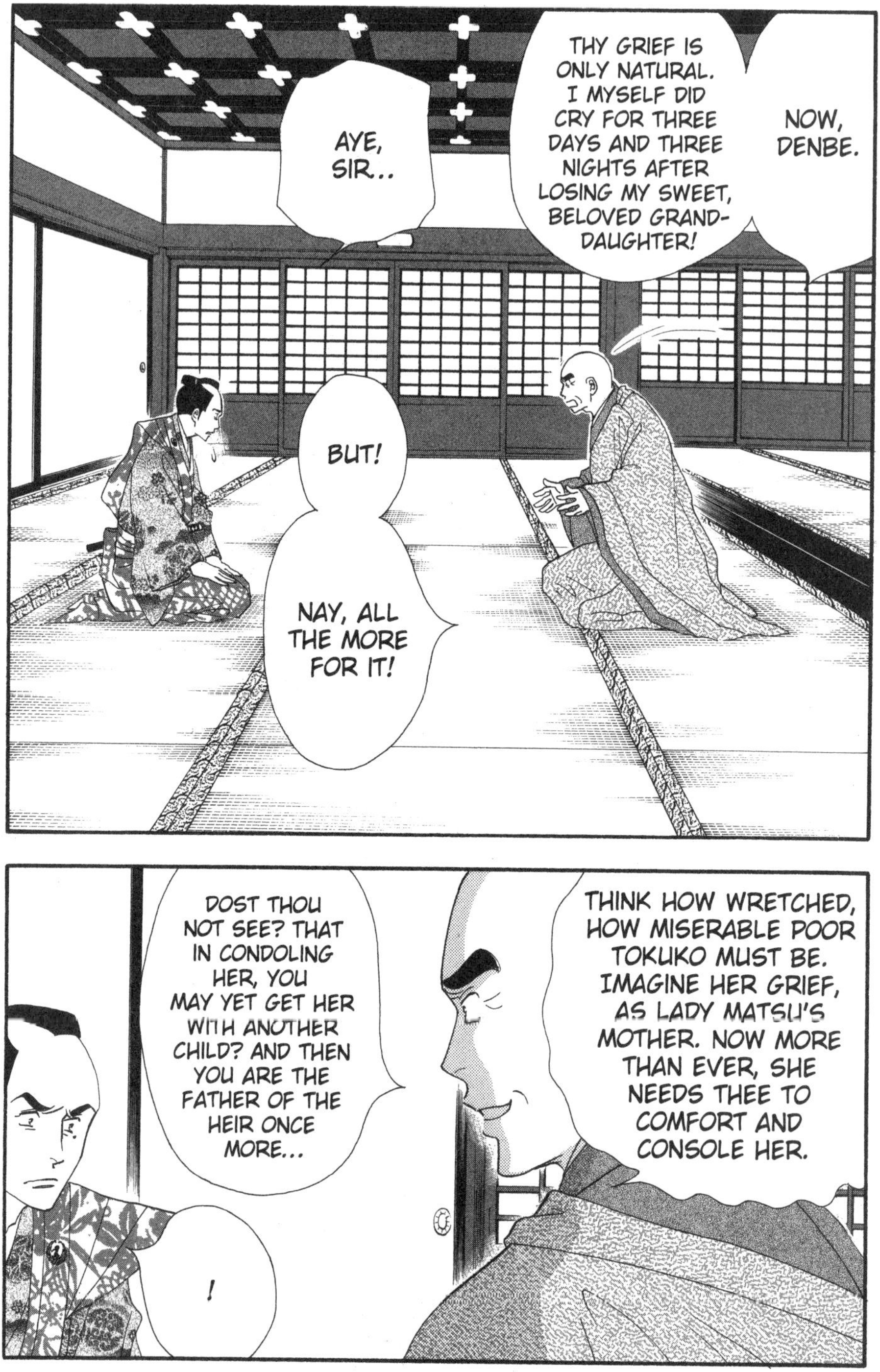
NOW, DENBE.
THY GRIEF IS ONLY NATURAL. I MYSELF DID CRY FOR THREE DAYS AND THREE NIGHTS AFTER LOSING MY SWEET, BELOVED GRAND-DAUGHTER!
AYE, SIR...
BUT!
NAY, ALL THE MORE FOR IT!
THINK HOW WRETCHED, HOW MISERABLE POOR TOKUKO MUST BE. IMAGINE HER GRIEF, AS LADY MATSU'S MOTHER. NOW MORE THAN EVER, SHE NEEDS THEE TO COMFORT AND CONSOLE HER.
DOST THOU NOT SEE? THAT IN CONDOLING HER, YOU MAY YET GET HER WITH ANOTHER CHILD? AND THEN YOU ARE THE FATHER OF THE HEIR ONCE MORE...
!

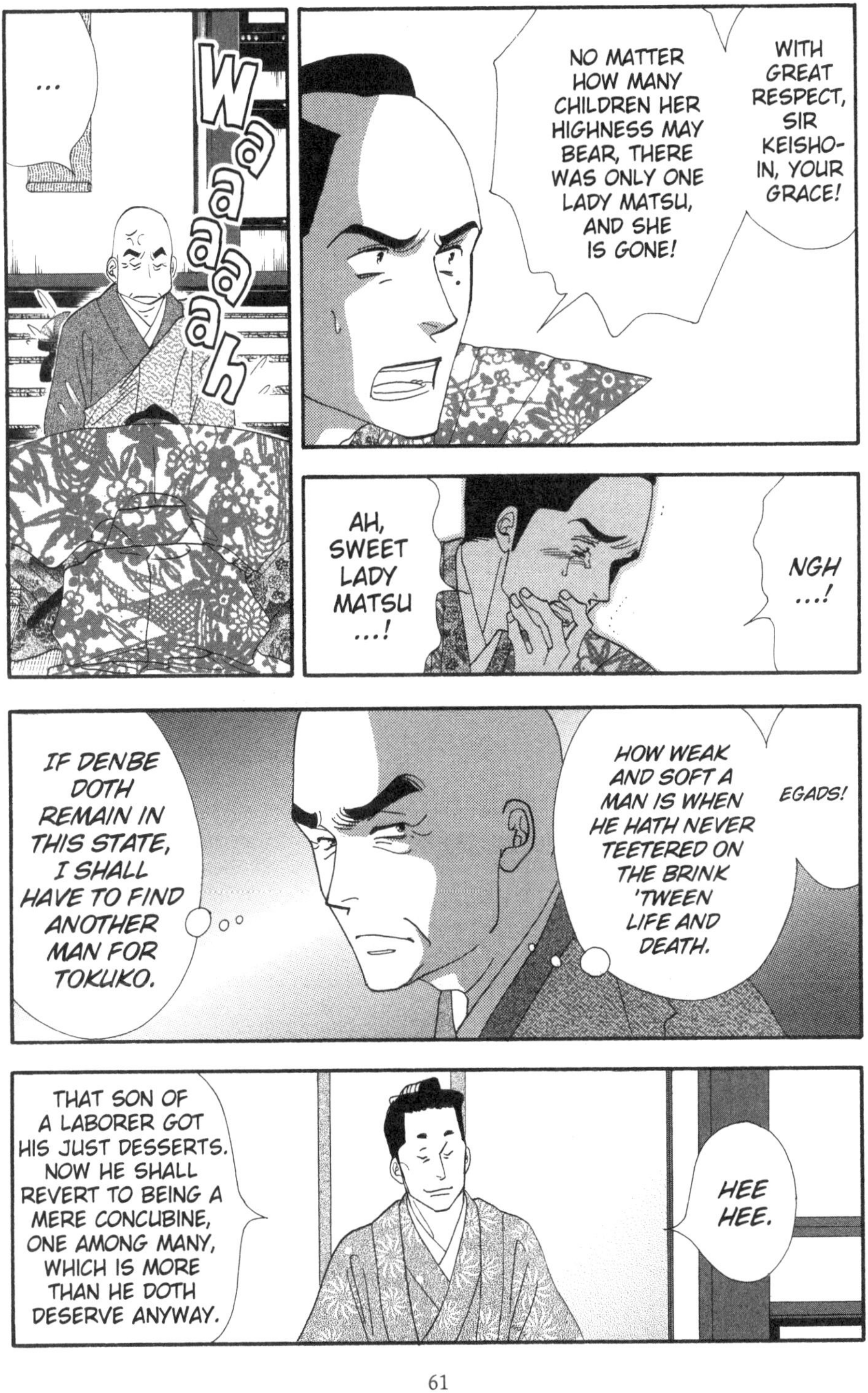
WITH GREAT RESPECT, SIR KEISHO-IN, YOUR GRACE!
NO MATTER HOW MANY CHILDREN HER HIGHNESS MAY BEAR, THERE WAS ONLY ONE LADY MATSU, AND SHE IS GONE!
NGH ...!
AH, SWEET LADY MATSU ...!
Waaaaaah
...
EGADS!
HOW WEAK AND SOFT A MAN IS WHEN HE HATH NEVER TEETERED ON THE BRINK 'TWEEN LIFE AND DEATH.
IF DENBE DOTH REMAIN IN THIS STATE, I SHALL HAVE TO FIND ANOTHER MAN FOR TOKUKO.
HEE HEE.
THAT SON OF A LABORER GOT HIS JUST DESSERTS. NOW HE SHALL REVERT TO BEING A MERE CONCUBINE, ONE AMONG MANY, WHICH IS MORE THAN HE DOTH DESERVE ANYWAY.

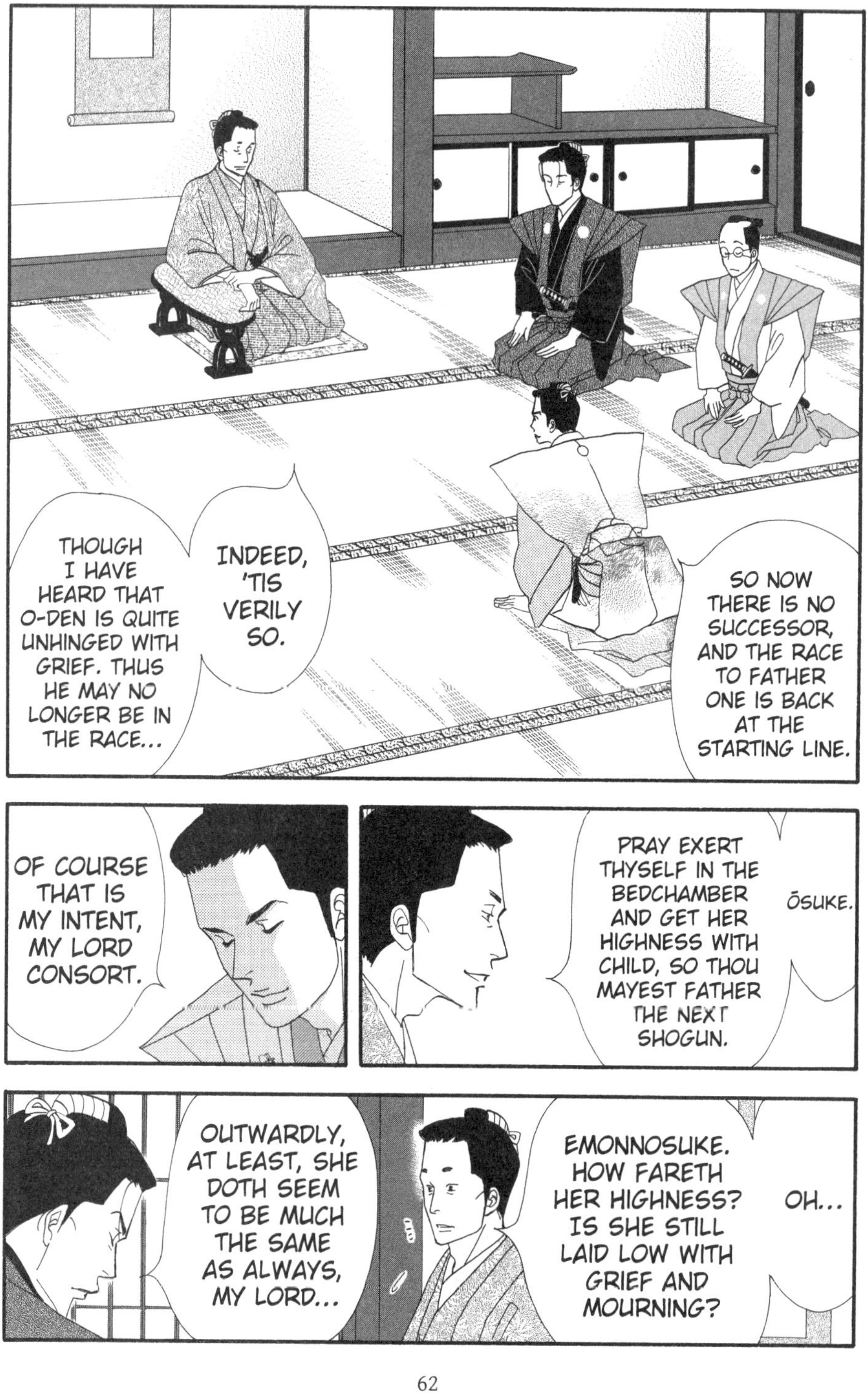
SO NOW THERE IS NO SUCCESSOR, AND THE RACE TO FATHER ONE IS BACK AT THE STARTING LINE.
INDEED, 'TIS VERILY SO.
THOUGH I HAVE HEARD THAT O-DEN IS QUITE UNHINGED WITH GRIEF. THUS HE MAY NO LONGER BE IN THE RACE...
ŌSUKE.
PRAY EXERT THYSELF IN THE BEDCHAMBER AND GET HER HIGHNESS WITH CHILD, SO THOU MAYEST FATHER THE NEXT SHOGUN.
OF COURSE THAT IS MY INTENT, MY LORD CONSORT.
OH...
EMONNOSUKE. HOW FARETH HER HIGHNESS? IS SHE STILL LAID LOW WITH GRIEF AND MOURNING?
OUTWARDLY, AT LEAST, SHE DOTH SEEM TO BE MUCH THE SAME AS ALWAYS, MY LORD...

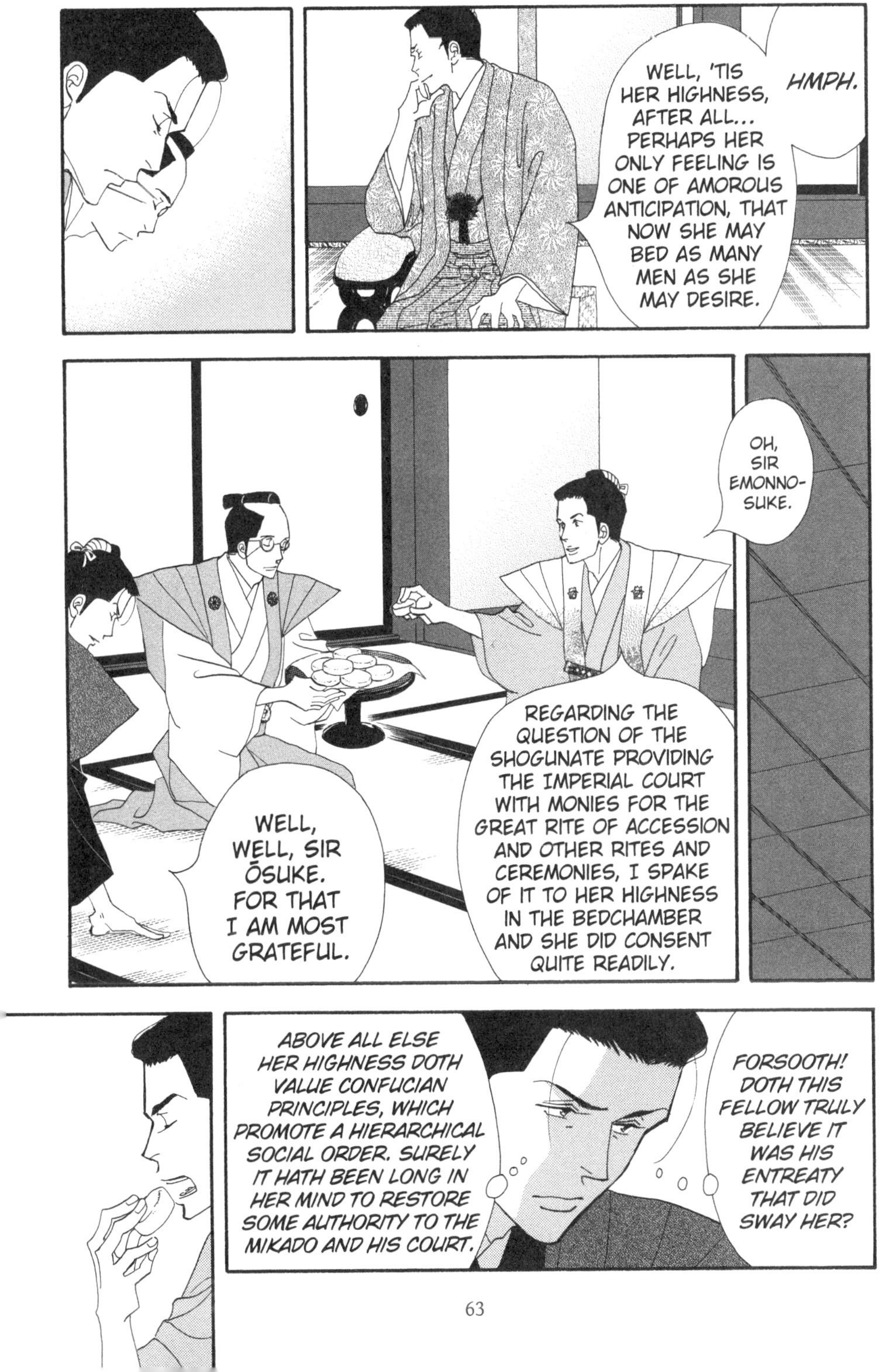
HMPH.
WELL, 'TIS HER HIGHNESS, AFTER ALL... PERHAPS HER ONLY FEELING IS ONE OF AMOROUS ANTICIPATION, THAT NOW SHE MAY BED AS MANY MEN AS SHE MAY DESIRE.
OH, SIR EMONNO-SUKE.
REGARDING THE QUESTION OF THE SHOGUNATE PROVIDING THE IMPERIAL COURT WITH MONIES FOR THE GREAT RITE OF ACCESSION AND OTHER RITES AND CEREMONIES, I SPAKE OF IT TO HER HIGHNESS IN THE BEDCHAMBER AND SHE DID CONSENT QUITE READILY.
WELL, WELL, SIR ŌSUKE. FOR THAT I AM MOST GRATEFUL.
FORSOOTH! DOTH THIS FELLOW TRULY BELIEVE IT WAS HIS ENTREATY THAT DID SWAY HER?
ABOVE ALL ELSE HER HIGHNESS DOTH VALUE CONFUCIAN PRINCIPLES, WHICH PROMOTE A HIERARCHICAL SOCIAL ORDER. SURELY IT HATH BEEN LONG IN HER MIND TO RESTORE SOME AUTHORITY TO THE MIKADO AND HIS COURT.

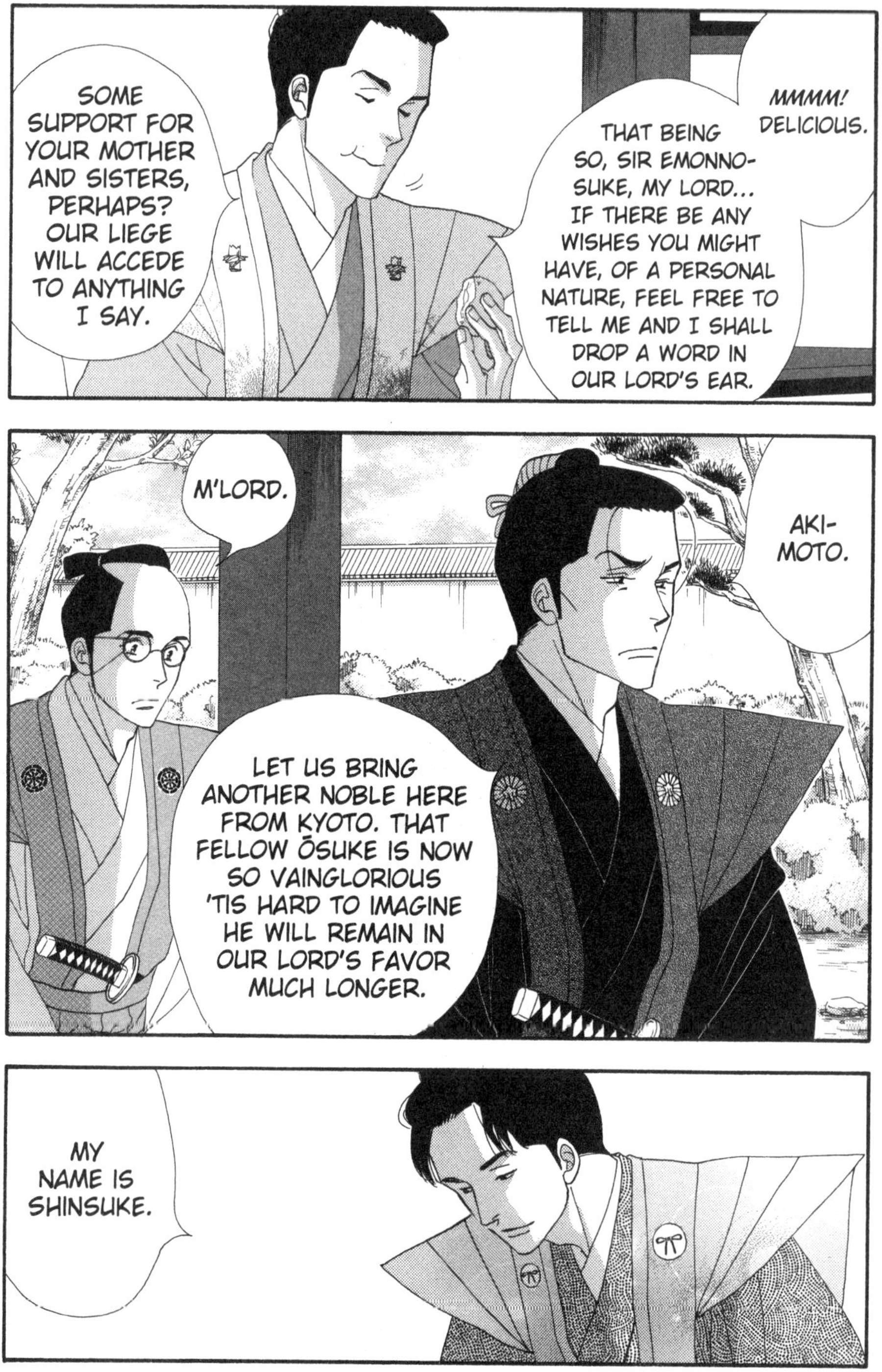
MMMM! DELICIOUS.
THAT BEING SO, SIR EMONNOSUKE, MY LORD... IF THERE BE ANY WISHES YOU MIGHT HAVE, OF A PERSONAL NATURE, FEEL FREE TO TELL ME AND I SHALL DROP A WORD IN OUR LORD'S EAR.
SOME SUPPORT FOR YOUR MOTHER AND SISTERS, PERHAPS? OUR LIEGE WILL ACCEDE TO ANYTHING I SAY.
AKI-MOTO.
M'LORD.
LET US BRING ANOTHER NOBLE HERE FROM KYOTO. THAT FELLOW ŌSUKE IS NOW SO VAINGLORIOUS 'TIS HARD TO IMAGINE HE WILL REMAIN IN OUR LORD'S FAVOR MUCH LONGER.
MY NAME IS SHINSUKE.

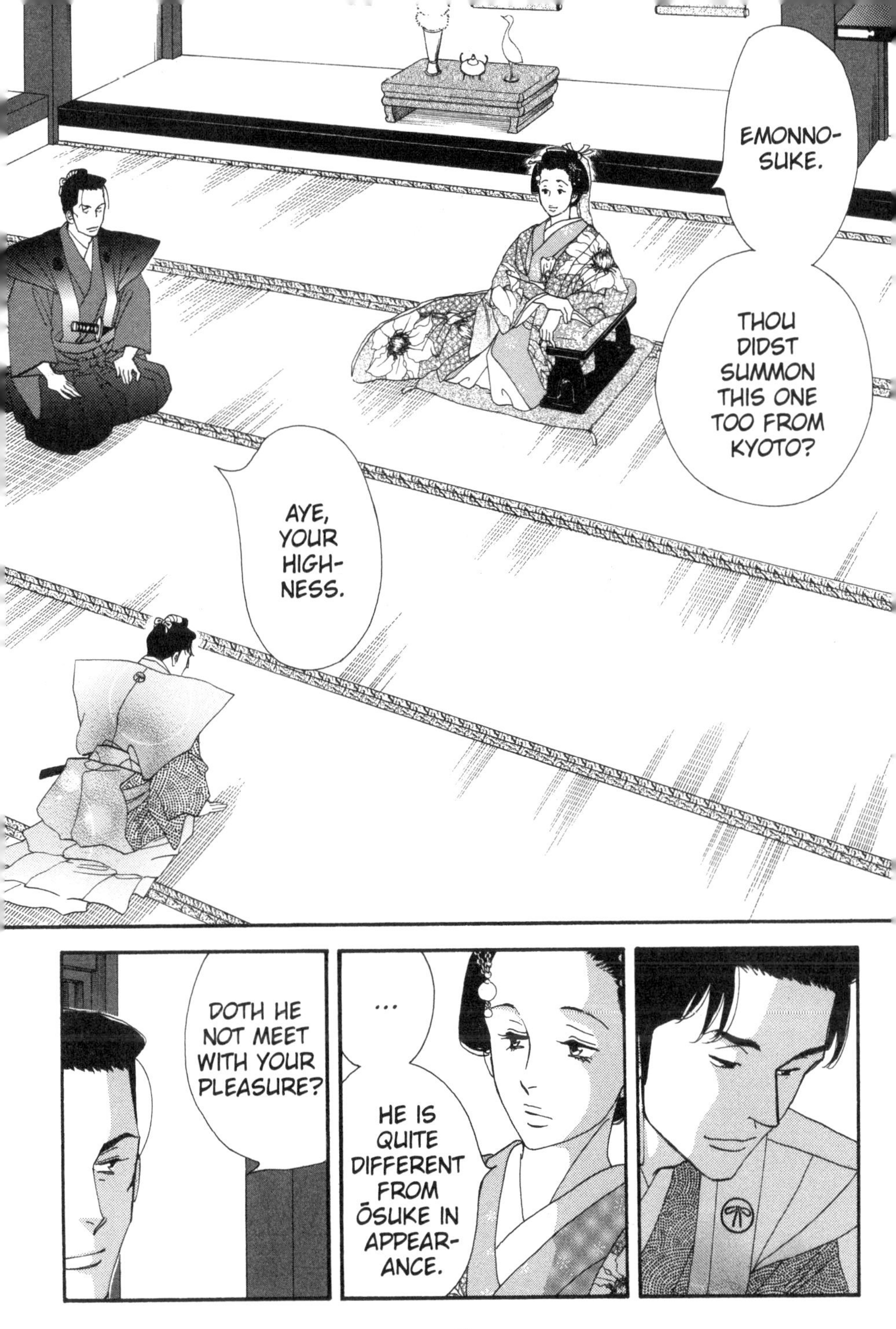
EMONNO-SUKE.
THOU DIDST SUMMON THIS ONE TOO FROM KYOTO?
AYE, YOUR HIGHNESS.
...
HE IS QUITE DIFFERENT FROM ŌSUKE IN APPEARANCE.
DOTH HE NOT MEET WITH YOUR PLEASURE?

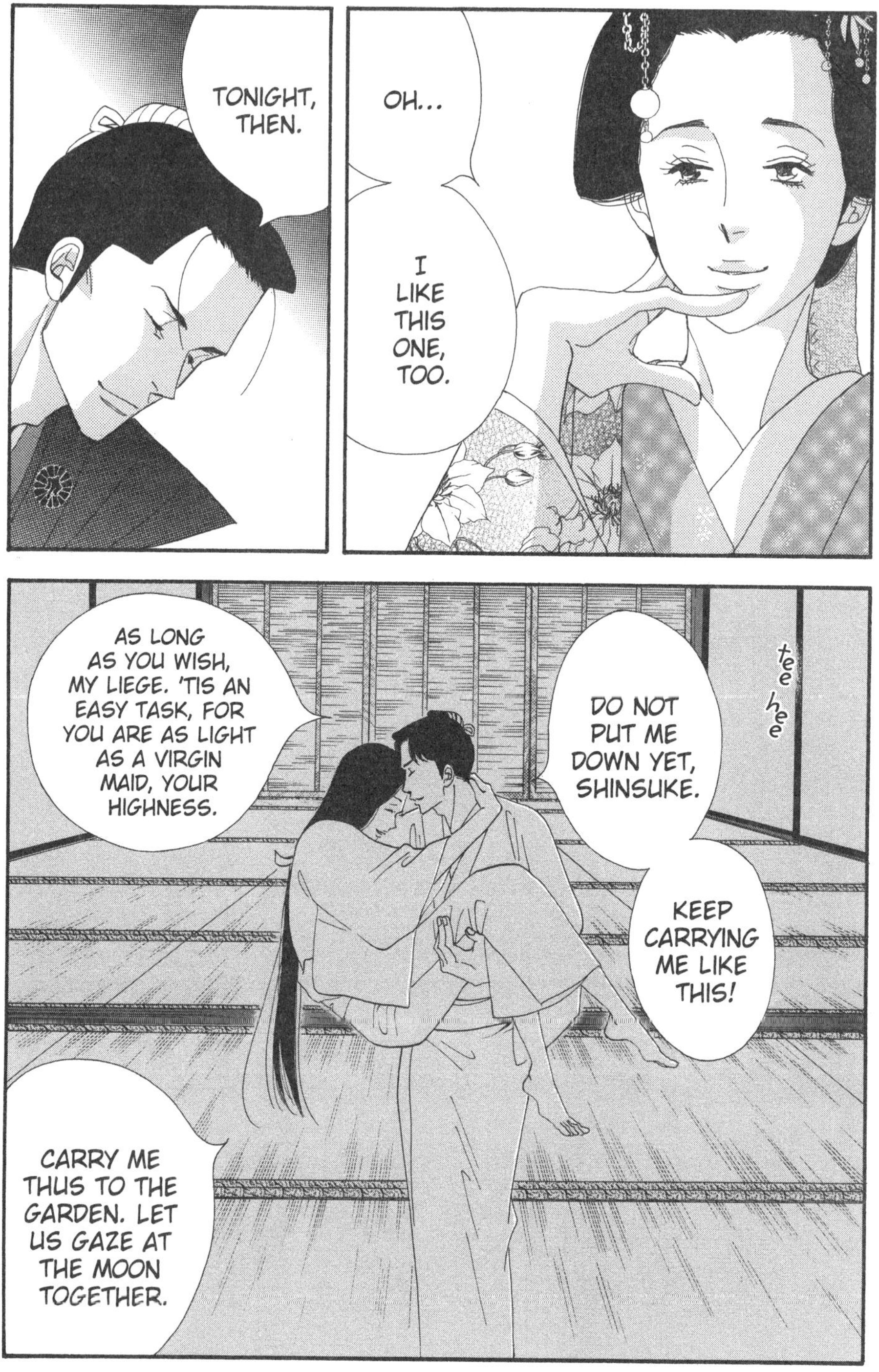
OH...
I LIKE THIS ONE, TOO.
TONIGHT, THEN.
tee hee
DO NOT PUT ME DOWN YET, SHINSUKE.
KEEP CARRYING ME LIKE THIS!
AS LONG AS YOU WISH, MY LIEGE. 'TIS AN EASY TASK, FOR YOU ARE AS LIGHT AS A VIRGIN MAID, YOUR HIGHNESS.
CARRY ME THUS TO THE GARDEN. LET US GAZE AT THE MOON TOGETHER.

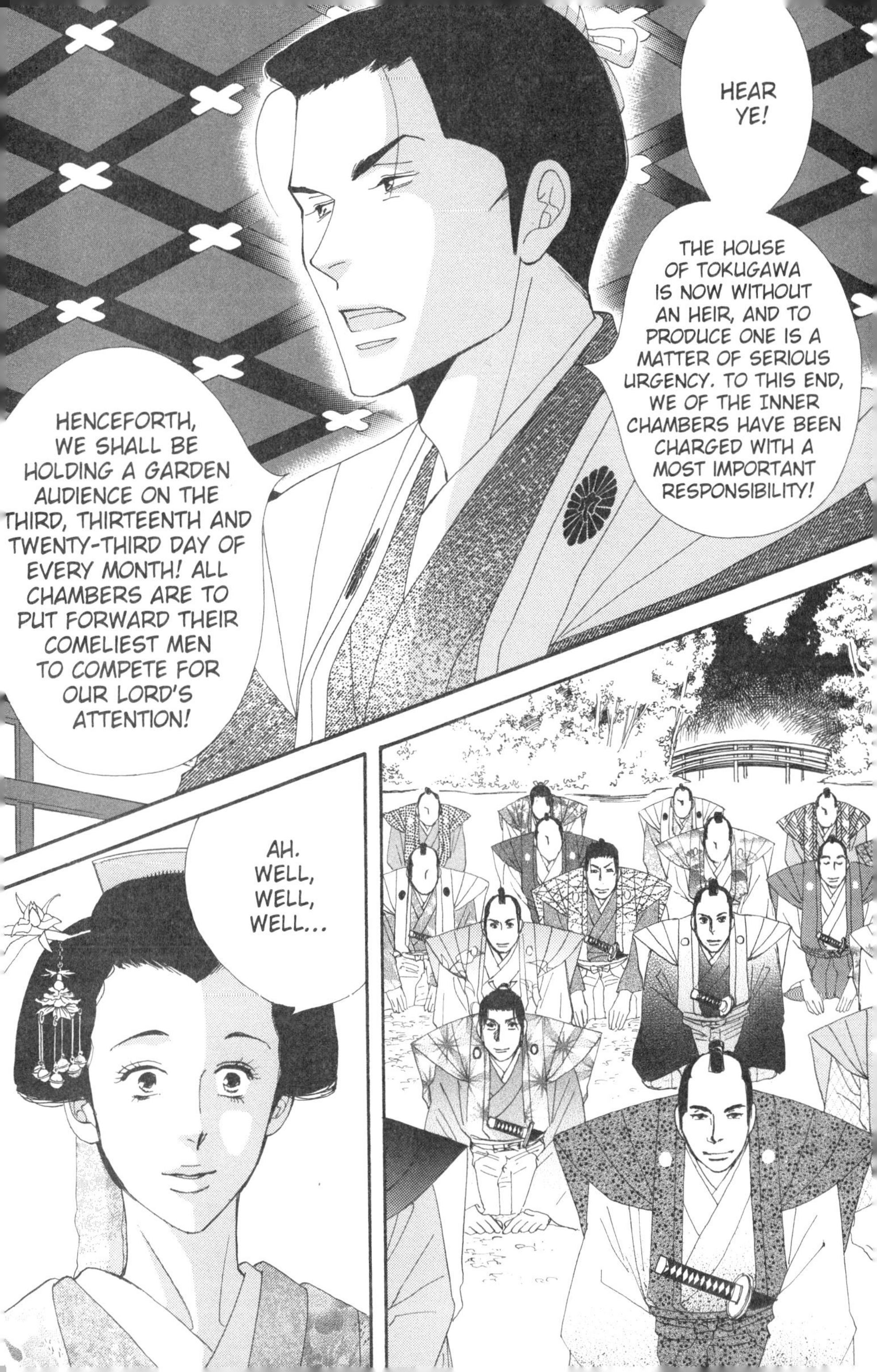
HEAR YE!
THE HOUSE OF TOKUGAWA IS NOW WITHOUT AN HEIR, AND TO PRODUCE ONE IS A MATTER OF SERIOUS URGENCY. TO THIS END, WE OF THE INNER CHAMBERS HAVE BEEN CHARGED WITH A MOST IMPORTANT RESPONSIBILITY!
HENCEFORTH, WE SHALL BE HOLDING A GARDEN AUDIENCE ON THE THIRD, THIRTEENTH AND TWENTY-THIRD DAY OF EVERY MONTH! ALL CHAMBERS ARE TO PUT FORWARD THEIR COMELIEST MEN TO COMPETE FOR OUR LORD'S ATTENTION!
AH. WELL, WELL, WELL...

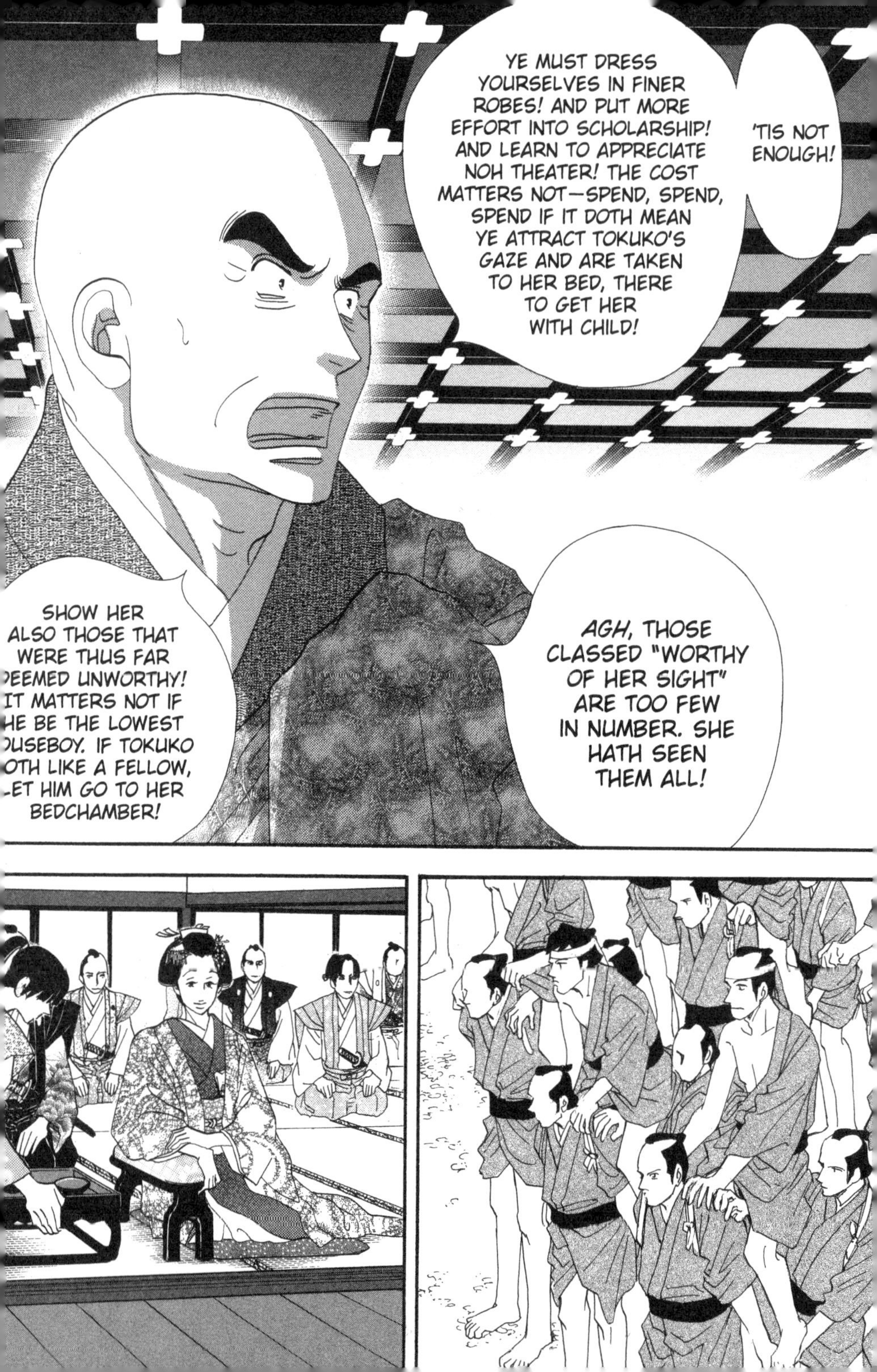
'TIS NOT ENOUGH!
YE MUST DRESS YOURSELVES IN FINER ROBES! AND PUT MORE EFFORT INTO SCHOLARSHIP! AND LEARN TO APPRECIATE NOH THEATER! THE COST MATTERS NOT—SPEND, SPEND, SPEND IF IT DOTH MEAN YE ATTRACT TOKUKO'S GAZE AND ARE TAKEN TO HER BED, THERE TO GET HER WITH CHILD!
AGH, THOSE CLASSED "WORTHY OF HER SIGHT" ARE TOO FEW IN NUMBER. SHE HATH SEEN THEM ALL!
SHOW HER ALSO THOSE THAT WERE THUS FAR EEMED UNWORTHY! IT MATTERS NOT IF HE BE THE LOWEST USEBOY. IF TOKUKO OTH LIKE A FELLOW, ET HIM GO TO HER BEDCHAMBER!

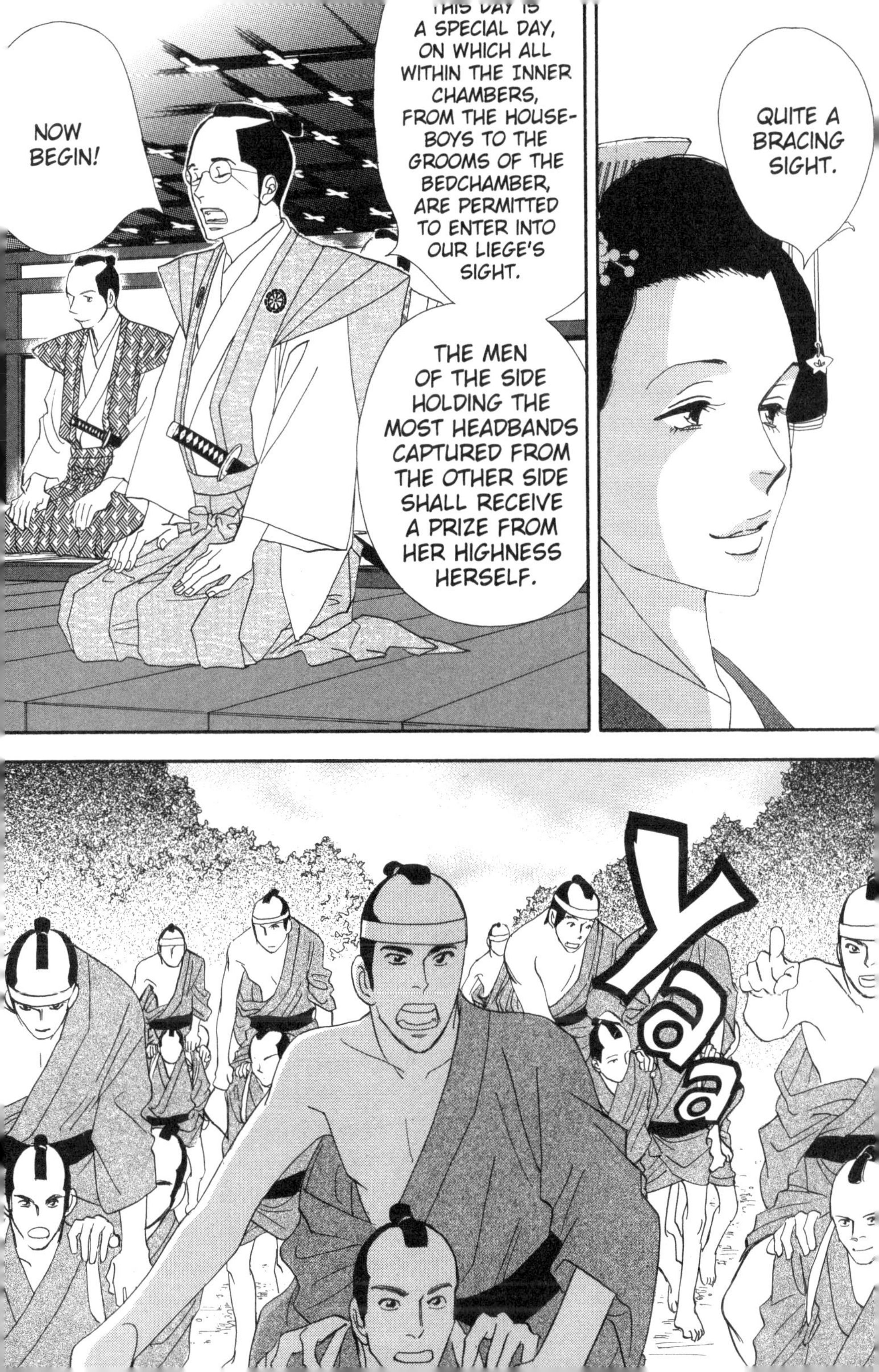
QUITE A BRACING SIGHT.
THIS DAY IS A SPECIAL DAY, ON WHICH ALL WITHIN THE INNER CHAMBERS, FROM THE HOUSE-BOYS TO THE GROOMS OF THE BEDCHAMBER, ARE PERMITTED TO ENTER INTO OUR LIEGE'S SIGHT.
THE MEN OF THE SIDE HOLDING THE MOST HEADBANDS CAPTURED FROM THE OTHER SIDE SHALL RECEIVE A PRIZE FROM HER HIGHNESS HERSELF.
NOW BEGIN!
Yaaa

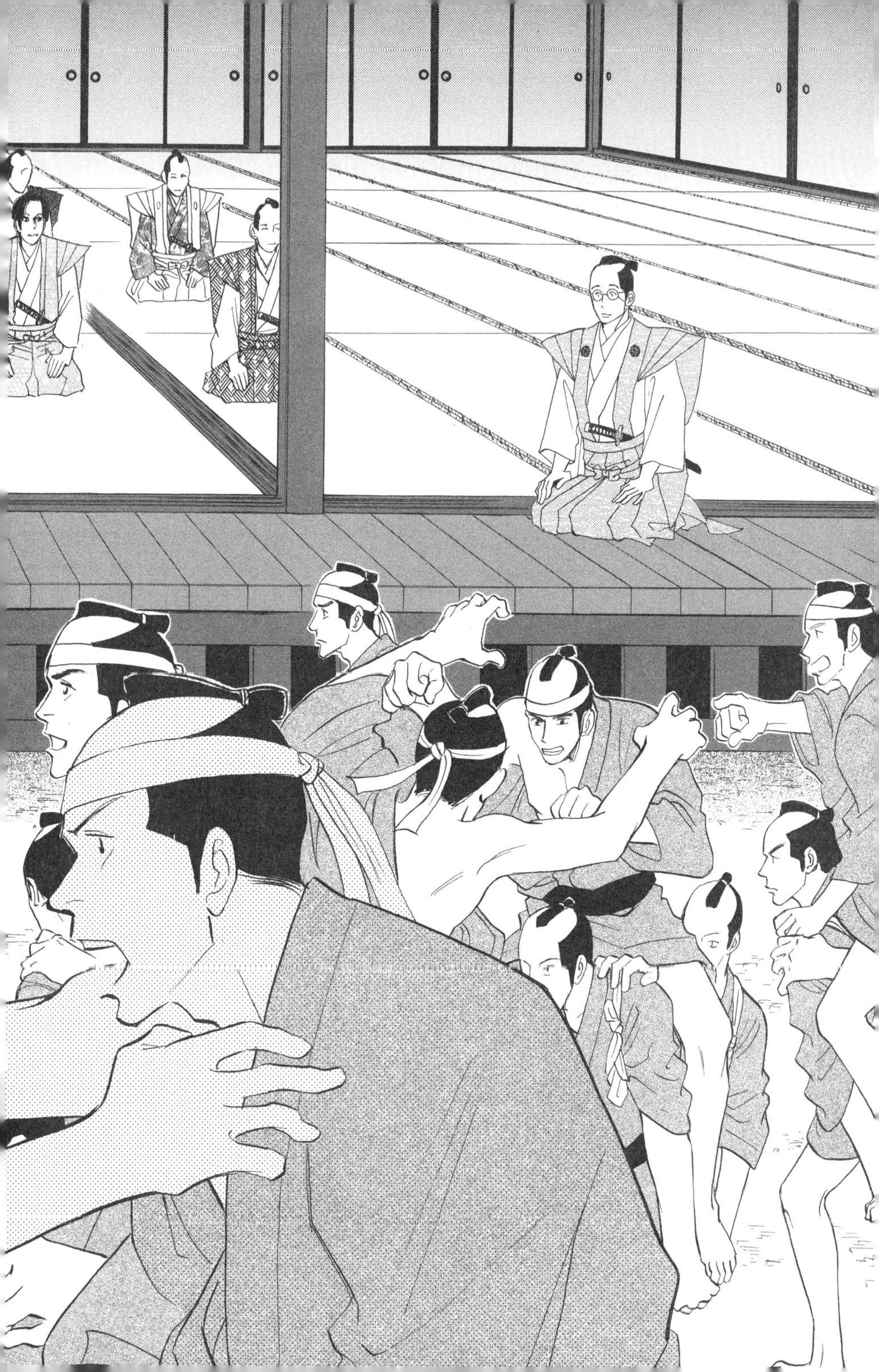

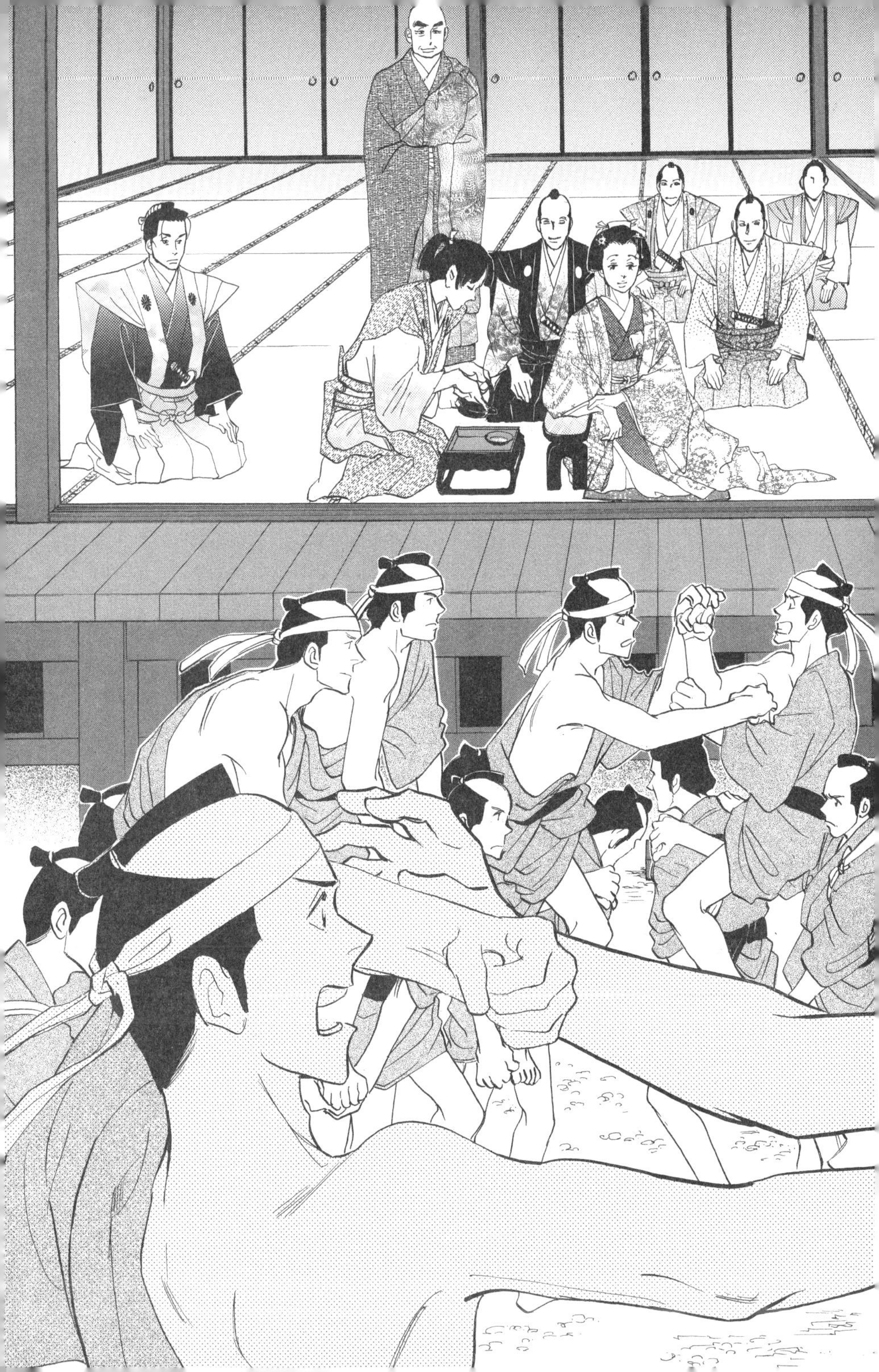

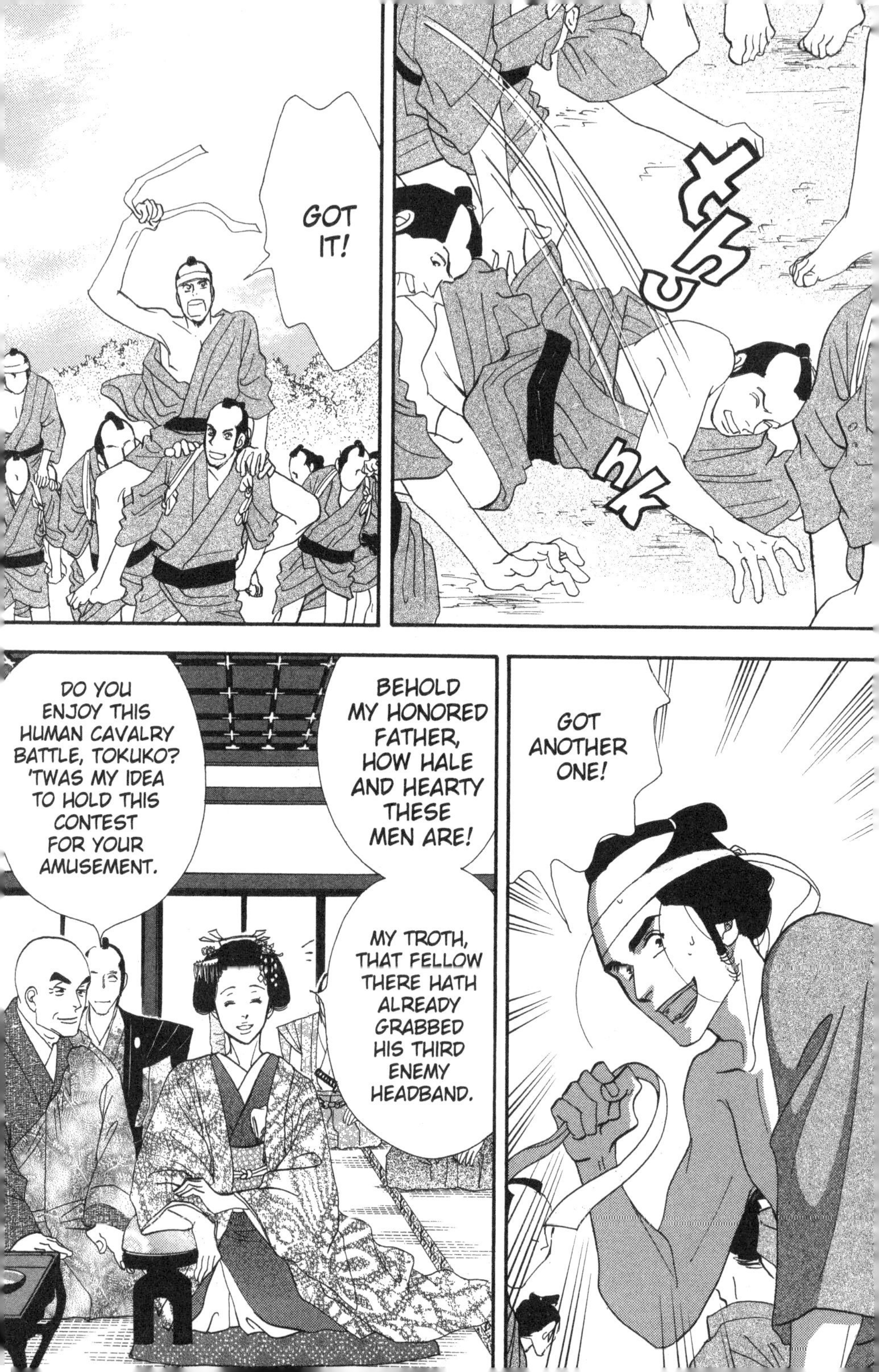
nk
GOT IT!
GOT ANOTHER ONE!
BEHOLD MY HONORED FATHER, HOW HALE AND HEARTY THESE MEN ARE!
DO YOU ENJOY THIS HUMAN CAVALRY BATTLE, TOKUKO? 'TWAS MY IDEA TO HOLD THIS CONTEST FOR YOUR AMUSEMENT.
MY TROTH, THAT FELLOW THERE HATH ALREADY GRABBED HIS THIRD ENEMY HEADBAND.

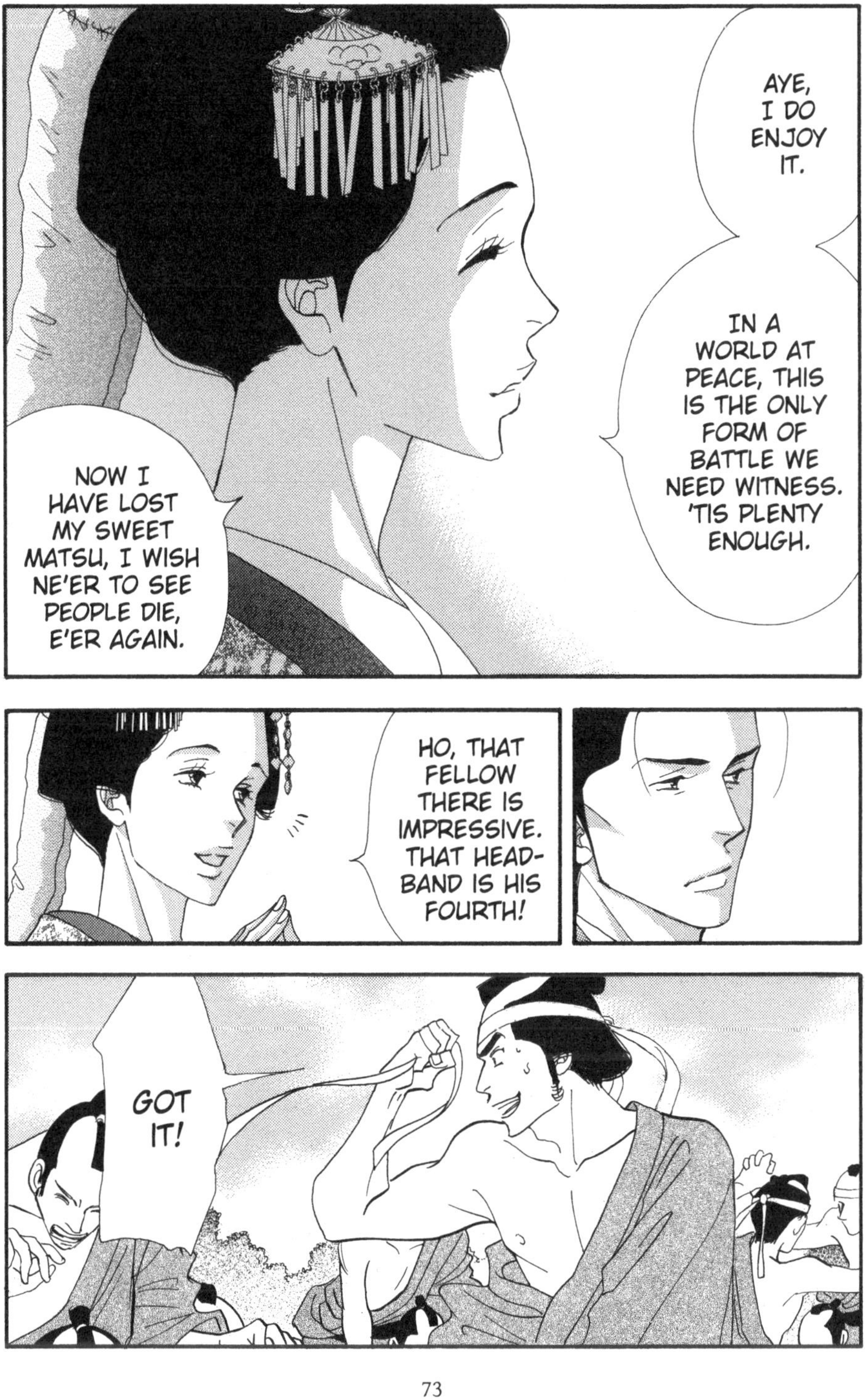
AYE, I DO ENJOY IT.
IN A WORLD AT PEACE, THIS IS THE ONLY FORM OF BATTLE WE NEED WITNESS. 'TIS PLENTY ENOUGH.
NOW I HAVE LOST MY SWEET MATSU, I WISH NE'ER TO SEE PEOPLE DIE, E'ER AGAIN.
HO, THAT FELLOW THERE IS IMPRESSIVE. THAT HEAD-BAND IS HIS FOURTH!
GOT IT!

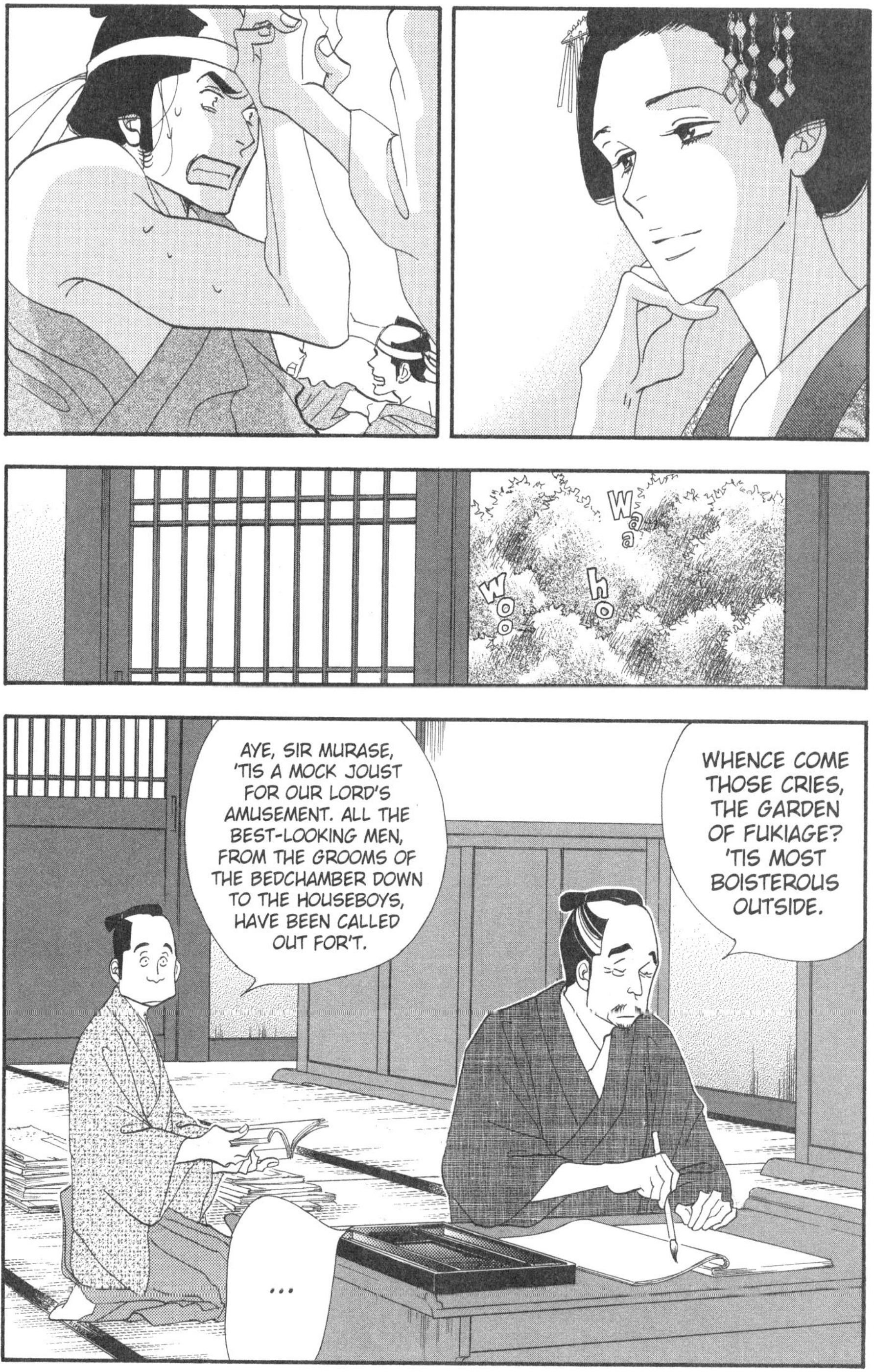
Waa
hoo
Woo
WHENCE COME THOSE CRIES, THE GARDEN OF FUKIAGE? 'TIS MOST BOISTEROUS OUTSIDE.
AYE, SIR MURASE, 'TIS A MOCK JOUST FOR OUR LORD'S AMUSEMENT. ALL THE BEST-LOOKING MEN, FROM THE GROOMS OF THE BEDCHAMBER DOWN TO THE HOUSEBOYS, HAVE BEEN CALLED OUT FOR'T.
...

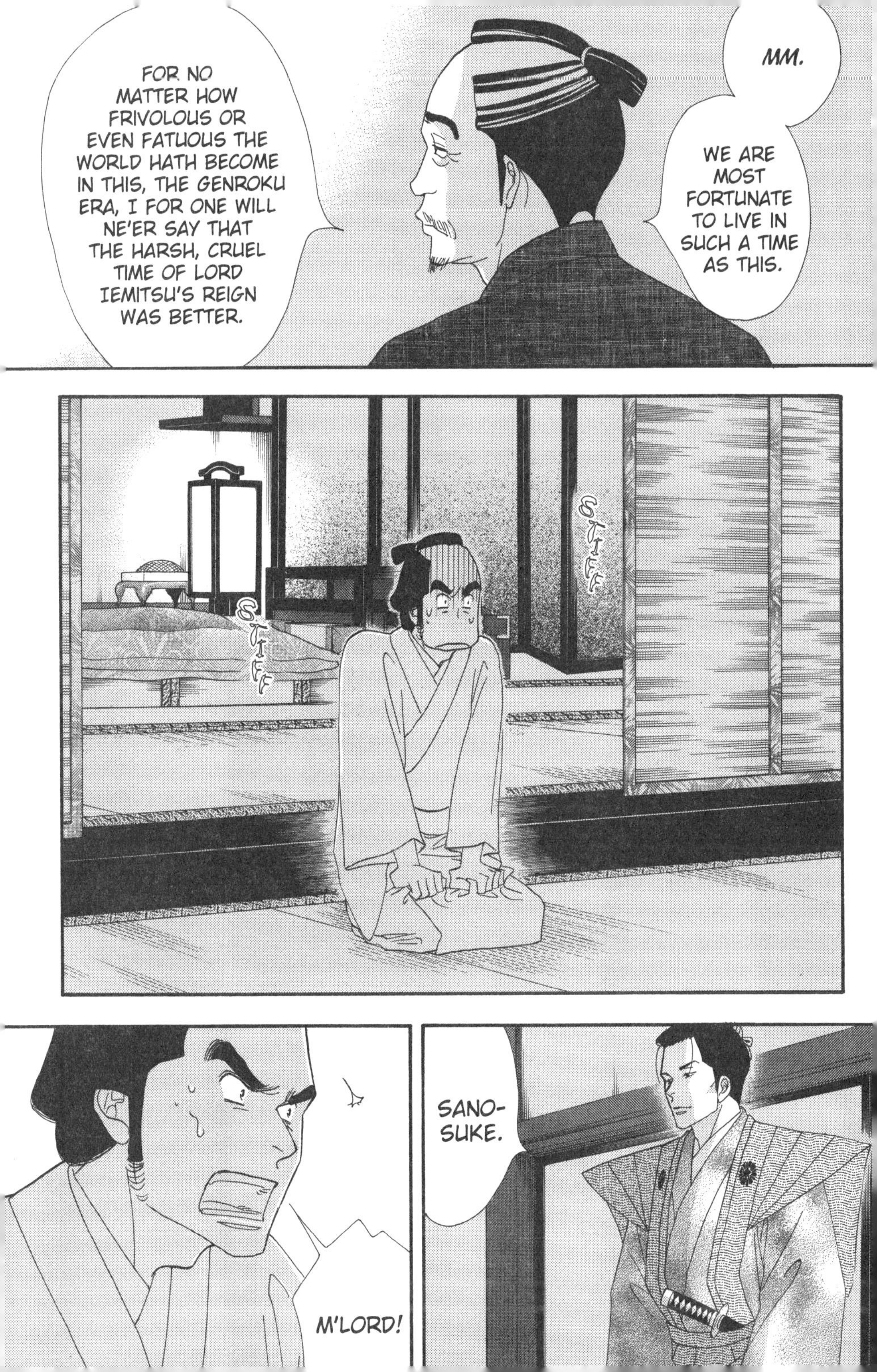
MM.
WE ARE MOST FORTUNATE TO LIVE IN SUCH A TIME AS THIS.
FOR NO MATTER HOW FRIVOLOUS OR EVEN FATUOUS THE WORLD HATH BECOME IN THIS, THE GENROKU ERA, I FOR ONE WILL NE'ER SAY THAT THE HARSH, CRUEL TIME OF LORD IEMITSU'S REIGN WAS BETTER.
STIFF
STIFF
SANO-SUKE.
M'LORD!

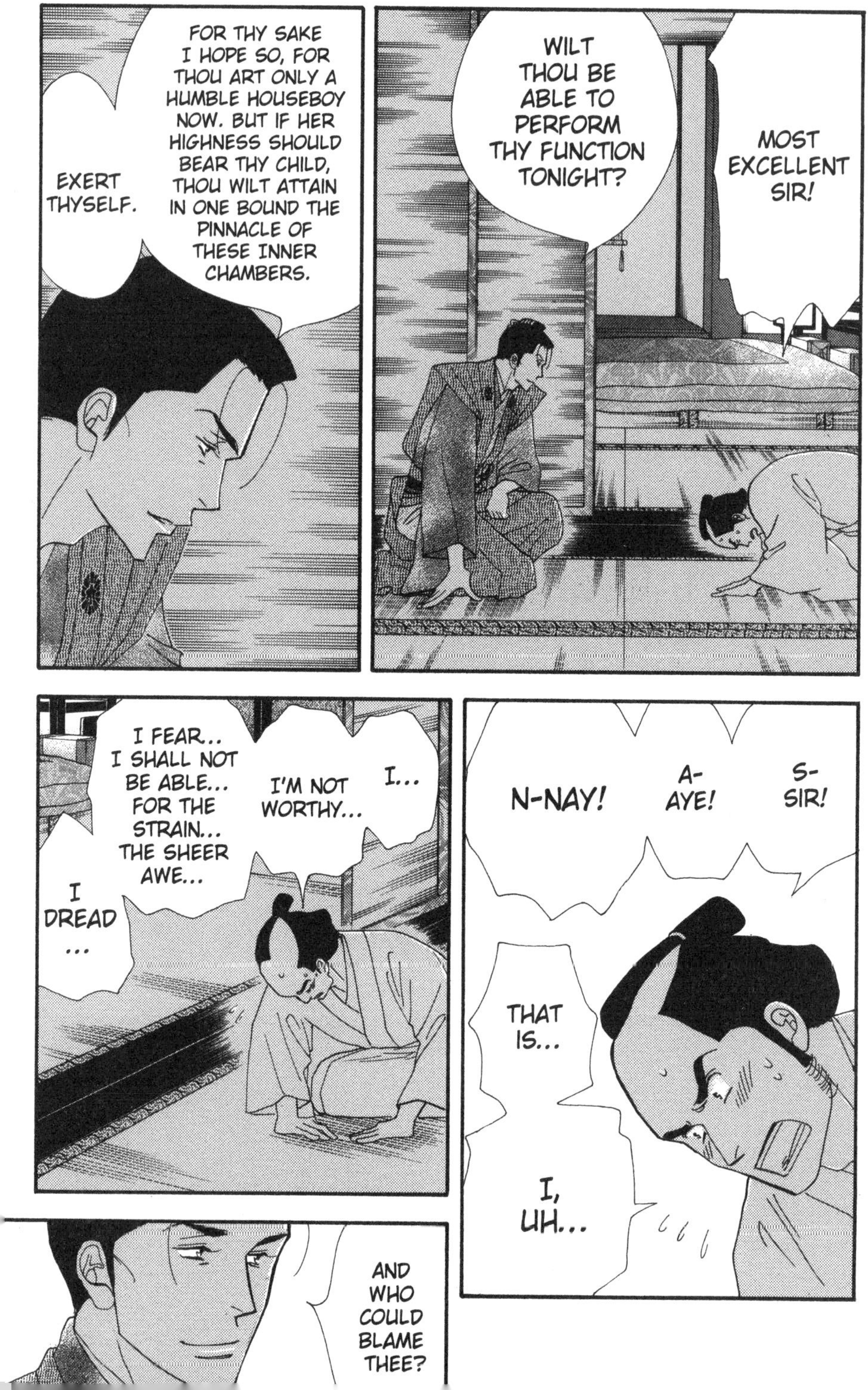
WILT THOU BE ABLE TO PERFORM THY FUNCTION TONIGHT?
MOST EXCELLENT SIR!
FOR THY SAKE I HOPE SO, FOR THOU ART ONLY A HUMBLE HOUSEBOY NOW. BUT IF HER HIGHNESS SHOULD BEAR THY CHILD, THOU WILT ATTAIN IN ONE BOUND THE PINNACLE OF THESE INNER CHAMBERS.
EXERT THYSELF.
S-SIR!
A-AYE!
N-NAY!
THAT IS...
I, UH...
I...
I'M NOT WORTHY...
I FEAR... I SHALL NOT BE ABLE... FOR THE STRAIN... THE SHEER AWE...
I DREAD...
AND WHO COULD BLAME THEE?

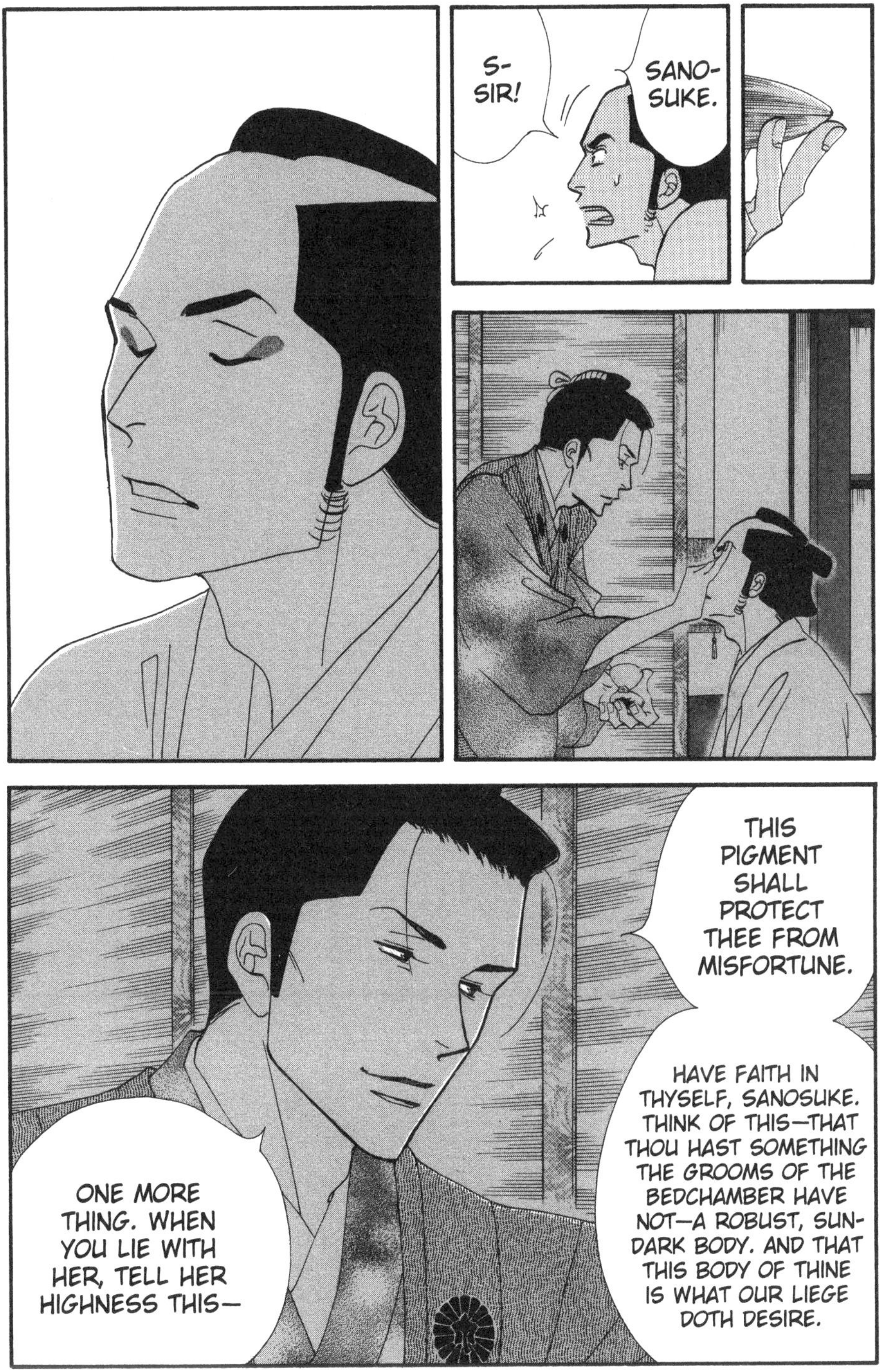
SANO-SUKE.
S-SIR!
THIS PIGMENT SHALL PROTECT THEE FROM MISFORTUNE.
HAVE FAITH IN THYSELF, SANOSUKE. THINK OF THIS—THAT THOU HAST SOMETHING THE GROOMS OF THE BEDCHAMBER HAVE NOT—A ROBUST, SUN-DARK BODY. AND THAT THIS BODY OF THINE IS WHAT OUR LIEGE DOTH DESIRE.
ONE MORE THING. WHEN YOU LIE WITH HER, TELL HER HIGHNESS THIS—

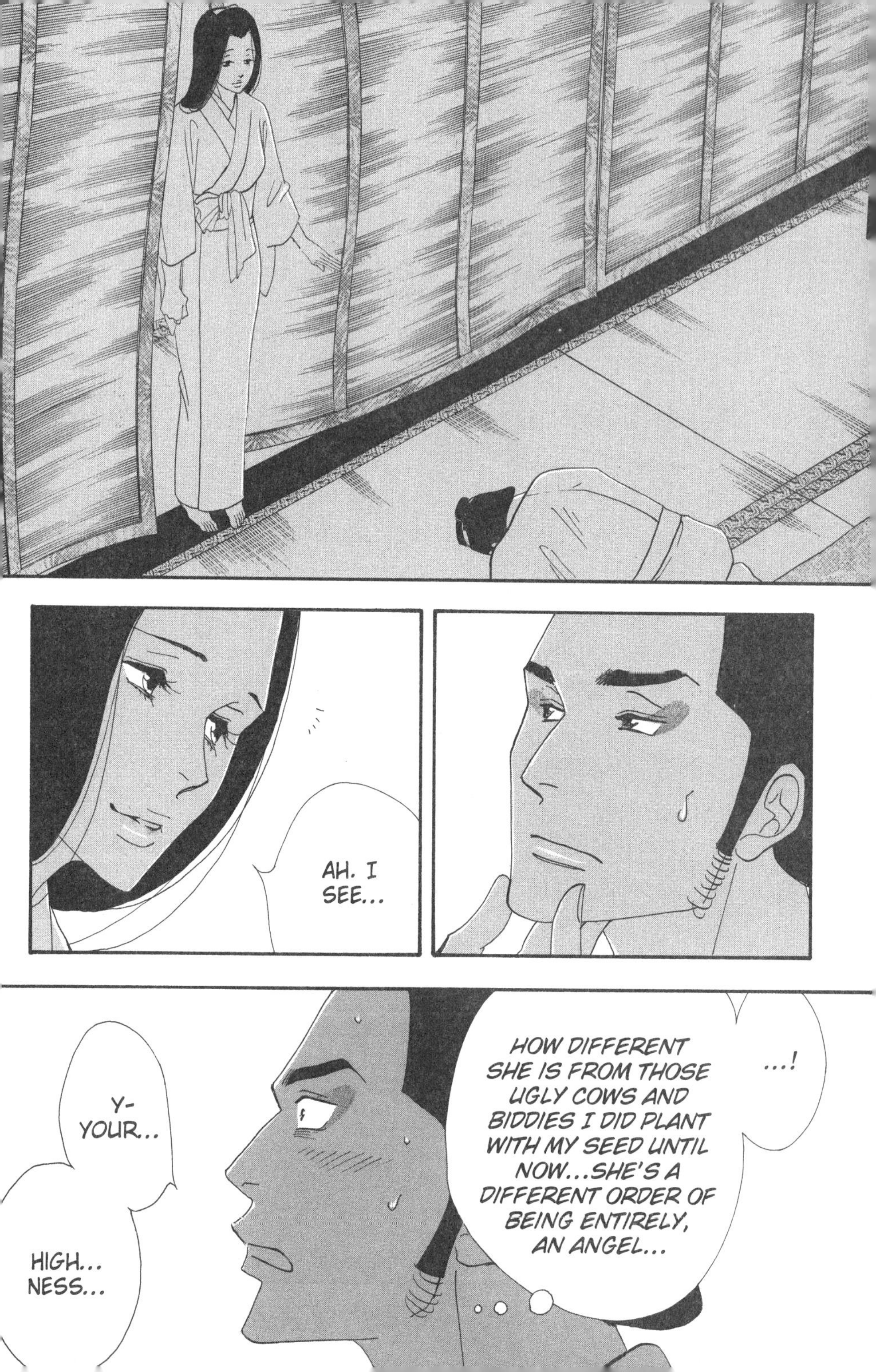
AH. I SEE...
...!
HOW DIFFERENT SHE IS FROM THOSE UGLY COWS AND BIDDIES I DID PLANT WITH MY SEED UNTIL NOW...SHE'S A DIFFERENT ORDER OF BEING ENTIRELY, AN ANGEL...
Y-YOUR...
HIGH...NESS...

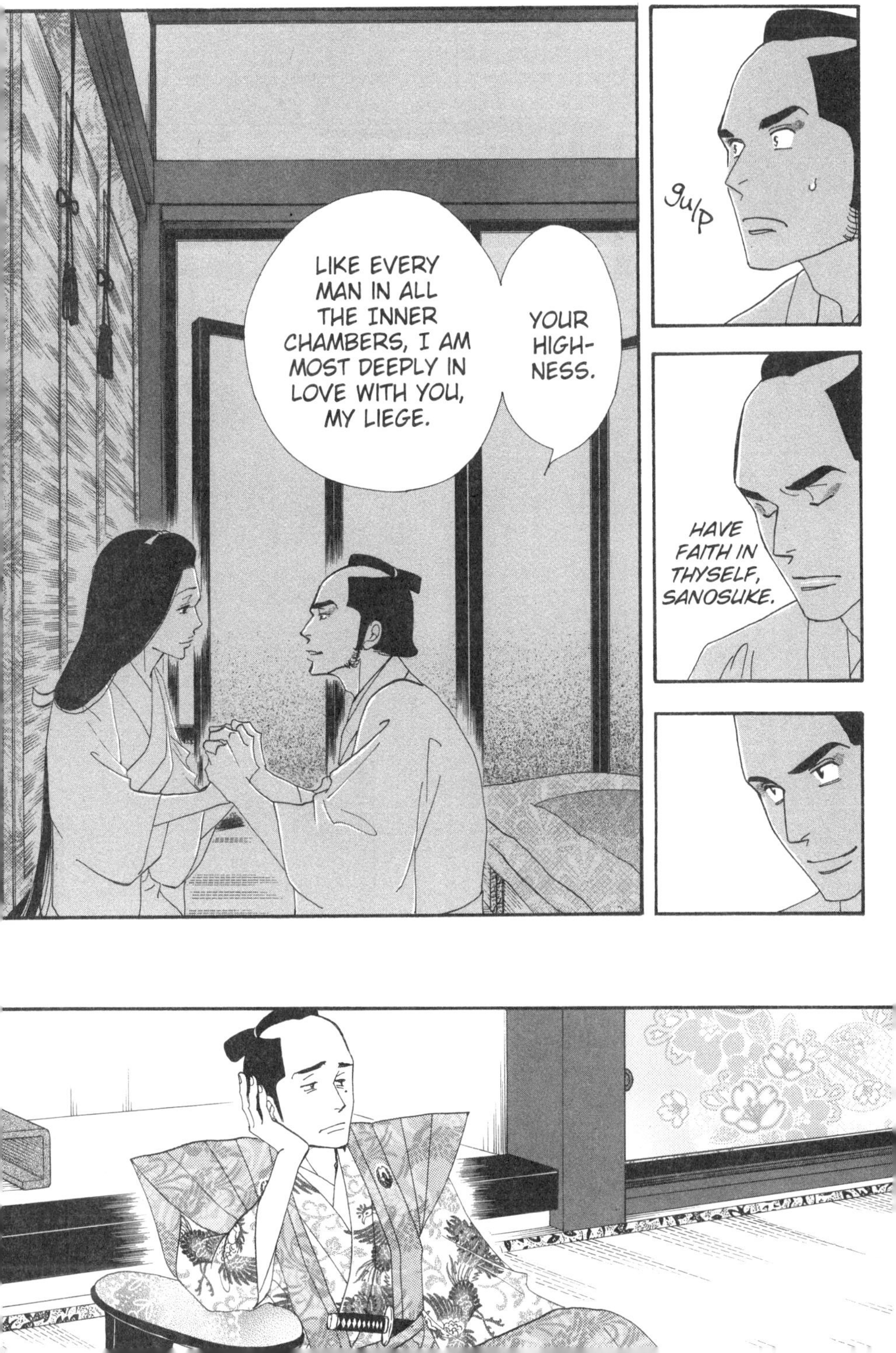
gulp
HAVE FAITH IN THYSELF, SANOSUKE.
YOUR HIGHNESS.
LIKE EVERY MAN IN ALL THE INNER CHAMBERS, I AM MOST DEEPLY IN LOVE WITH YOU, MY LIEGE.

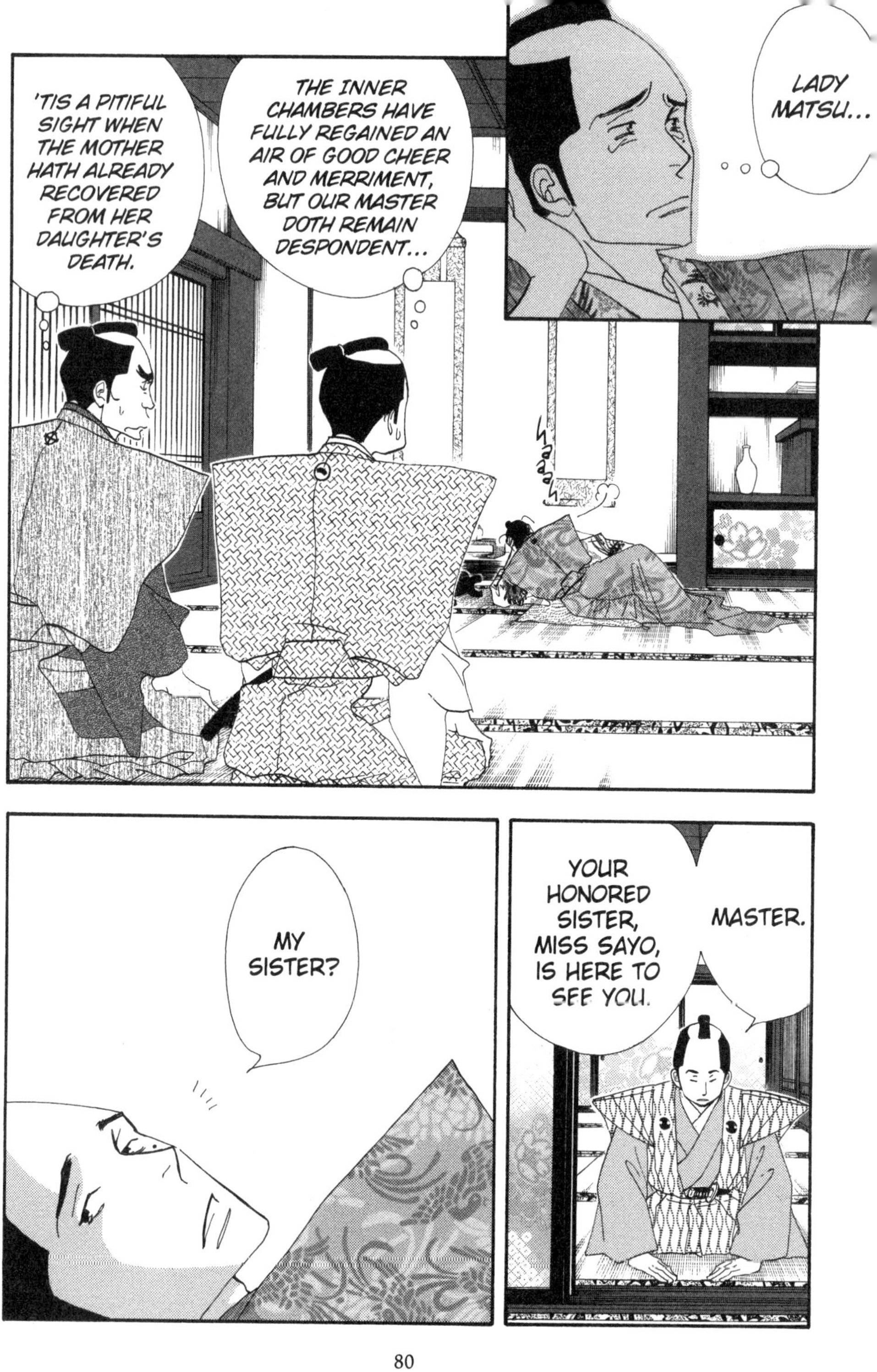
LADY MATSU...
THE INNER CHAMBERS HAVE FULLY REGAINED AN AIR OF GOOD CHEER AND MERRIMENT, BUT OUR MASTER DOTH REMAIN DESPONDENT...
'TIS A PITIFUL SIGHT WHEN THE MOTHER HATH ALREADY RECOVERED FROM HER DAUGHTER'S DEATH.
MASTER.
YOUR HONORED SISTER, MISS SAYO, IS HERE TO SEE YOU.
MY SISTER?

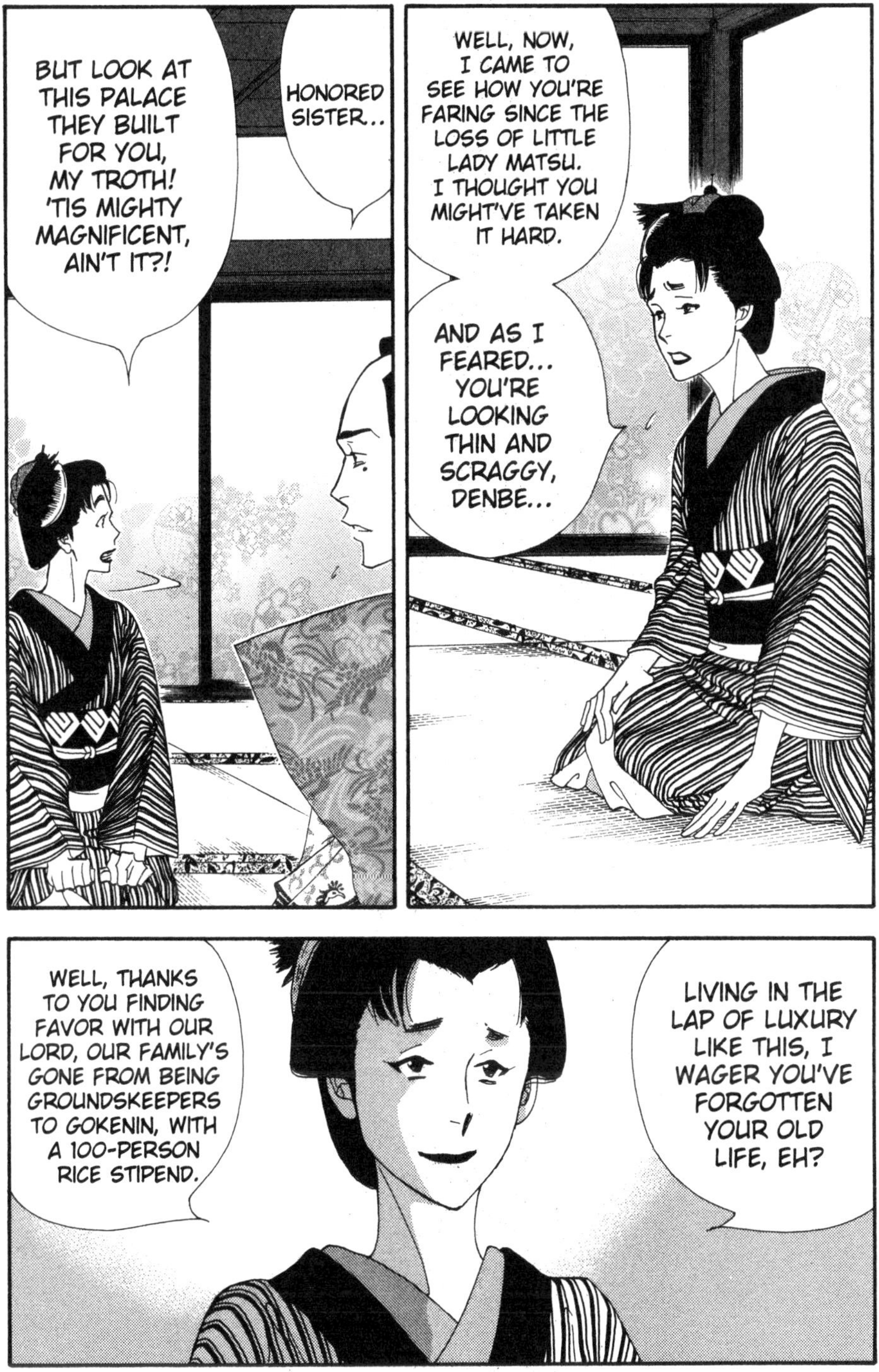
WELL, NOW, I CAME TO SEE HOW YOU'RE FARING SINCE THE LOSS OF LITTLE LADY MATSU. I THOUGHT YOU MIGHT'VE TAKEN IT HARD.
AND AS I FEARED... YOU'RE LOOKING THIN AND SCRAGGY, DENBE...
HONORED SISTER...
BUT LOOK AT THIS PALACE THEY BUILT FOR YOU, MY TROTH! 'TIS MIGHTY MAGNIFICENT, AIN'T IT?!
LIVING IN THE LAP OF LUXURY LIKE THIS, I WAGER YOU'VE FORGOTTEN YOUR OLD LIFE, EH?
WELL, THANKS TO YOU FINDING FAVOR WITH OUR LORD, OUR FAMILY'S GONE FROM BEING GROUNDSKEEPERS TO GOKENIN, WITH A 100-PERSON RICE STIPEND.

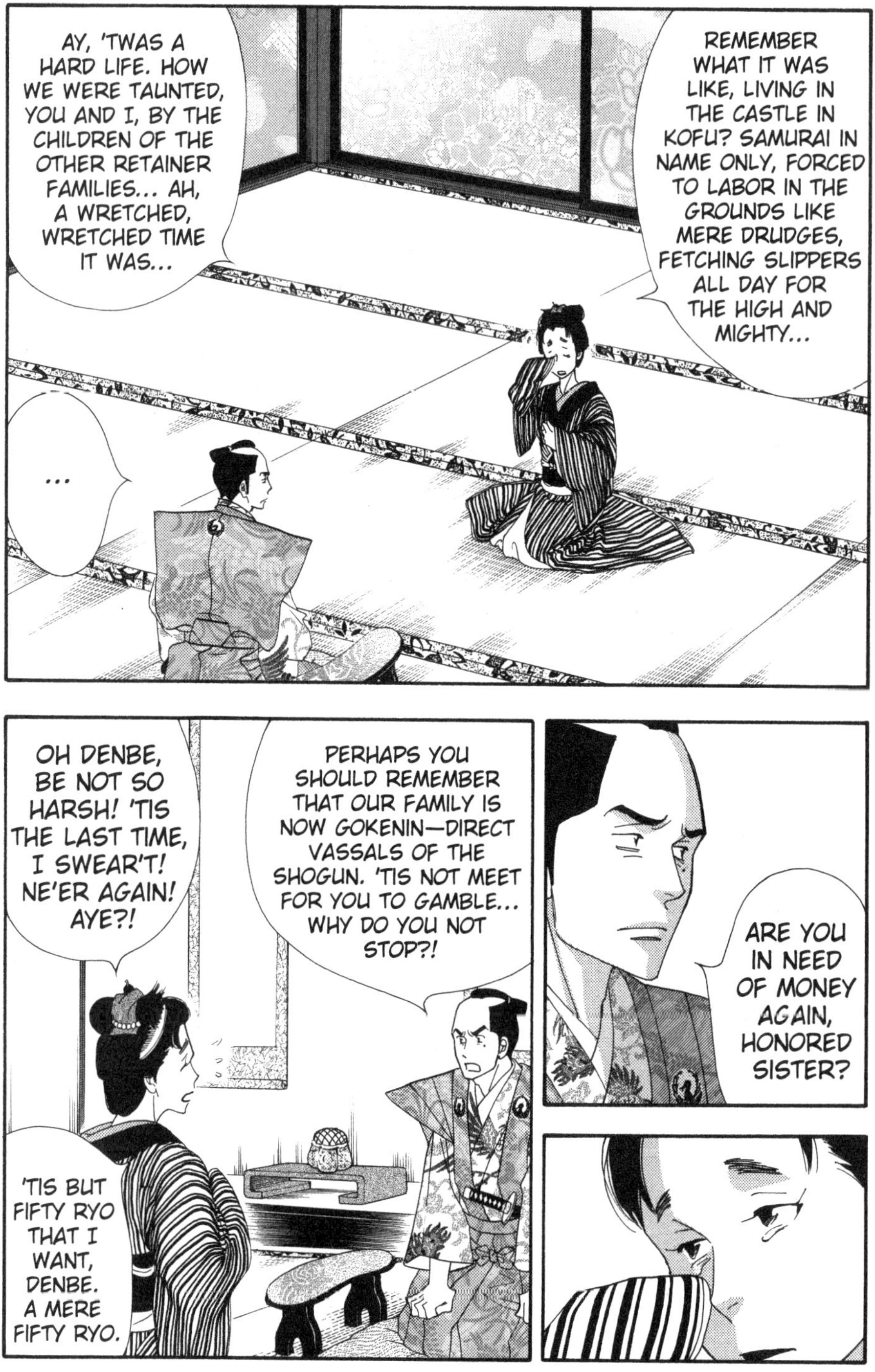
REMEMBER WHAT IT WAS LIKE, LIVING IN THE CASTLE IN KOFU? SAMURAI IN NAME ONLY, FORCED TO LABOR IN THE GROUNDS LIKE MERE DRUDGES, FETCHING SLIPPERS ALL DAY FOR THE HIGH AND MIGHTY...
AY, 'TWAS A HARD LIFE. HOW WE WERE TAUNTED, YOU AND I, BY THE CHILDREN OF THE OTHER RETAINER FAMILIES... AH, A WRETCHED, WRETCHED TIME IT WAS...
...
ARE YOU IN NEED OF MONEY AGAIN, HONORED SISTER?
PERHAPS YOU SHOULD REMEMBER THAT OUR FAMILY IS NOW GOKENIN—DIRECT VASSALS OF THE SHOGUN. 'TIS NOT MEET FOR YOU TO GAMBLE... WHY DO YOU NOT STOP?!
OH DENBE, BE NOT SO HARSH! 'TIS THE LAST TIME, I SWEAR'T! NE'ER AGAIN! AYE?!
'TIS BUT FIFTY RYO THAT I WANT, DENBE. A MERE FIFTY RYO.

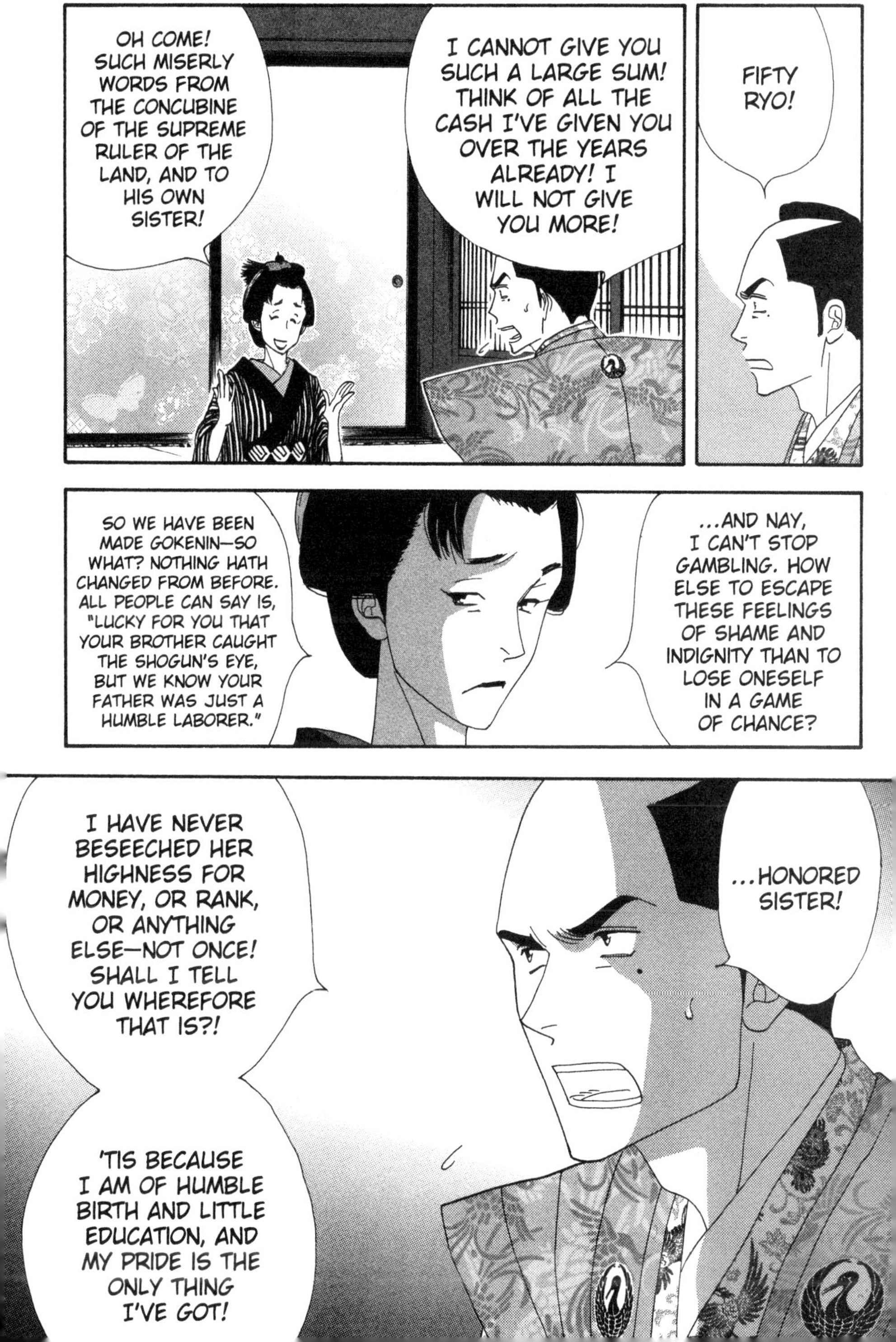
FIFTY RYO!
I CANNOT GIVE YOU SUCH A LARGE SUM! THINK OF ALL THE CASH I'VE GIVEN YOU OVER THE YEARS ALREADY! I WILL NOT GIVE YOU MORE!
OH COME! SUCH MISERLY WORDS FROM THE CONCUBINE OF THE SUPREME RULER OF THE LAND, AND TO HIS OWN SISTER!
...AND NAY, I CAN'T STOP GAMBLING. HOW ELSE TO ESCAPE THESE FEELINGS OF SHAME AND INDIGNITY THAN TO LOSE ONESELF IN A GAME OF CHANCE?
SO WE HAVE BEEN MADE GOKENIN—SO WHAT? NOTHING HATH CHANGED FROM BEFORE. ALL PEOPLE CAN SAY IS, "LUCKY FOR YOU THAT YOUR BROTHER CAUGHT THE SHOGUN'S EYE, BUT WE KNOW YOUR FATHER WAS JUST A HUMBLE LABORER."
...HONORED SISTER!
I HAVE NEVER BESEECHED HER HIGHNESS FOR MONEY, OR RANK, OR ANYTHING ELSE—NOT ONCE! SHALL I TELL YOU WHEREFORE THAT IS?!
'TIS BECAUSE I AM OF HUMBLE BIRTH AND LITTLE EDUCATION, AND MY PRIDE IS THE ONLY THING I'VE GOT!

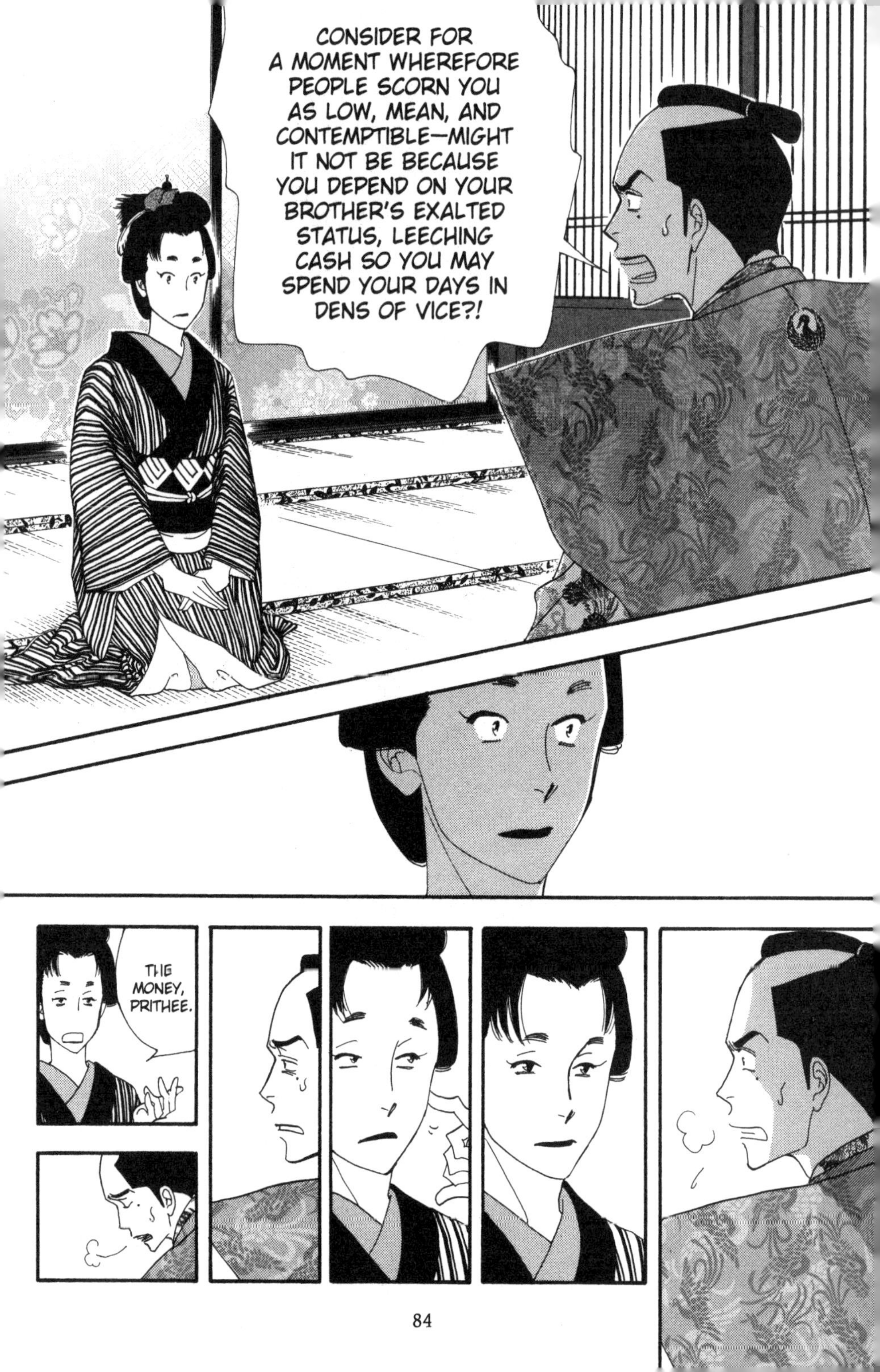
CONSIDER FOR A MOMENT WHEREFORE PEOPLE SCORN YOU AS LOW, MEAN, AND CONTEMPTIBLE—MIGHT IT NOT BE BECAUSE YOU DEPEND ON YOUR BROTHER'S EXALTED STATUS, LEECHING CASH SO YOU MAY SPEND YOUR DAYS IN DENS OF VICE?!
THE MONEY, PRITHEE.

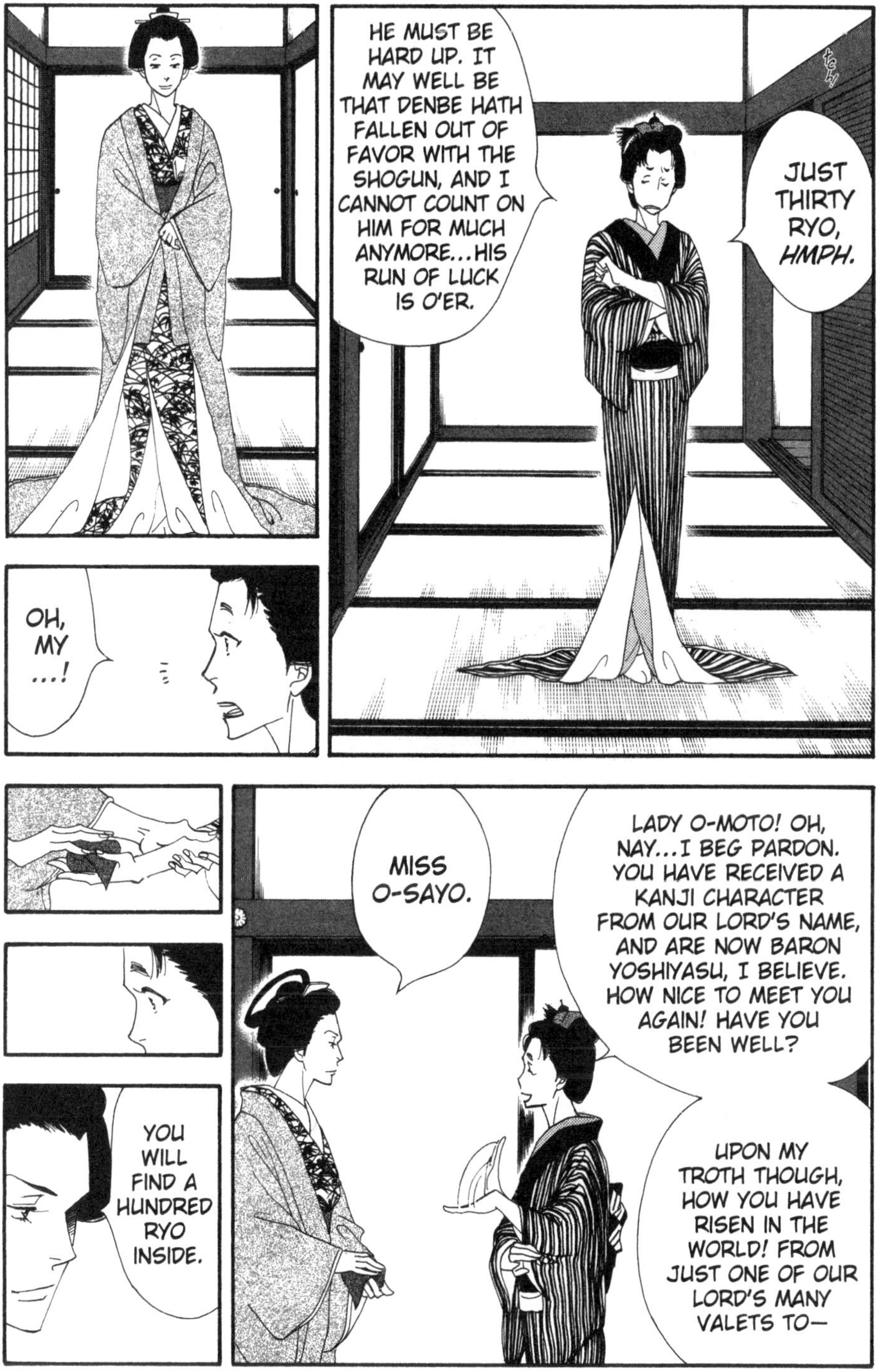
JUST THIRTY RYO, *HMPH.*
HE MUST BE HARD UP. IT MAY WELL BE THAT DENBE HATH FALLEN OUT OF FAVOR WITH THE SHOGUN, AND I CANNOT COUNT ON HIM FOR MUCH ANYMORE...HIS RUN OF LUCK IS O'ER.
OH, MY ...!
LADY O-MOTO! OH, NAY...I BEG PARDON. YOU HAVE RECEIVED A KANJI CHARACTER FROM OUR LORD'S NAME, AND ARE NOW BARON YOSHIYASU, I BELIEVE. HOW NICE TO MEET YOU AGAIN! HAVE YOU BEEN WELL?
MISS O-SAYO.
UPON MY TROTH THOUGH, HOW YOU HAVE RISEN IN THE WORLD! FROM JUST ONE OF OUR LORD'S MANY VALETS TO—
YOU WILL FIND A HUNDRED RYO INSIDE.

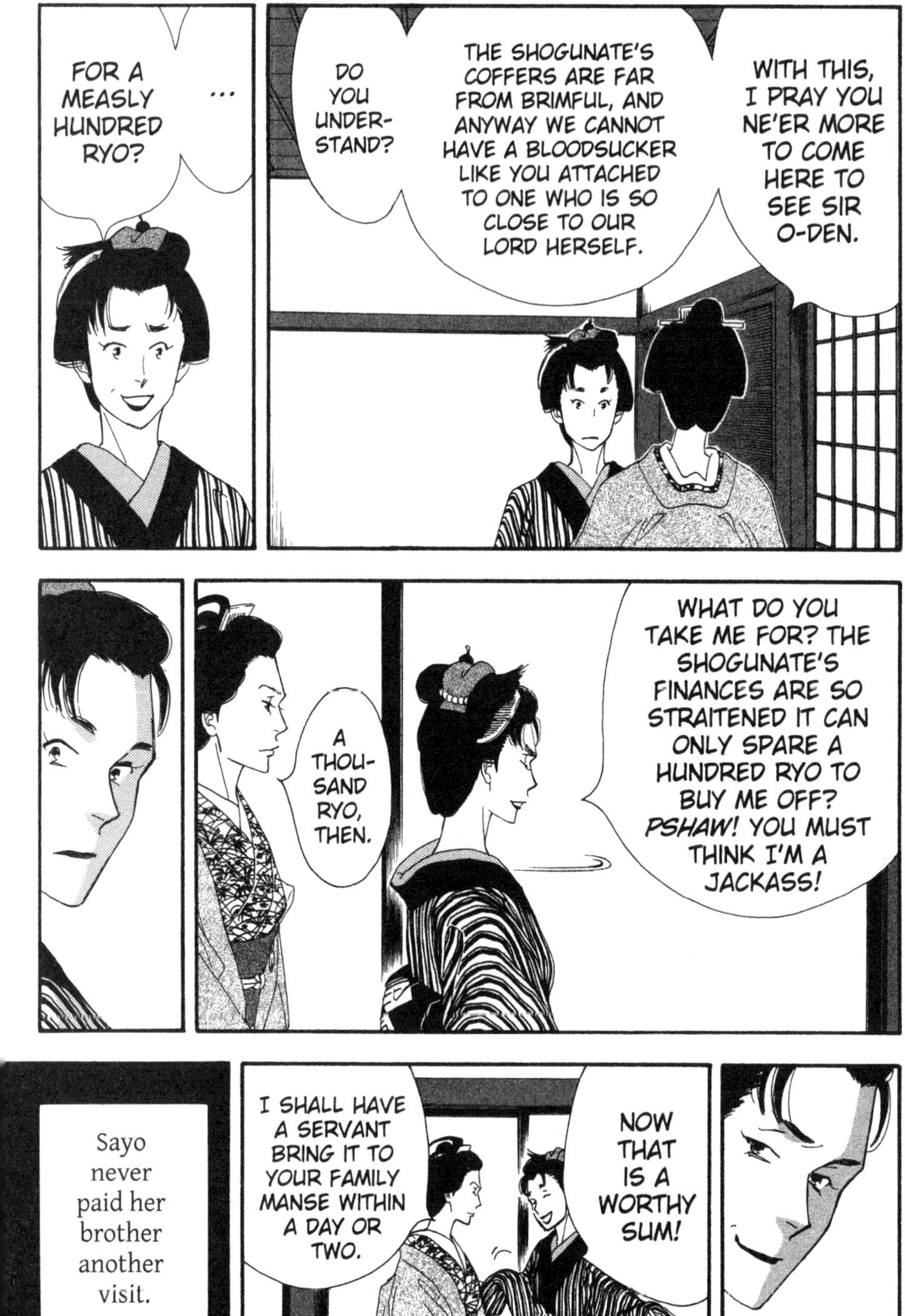
WITH THIS, I PRAY YOU NE'ER MORE TO COME HERE TO SEE SIR O-DEN.
THE SHOGUNATE'S COFFERS ARE FAR FROM BRIMFUL, AND ANYWAY WE CANNOT HAVE A BLOODSUCKER LIKE YOU ATTACHED TO ONE WHO IS SO CLOSE TO OUR LORD HERSELF.
DO YOU UNDER-STAND?
...
FOR A MEASLY HUNDRED RYO?
WHAT DO YOU TAKE ME FOR? THE SHOGUNATE'S FINANCES ARE SO STRAITENED IT CAN ONLY SPARE A HUNDRED RYO TO BUY ME OFF? *PSHAW!* YOU MUST THINK I'M A JACKASS!
A THOU-SAND RYO, THEN.
NOW THAT IS A WORTHY SUM!
I SHALL HAVE A SERVANT BRING IT TO YOUR FAMILY MANSE WITHIN A DAY OR TWO.
Sayo never paid her brother another visit.

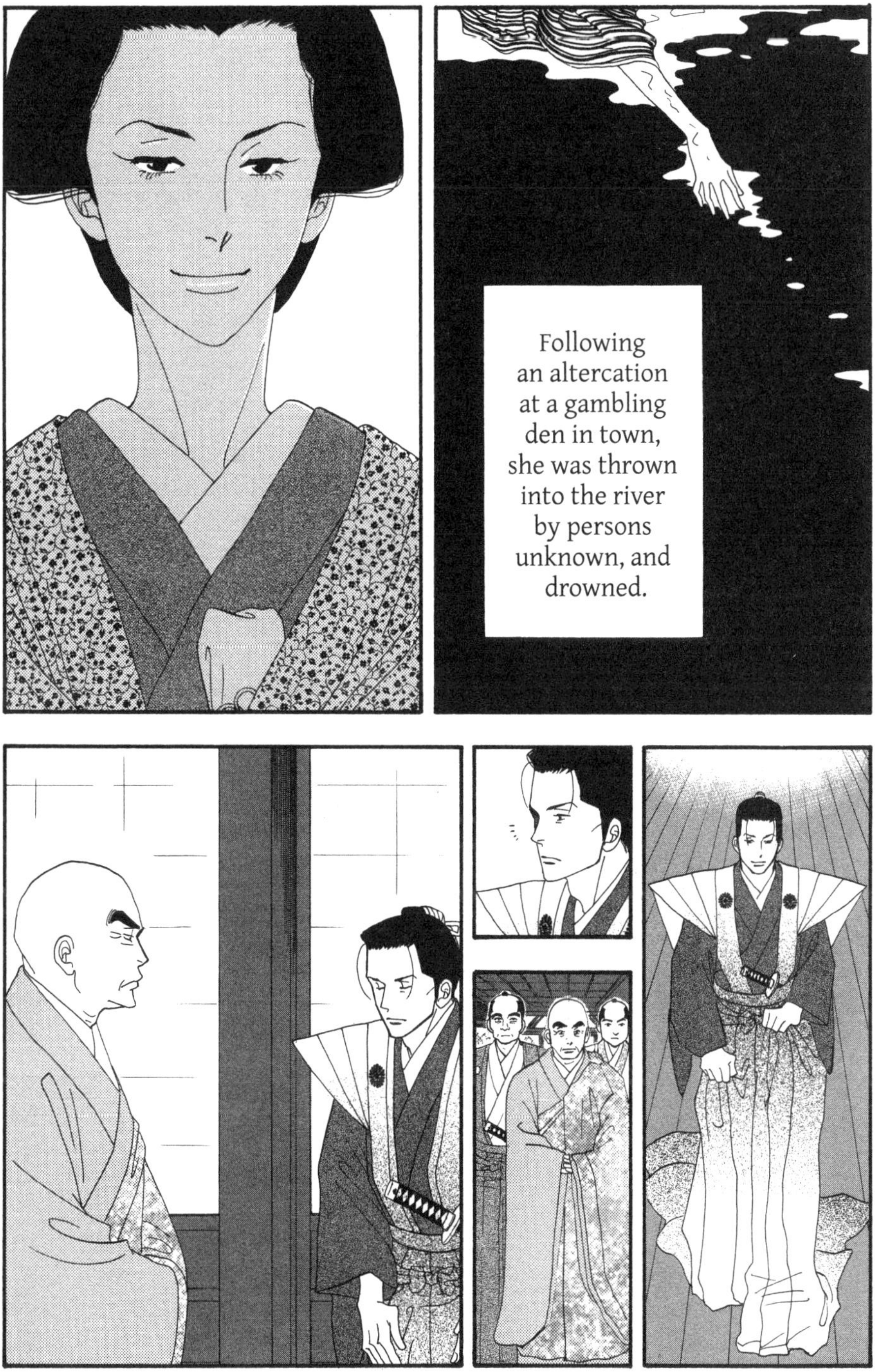
Following an altercation at a gambling den in town, she was thrown into the river by persons unknown, and drowned.

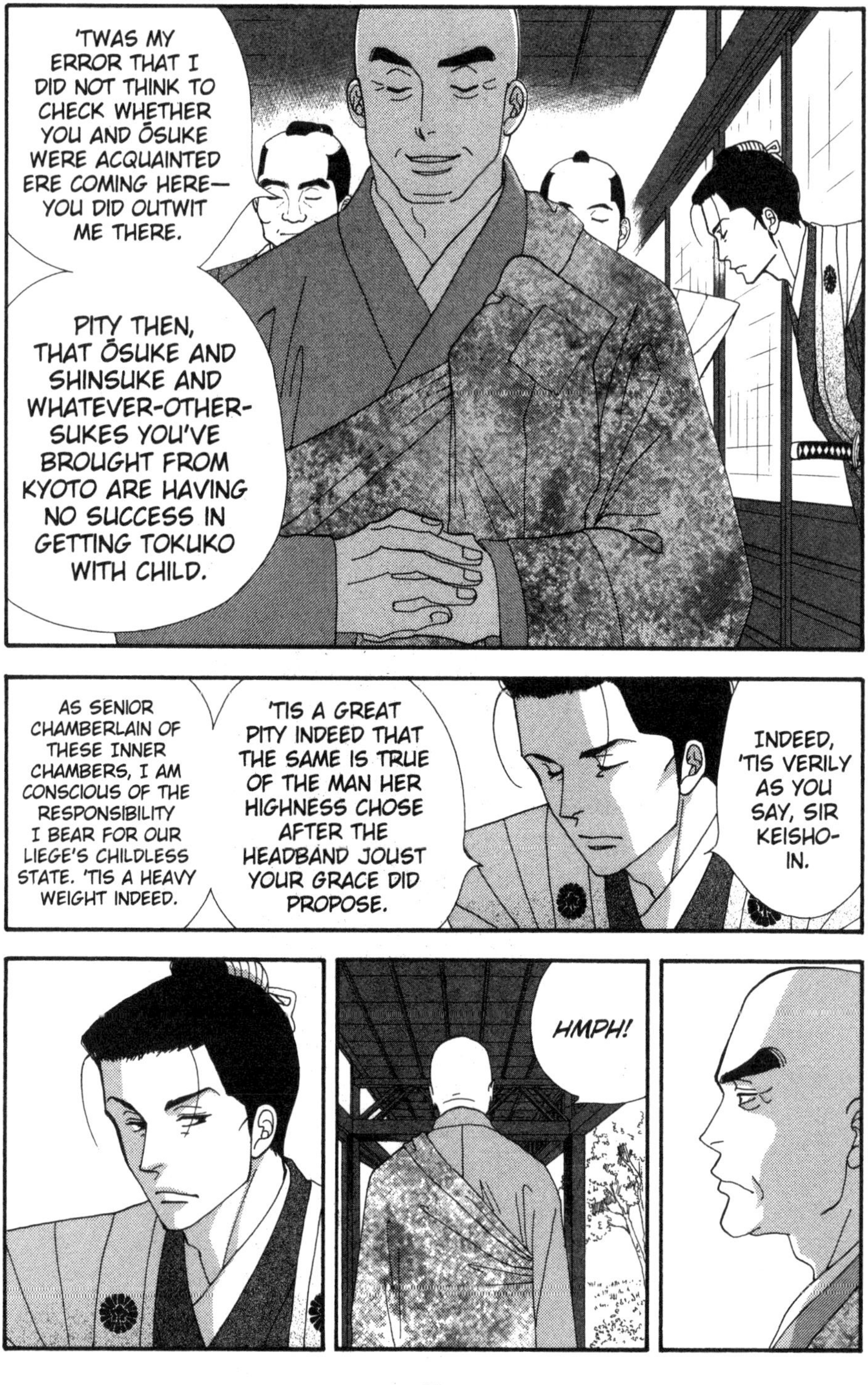
'TWAS MY ERROR THAT I DID NOT THINK TO CHECK WHETHER YOU AND ŌSUKE WERE ACQUAINTED ERE COMING HERE—YOU DID OUTWIT ME THERE.
PITY THEN, THAT ŌSUKE AND SHINSUKE AND WHATEVER-OTHER-SUKES YOU'VE BROUGHT FROM KYOTO ARE HAVING NO SUCCESS IN GETTING TOKUKO WITH CHILD.
INDEED, 'TIS VERILY AS YOU SAY, SIR KEISHO-IN.
'TIS A GREAT PITY INDEED THAT THE SAME IS TRUE OF THE MAN HER HIGHNESS CHOSE AFTER THE HEADBAND JOUST YOUR GRACE DID PROPOSE.
AS SENIOR CHAMBERLAIN OF THESE INNER CHAMBERS, I AM CONSCIOUS OF THE RESPONSIBILITY I BEAR FOR OUR LIEGE'S CHILDLESS STATE. 'TIS A HEAVY WEIGHT INDEED.
HMPH!

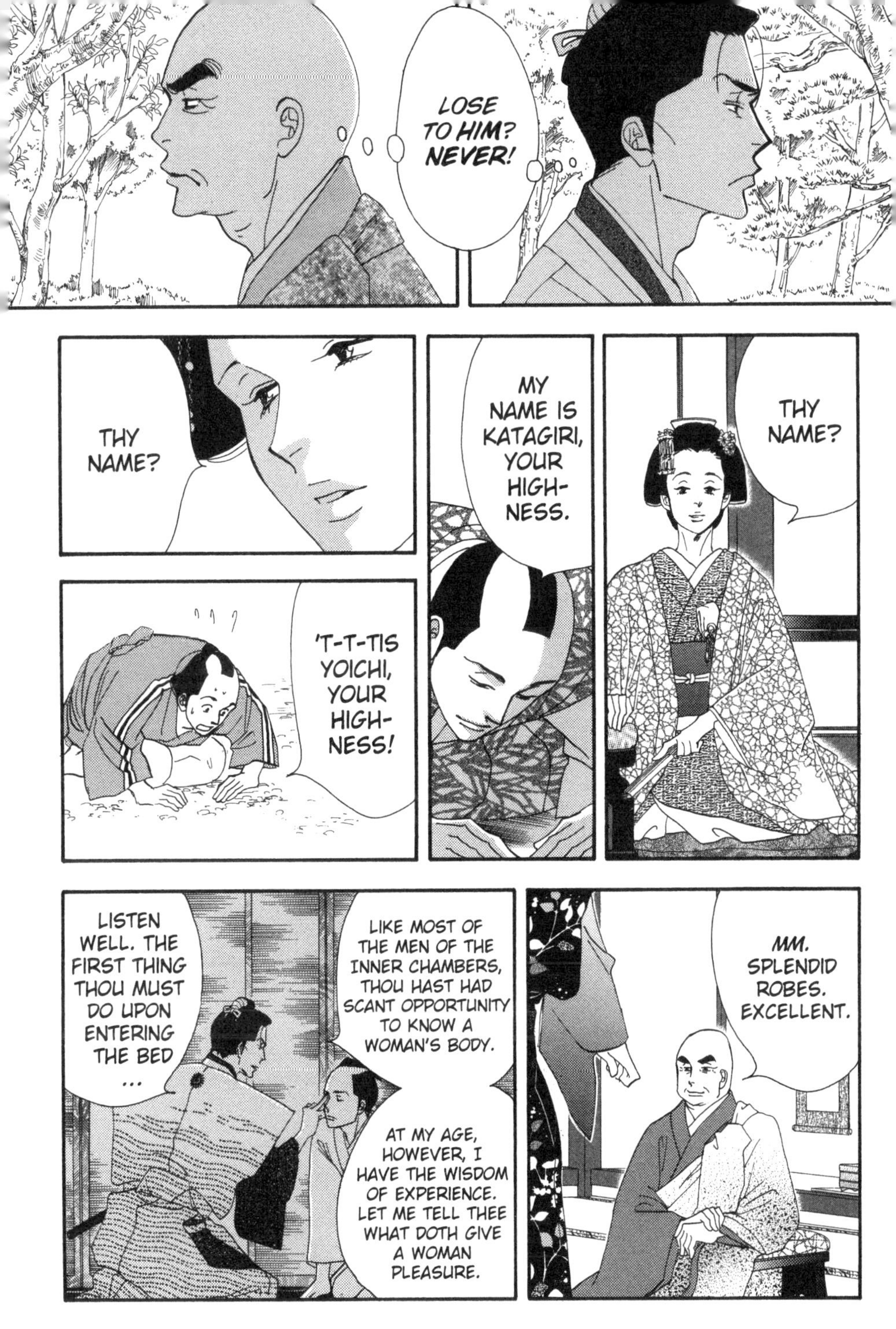
LOSE TO HIM? NEVER!
THY NAME?
MY NAME IS KATAGIRI, YOUR HIGH-NESS.
THY NAME?
'T-T-TIS YOICHI, YOUR HIGH-NESS!
MM. SPLENDID ROBES. EXCELLENT.
LIKE MOST OF THE MEN OF THE INNER CHAMBERS, THOU HAST HAD SCANT OPPORTUNITY TO KNOW A WOMAN'S BODY.
AT MY AGE, HOWEVER, I HAVE THE WISDOM OF EXPERIENCE. LET ME TELL THEE WHAT DOTH GIVE A WOMAN PLEASURE.
LISTEN WELL. THE FIRST THING THOU MUST DO UPON ENTERING THE BED ...

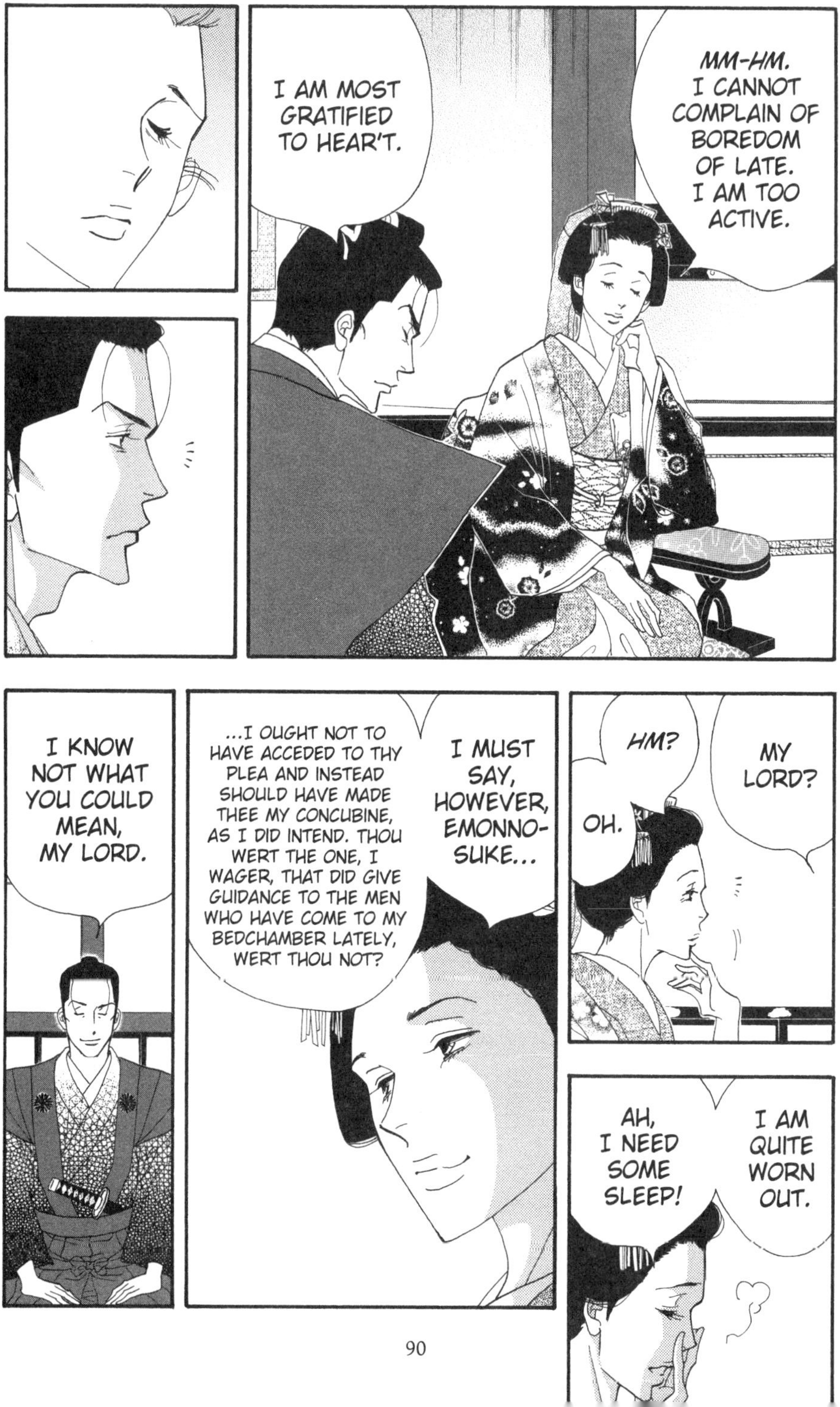
MM-HM. I CANNOT COMPLAIN OF BOREDOM OF LATE. I AM TOO ACTIVE.
I AM MOST GRATIFIED TO HEAR'T.
MY LORD?
HM?
OH.
I AM QUITE WORN OUT.
AH, I NEED SOME SLEEP!
I MUST SAY, HOWEVER, EMONNO-SUKE...
...I OUGHT NOT TO HAVE ACCEDED TO THY PLEA AND INSTEAD SHOULD HAVE MADE THEE MY CONCUBINE, AS I DID INTEND. THOU WERT THE ONE, I WAGER, THAT DID GIVE GUIDANCE TO THE MEN WHO HAVE COME TO MY BEDCHAMBER LATELY, WERT THOU NOT?
I KNOW NOT WHAT YOU COULD MEAN, MY LORD.

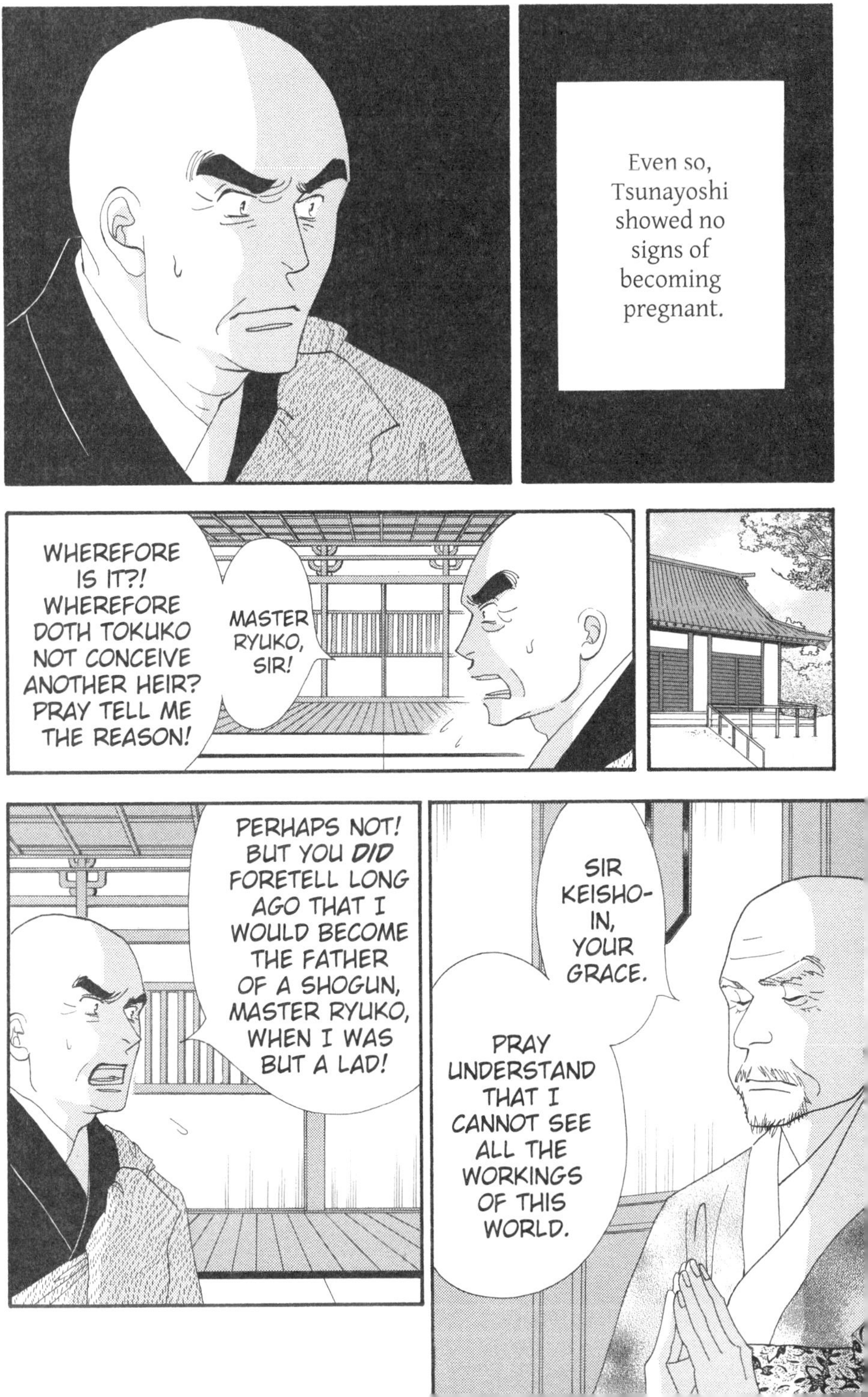
Even so, Tsunayoshi showed no signs of becoming pregnant.
MASTER RYUKO, SIR!
WHEREFORE IS IT?! WHEREFORE DOTH TOKUKO NOT CONCEIVE ANOTHER HEIR? PRAY TELL ME THE REASON!
SIR KEISHO-IN, YOUR GRACE.
PRAY UNDERSTAND THAT I CANNOT SEE ALL THE WORKINGS OF THIS WORLD.
PERHAPS NOT! BUT YOU *DID* FORETELL LONG AGO THAT I WOULD BECOME THE FATHER OF A SHOGUN, MASTER RYUKO, WHEN I WAS BUT A LAD!

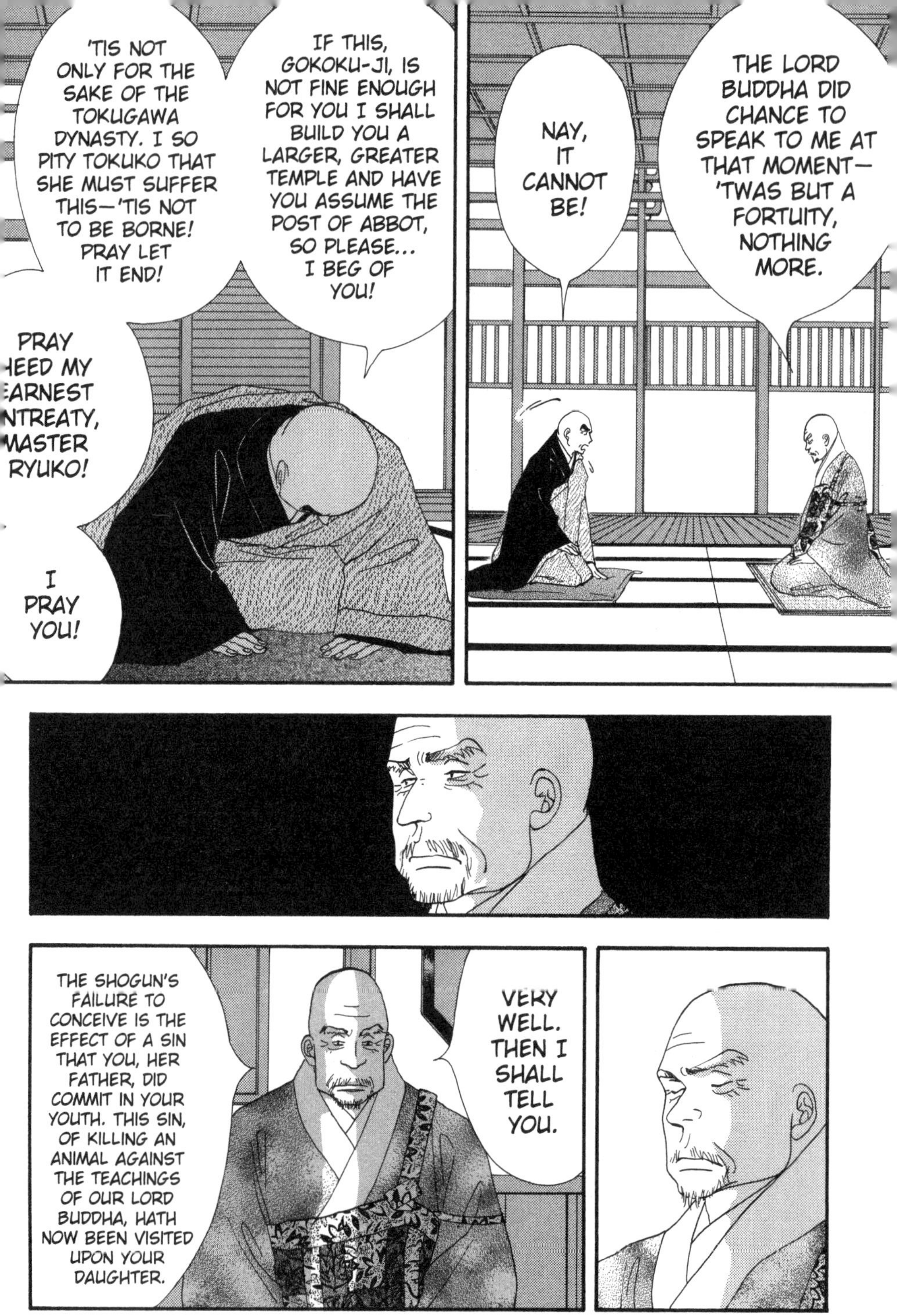
THE LORD BUDDHA DID CHANCE TO SPEAK TO ME AT THAT MOMENT—'TWAS BUT A FORTUITY, NOTHING MORE.
NAY, IT CANNOT BE!
IF THIS, GOKOKU-JI, IS NOT FINE ENOUGH FOR YOU I SHALL BUILD YOU A LARGER, GREATER TEMPLE AND HAVE YOU ASSUME THE POST OF ABBOT, SO PLEASE... I BEG OF YOU!
'TIS NOT ONLY FOR THE SAKE OF THE TOKUGAWA DYNASTY. I SO PITY TOKUKO THAT SHE MUST SUFFER THIS—'TIS NOT TO BE BORNE! PRAY LET IT END!
PRAY HEED MY ARNEST NTREATY, MASTER RYUKO!
I PRAY YOU!
VERY WELL. THEN I SHALL TELL YOU.
THE SHOGUN'S FAILURE TO CONCEIVE IS THE EFFECT OF A SIN THAT YOU, HER FATHER, DID COMMIT IN YOUR YOUTH. THIS SIN, OF KILLING AN ANIMAL AGAINST THE TEACHINGS OF OUR LORD BUDDHA, HATH NOW BEEN VISITED UPON YOUR DAUGHTER.

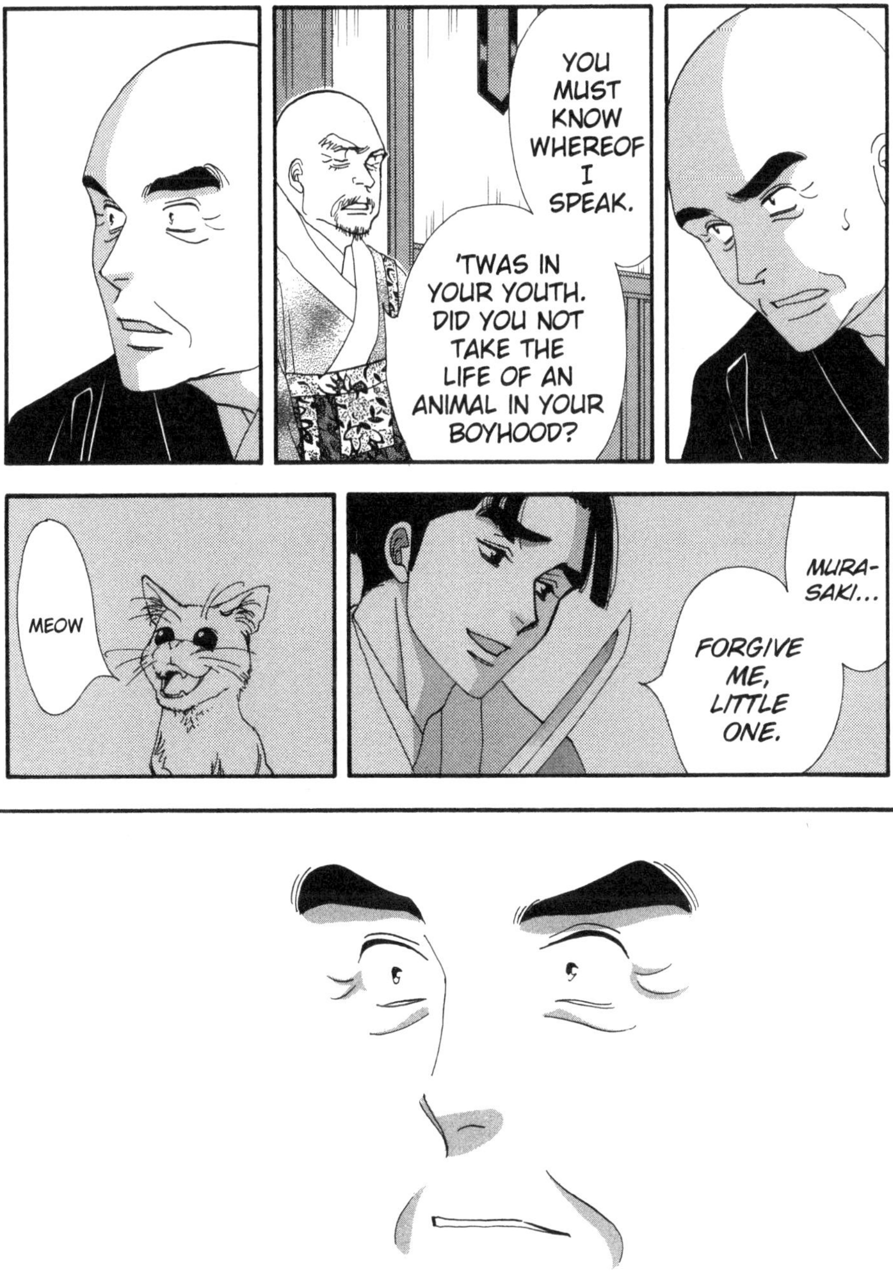
YOU MUST KNOW WHEREOF I SPEAK.
'TWAS IN YOUR YOUTH. DID YOU NOT TAKE THE LIFE OF AN ANIMAL IN YOUR BOYHOOD?
MURA-SAKI...
FORGIVE ME, LITTLE ONE.
MEOW

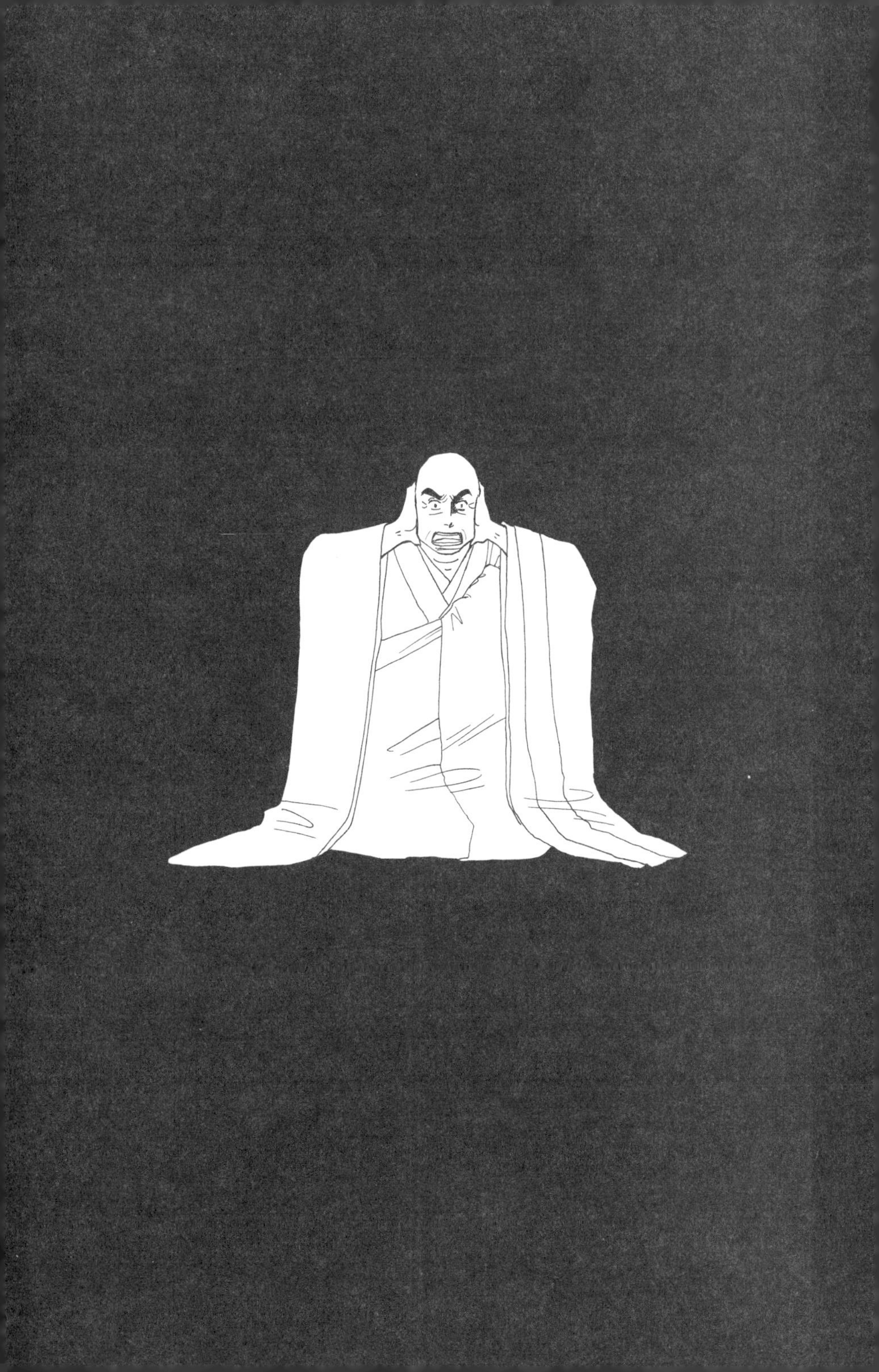

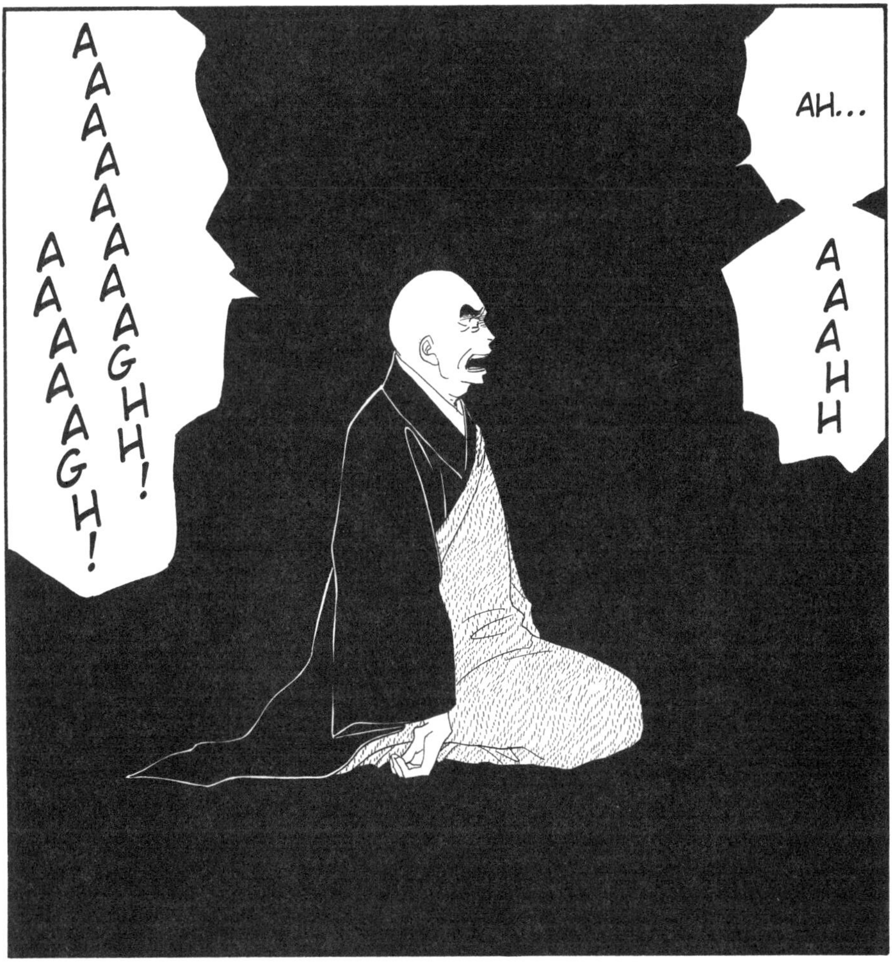
AH...
AAAHH
AAAAAAAAGHH!
AAAAAGH!

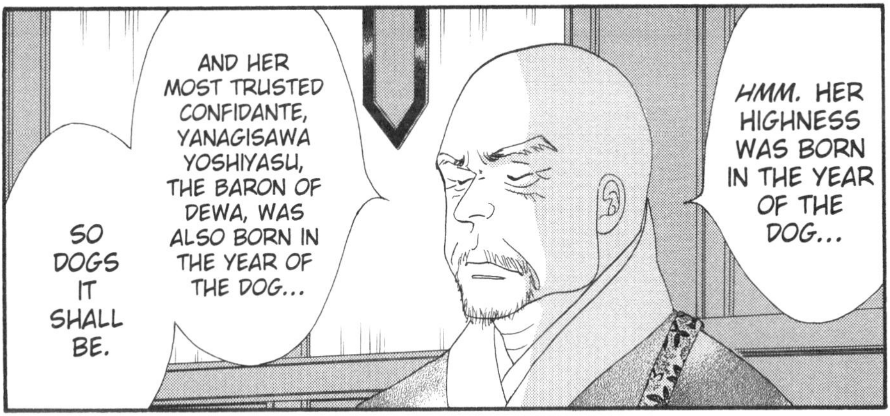
HMM. HER HIGHNESS WAS BORN IN THE YEAR OF THE DOG...
AND HER MOST TRUSTED CONFIDANTE, YANAGISAWA YOSHIYASU, THE BARON OF DEWA, WAS ALSO BORN IN THE YEAR OF THE DOG...
SO DOGS IT SHALL BE.

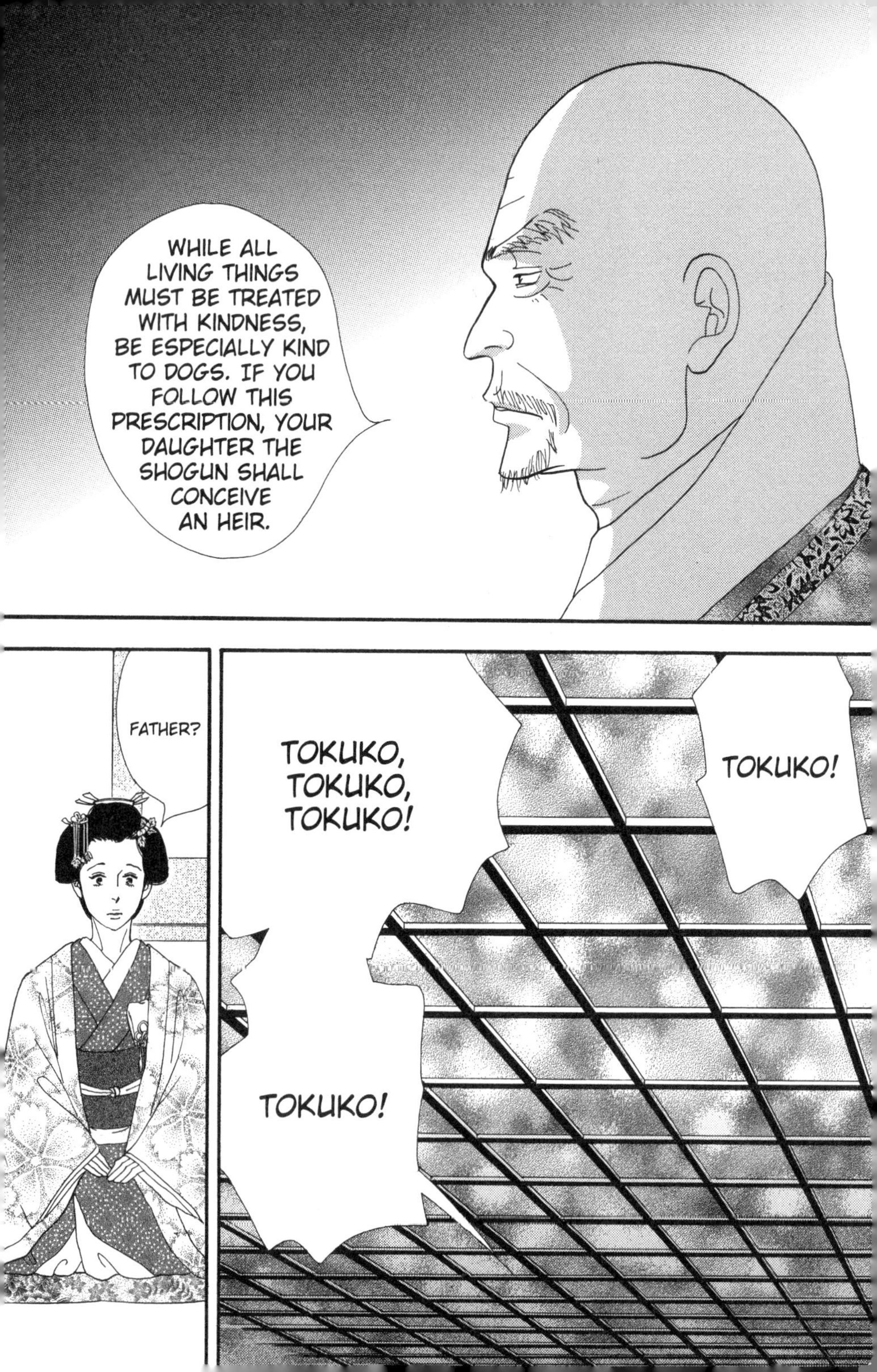
WHILE ALL LIVING THINGS MUST BE TREATED WITH KINDNESS, BE ESPECIALLY KIND TO DOGS. IF YOU FOLLOW THIS PRESCRIPTION, YOUR DAUGHTER THE SHOGUN SHALL CONCEIVE AN HEIR.
TOKUKO!
TOKUKO, TOKUKO, TOKUKO!
TOKUKO!
FATHER?

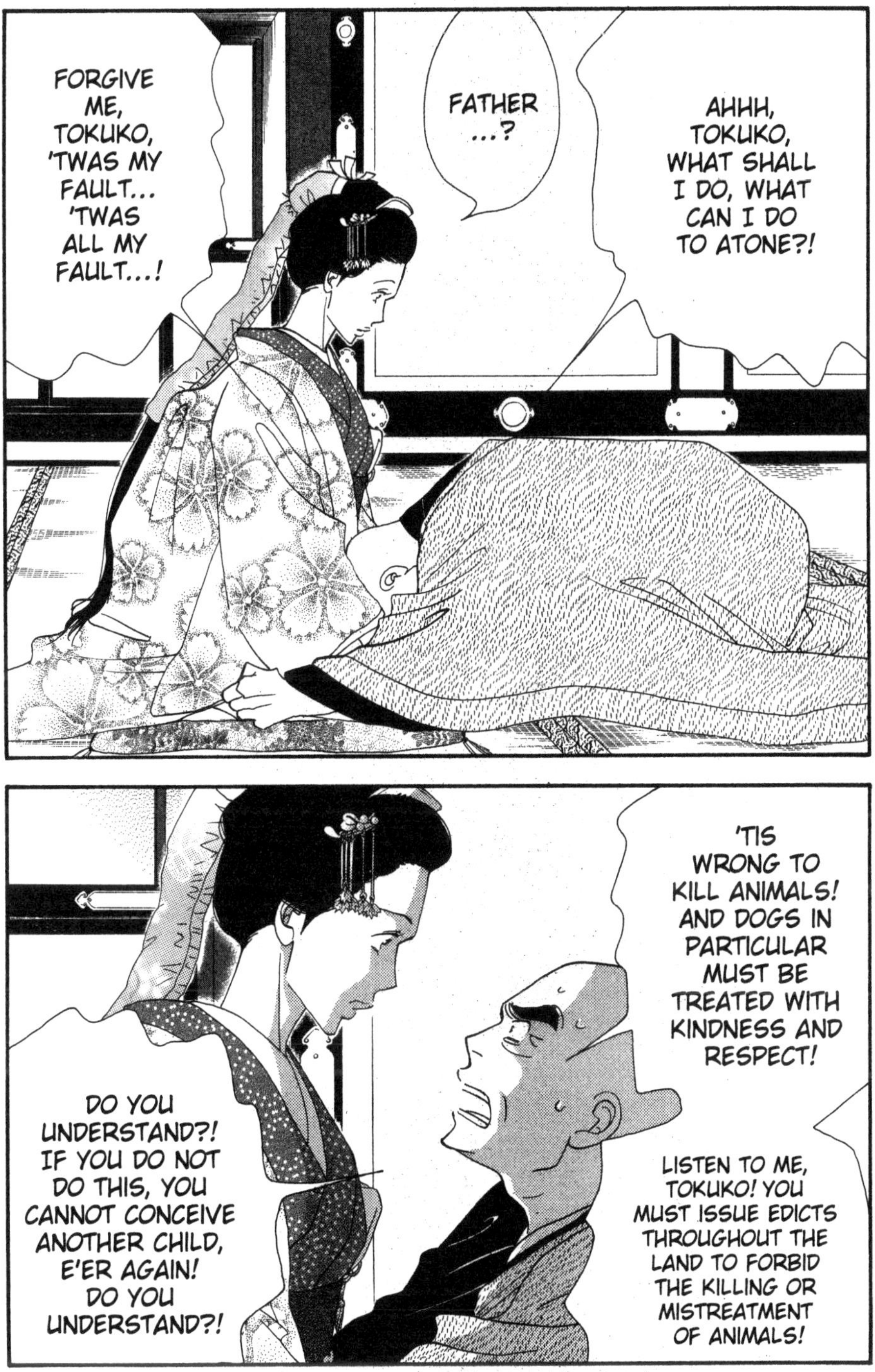
AHHH, TOKUKO, WHAT SHALL I DO, WHAT CAN I DO TO ATONE?!
FATHER ...?
FORGIVE ME, TOKUKO, 'TWAS MY FAULT... 'TWAS ALL MY FAULT...!
'TIS WRONG TO KILL ANIMALS! AND DOGS IN PARTICULAR MUST BE TREATED WITH KINDNESS AND RESPECT!
LISTEN TO ME, TOKUKO! YOU MUST ISSUE EDICTS THROUGHOUT THE LAND TO FORBID THE KILLING OR MISTREATMENT OF ANIMALS!
DO YOU UNDERSTAND?! IF YOU DO NOT DO THIS, YOU CANNOT CONCEIVE ANOTHER CHILD, E'ER AGAIN! DO YOU UNDERSTAND?!

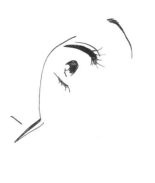

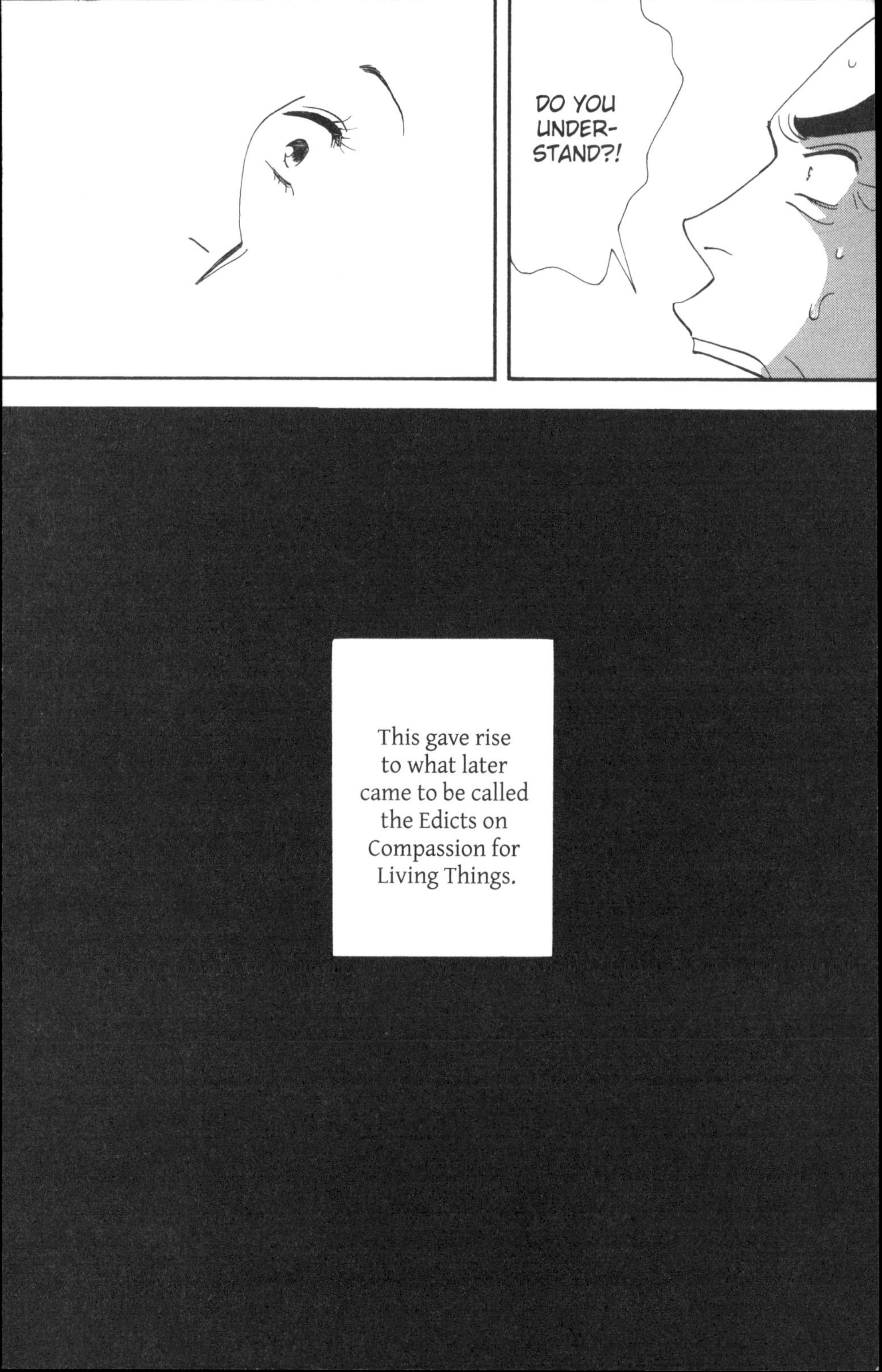
DO YOU UNDER-STAND?!
This gave rise to what later came to be called the Edicts on Compassion for Living Things.

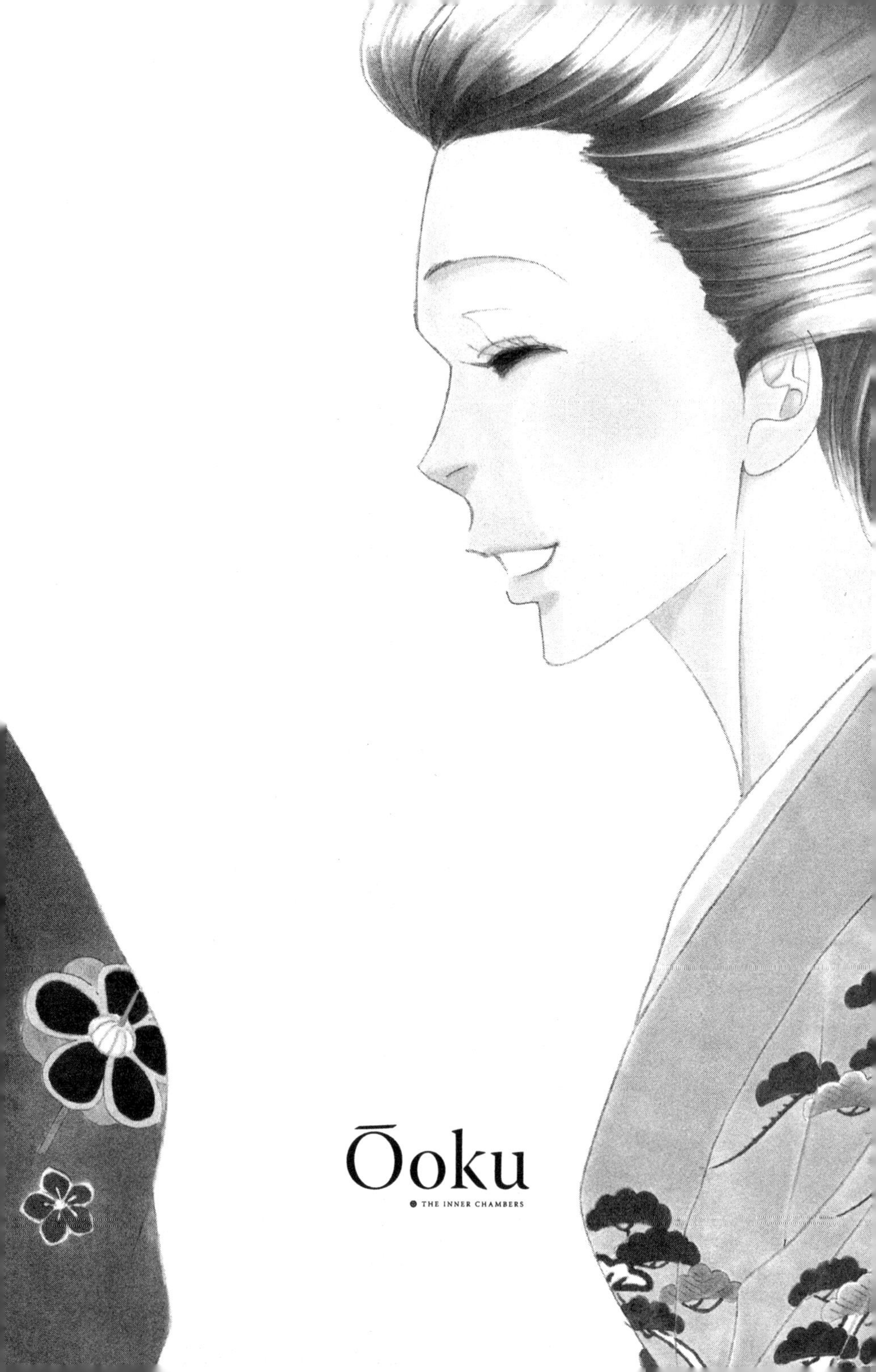
Ōoku
THE INNER CHAMBERS

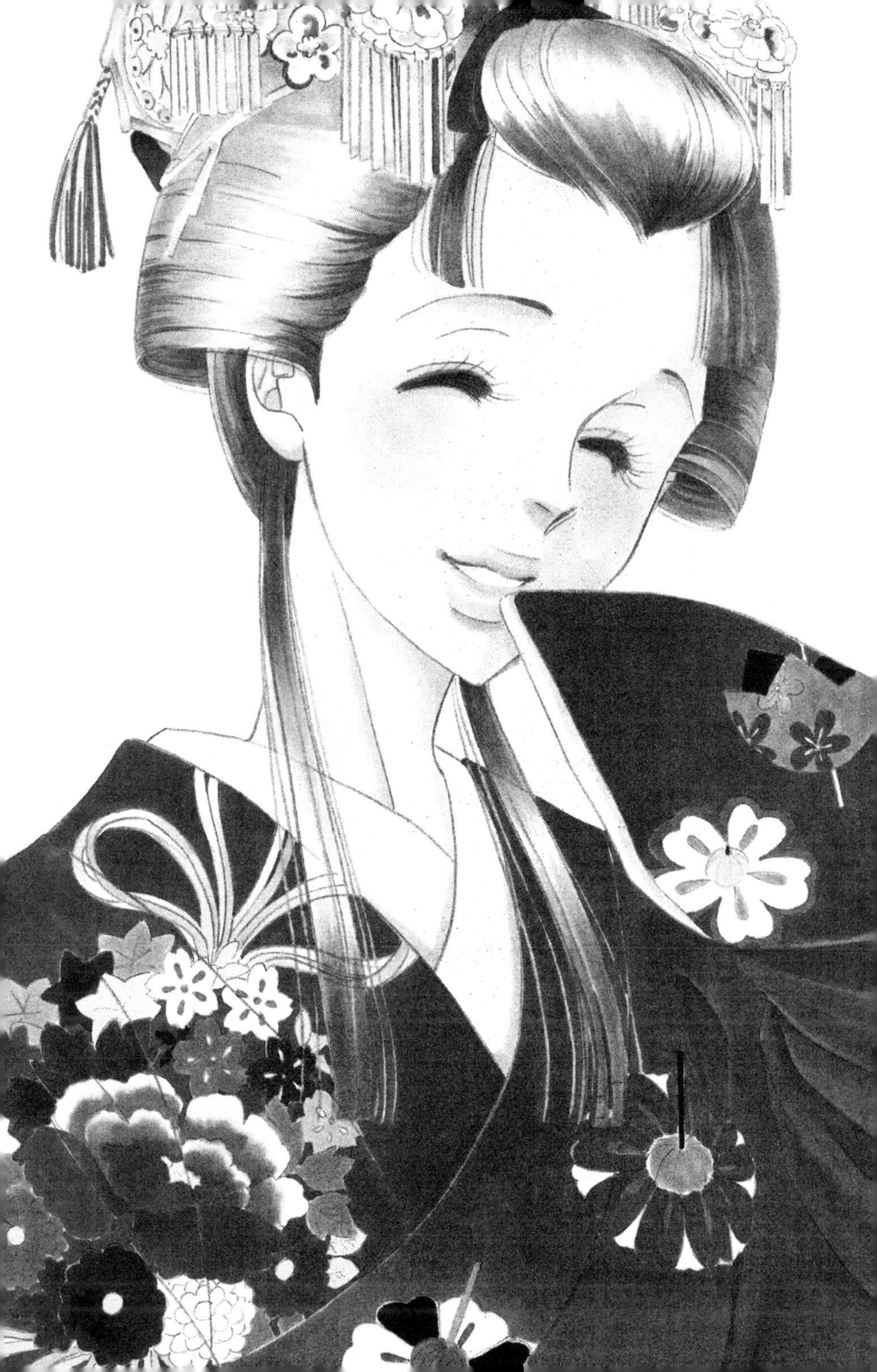

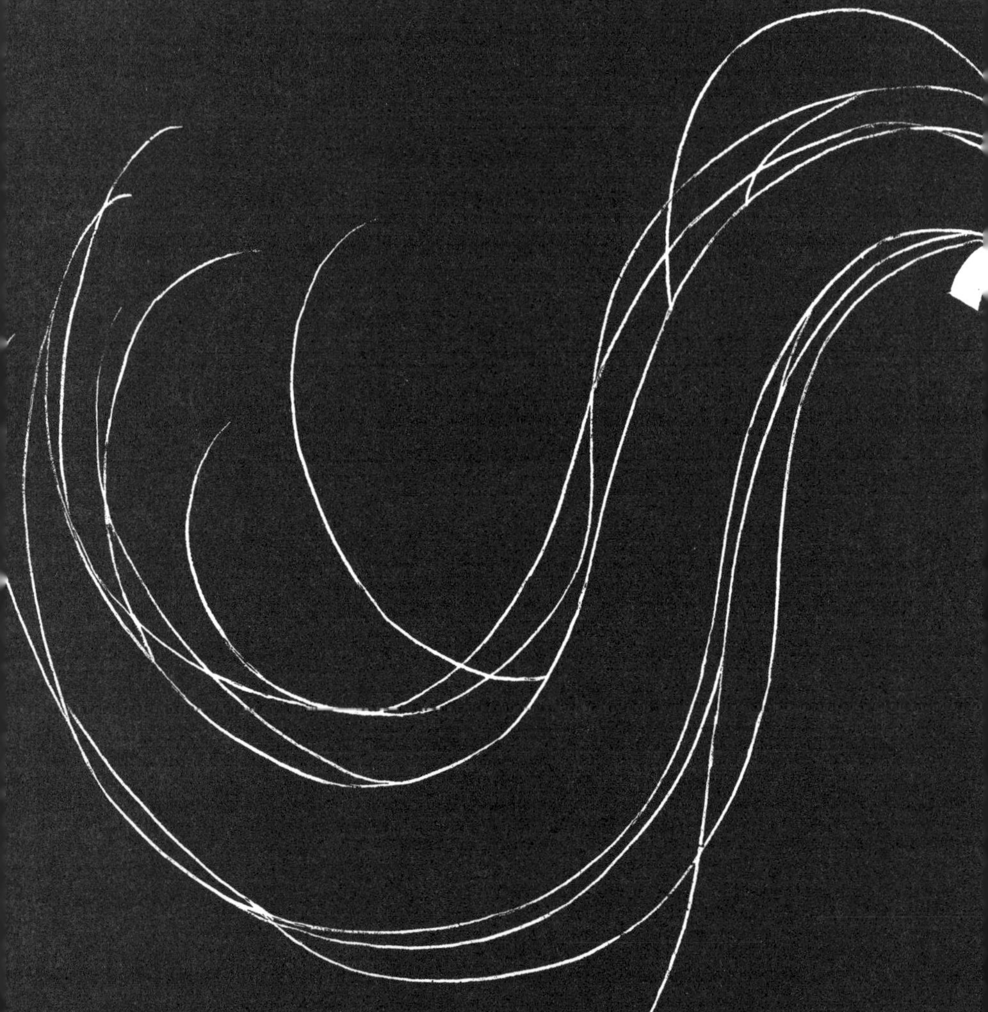

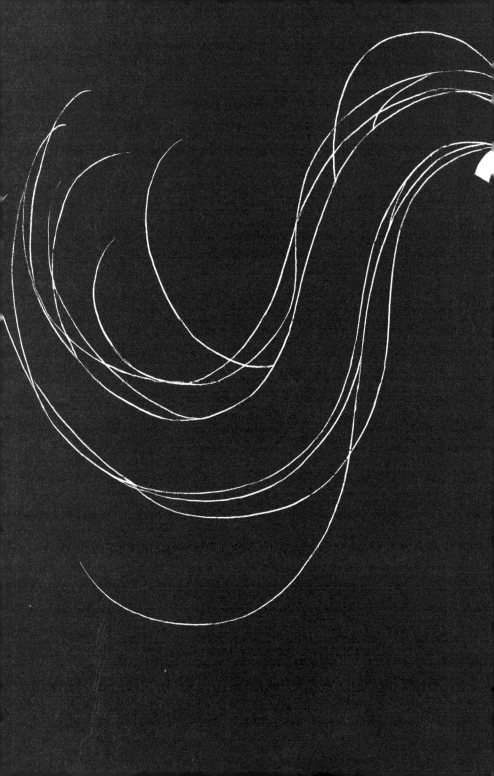

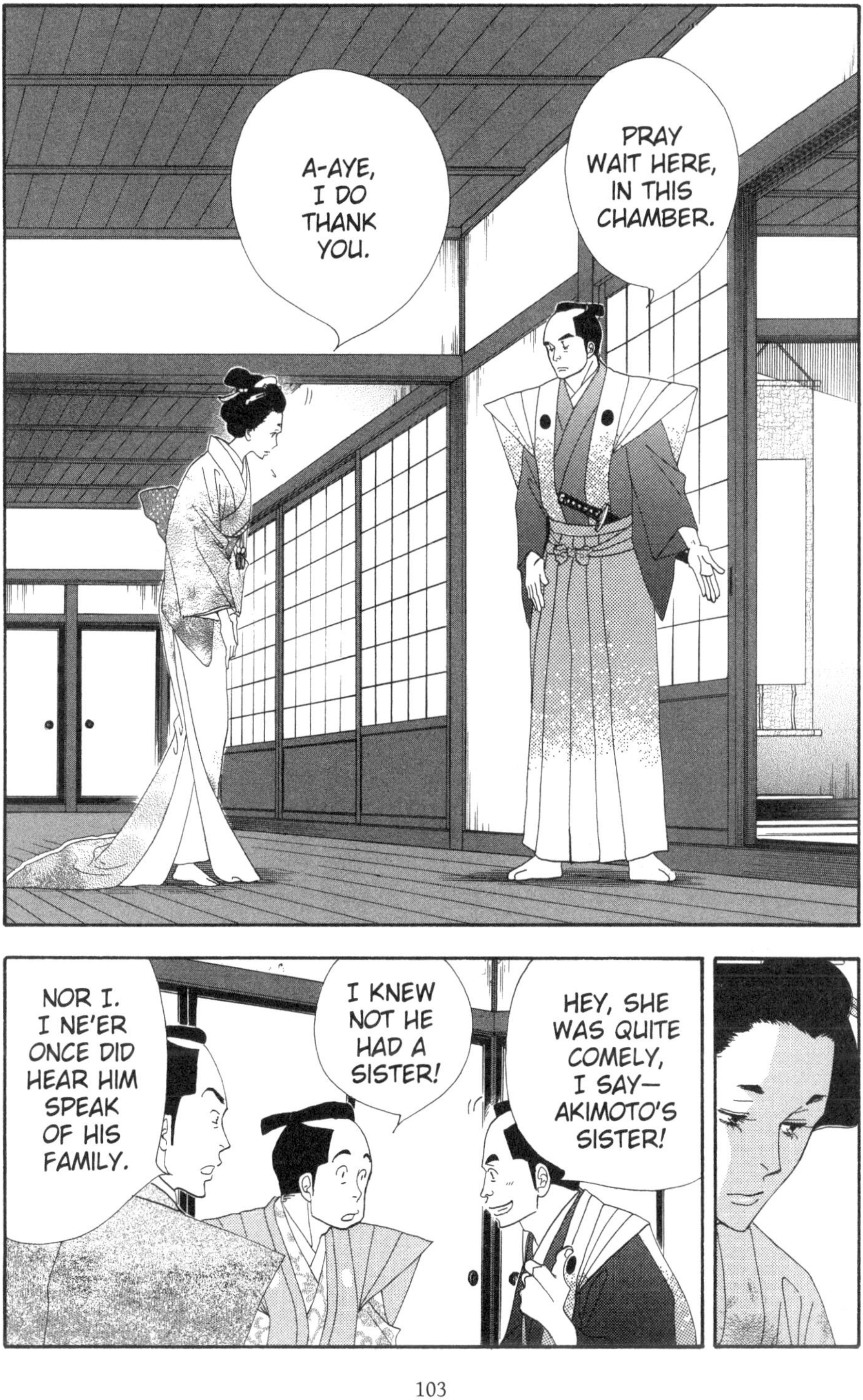
PRAY WAIT HERE, IN THIS CHAMBER.
A-AYE, I DO THANK YOU.
HEY, SHE WAS QUITE COMELY, I SAY—AKIMOTO'S SISTER!
I KNEW NOT HE HAD A SISTER!
NOR I. I NE'ER ONCE DID HEAR HIM SPEAK OF HIS FAMILY.

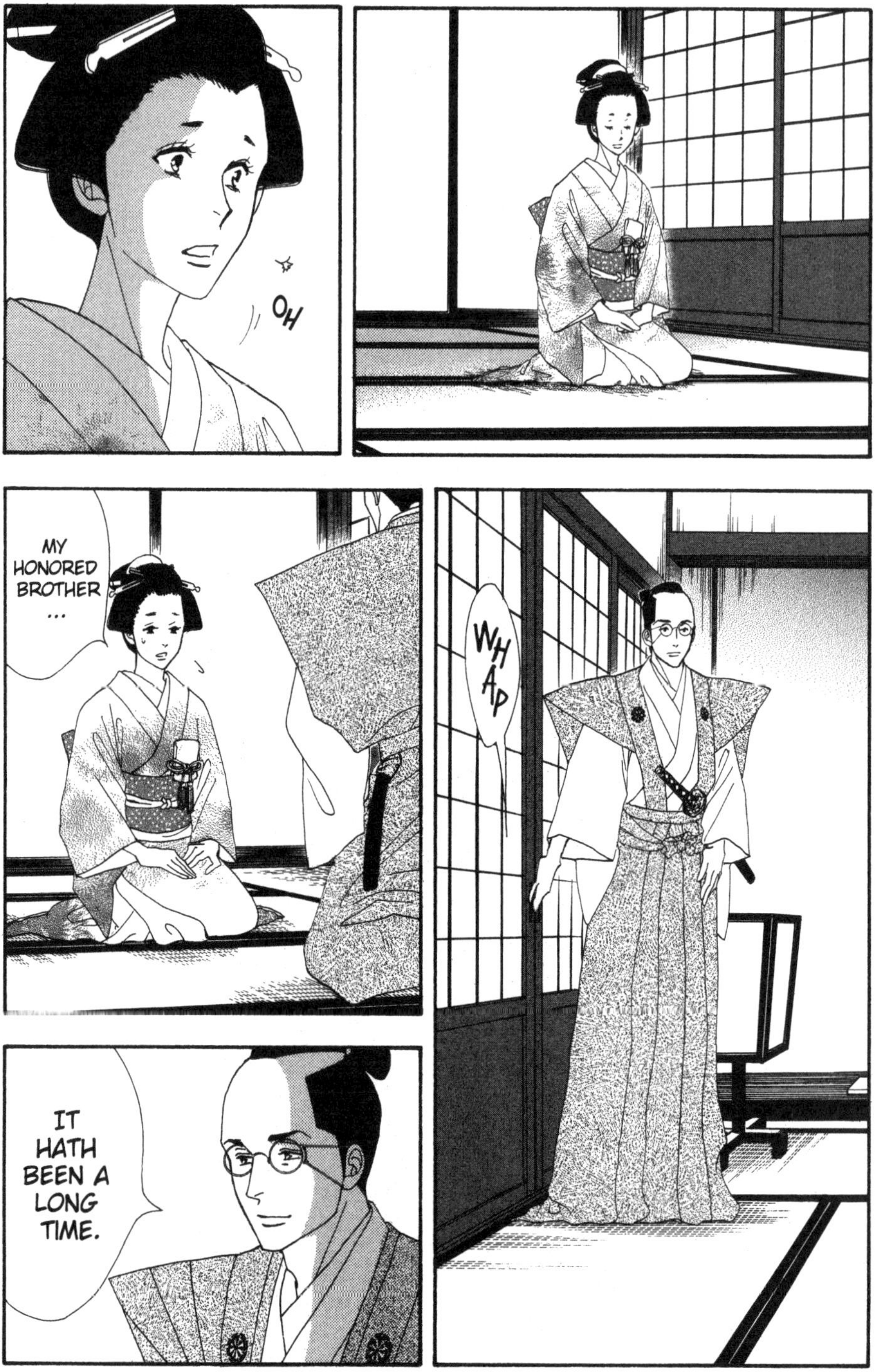
OH
WHAP
MY HONORED BROTHER ...
IT HATH BEEN A LONG TIME.

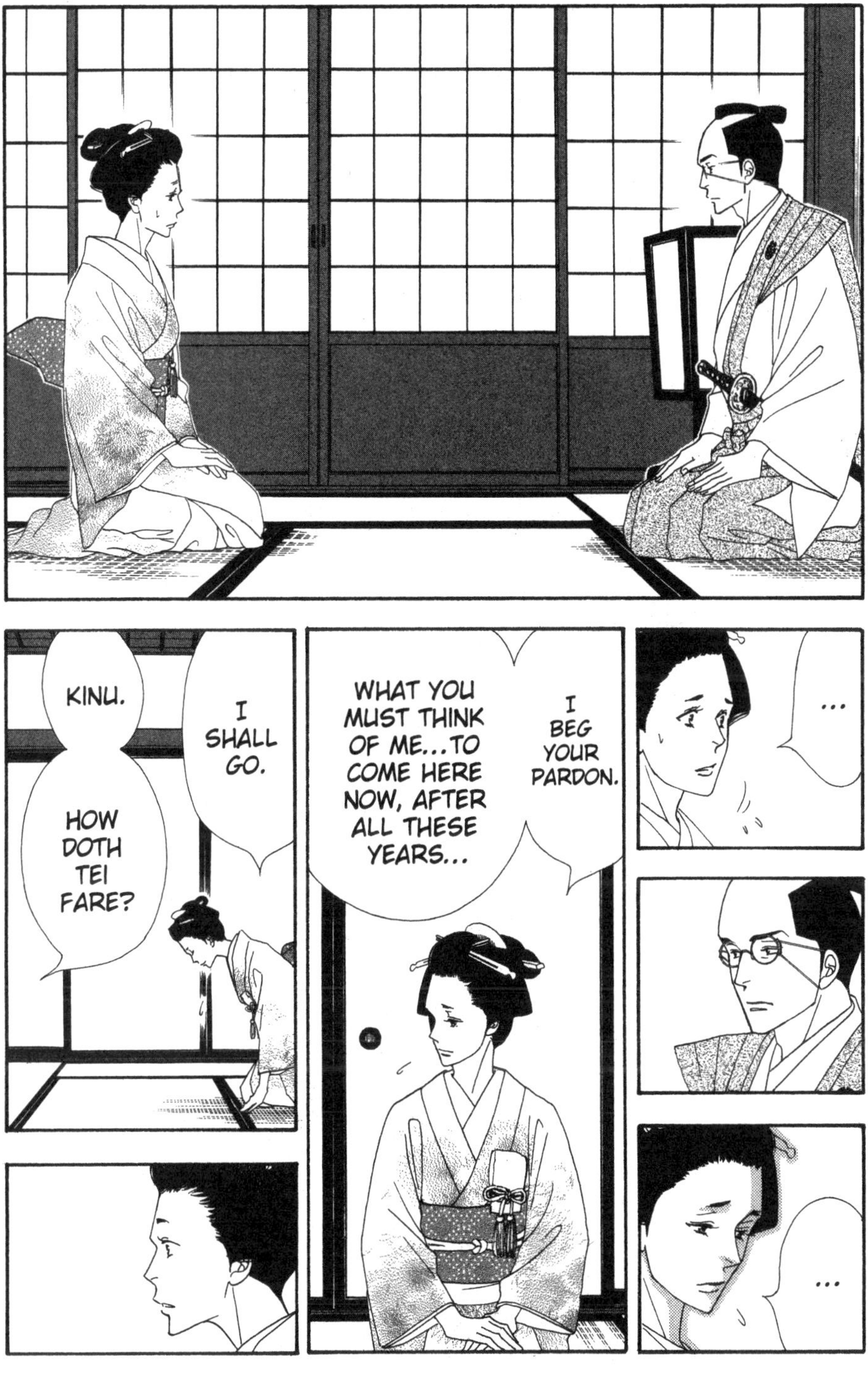
...
...
I BEG YOUR PARDON.
WHAT YOU MUST THINK OF ME...TO COME HERE NOW, AFTER ALL THESE YEARS...
I SHALL GO.
KINU.
HOW DOTH TEI FARE?

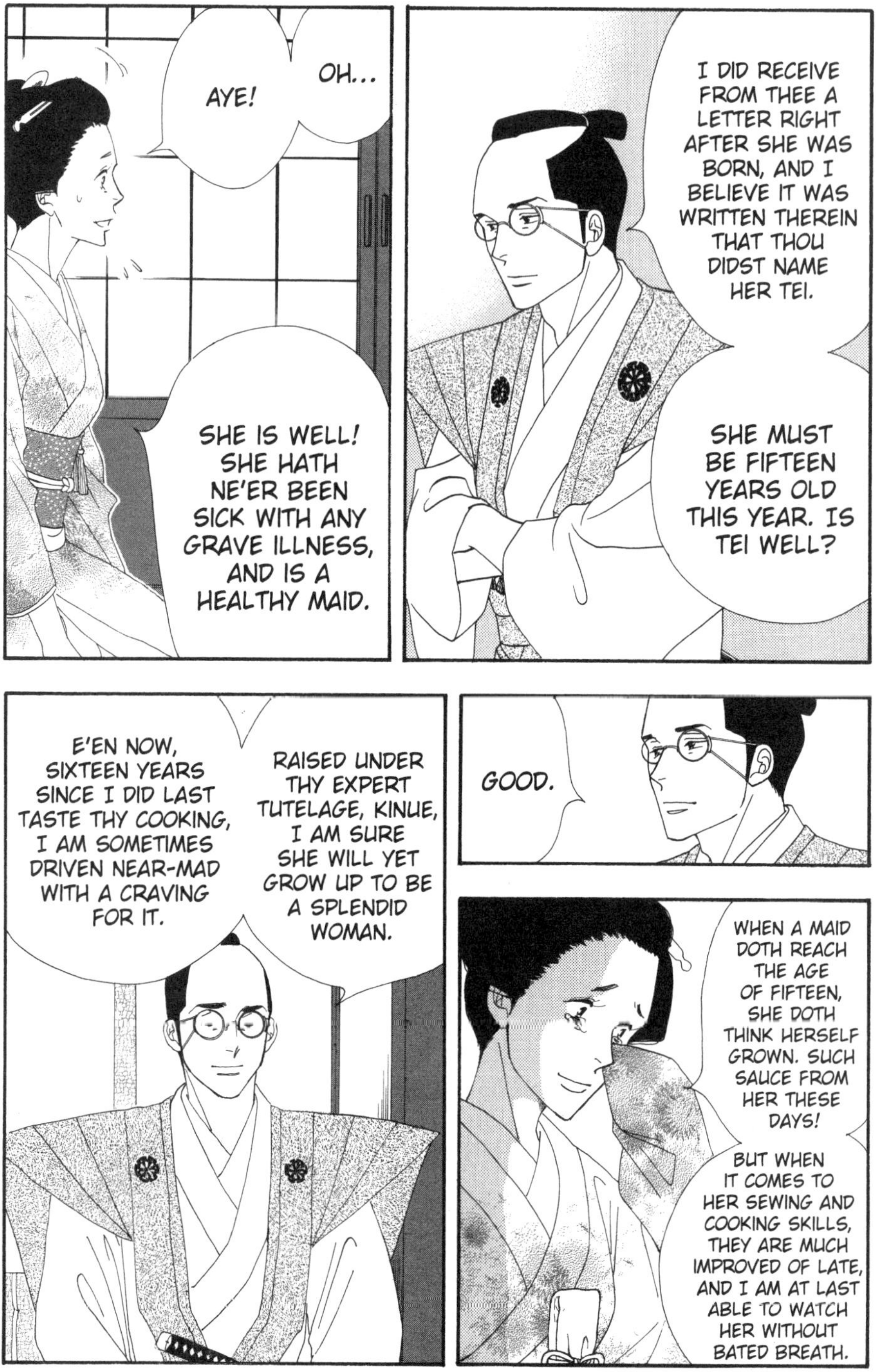
I DID RECEIVE FROM THEE A LETTER RIGHT AFTER SHE WAS BORN, AND I BELIEVE IT WAS WRITTEN THEREIN THAT THOU DIDST NAME HER TEI.
SHE MUST BE FIFTEEN YEARS OLD THIS YEAR. IS TEI WELL?
OH...
AYE!
SHE IS WELL! SHE HATH NE'ER BEEN SICK WITH ANY GRAVE ILLNESS, AND IS A HEALTHY MAID.
GOOD.
WHEN A MAID DOTH REACH THE AGE OF FIFTEEN, SHE DOTH THINK HERSELF GROWN. SUCH SAUCE FROM HER THESE DAYS!
BUT WHEN IT COMES TO HER SEWING AND COOKING SKILLS, THEY ARE MUCH IMPROVED OF LATE, AND I AM AT LAST ABLE TO WATCH HER WITHOUT BATED BREATH.
RAISED UNDER THY EXPERT TUTELAGE, KINUE, I AM SURE SHE WILL YET GROW UP TO BE A SPLENDID WOMAN.
E'EN NOW, SIXTEEN YEARS SINCE I DID LAST TASTE THY COOKING, I AM SOMETIMES DRIVEN NEAR-MAD WITH A CRAVING FOR IT.

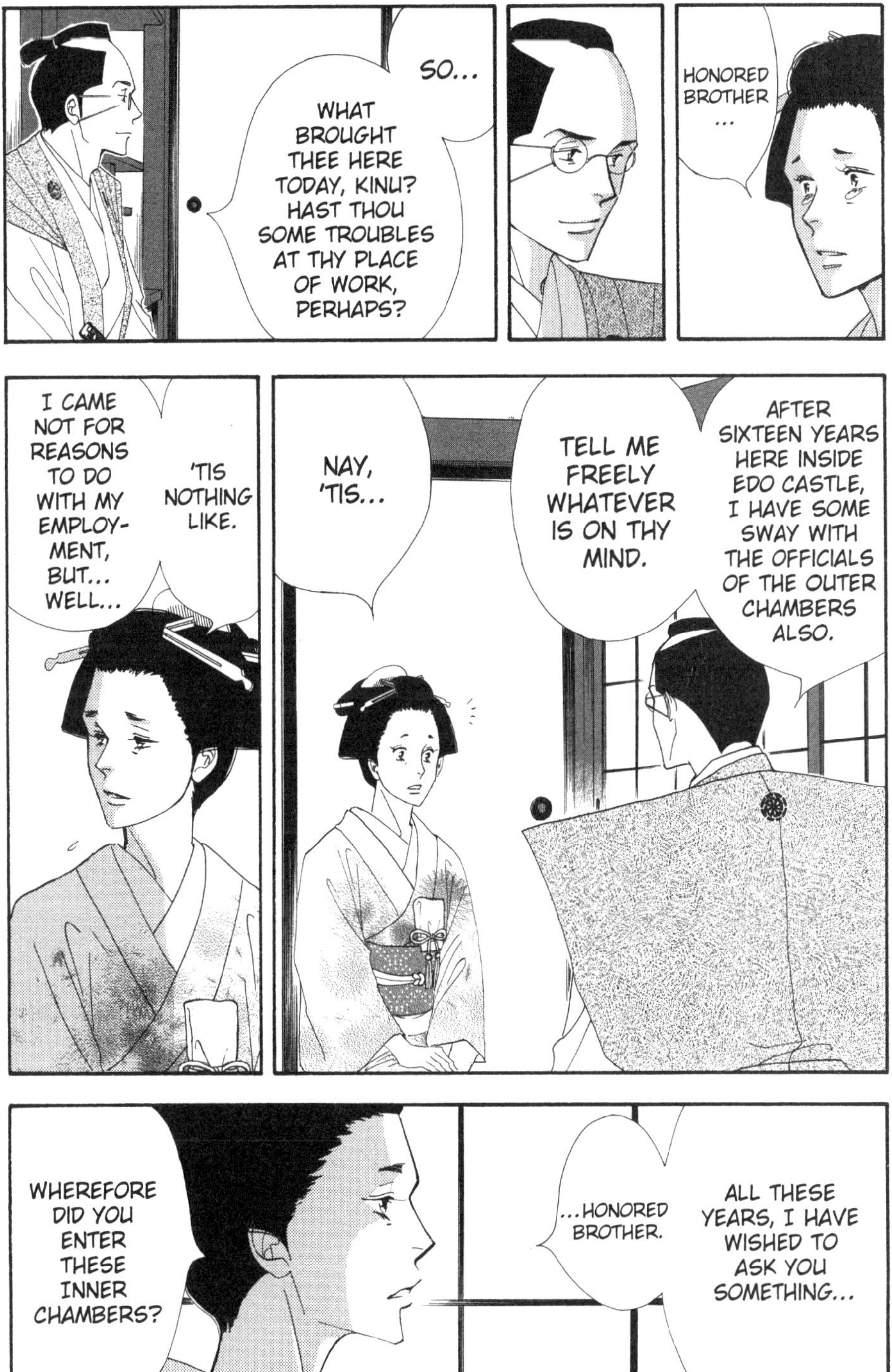
HONORED BROTHER ...
SO...
WHAT BROUGHT THEE HERE TODAY, KINU? HAST THOU SOME TROUBLES AT THY PLACE OF WORK, PERHAPS?
AFTER SIXTEEN YEARS HERE INSIDE EDO CASTLE, I HAVE SOME SWAY WITH THE OFFICIALS OF THE OUTER CHAMBERS ALSO.
TELL ME FREELY WHATEVER IS ON THY MIND.
NAY, 'TIS...
'TIS NOTHING LIKE.
I CAME NOT FOR REASONS TO DO WITH MY EMPLOY-MENT, BUT... WELL...
ALL THESE YEARS, I HAVE WISHED TO ASK YOU SOMETHING...
...HONORED BROTHER.
WHEREFORE DID YOU ENTER THESE INNER CHAMBERS?

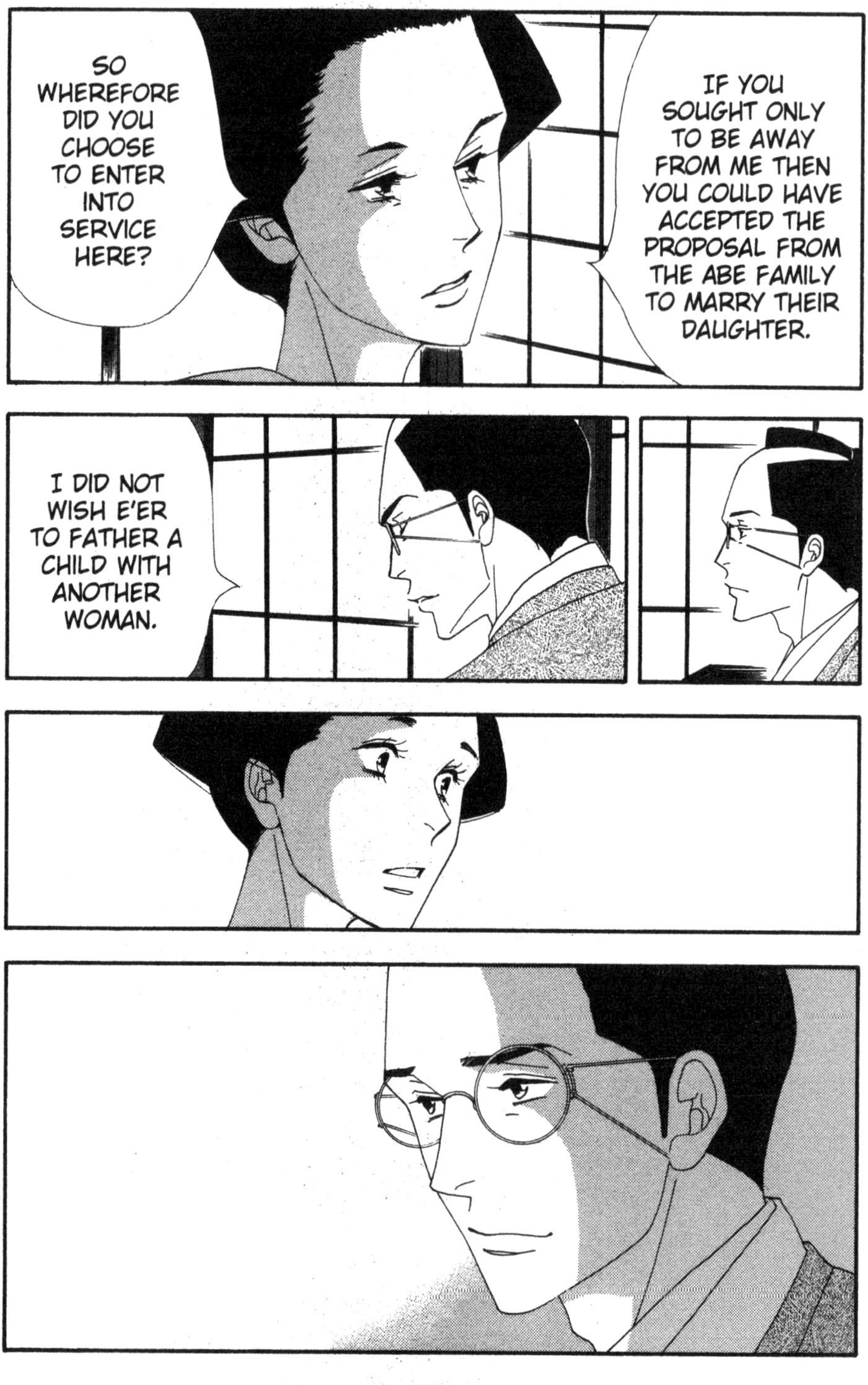
IF YOU SOUGHT ONLY TO BE AWAY FROM ME THEN YOU COULD HAVE ACCEPTED THE PROPOSAL FROM THE ABE FAMILY TO MARRY THEIR DAUGHTER.
SO WHEREFORE DID YOU CHOOSE TO ENTER INTO SERVICE HERE?
I DID NOT WISH E'ER TO FATHER A CHILD WITH ANOTHER WOMAN.

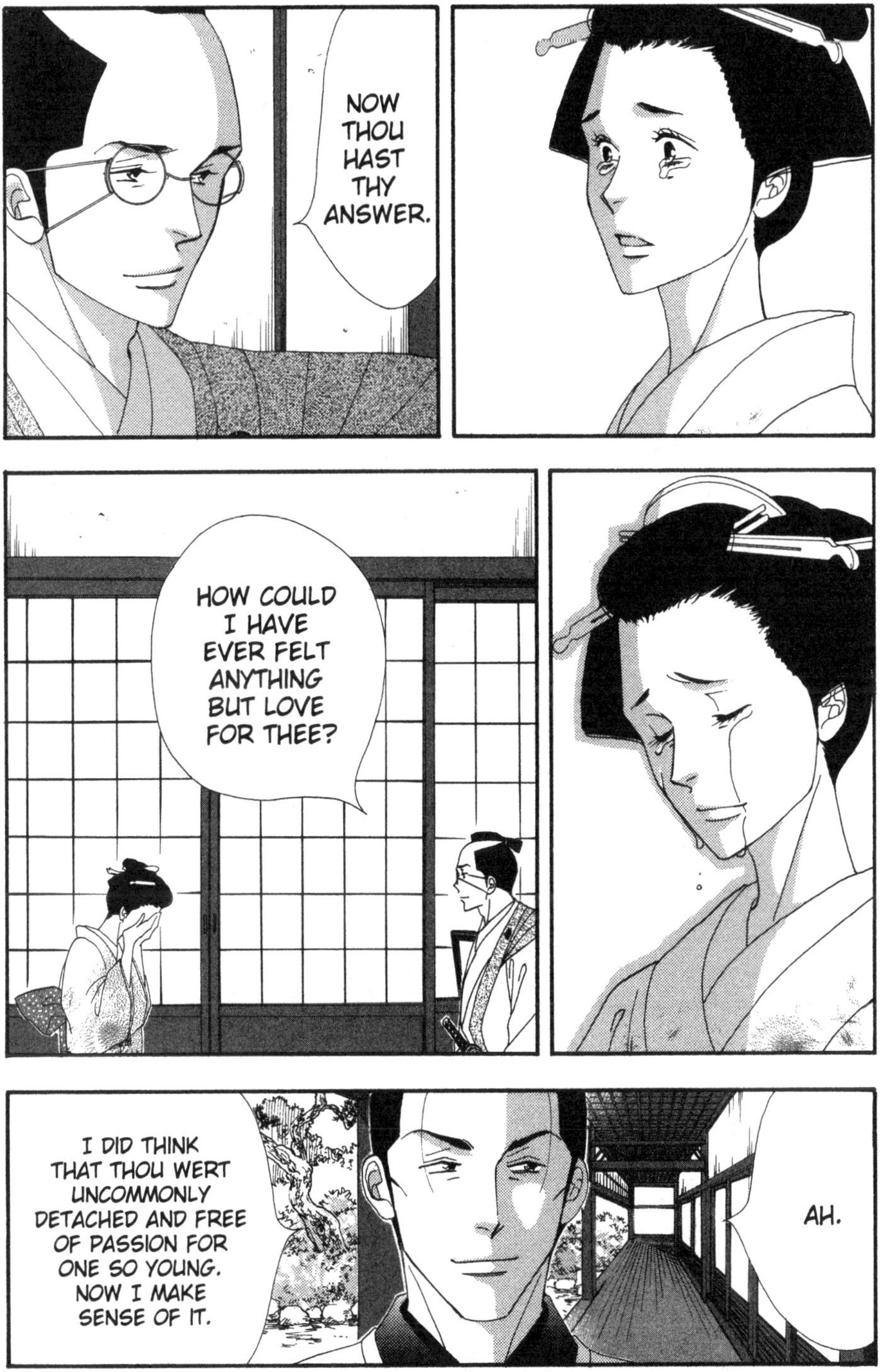
NOW THOU HAST THY ANSWER.
HOW COULD I HAVE EVER FELT ANYTHING BUT LOVE FOR THEE?
AH.
I DID THINK THAT THOU WERT UNCOMMONLY DETACHED AND FREE OF PASSION FOR ONE SO YOUNG. NOW I MAKE SENSE OF IT.

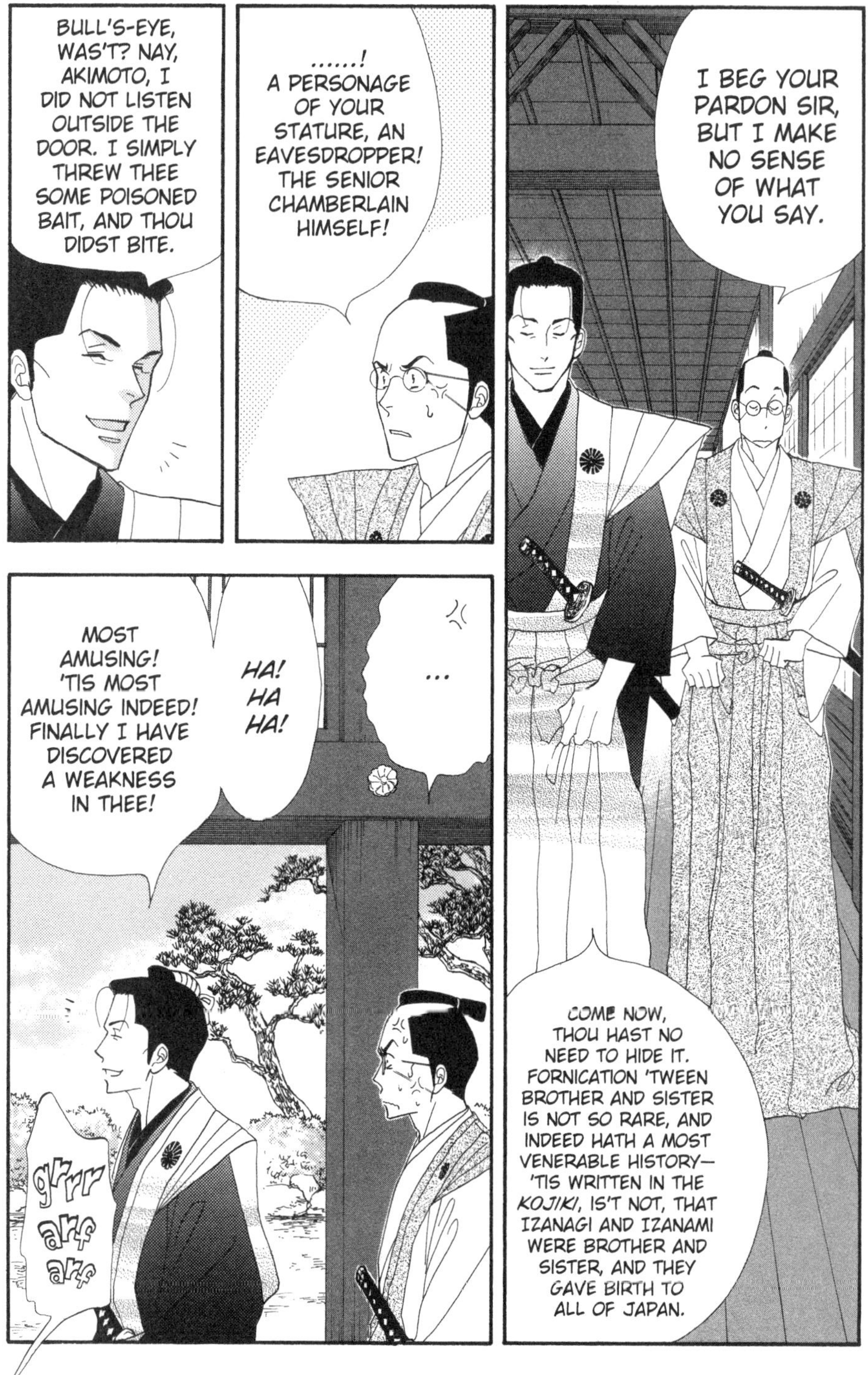
I BEG YOUR PARDON SIR, BUT I MAKE NO SENSE OF WHAT YOU SAY.
COME NOW, THOU HAST NO NEED TO HIDE IT. FORNICATION 'TWEEN BROTHER AND SISTER IS NOT SO RARE, AND INDEED HATH A MOST VENERABLE HISTORY— 'TIS WRITTEN IN THE *KOJIKI*, IS'T NOT, THAT IZANAGI AND IZANAMI WERE BROTHER AND SISTER, AND THEY GAVE BIRTH TO ALL OF JAPAN.
......! A PERSONAGE OF YOUR STATURE, AN EAVESDROPPER! THE SENIOR CHAMBERLAIN HIMSELF!
BULL'S-EYE, WAS'T? NAY, AKIMOTO, I DID NOT LISTEN OUTSIDE THE DOOR. I SIMPLY THREW THEE SOME POISONED BAIT, AND THOU DIDST BITE.
...
HA! HA HA!
MOST AMUSING! 'TIS MOST AMUSING INDEED! FINALLY I HAVE DISCOVERED A WEAKNESS IN THEE!
grrr arf arf

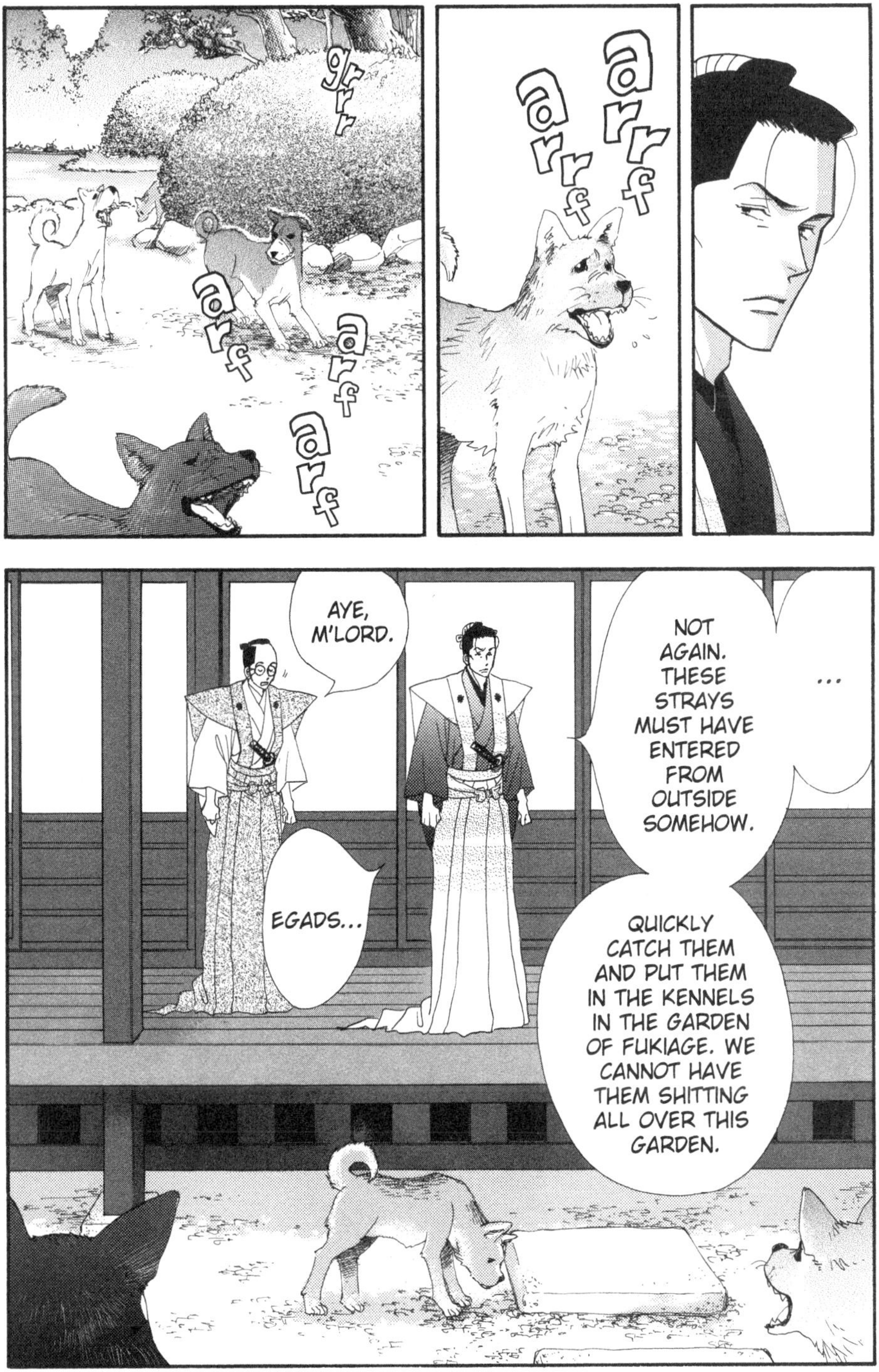
arrf
arrf
grrr
arf
arf
arf
...
NOT AGAIN. THESE STRAYS MUST HAVE ENTERED FROM OUTSIDE SOMEHOW.
QUICKLY CATCH THEM AND PUT THEM IN THE KENNELS IN THE GARDEN OF FUKIAGE. WE CANNOT HAVE THEM SHITTING ALL OVER THIS GARDEN.
AYE, M'LORD.
EGADS...

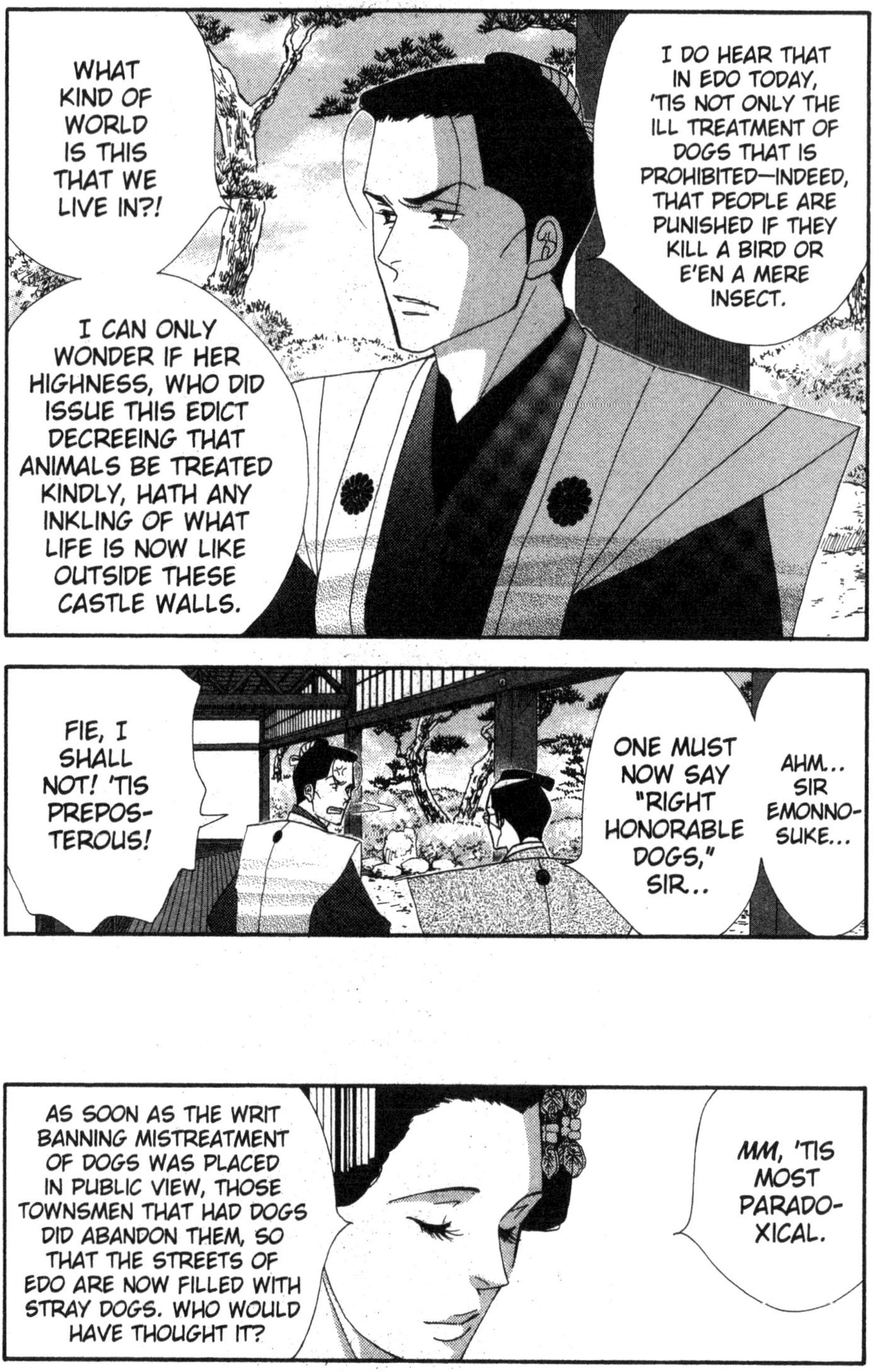
I DO HEAR THAT IN EDO TODAY, 'TIS NOT ONLY THE ILL TREATMENT OF DOGS THAT IS PROHIBITED—INDEED, THAT PEOPLE ARE PUNISHED IF THEY KILL A BIRD OR E'EN A MERE INSECT.
WHAT KIND OF WORLD IS THIS THAT WE LIVE IN?!
I CAN ONLY WONDER IF HER HIGHNESS, WHO DID ISSUE THIS EDICT DECREEING THAT ANIMALS BE TREATED KINDLY, HATH ANY INKLING OF WHAT LIFE IS NOW LIKE OUTSIDE THESE CASTLE WALLS.
AHM.. SIR EMONNOSUKE...
ONE MUST NOW SAY "RIGHT HONORABLE DOGS," SIR..
FIE, I SHALL NOT! 'TIS PREPOSTEROUS!
MM, 'TIS MOST PARADOXICAL.
AS SOON AS THE WRIT BANNING MISTREATMENT OF DOGS WAS PLACED IN PUBLIC VIEW, THOSE TOWNSMEN THAT HAD DOGS DID ABANDON THEM, SO THAT THE STREETS OF EDO ARE NOW FILLED WITH STRAY DOGS. WHO WOULD HAVE THOUGHT IT?

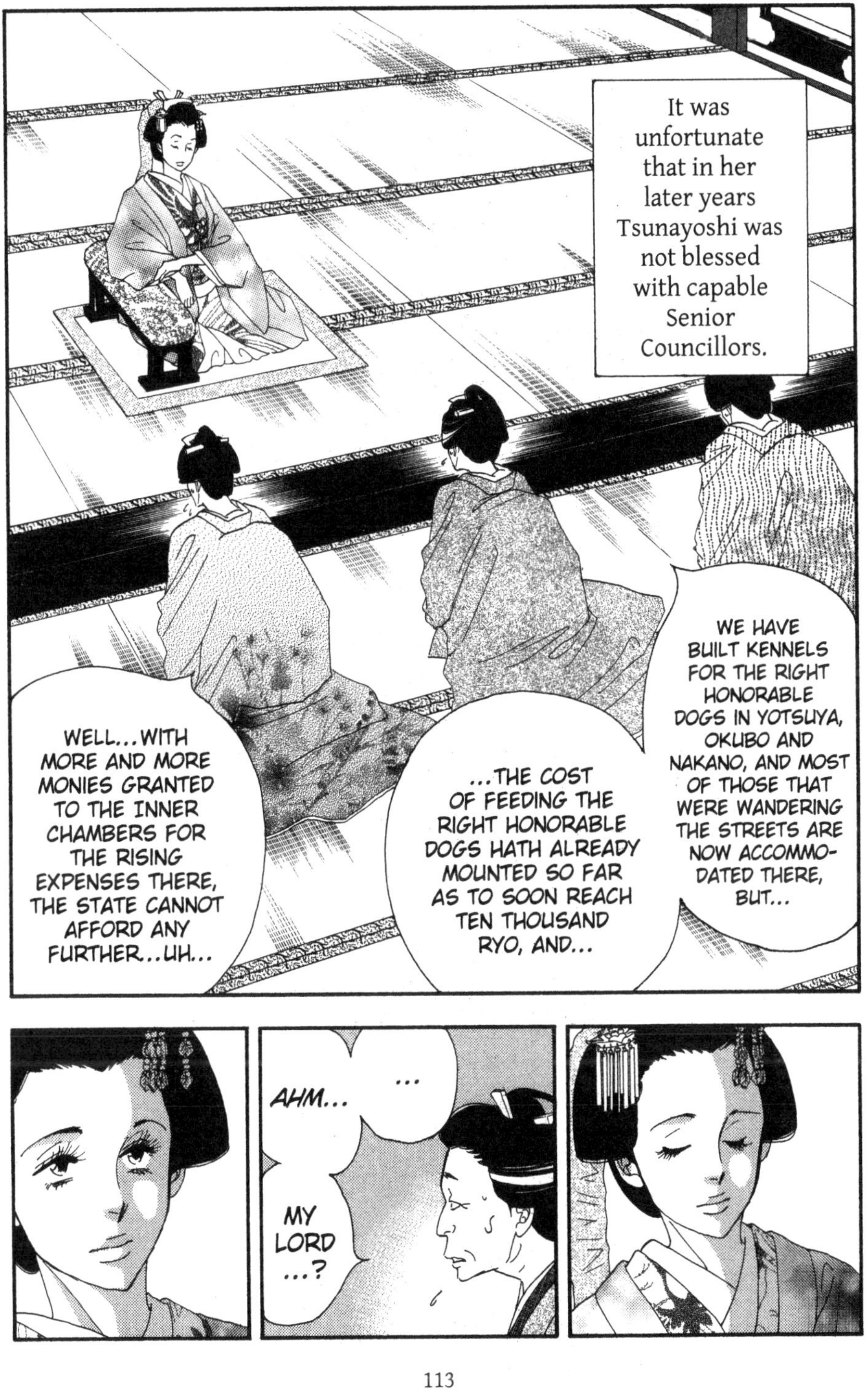
It was unfortunate that in her later years Tsunayoshi was not blessed with capable Senior Councillors.
WE HAVE BUILT KENNELS FOR THE RIGHT HONORABLE DOGS IN YOTSUYA, OKUBO AND NAKANO, AND MOST OF THOSE THAT WERE WANDERING THE STREETS ARE NOW ACCOMMO-DATED THERE, BUT...
...THE COST OF FEEDING THE RIGHT HONORABLE DOGS HATH ALREADY MOUNTED SO FAR AS TO SOON REACH TEN THOUSAND RYO, AND...
WELL...WITH MORE AND MORE MONIES GRANTED TO THE INNER CHAMBERS FOR THE RISING EXPENSES THERE, THE STATE CANNOT AFFORD ANY FURTHER...UH...
...
AHM...
MY LORD ...?

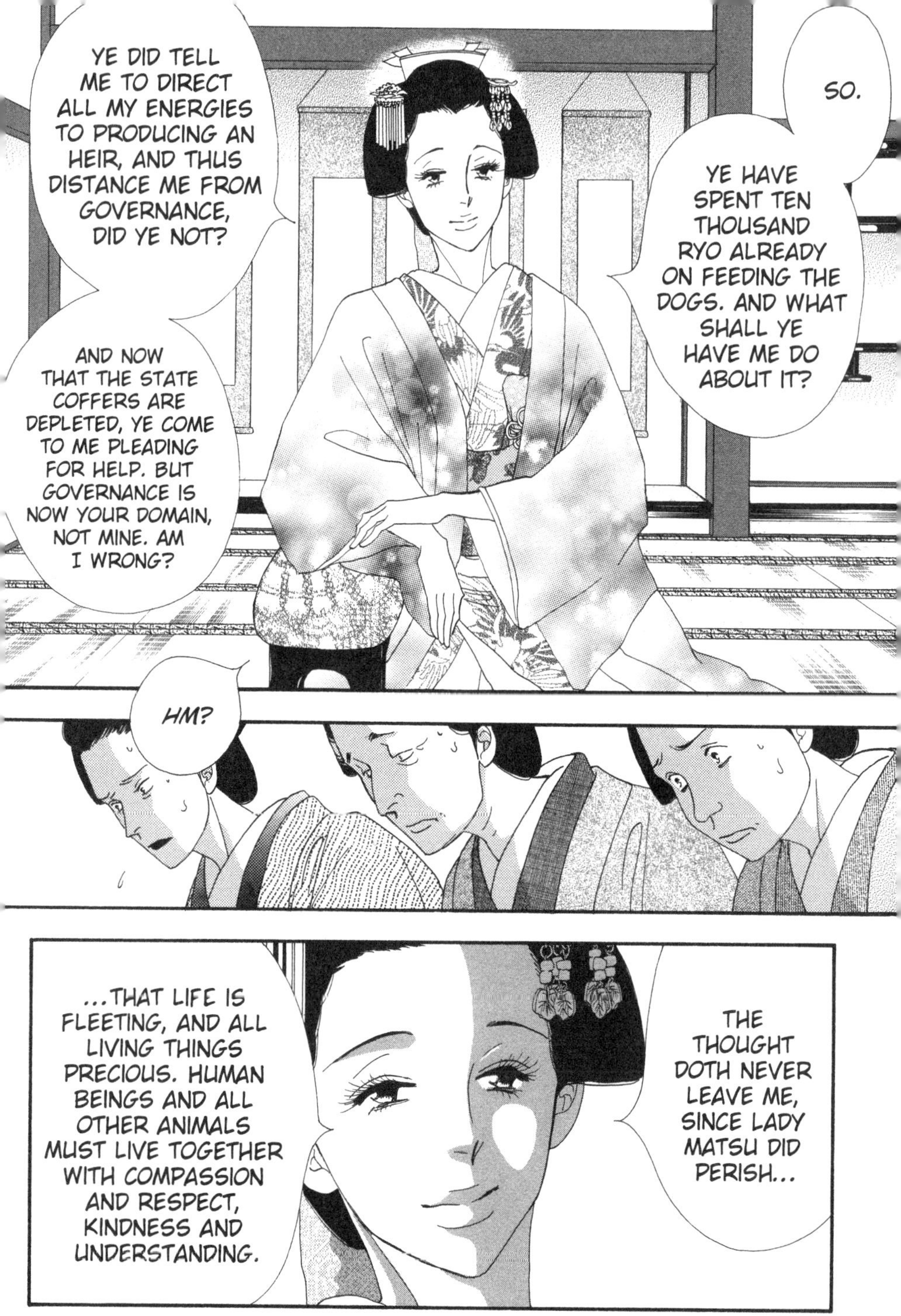
SO.
YE HAVE SPENT TEN THOUSAND RYO ALREADY ON FEEDING THE DOGS. AND WHAT SHALL YE HAVE ME DO ABOUT IT?
YE DID TELL ME TO DIRECT ALL MY ENERGIES TO PRODUCING AN HEIR, AND THUS DISTANCE ME FROM GOVERNANCE, DID YE NOT?
AND NOW THAT THE STATE COFFERS ARE DEPLETED, YE COME TO ME PLEADING FOR HELP. BUT GOVERNANCE IS NOW YOUR DOMAIN, NOT MINE. AM I WRONG?
HM?
THE THOUGHT DOTH NEVER LEAVE ME, SINCE LADY MATSU DID PERISH...
...THAT LIFE IS FLEETING, AND ALL LIVING THINGS PRECIOUS. HUMAN BEINGS AND ALL OTHER ANIMALS MUST LIVE TOGETHER WITH COMPASSION AND RESPECT, KINDNESS AND UNDERSTANDING.

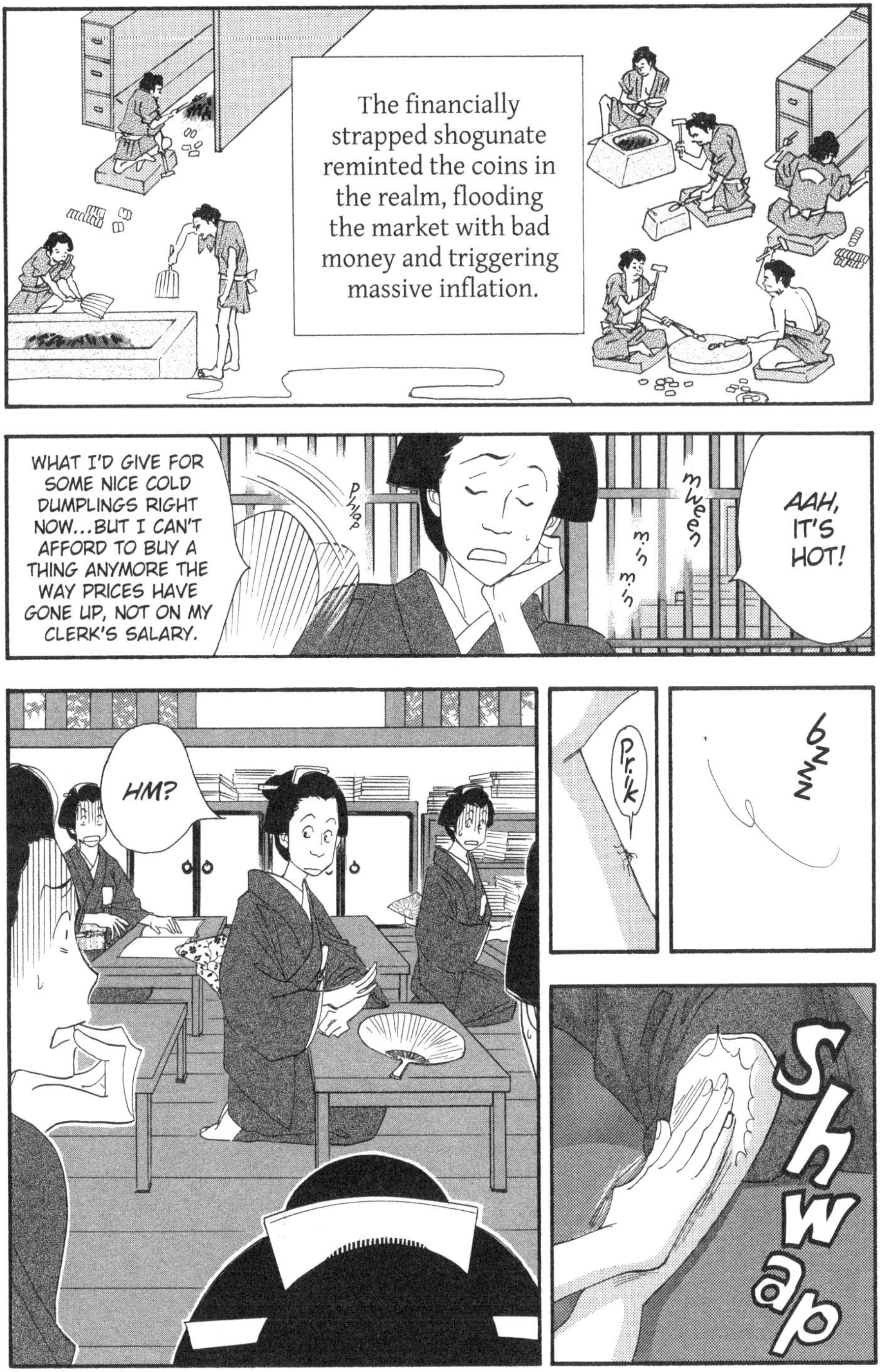
The financially strapped shogunate reminted the coins in the realm, flooding the market with bad money and triggering massive inflation.
AAH, IT'S HOT!
mween
min min
phlap
WHAT I'D GIVE FOR SOME NICE COLD DUMPLINGS RIGHT NOW...BUT I CAN'T AFFORD TO BUY A THING ANYMORE THE WAY PRICES HAVE GONE UP, NOT ON MY CLERK'S SALARY.
bzzz
Prik
Shwap
HM?

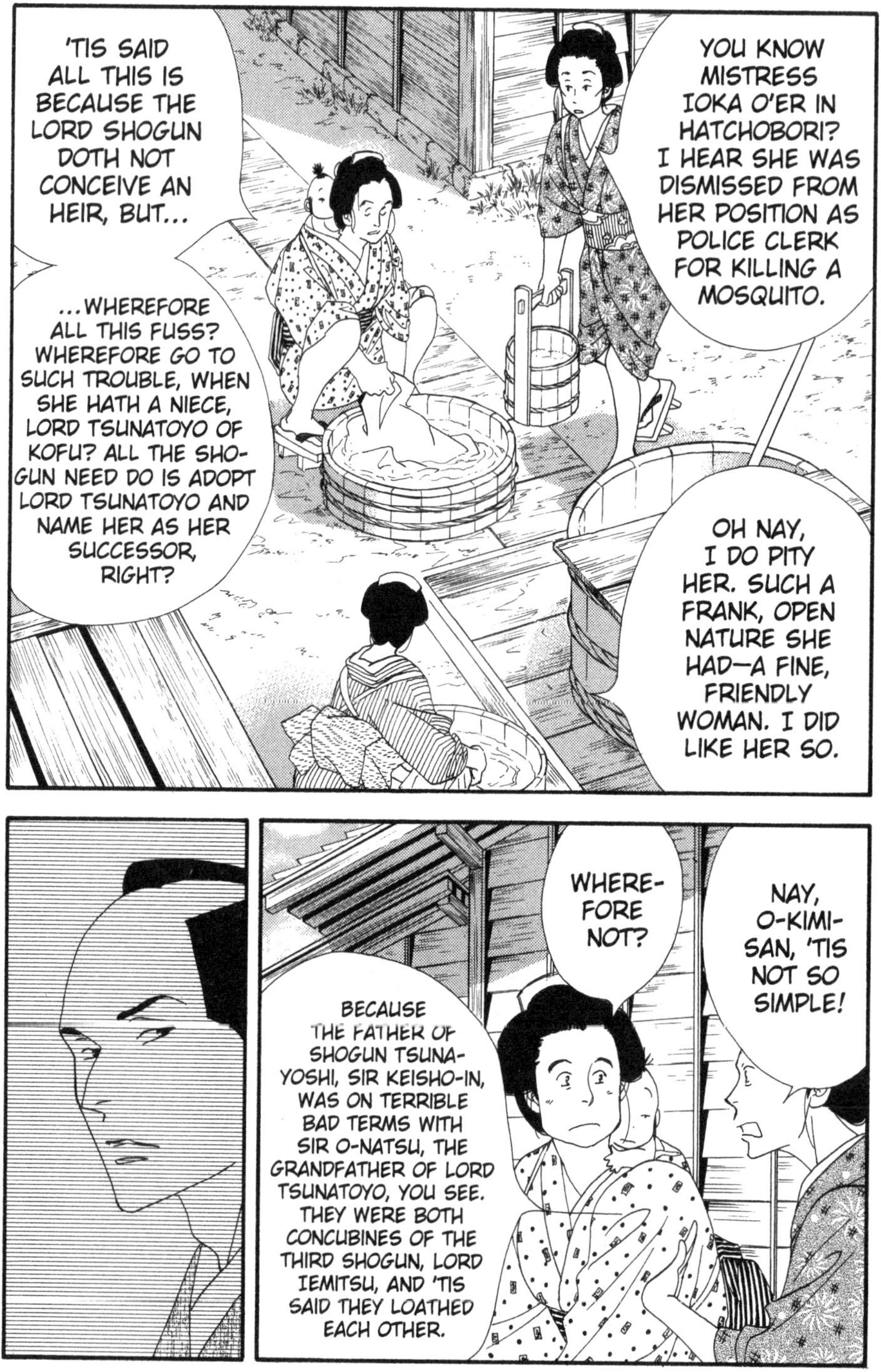
YOU KNOW MISTRESS IOKA O'ER IN HATCHOBORI? I HEAR SHE WAS DISMISSED FROM HER POSITION AS POLICE CLERK FOR KILLING A MOSQUITO.
OH NAY, I DO PITY HER. SUCH A FRANK, OPEN NATURE SHE HAD—A FINE, FRIENDLY WOMAN. I DID LIKE HER SO.
'TIS SAID ALL THIS IS BECAUSE THE LORD SHOGUN DOTH NOT CONCEIVE AN HEIR, BUT...
...WHEREFORE ALL THIS FUSS? WHEREFORE GO TO SUCH TROUBLE, WHEN SHE HATH A NIECE, LORD TSUNATOYO OF KOFU? ALL THE SHO-GUN NEED DO IS ADOPT LORD TSUNATOYO AND NAME HER AS HER SUCCESSOR, RIGHT?
NAY, O-KIMI-SAN, 'TIS NOT SO SIMPLE!
WHERE-FORE NOT?
BECAUSE THE FATHER OF SHOGUN TSUNA-YOSHI, SIR KEISHO-IN, WAS ON TERRIBLE BAD TERMS WITH SIR O-NATSU, THE GRANDFATHER OF LORD TSUNATOYO, YOU SEE. THEY WERE BOTH CONCUBINES OF THE THIRD SHOGUN, LORD IEMITSU, AND 'TIS SAID THEY LOATHED EACH OTHER.

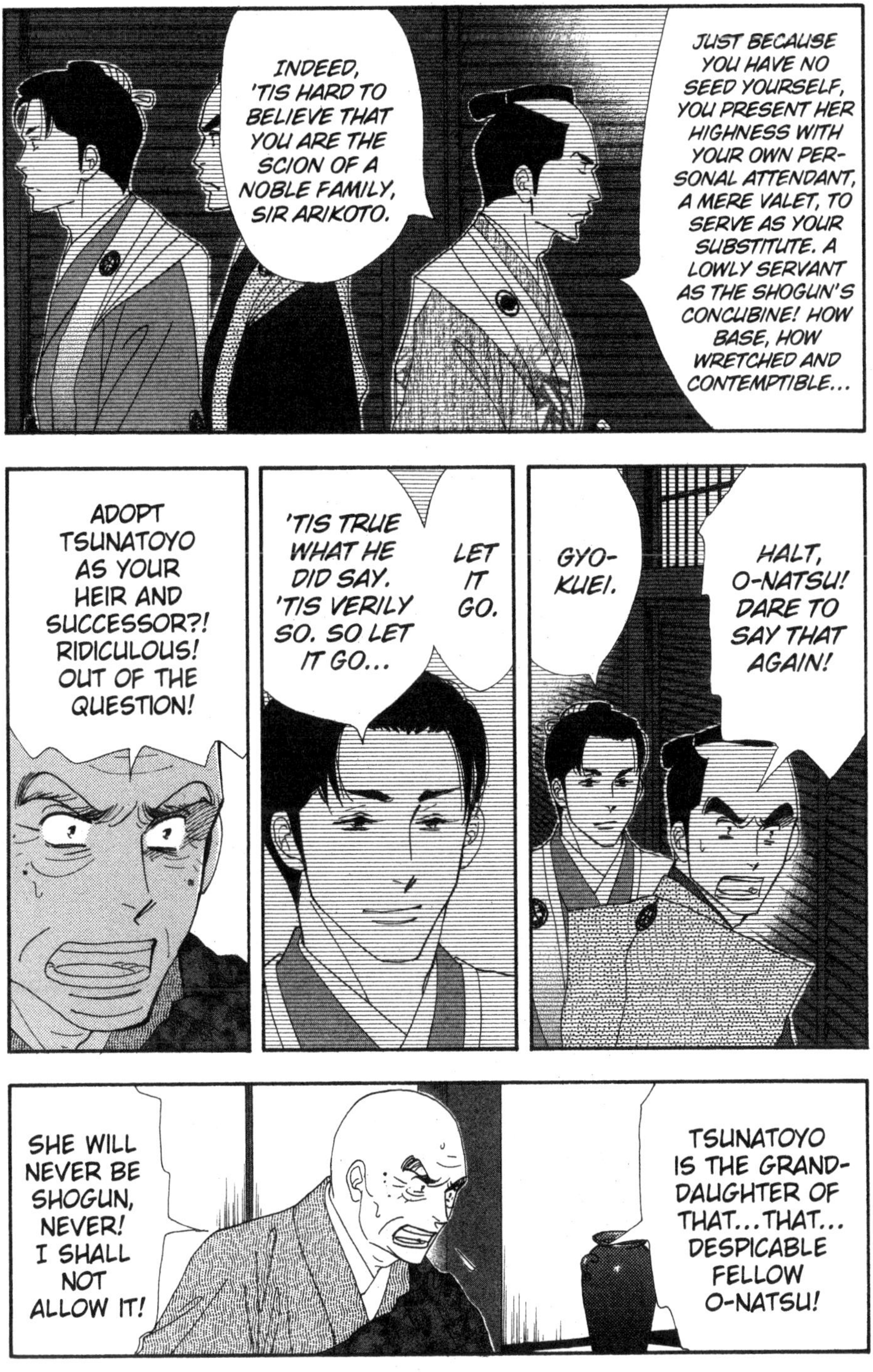
JUST BECAUSE YOU HAVE NO SEED YOURSELF, YOU PRESENT HER HIGHNESS WITH YOUR OWN PERSONAL ATTENDANT, A MERE VALET, TO SERVE AS YOUR SUBSTITUTE. A LOWLY SERVANT AS THE SHOGUN'S CONCUBINE! HOW BASE, HOW WRETCHED AND CONTEMPTIBLE...
INDEED, 'TIS HARD TO BELIEVE THAT YOU ARE THE SCION OF A NOBLE FAMILY, SIR ARIKOTO.
HALT, O-NATSU! DARE TO SAY THAT AGAIN!
GYO-KUEI.
LET IT GO.
'TIS TRUE WHAT HE DID SAY. 'TIS VERILY SO. SO LET IT GO...
ADOPT TSUNATOYO AS YOUR HEIR AND SUCCESSOR?! RIDICULOUS! OUT OF THE QUESTION!
TSUNATOYO IS THE GRAND-DAUGHTER OF THAT...THAT... DESPICABLE FELLOW O-NATSU!
SHE WILL NEVER BE SHOGUN, NEVER! I SHALL NOT ALLOW IT!

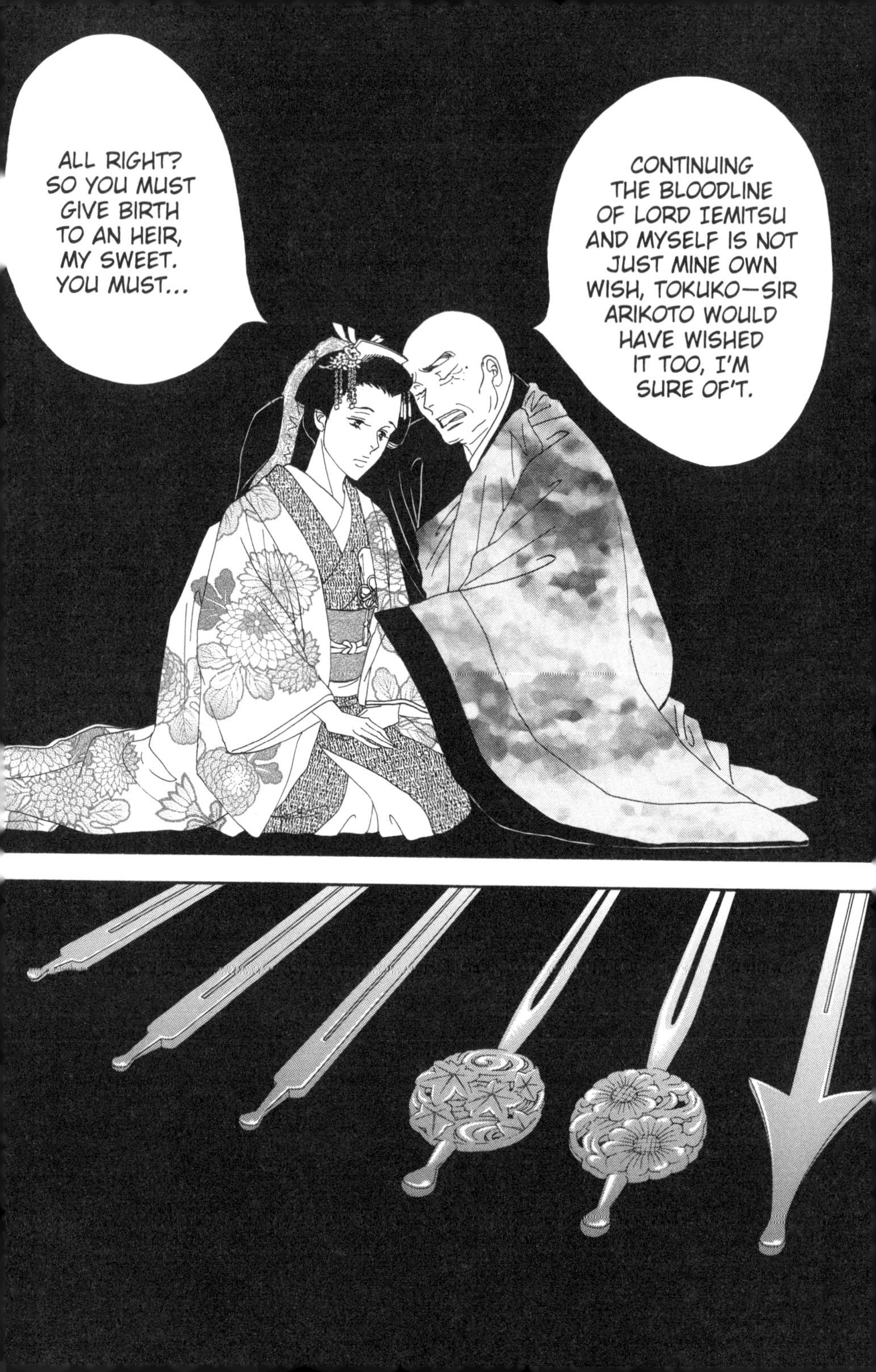
CONTINUING THE BLOODLINE OF LORD IEMITSU AND MYSELF IS NOT JUST MINE OWN WISH, TOKUKO—SIR ARIKOTO WOULD HAVE WISHED IT TOO, I'M SURE OF'T.
ALL RIGHT? SO YOU MUST GIVE BIRTH TO AN HEIR, MY SWEET. YOU MUST...

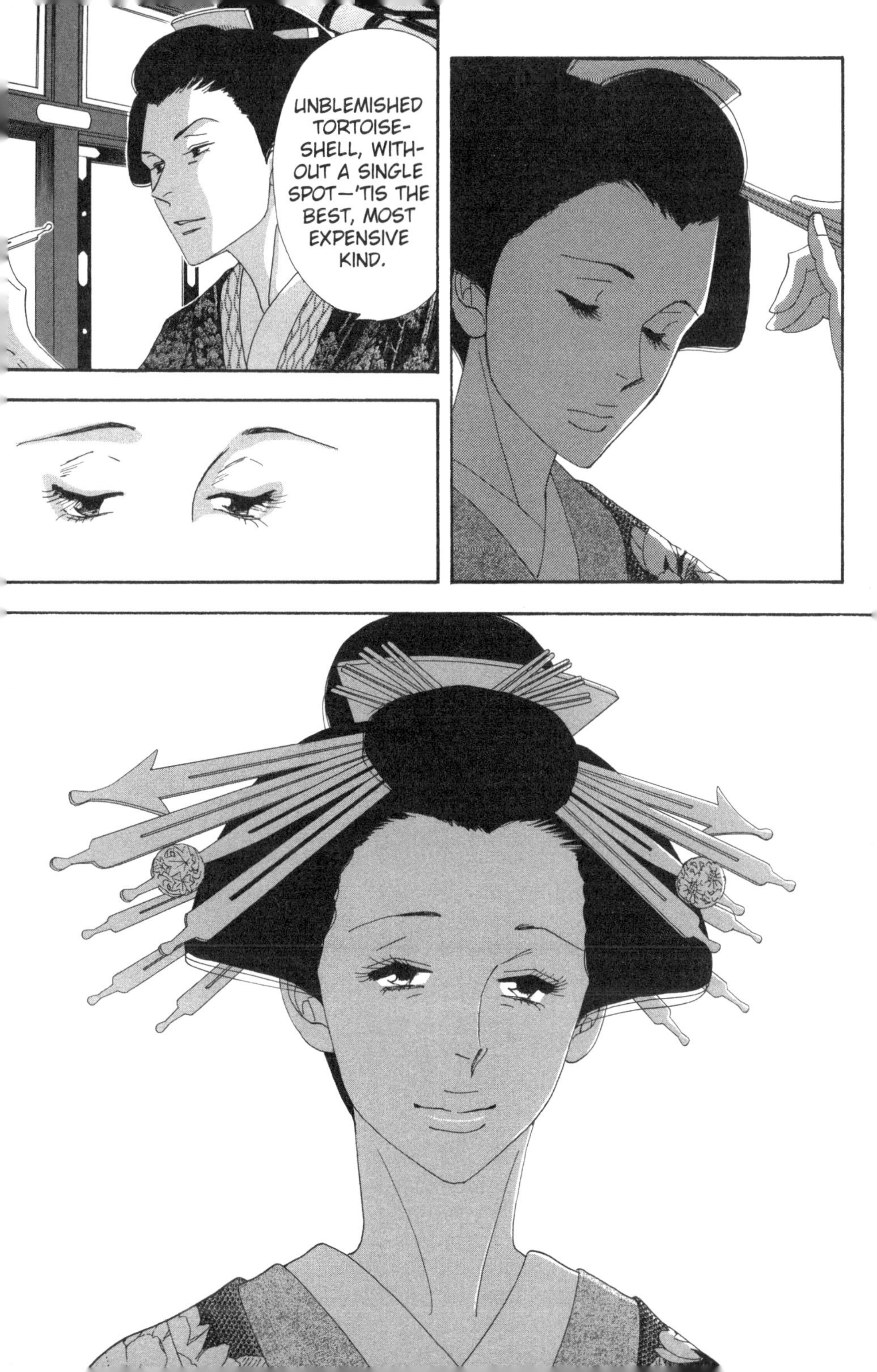
UNBLEMISHED TORTOISE-SHELL, WITH-OUT A SINGLE SPOT—'TIS THE BEST, MOST EXPENSIVE KIND.

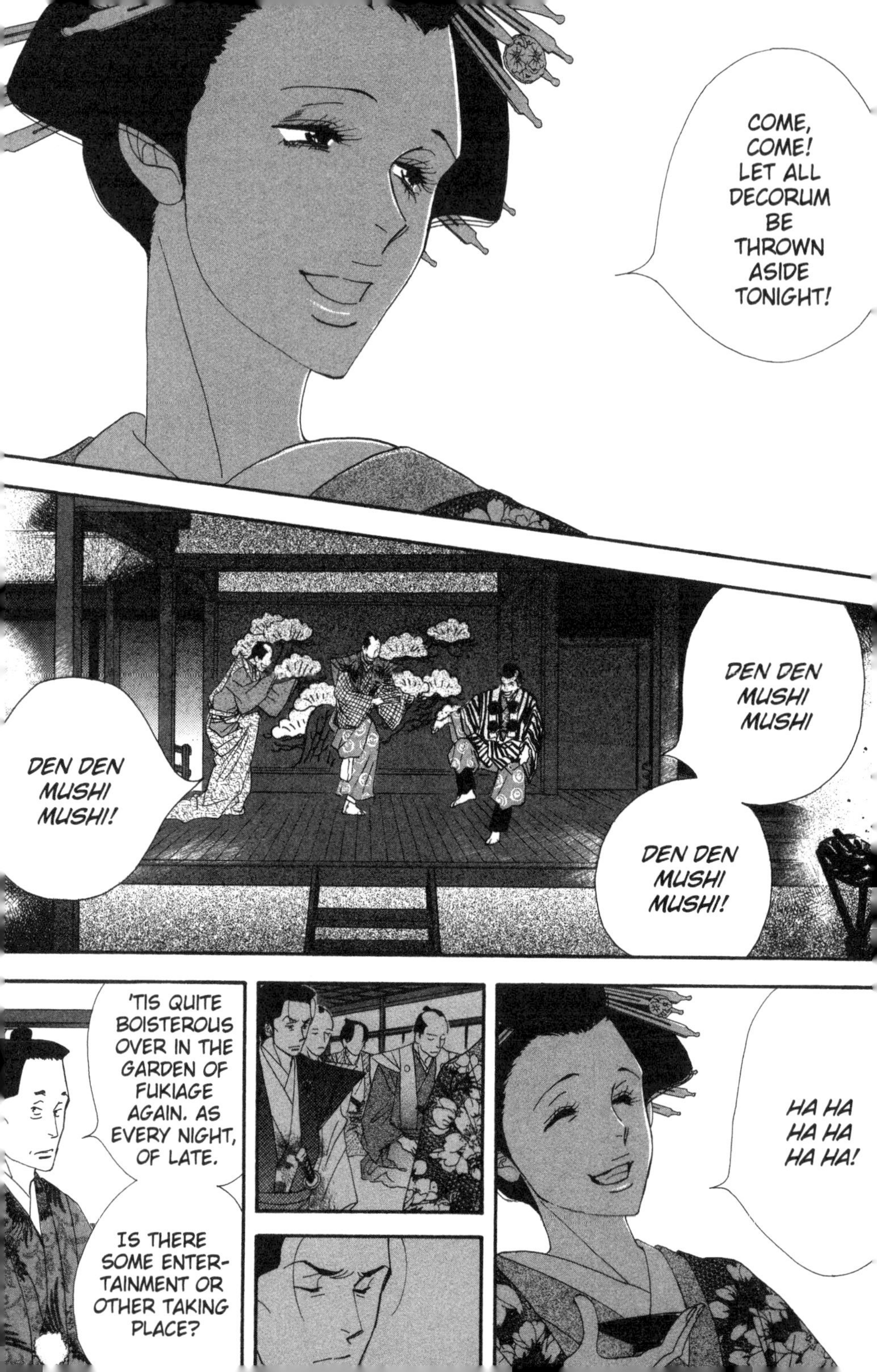
COME, COME! LET ALL DECORUM BE THROWN ASIDE TONIGHT!
DEN DEN MUSHI MUSHI
DEN DEN MUSHI MUSHI!
DEN DEN MUSHI MUSHI!
HA HA HA HA HA HA!
'TIS QUITE BOISTEROUS OVER IN THE GARDEN OF FUKIAGE AGAIN. AS EVERY NIGHT, OF LATE.
IS THERE SOME ENTER-TAINMENT OR OTHER TAKING PLACE?

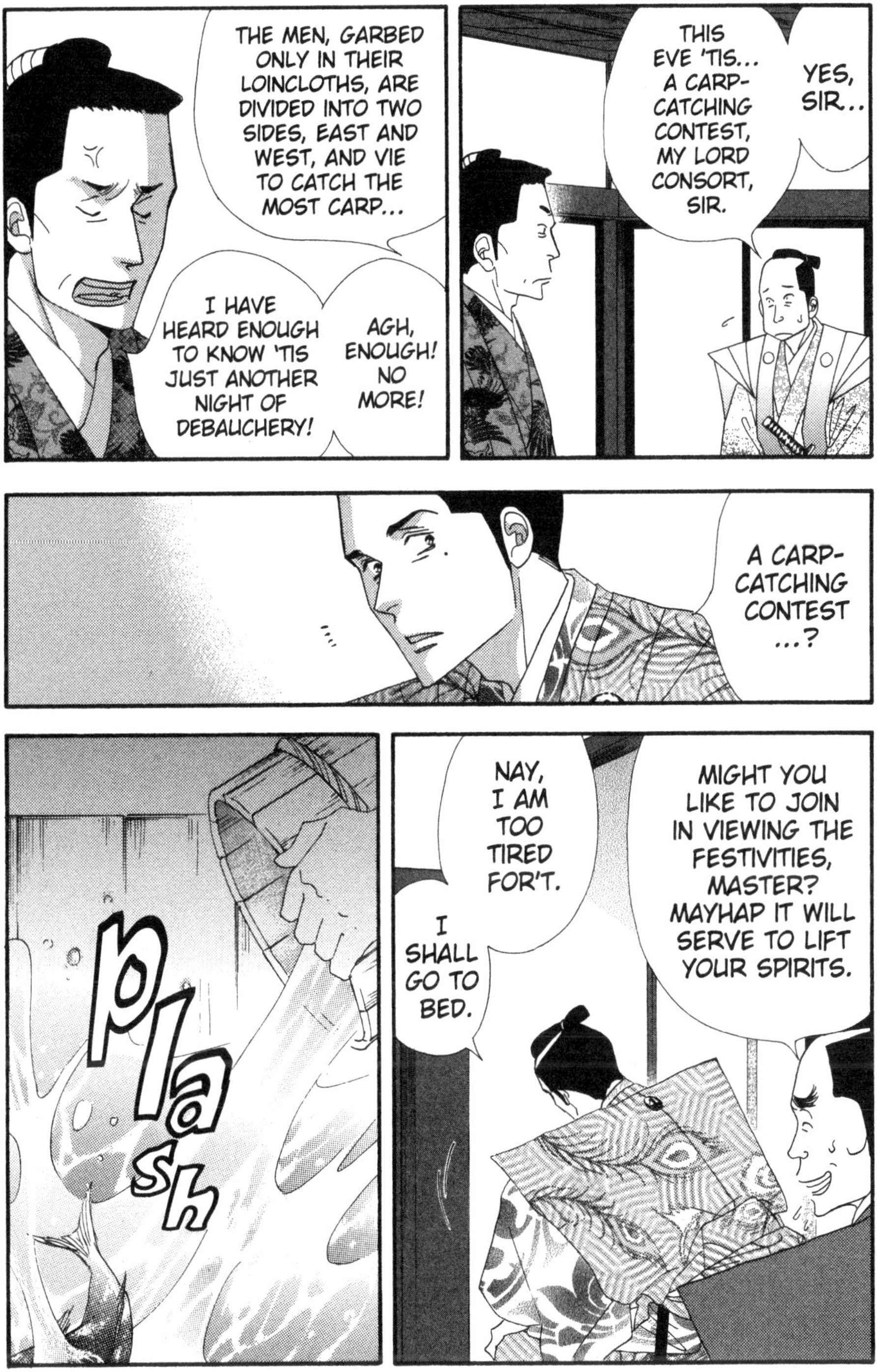
YES, SIR...
THIS EVE 'TIS... A CARP-CATCHING CONTEST, MY LORD CONSORT, SIR.
THE MEN, GARBED ONLY IN THEIR LOINCLOTHS, ARE DIVIDED INTO TWO SIDES, EAST AND WEST, AND VIE TO CATCH THE MOST CARP...
AGH, ENOUGH! NO MORE!
I HAVE HEARD ENOUGH TO KNOW 'TIS JUST ANOTHER NIGHT OF DEBAUCHERY!
A CARP-CATCHING CONTEST ...?
...
MIGHT YOU LIKE TO JOIN IN VIEWING THE FESTIVITIES, MASTER? MAYHAP IT WILL SERVE TO LIFT YOUR SPIRITS.
NAY, I AM TOO TIRED FOR'T.
I SHALL GO TO BED.
plash

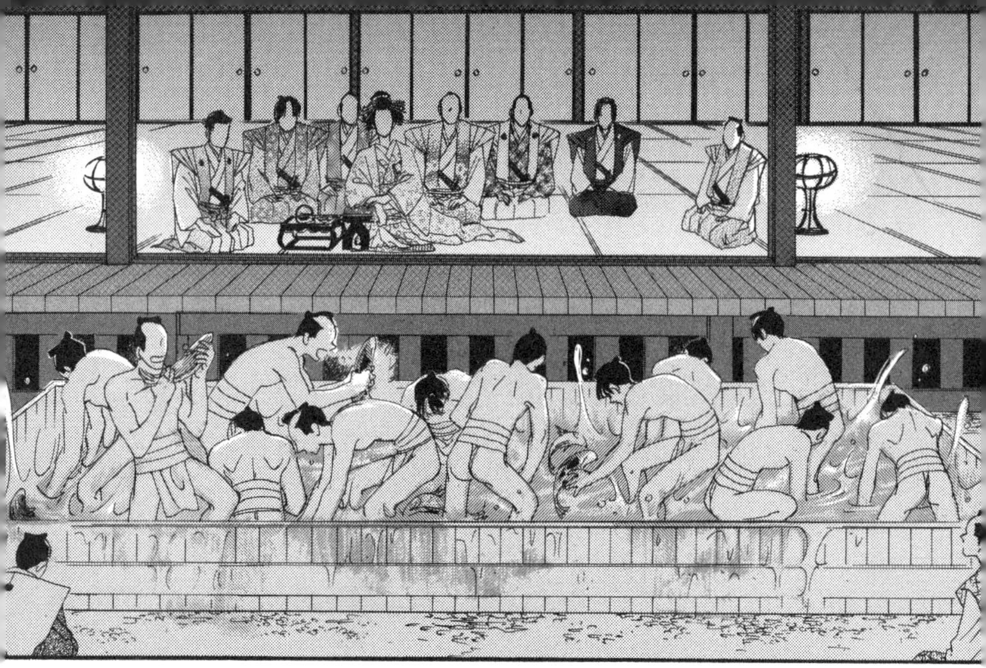

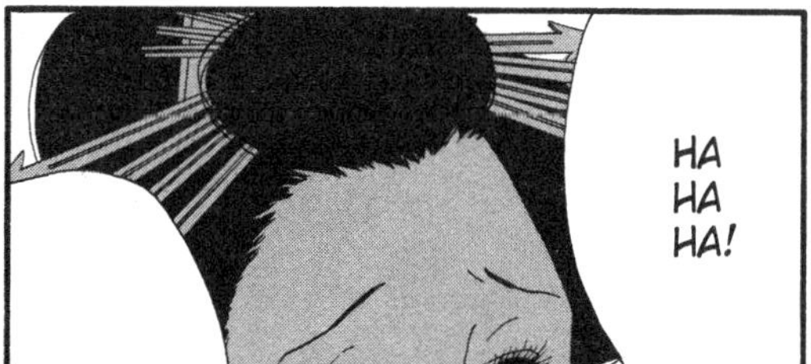
HA HA HA!
OH HO HO HO HO HO HO!

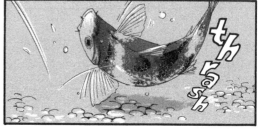

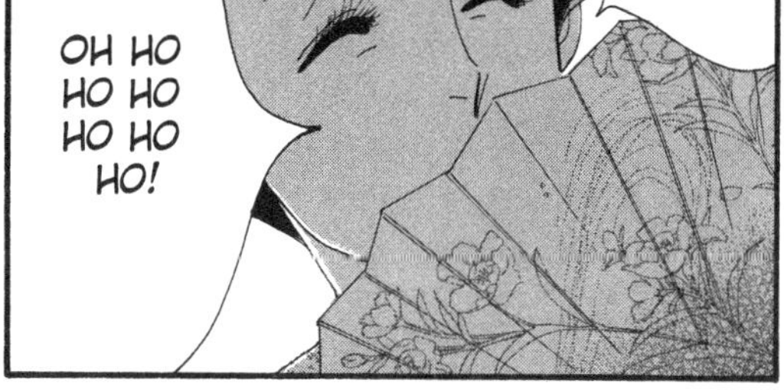
thrash

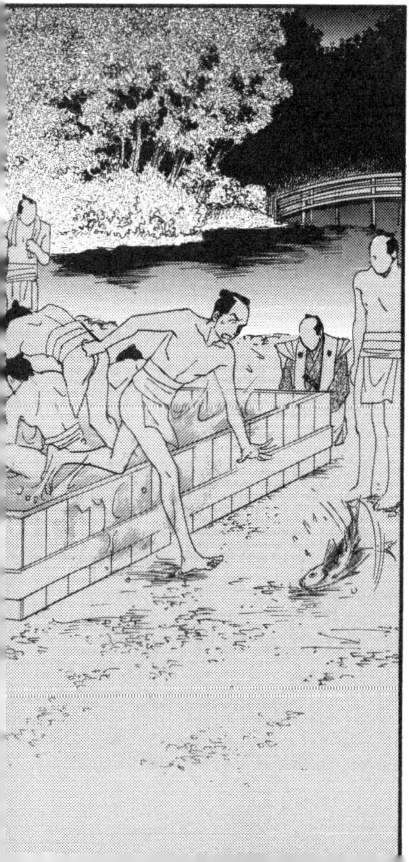

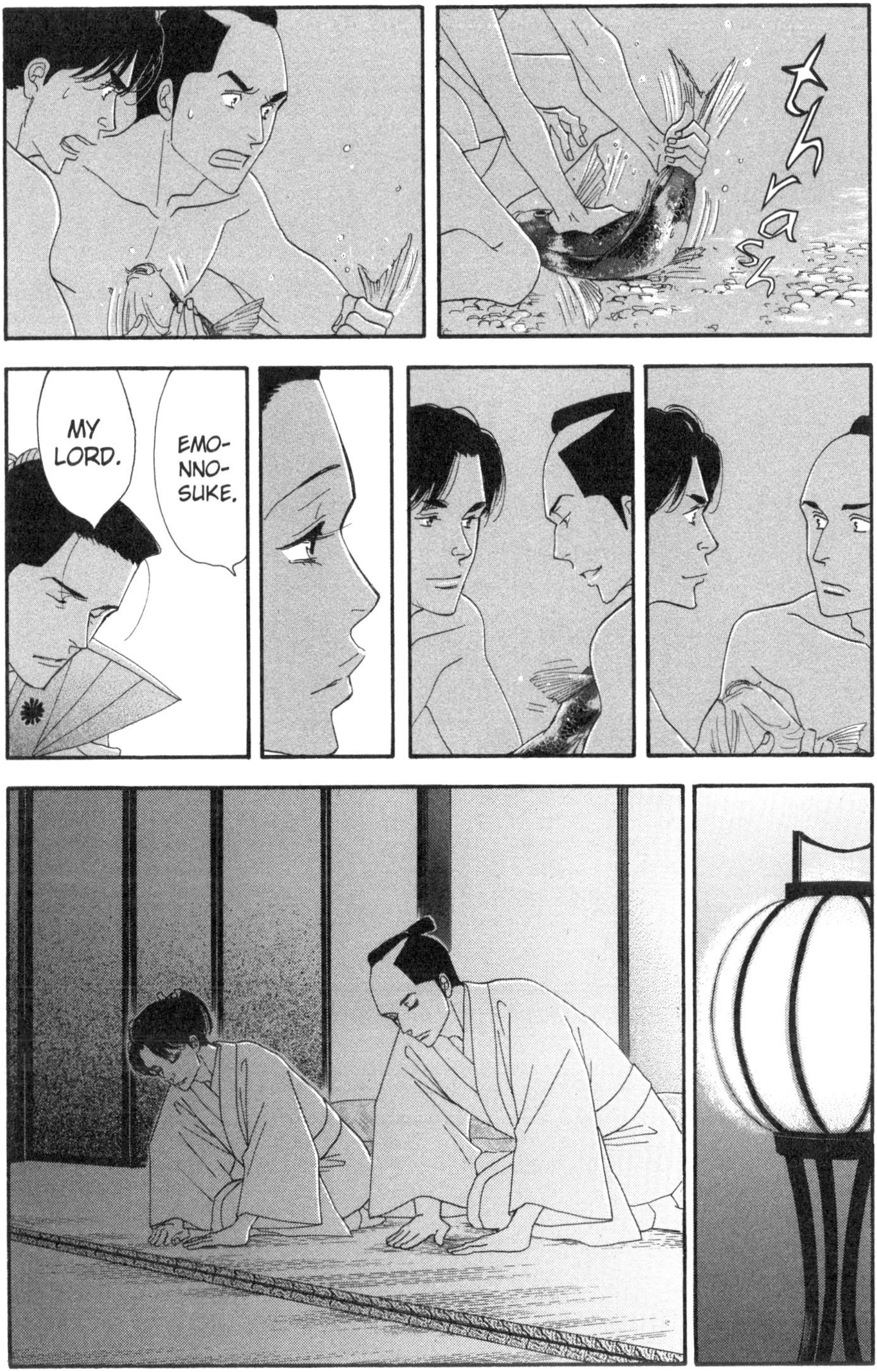
thrash
EMO-NNO-SUKE.
MY LORD.

YOUR.. HIGH-
NESS...

AWGH...

NGH...!

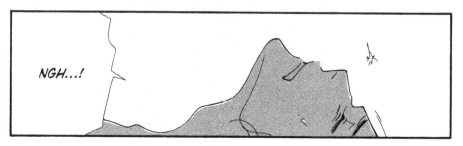

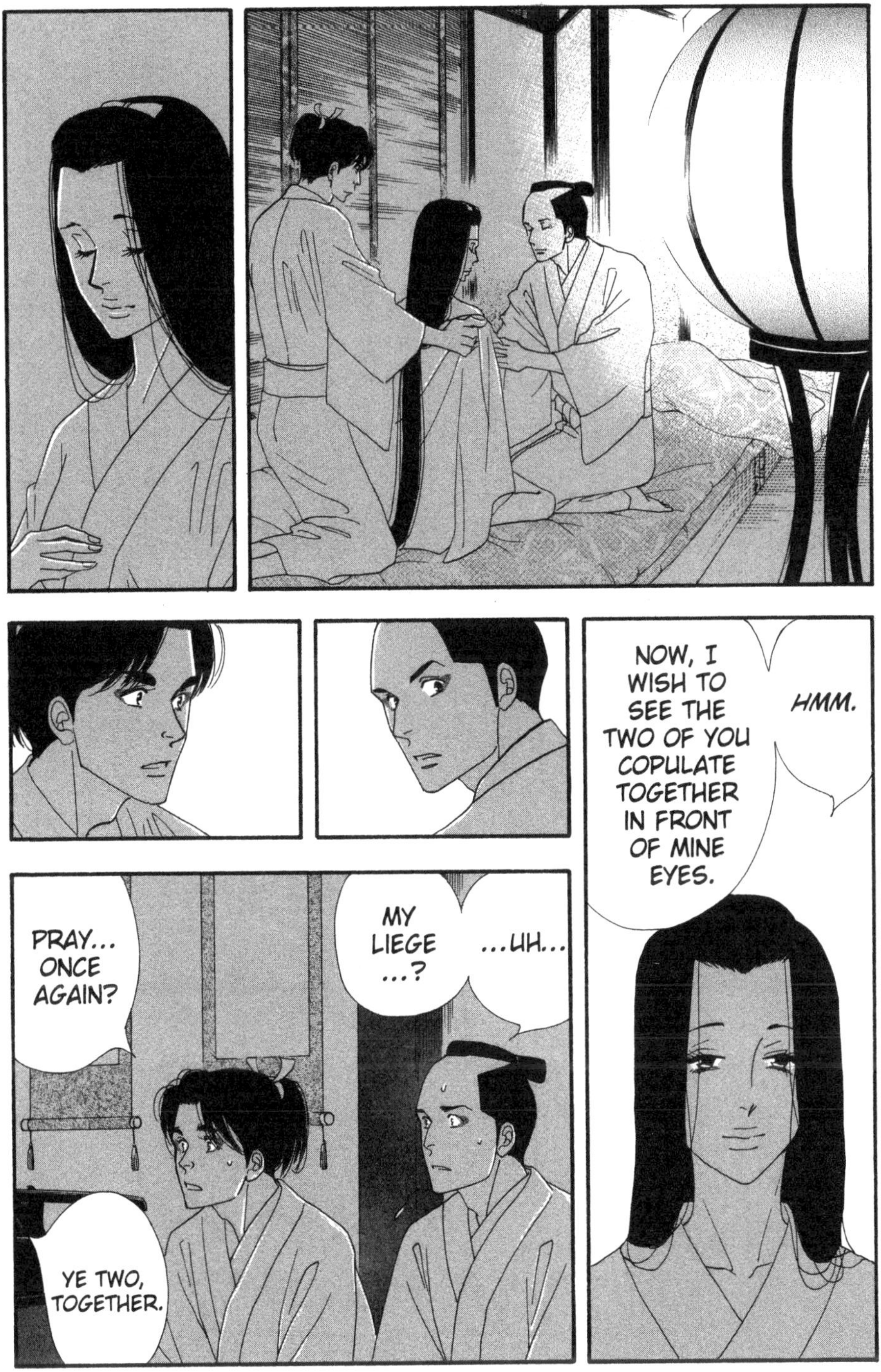
HMM.
NOW, I WISH TO SEE THE TWO OF YOU COPULATE TOGETHER IN FRONT OF MINE EYES.
...UH...
MY LIEGE ...?
PRAY... ONCE AGAIN?
YE TWO, TOGETHER.

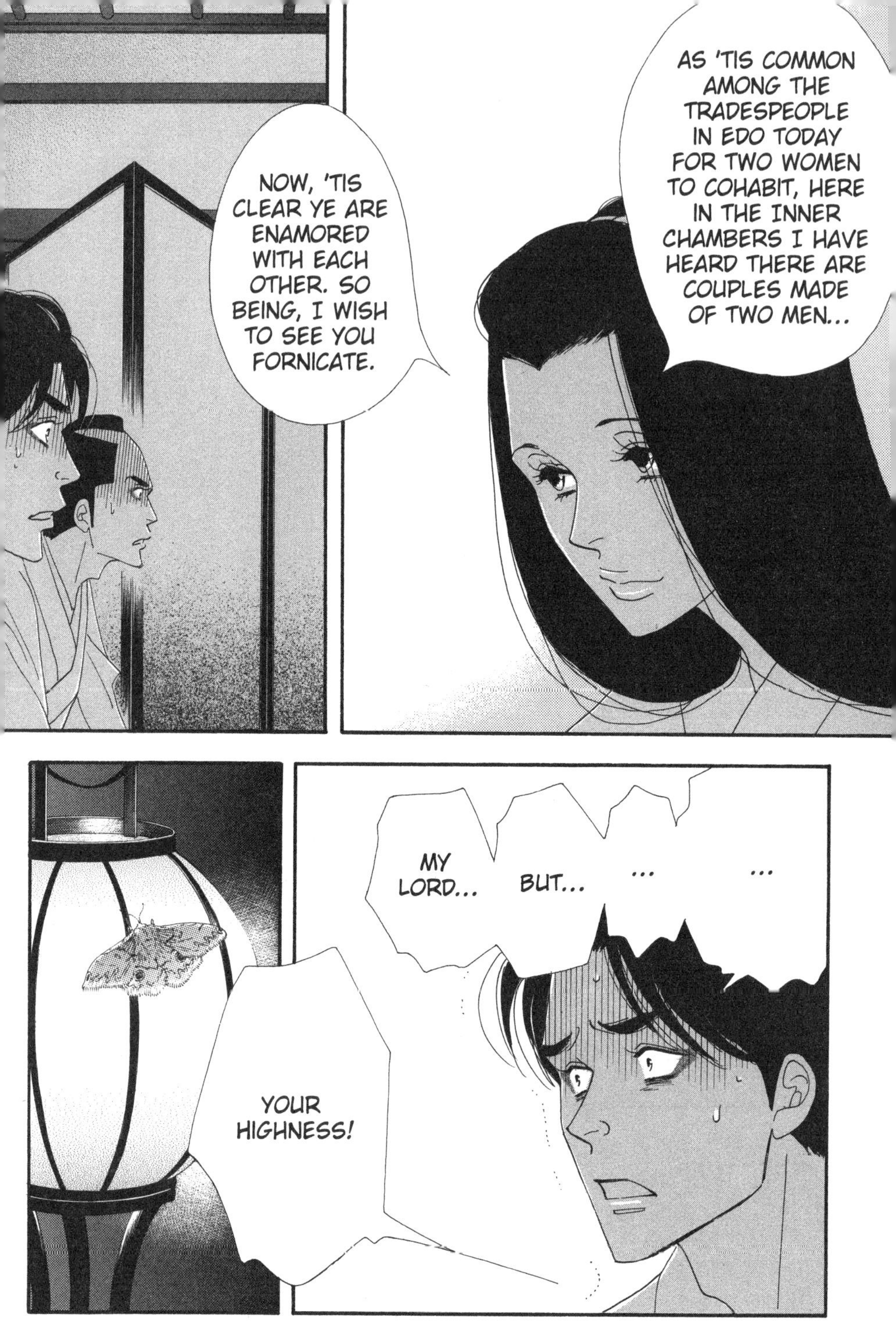
AS 'TIS COMMON AMONG THE TRADESPEOPLE IN EDO TODAY FOR TWO WOMEN TO COHABIT, HERE IN THE INNER CHAMBERS I HAVE HEARD THERE ARE COUPLES MADE OF TWO MEN...
NOW, 'TIS CLEAR YE ARE ENAMORED WITH EACH OTHER. SO BEING, I WISH TO SEE YOU FORNICATE.
MY LORD... BUT... ... ...
YOUR HIGHNESS!

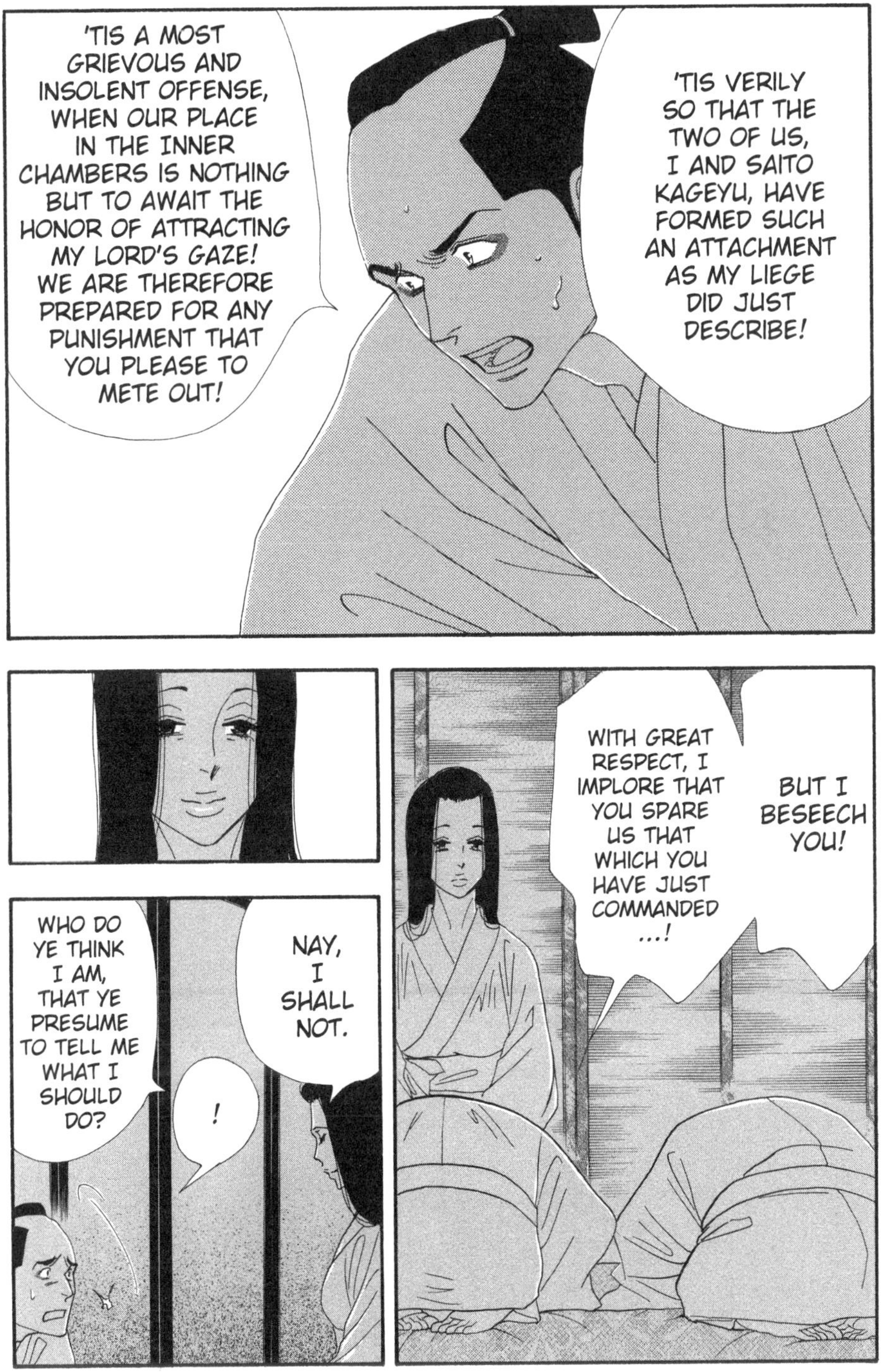
'TIS VERILY SO THAT THE TWO OF US, I AND SAITO KAGEYU, HAVE FORMED SUCH AN ATTACHMENT AS MY LIEGE DID JUST DESCRIBE!
'TIS A MOST GRIEVOUS AND INSOLENT OFFENSE, WHEN OUR PLACE IN THE INNER CHAMBERS IS NOTHING BUT TO AWAIT THE HONOR OF ATTRACTING MY LORD'S GAZE! WE ARE THEREFORE PREPARED FOR ANY PUNISHMENT THAT YOU PLEASE TO METE OUT!
BUT I BESEECH YOU!
WITH GREAT RESPECT, I IMPLORE THAT YOU SPARE US THAT WHICH YOU HAVE JUST COMMANDED ...!
NAY, I SHALL NOT.
!
WHO DO YE THINK I AM, THAT YE PRESUME TO TELL ME WHAT I SHOULD DO?

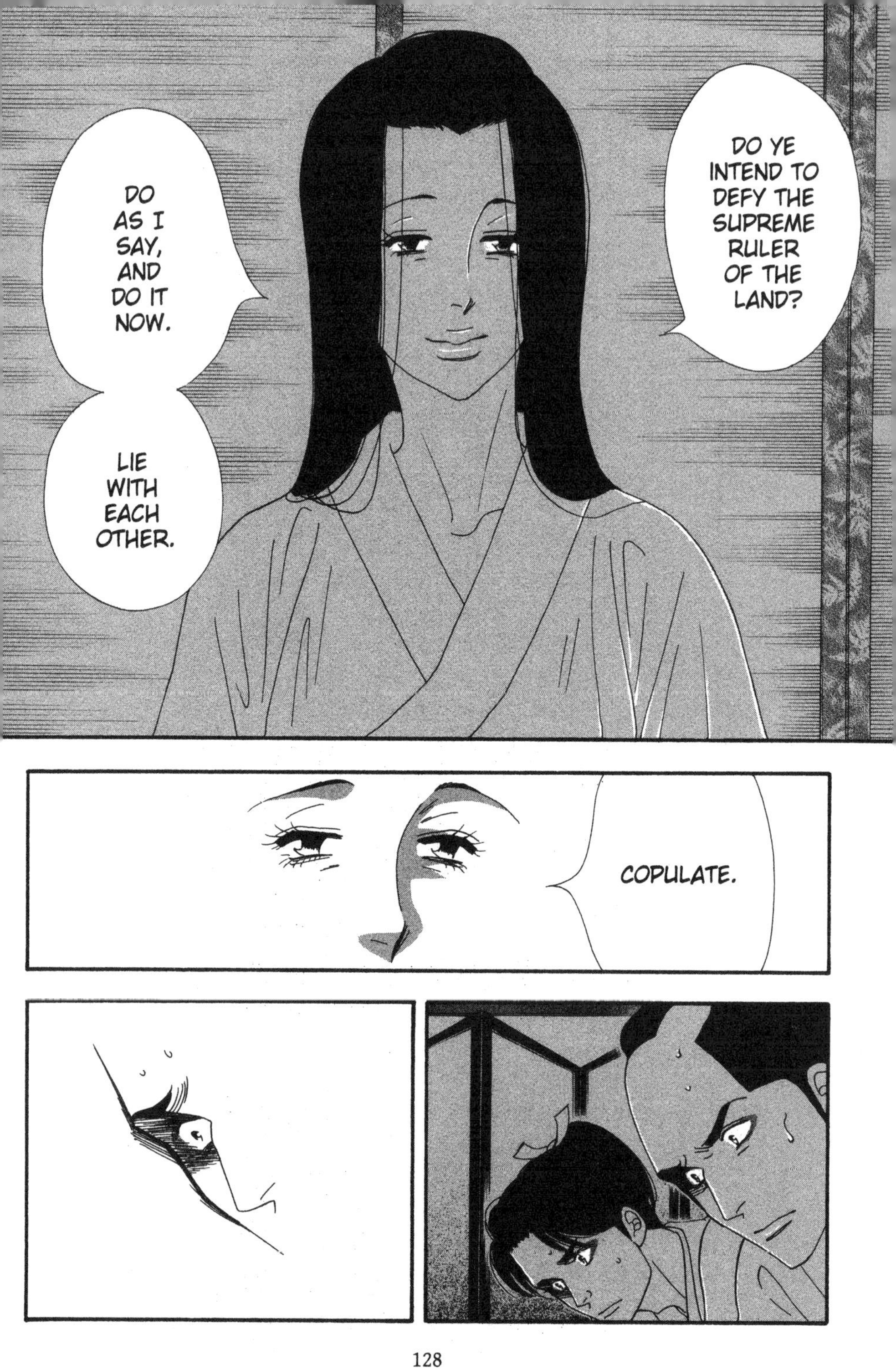
DO YE INTEND TO DEFY THE SUPREME RULER OF THE LAND?
DO AS I SAY, AND DO IT NOW.
LIE WITH EACH OTHER.
COPULATE.

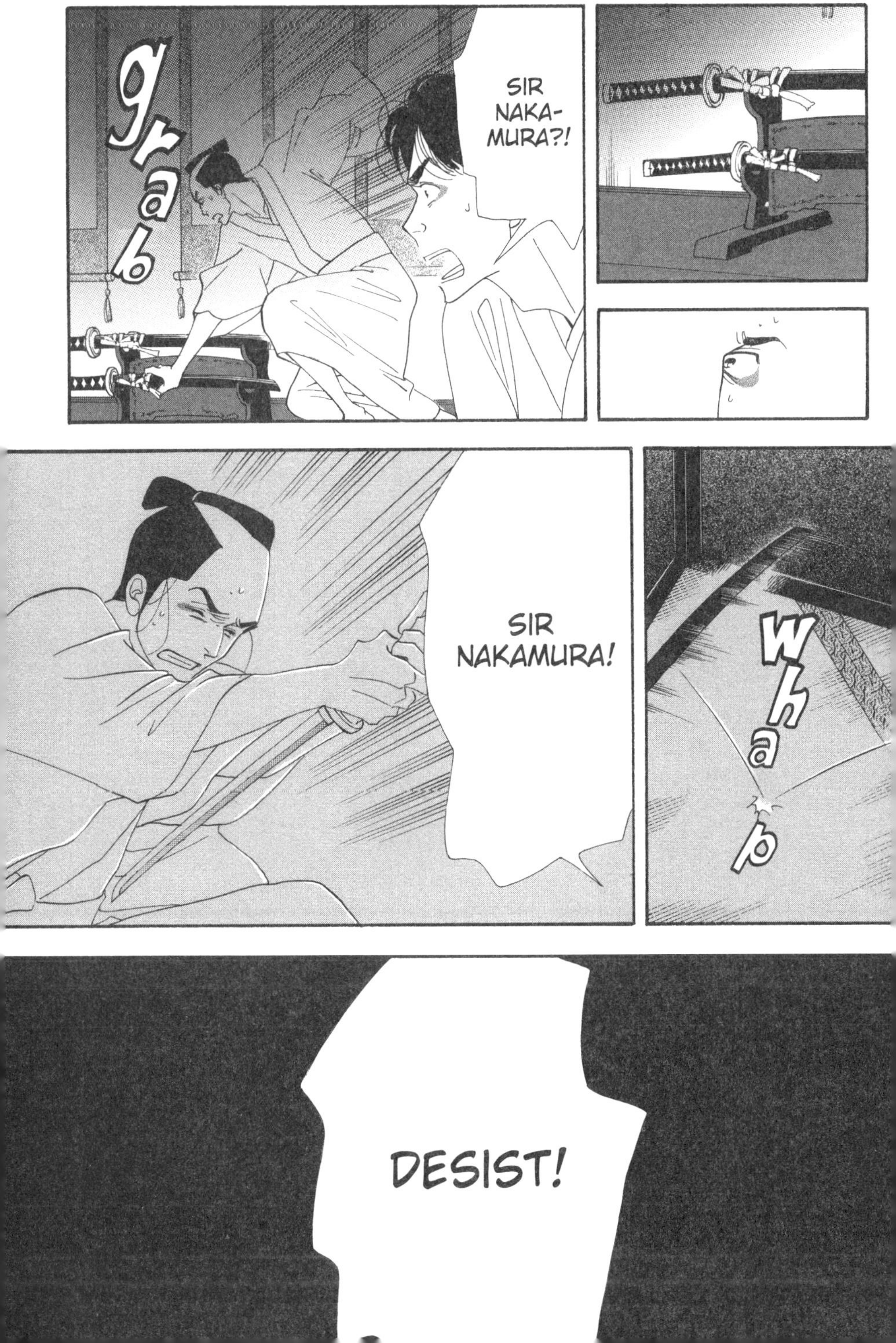
SIR NAKA-MURA?!
grab
whap
SIR NAKAMURA!
DESIST!

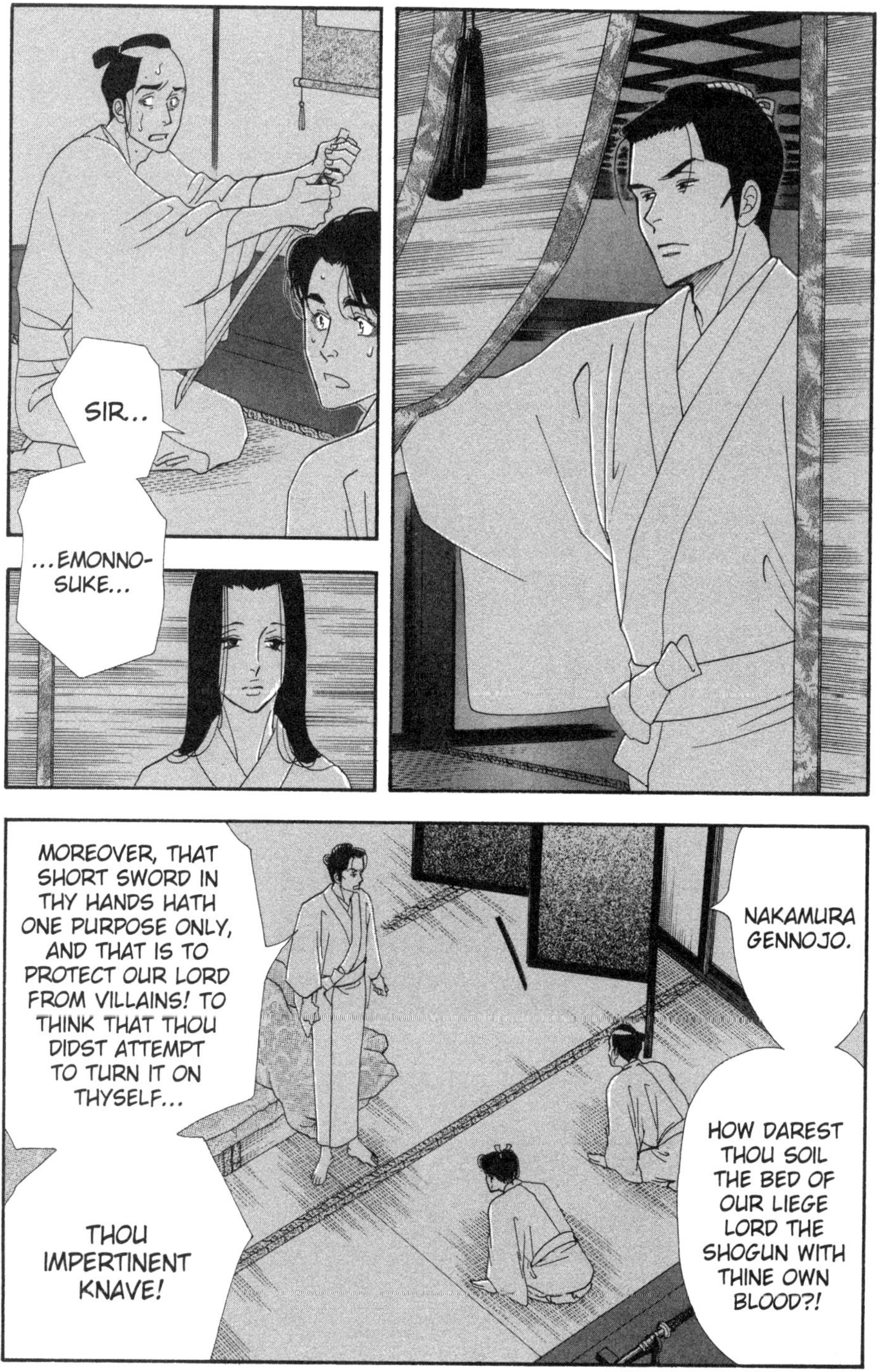
SIR...
...EMONNO-SUKE...
NAKAMURA GENNOJO.
HOW DAREST THOU SOIL THE BED OF OUR LIEGE LORD THE SHOGUN WITH THINE OWN BLOOD?!
MOREOVER, THAT SHORT SWORD IN THY HANDS HATH ONE PURPOSE ONLY, AND THAT IS TO PROTECT OUR LORD FROM VILLAINS! TO THINK THAT THOU DIDST ATTEMPT TO TURN IT ON THYSELF...
THOU IMPERTINENT KNAVE!

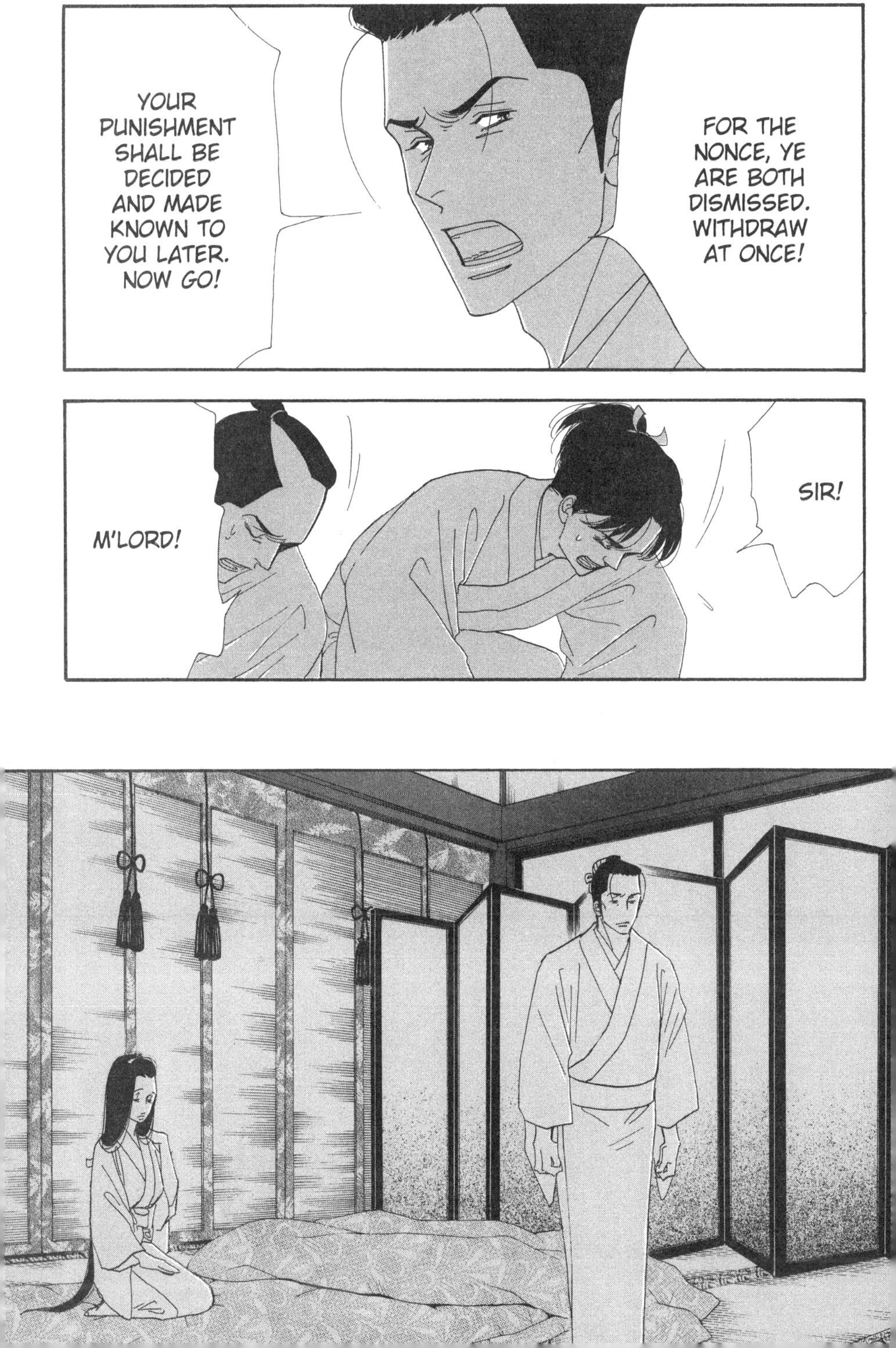
FOR THE NONCE, YE ARE BOTH DISMISSED. WITHDRAW AT ONCE!
YOUR PUNISHMENT SHALL BE DECIDED AND MADE KNOWN TO YOU LATER. NOW GO!
SIR!
M'LORD!

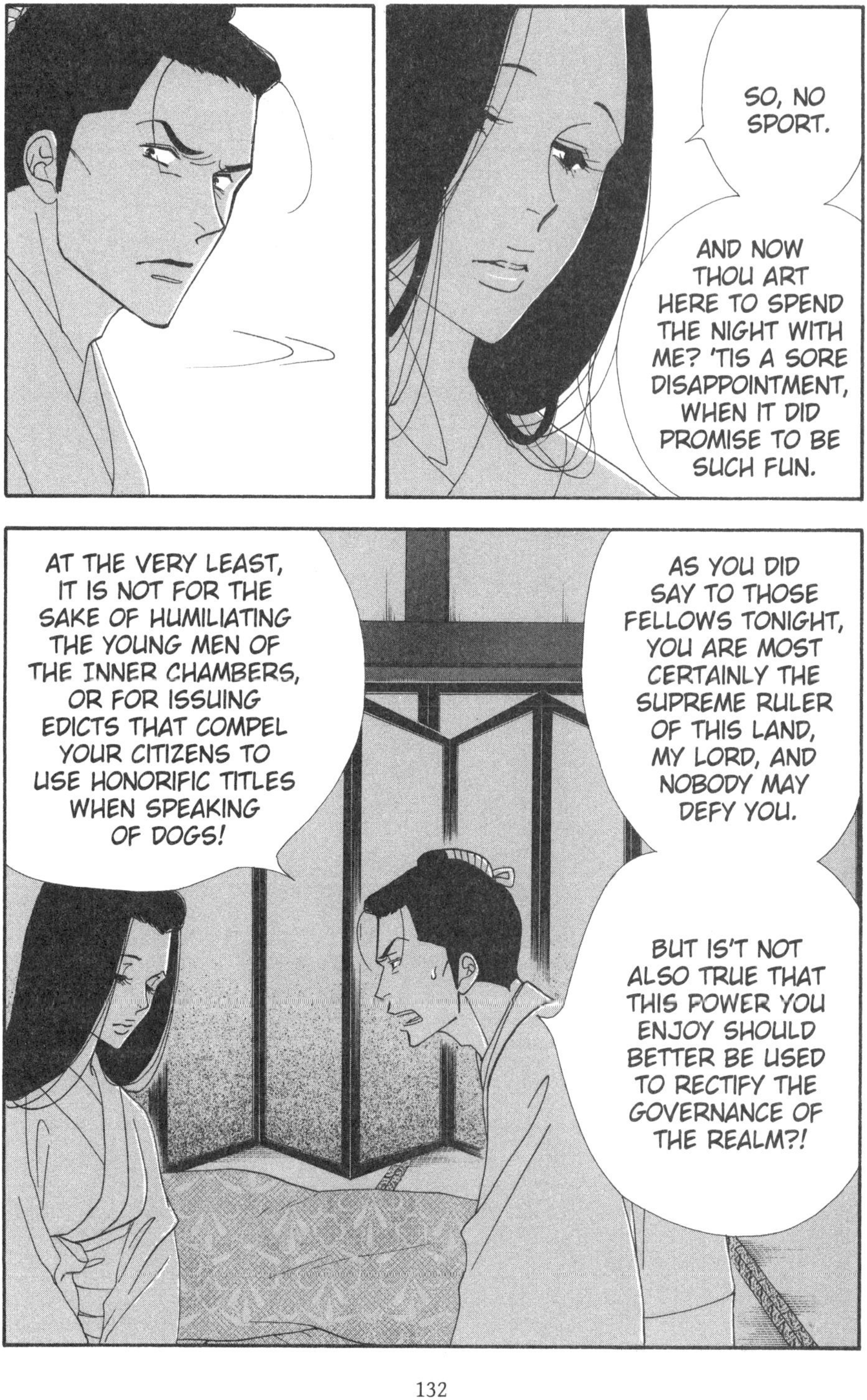
SO, NO SPORT.
AND NOW THOU ART HERE TO SPEND THE NIGHT WITH ME? 'TIS A SORE DISAPPOINTMENT, WHEN IT DID PROMISE TO BE SUCH FUN.
AS YOU DID SAY TO THOSE FELLOWS TONIGHT, YOU ARE MOST CERTAINLY THE SUPREME RULER OF THIS LAND, MY LORD, AND NOBODY MAY DEFY YOU.
BUT IS'T NOT ALSO TRUE THAT THIS POWER YOU ENJOY SHOULD BETTER BE USED TO RECTIFY THE GOVERNANCE OF THE REALM?!
AT THE VERY LEAST, IT IS NOT FOR THE SAKE OF HUMILIATING THE YOUNG MEN OF THE INNER CHAMBERS, OR FOR ISSUING EDICTS THAT COMPEL YOUR CITIZENS TO USE HONORIFIC TITLES WHEN SPEAKING OF DOGS!

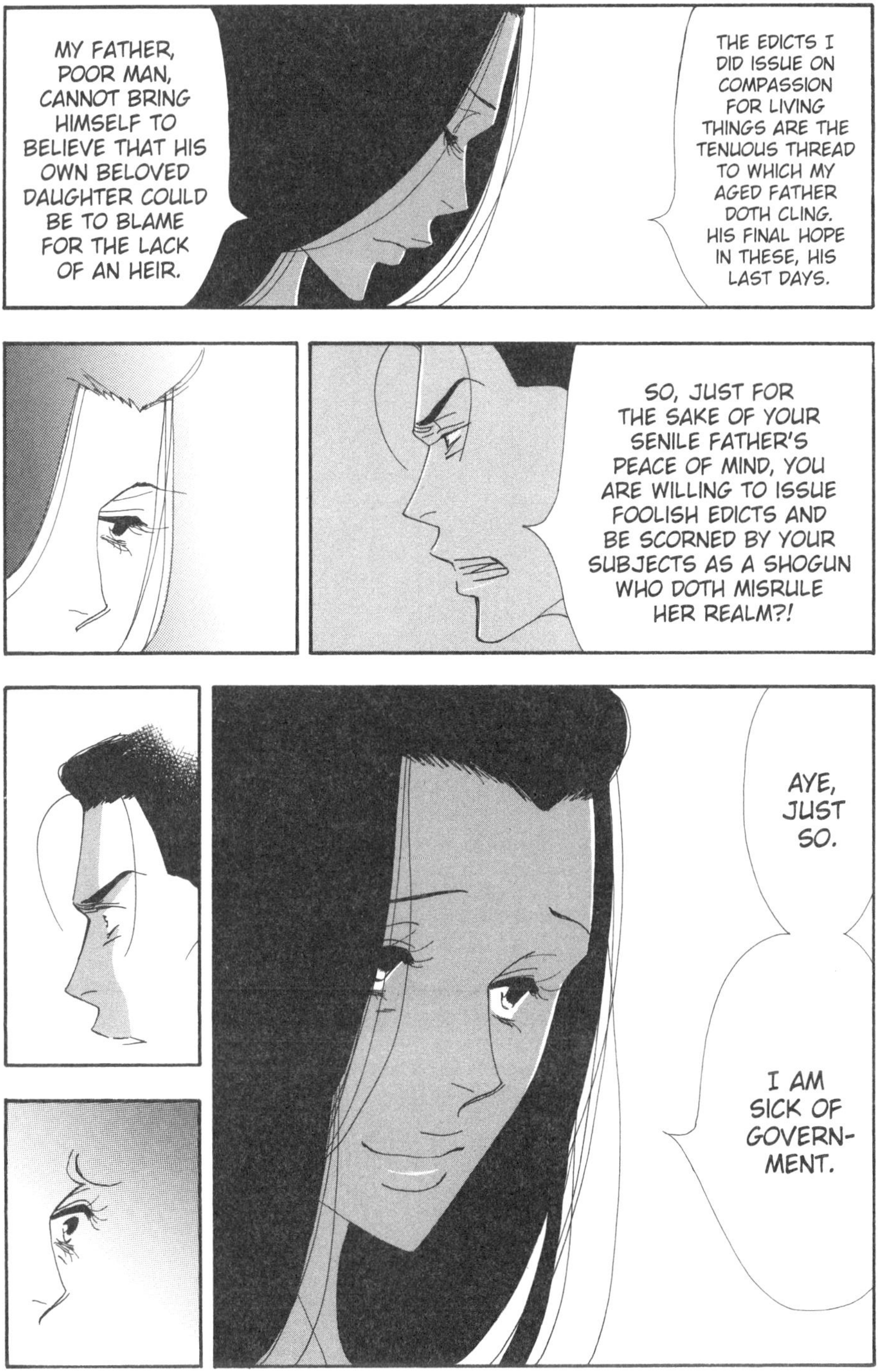
THE EDICTS I DID ISSUE ON COMPASSION FOR LIVING THINGS ARE THE TENUOUS THREAD TO WHICH MY AGED FATHER DOTH CLING. HIS FINAL HOPE IN THESE, HIS LAST DAYS.
MY FATHER, POOR MAN, CANNOT BRING HIMSELF TO BELIEVE THAT HIS OWN BELOVED DAUGHTER COULD BE TO BLAME FOR THE LACK OF AN HEIR.
SO, JUST FOR THE SAKE OF YOUR SENILE FATHER'S PEACE OF MIND, YOU ARE WILLING TO ISSUE FOOLISH EDICTS AND BE SCORNED BY YOUR SUBJECTS AS A SHOGUN WHO DOTH MISRULE HER REALM?!
AYE, JUST SO.
I AM SICK OF GOVERN-MENT.

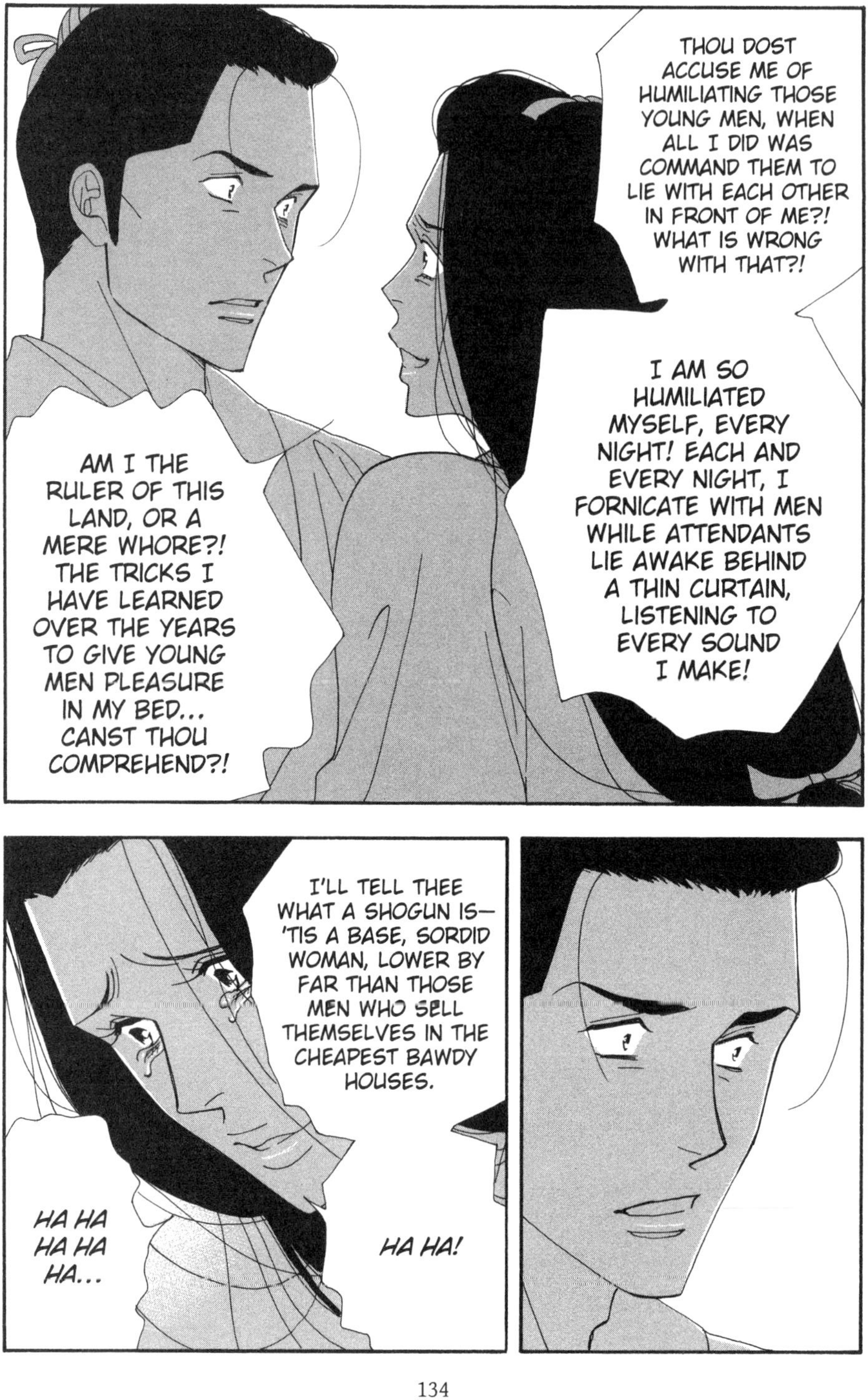
THOU DOST ACCUSE ME OF HUMILIATING THOSE YOUNG MEN, WHEN ALL I DID WAS COMMAND THEM TO LIE WITH EACH OTHER IN FRONT OF ME?! WHAT IS WRONG WITH THAT?!
I AM SO HUMILIATED MYSELF, EVERY NIGHT! EACH AND EVERY NIGHT, I FORNICATE WITH MEN WHILE ATTENDANTS LIE AWAKE BEHIND A THIN CURTAIN, LISTENING TO EVERY SOUND I MAKE!
AM I THE RULER OF THIS LAND, OR A MERE WHORE?! THE TRICKS I HAVE LEARNED OVER THE YEARS TO GIVE YOUNG MEN PLEASURE IN MY BED... CANST THOU COMPREHEND?!
I'LL TELL THEE WHAT A SHOGUN IS— 'TIS A BASE, SORDID WOMAN, LOWER BY FAR THAN THOSE MEN WHO SELL THEMSELVES IN THE CHEAPEST BAWDY HOUSES.
HA HA!
HA HA HA HA HA...

WHEREFORE DIDST THOU DIE...

OH, MATSU...

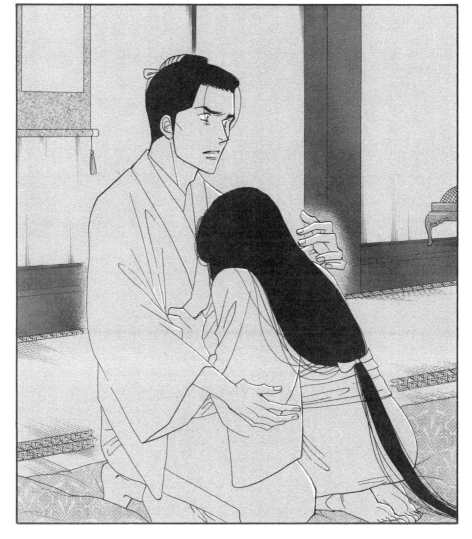

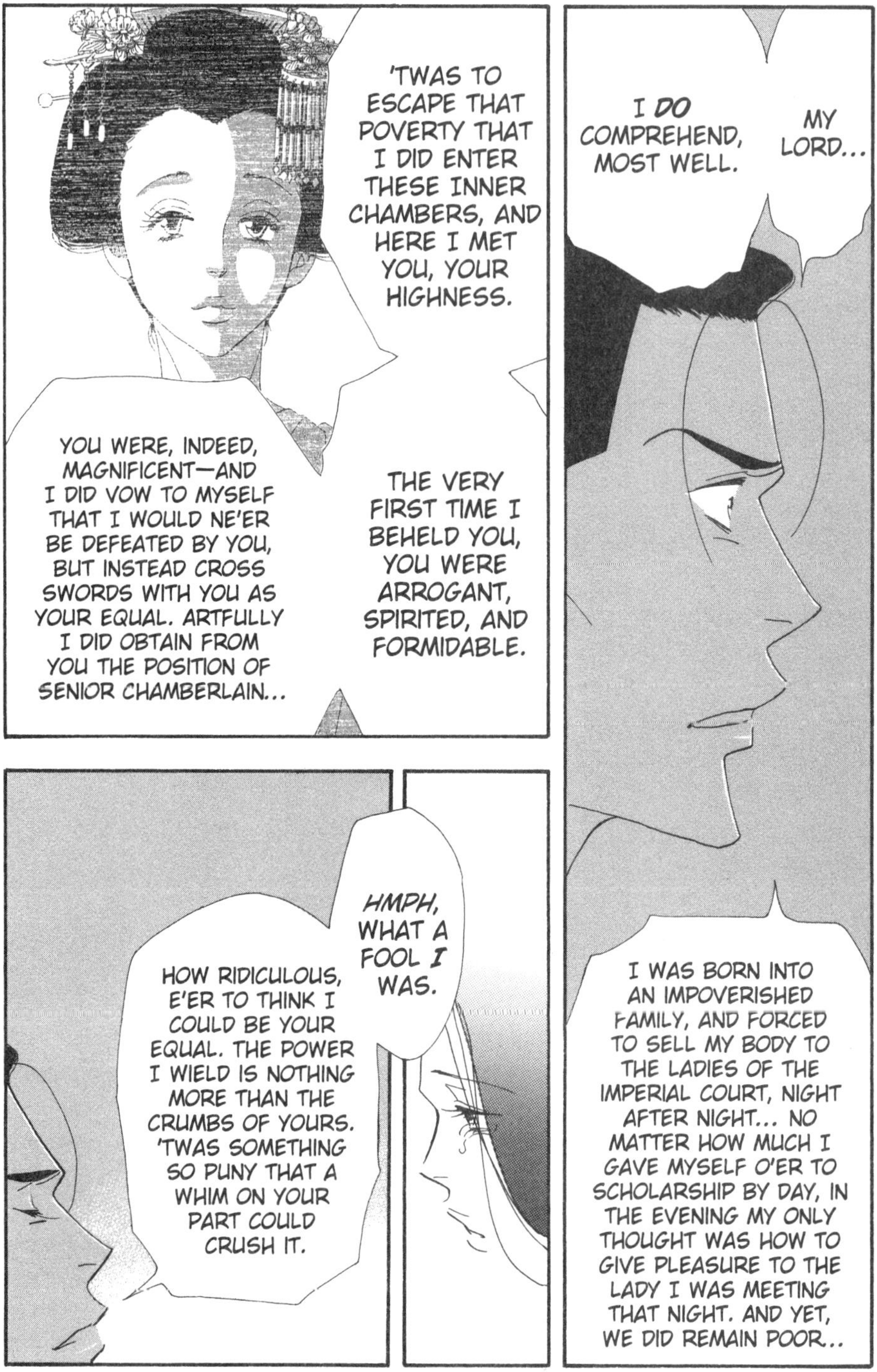
MY LORD...
I DO COMPREHEND, MOST WELL.
I WAS BORN INTO AN IMPOVERISHED FAMILY, AND FORCED TO SELL MY BODY TO THE LADIES OF THE IMPERIAL COURT, NIGHT AFTER NIGHT... NO MATTER HOW MUCH I GAVE MYSELF O'ER TO SCHOLARSHIP BY DAY, IN THE EVENING MY ONLY THOUGHT WAS HOW TO GIVE PLEASURE TO THE LADY I WAS MEETING THAT NIGHT. AND YET, WE DID REMAIN POOR..
'TWAS TO ESCAPE THAT POVERTY THAT I DID ENTER THESE INNER CHAMBERS, AND HERE I MET YOU, YOUR HIGHNESS.
THE VERY FIRST TIME I BEHELD YOU, YOU WERE ARROGANT, SPIRITED, AND FORMIDABLE.
YOU WERE, INDEED, MAGNIFICENT—AND I DID VOW TO MYSELF THAT I WOULD NE'ER BE DEFEATED BY YOU, BUT INSTEAD CROSS SWORDS WITH YOU AS YOUR EQUAL. ARTFULLY I DID OBTAIN FROM YOU THE POSITION OF SENIOR CHAMBERLAIN...
HMPH, WHAT A FOOL I WAS.
HOW RIDICULOUS, E'ER TO THINK I COULD BE YOUR EQUAL. THE POWER I WIELD IS NOTHING MORE THAN THE CRUMBS OF YOURS. 'TWAS SOMETHING SO PUNY THAT A WHIM ON YOUR PART COULD CRUSH IT.

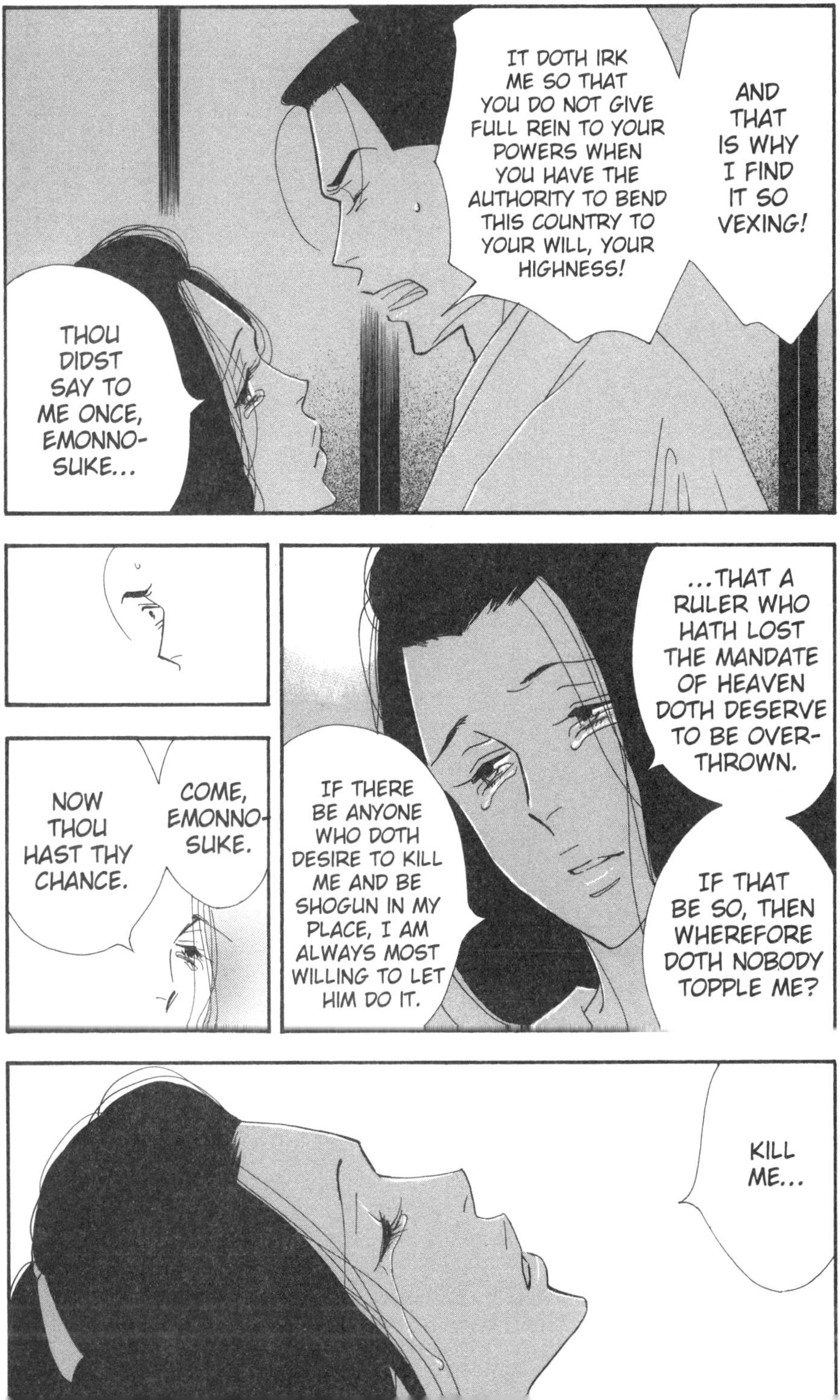
IT DOTH IRK ME SO THAT YOU DO NOT GIVE FULL REIN TO YOUR POWERS WHEN YOU HAVE THE AUTHORITY TO BEND THIS COUNTRY TO YOUR WILL, YOUR HIGHNESS!
AND THAT IS WHY I FIND IT SO VEXING!
THOU DIDST SAY TO ME ONCE, EMONNO-SUKE...
...THAT A RULER WHO HATH LOST THE MANDATE OF HEAVEN DOTH DESERVE TO BE OVER-THROWN.
IF THAT BE SO, THEN WHEREFORE DOTH NOBODY TOPPLE ME?
IF THERE BE ANYONE WHO DOTH DESIRE TO KILL ME AND BE SHOGUN IN MY PLACE, I AM ALWAYS MOST WILLING TO LET HIM DO IT.
COME, EMONNO-SUKE.
NOW THOU HAST THY CHANCE.
KILL ME...

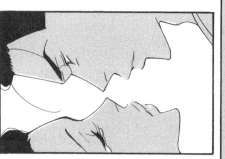

YOUR HIGH-NESS...

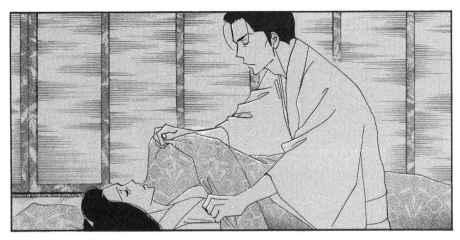

...SLEEP, MY LORD, I PRAY YOU.

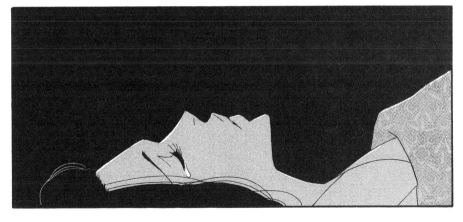

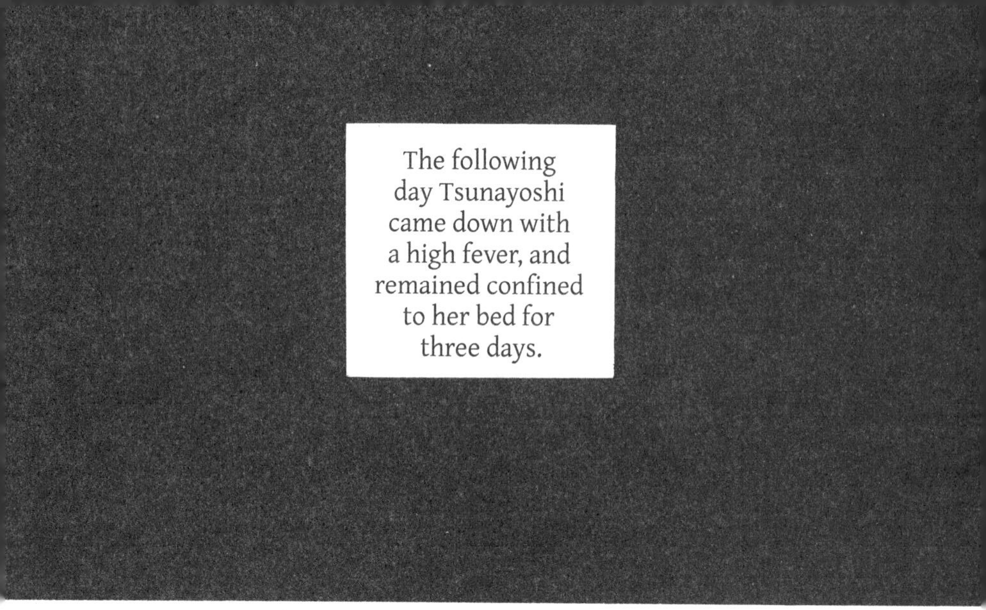
The following day Tsunayoshi came down with a high fever, and remained confined to her bed for three days.

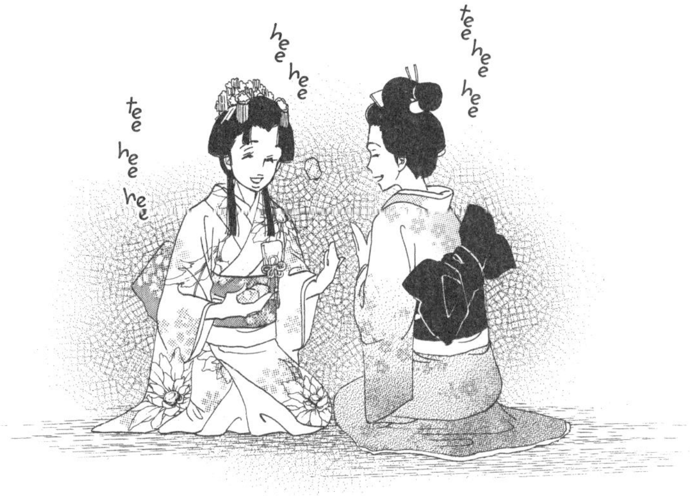
tee hee hee
hee hee
tee hee hee

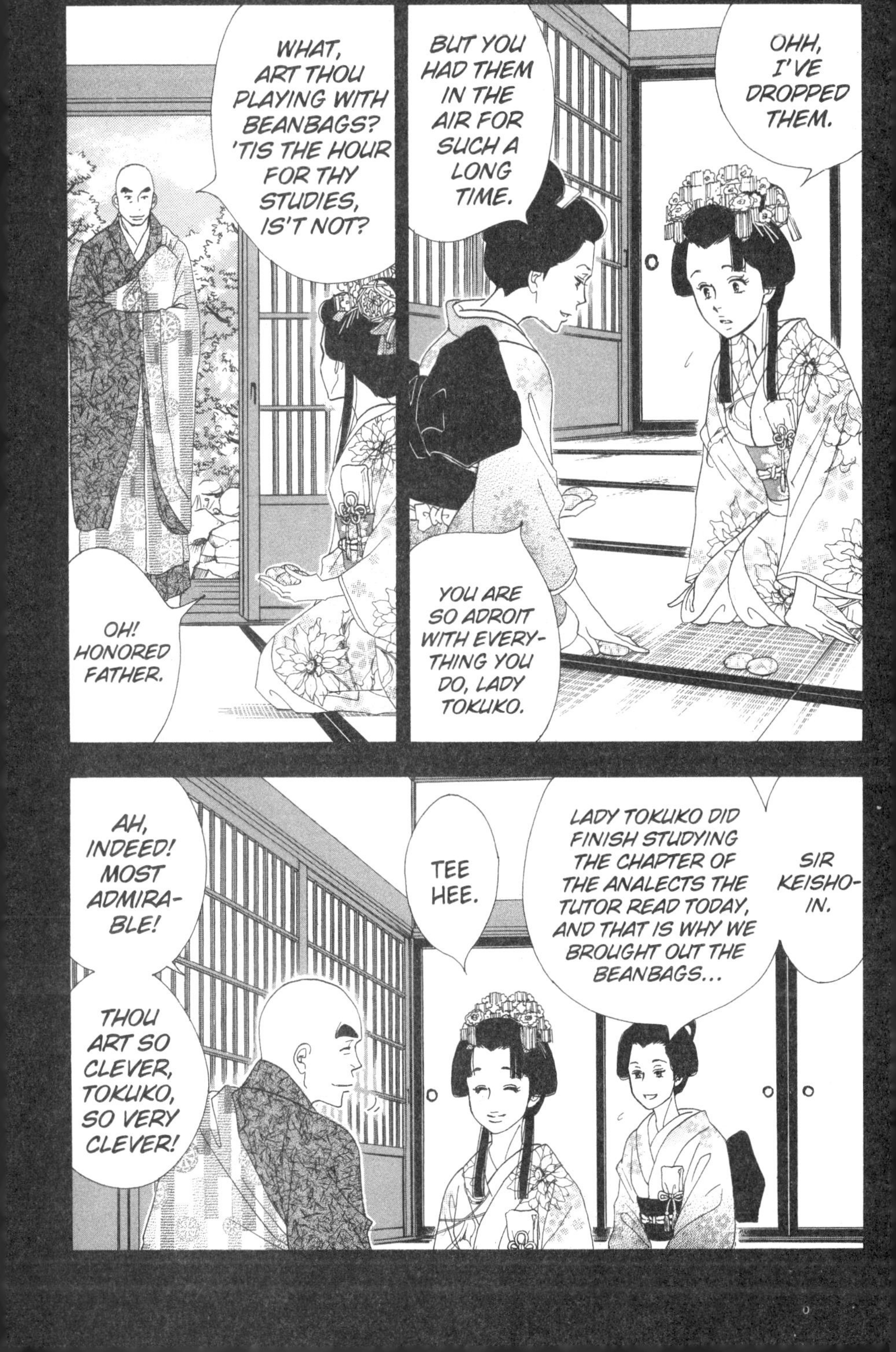
OHH, I'VE DROPPED THEM.
BUT YOU HAD THEM IN THE AIR FOR SUCH A LONG TIME.
YOU ARE SO ADROIT WITH EVERY-THING YOU DO, LADY TOKUKO.
WHAT, ART THOU PLAYING WITH BEANBAGS? 'TIS THE HOUR FOR THY STUDIES, IS'T NOT?
OH! HONORED FATHER.
SIR KEISHO-IN.
LADY TOKUKO DID FINISH STUDYING THE CHAPTER OF THE ANALECTS THE TUTOR READ TODAY, AND THAT IS WHY WE BROUGHT OUT THE BEANBAGS...
TEE HEE.
AH, INDEED! MOST ADMIRA-BLE!
THOU ART SO CLEVER, TOKUKO, SO VERY CLEVER!

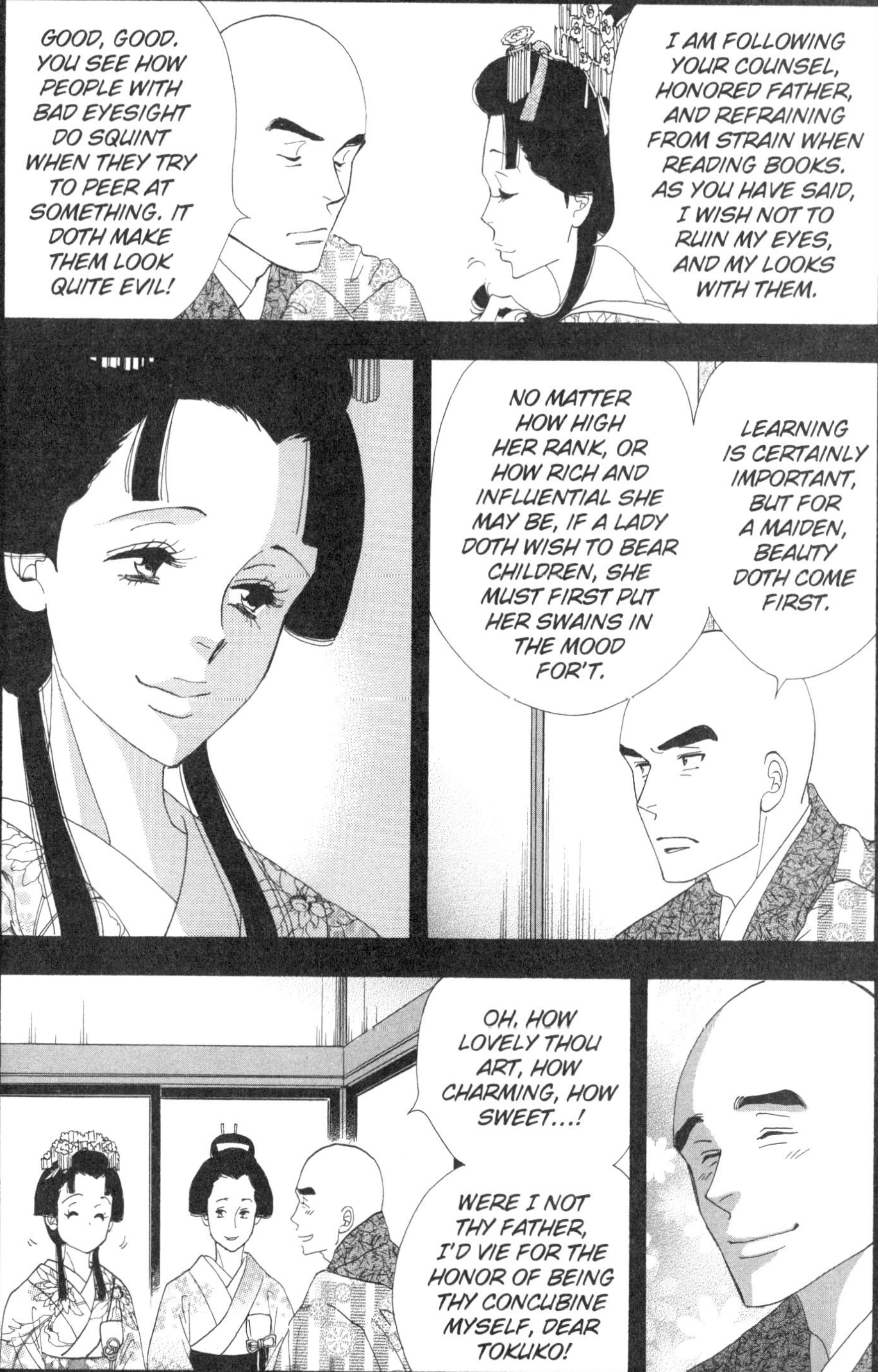
I AM FOLLOWING YOUR COUNSEL, HONORED FATHER, AND REFRAINING FROM STRAIN WHEN READING BOOKS. AS YOU HAVE SAID, I WISH NOT TO RUIN MY EYES, AND MY LOOKS WITH THEM.
GOOD, GOOD. YOU SEE HOW PEOPLE WITH BAD EYESIGHT DO SQUINT WHEN THEY TRY TO PEER AT SOMETHING. IT DOTH MAKE THEM LOOK QUITE EVIL!
LEARNING IS CERTAINLY IMPORTANT, BUT FOR A MAIDEN, BEAUTY DOTH COME FIRST.
NO MATTER HOW HIGH HER RANK, OR HOW RICH AND INFLUENTIAL SHE MAY BE, IF A LADY DOTH WISH TO BEAR CHILDREN, SHE MUST FIRST PUT HER SWAINS IN THE MOOD FOR'T.
OH, HOW LOVELY THOU ART, HOW CHARMING, HOW SWEET...!
WERE I NOT THY FATHER, I'D VIE FOR THE HONOR OF BEING THY CONCUBINE MYSELF, DEAR TOKUKO!

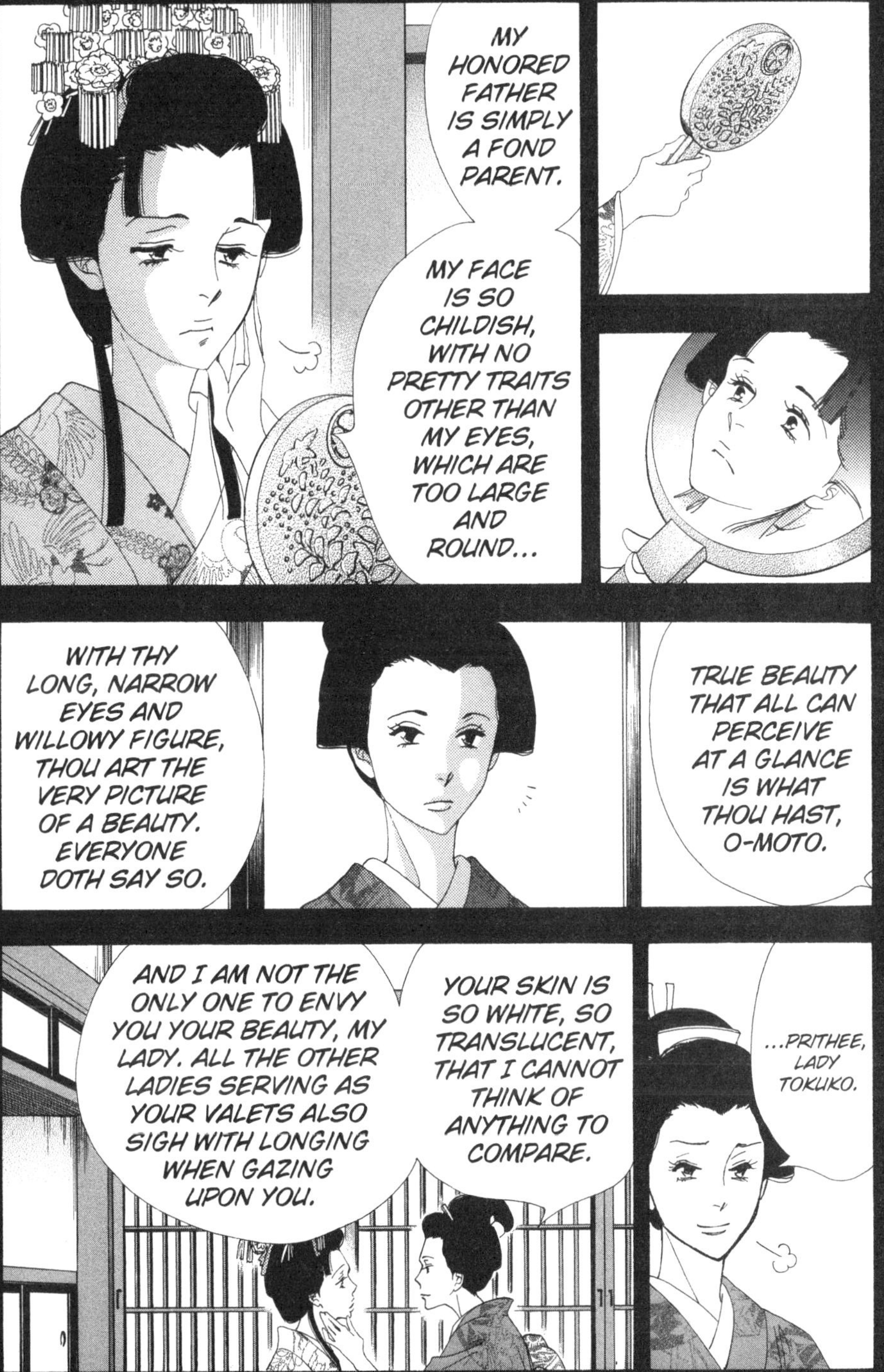
MY HONORED FATHER IS SIMPLY A FOND PARENT.
MY FACE IS SO CHILDISH, WITH NO PRETTY TRAITS OTHER THAN MY EYES, WHICH ARE TOO LARGE AND ROUND...
TRUE BEAUTY THAT ALL CAN PERCEIVE AT A GLANCE IS WHAT THOU HAST, O-MOTO.
WITH THY LONG, NARROW EYES AND WILLOWY FIGURE, THOU ART THE VERY PICTURE OF A BEAUTY. EVERYONE DOTH SAY SO.
...PRITHEE, LADY TOKUKO.
YOUR SKIN IS SO WHITE, SO TRANSLUCENT, THAT I CANNOT THINK OF ANYTHING TO COMPARE.
AND I AM NOT THE ONLY ONE TO ENVY YOU YOUR BEAUTY, MY LADY. ALL THE OTHER LADIES SERVING AS YOUR VALETS ALSO SIGH WITH LONGING WHEN GAZING UPON YOU.

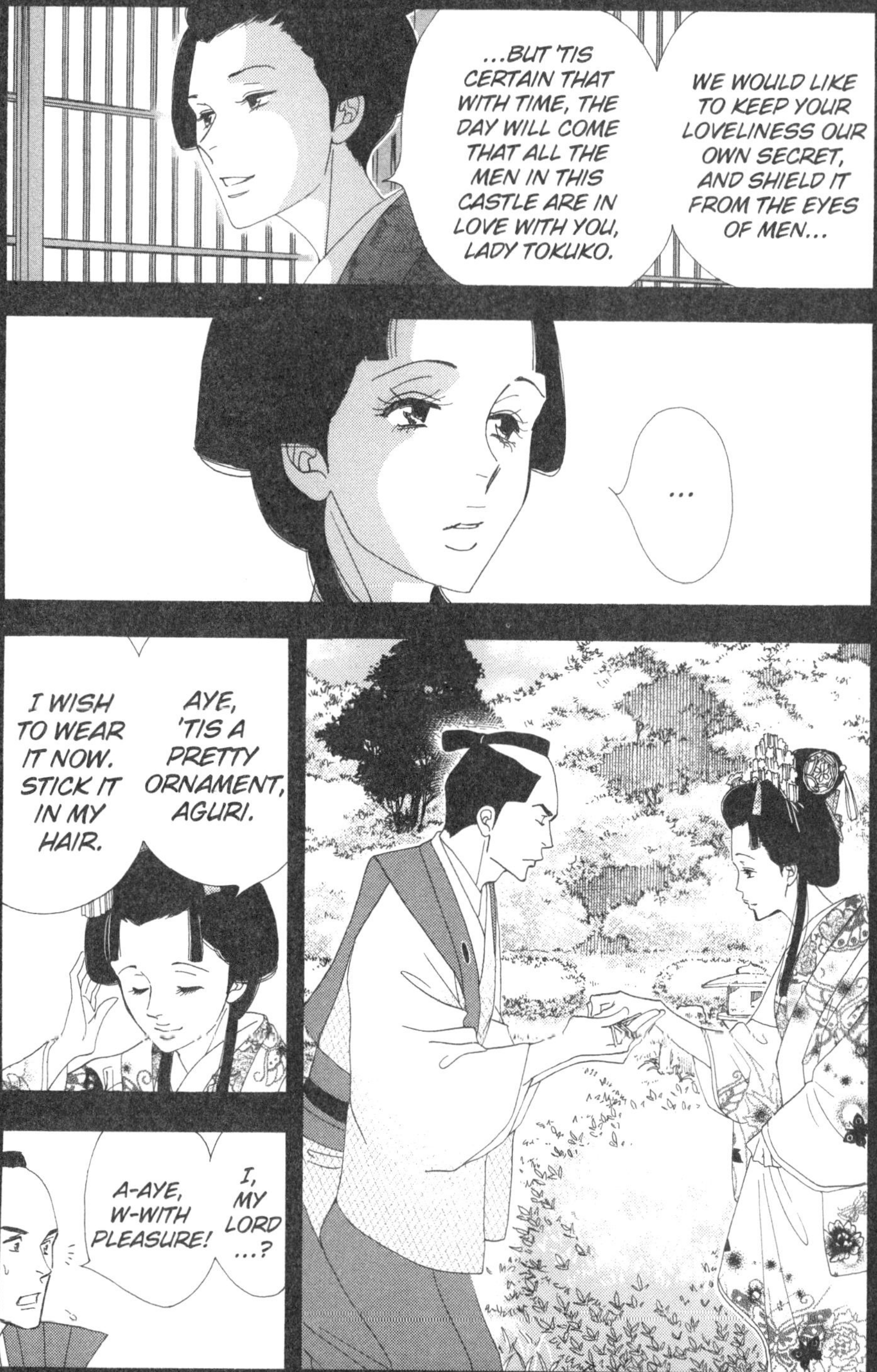
WE WOULD LIKE TO KEEP YOUR LOVELINESS OUR OWN SECRET, AND SHIELD IT FROM THE EYES OF MEN...
...BUT 'TIS CERTAIN THAT WITH TIME, THE DAY WILL COME THAT ALL THE MEN IN THIS CASTLE ARE IN LOVE WITH YOU, LADY TOKUKO.
...
AYE, 'TIS A PRETTY ORNAMENT, AGURI.
I WISH TO WEAR IT NOW. STICK IT IN MY HAIR.
I, MY LORD ...?
A-AYE, W-WITH PLEASURE!

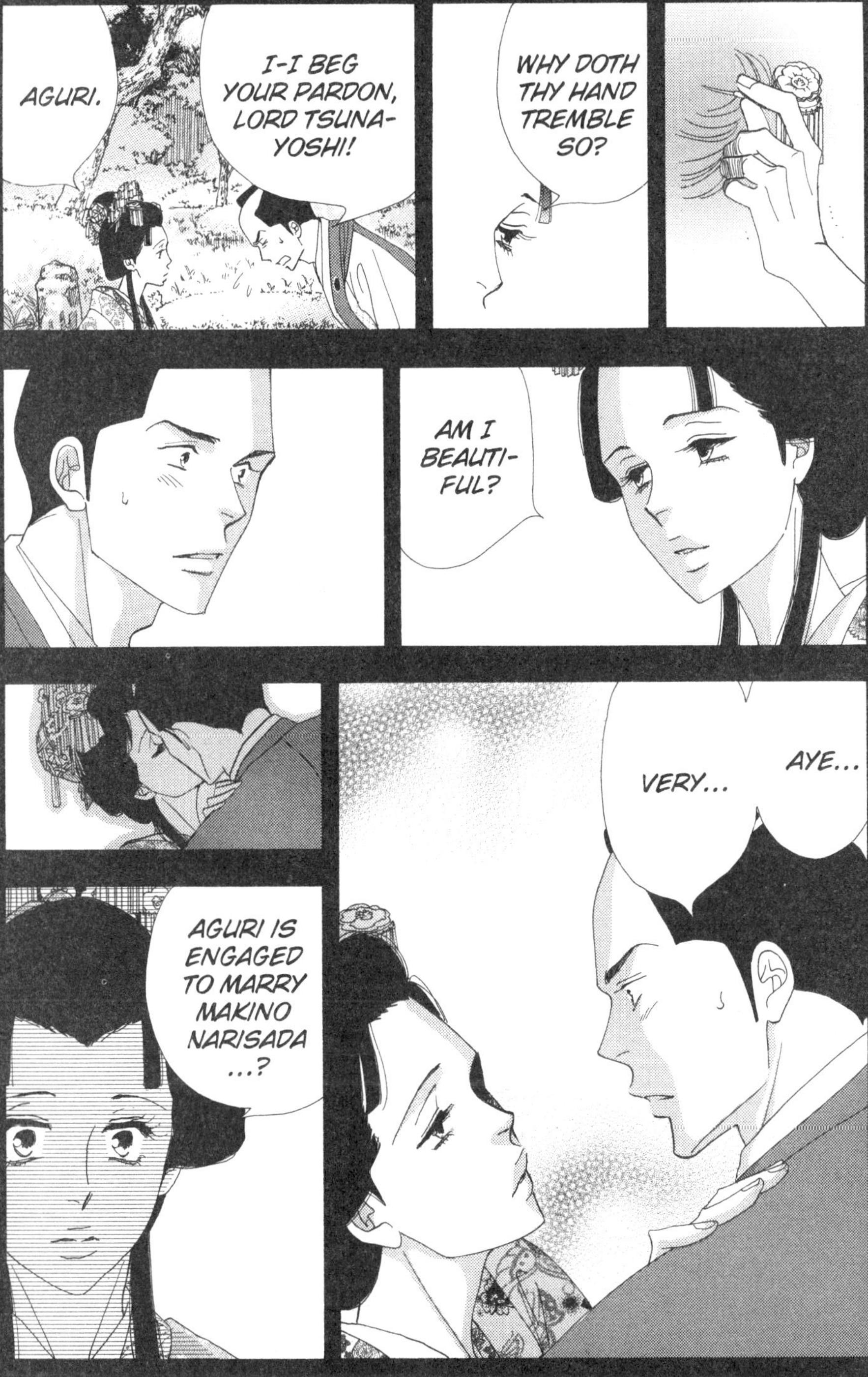
WHY DOTH THY HAND TREMBLE SO?
I-I BEG YOUR PARDON, LORD TSUNA-YOSHI!
AGURI.
AM I BEAUTI-FUL?
AYE...
VERY...
AGURI IS ENGAGED TO MARRY MAKINO NARISADA ...?

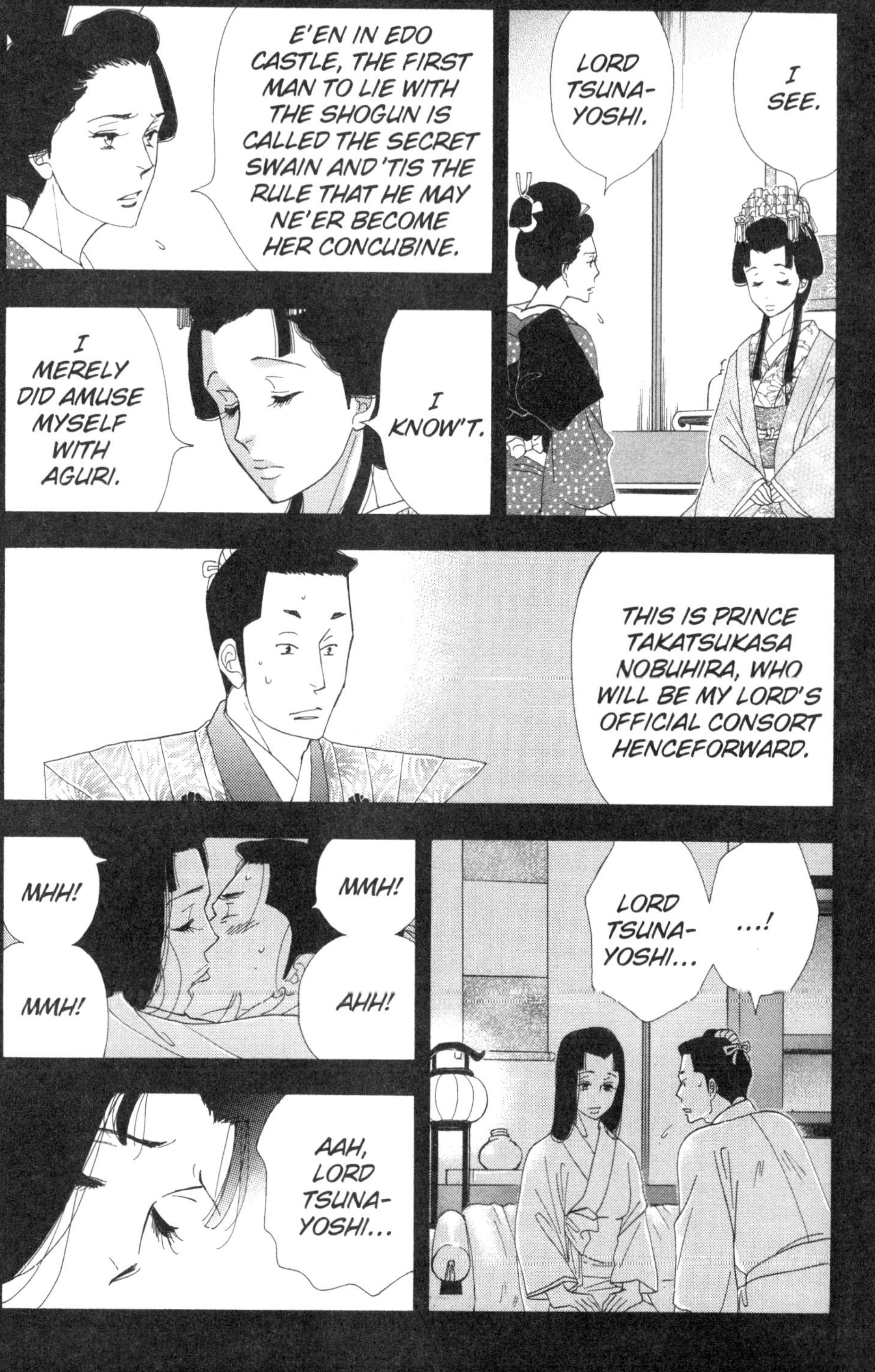
I SEE.
LORD TSUNA-YOSHI.
E'EN IN EDO CASTLE, THE FIRST MAN TO LIE WITH THE SHOGUN IS CALLED THE SECRET SWAIN AND 'TIS THE RULE THAT HE MAY NE'ER BECOME HER CONCUBINE.
I KNOW'T.
I MERELY DID AMUSE MYSELF WITH AGURI.
THIS IS PRINCE TAKATSUKASA NOBUHIRA, WHO WILL BE MY LORD'S OFFICIAL CONSORT HENCEFORWARD.
...!
LORD TSUNA-YOSHI...
MMH!
MHH!
AHH!
MMH!
AAH, LORD TSUNA-YOSHI...

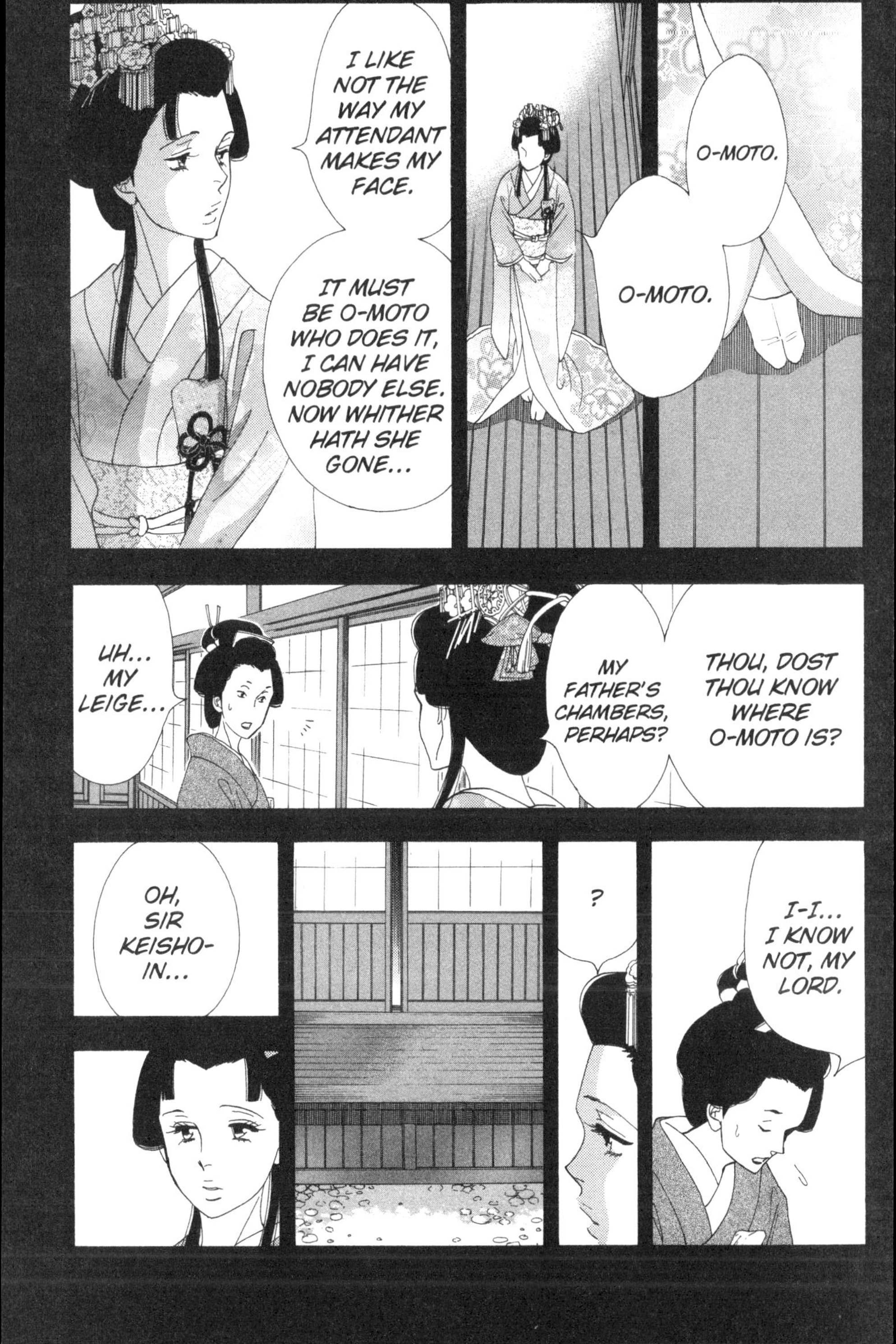
O-MOTO.
O-MOTO.
I LIKE NOT THE WAY MY ATTENDANT MAKES MY FACE.
IT MUST BE O-MOTO WHO DOES IT, I CAN HAVE NOBODY ELSE. NOW WHITHER HATH SHE GONE...
THOU, DOST THOU KNOW WHERE O-MOTO IS?
MY FATHER'S CHAMBERS, PERHAPS?
UH... MY LEIGE...
I-I... I KNOW NOT, MY LORD.
?
OH, SIR KEISHO-IN...

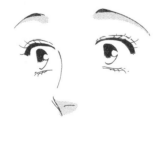

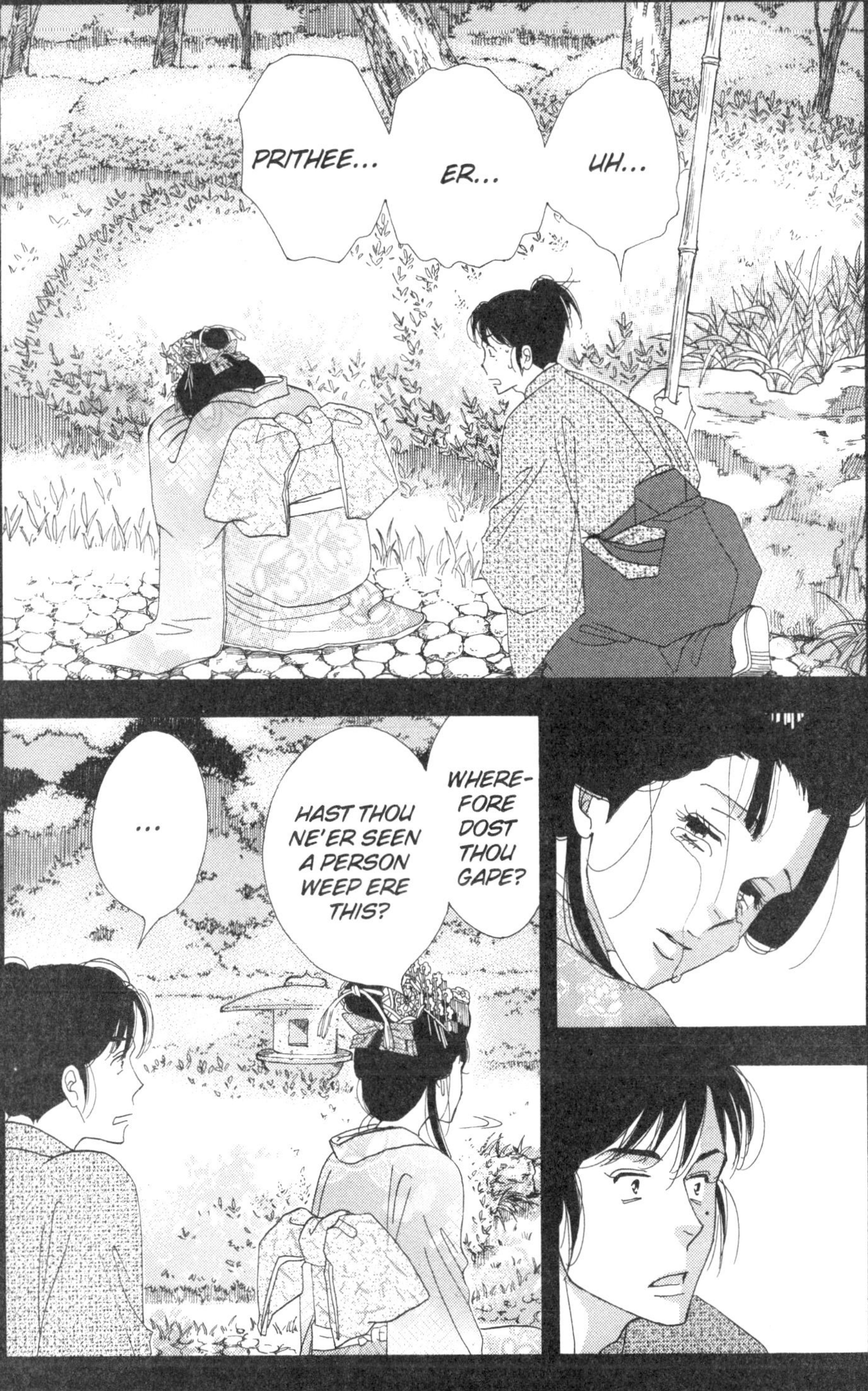
UH...
ER...
PRITHEE...
WHERE-FORE DOST THOU GAPE?
HAST THOU NE'ER SEEN A PERSON WEEP ERE THIS?
...

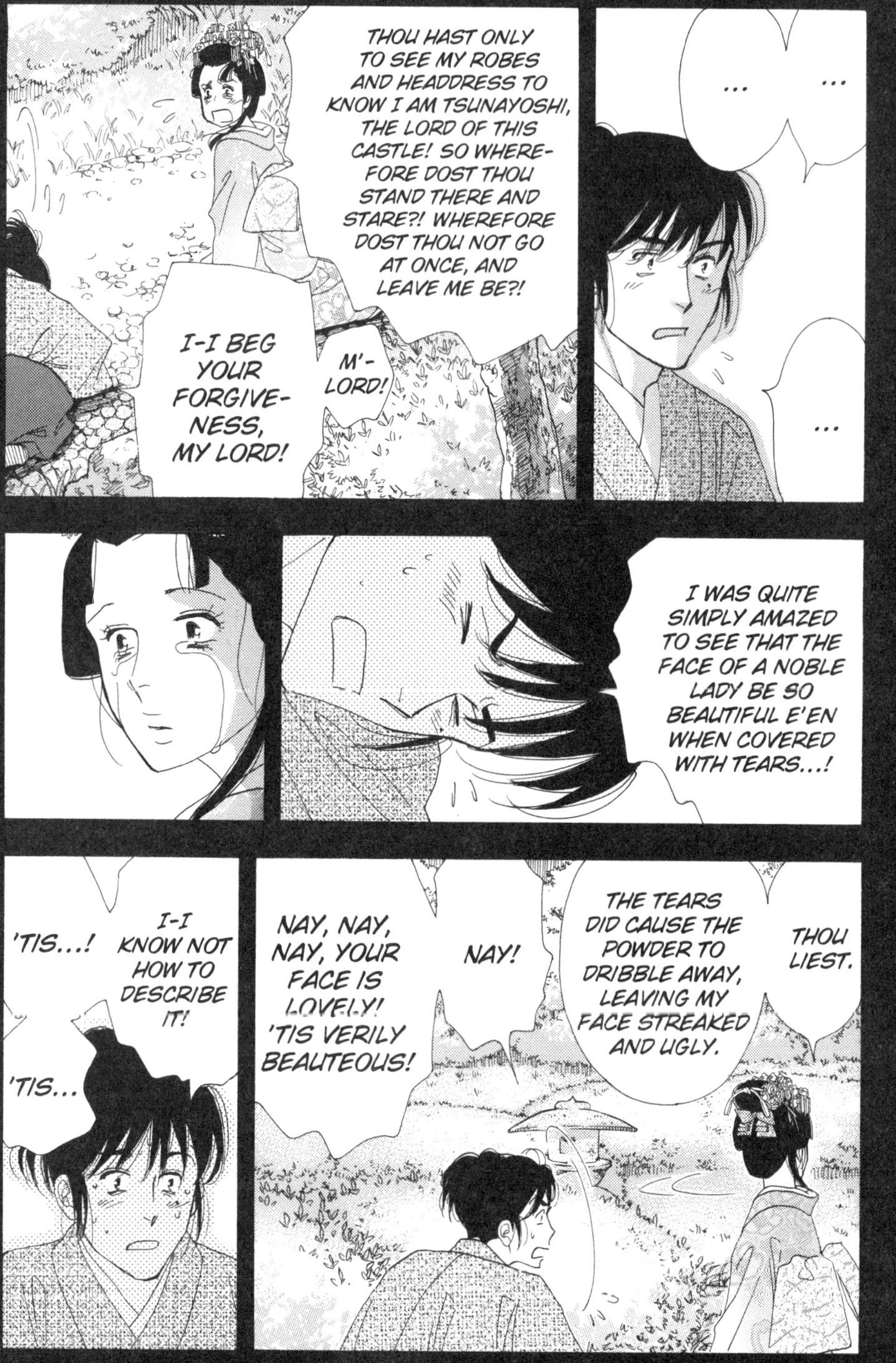
...
...
...
THOU HAST ONLY TO SEE MY ROBES AND HEADDRESS TO KNOW I AM TSUNAYOSHI, THE LORD OF THIS CASTLE! SO WHEREFORE DOST THOU STAND THERE AND STARE?! WHEREFORE DOST THOU NOT GO AT ONCE, AND LEAVE ME BE?!
M'-LORD!
I-I BEG YOUR FORGIVENESS, MY LORD!
I WAS QUITE SIMPLY AMAZED TO SEE THAT THE FACE OF A NOBLE LADY BE SO BEAUTIFUL E'EN WHEN COVERED WITH TEARS...!
THOU LIEST.
THE TEARS DID CAUSE THE POWDER TO DRIBBLE AWAY, LEAVING MY FACE STREAKED AND UGLY.
NAY!
NAY, NAY, NAY, YOUR FACE IS LOVELY! 'TIS VERILY BEAUTEOUS!
I-I KNOW NOT HOW TO DESCRIBE IT!
'TIS...!
'TIS...

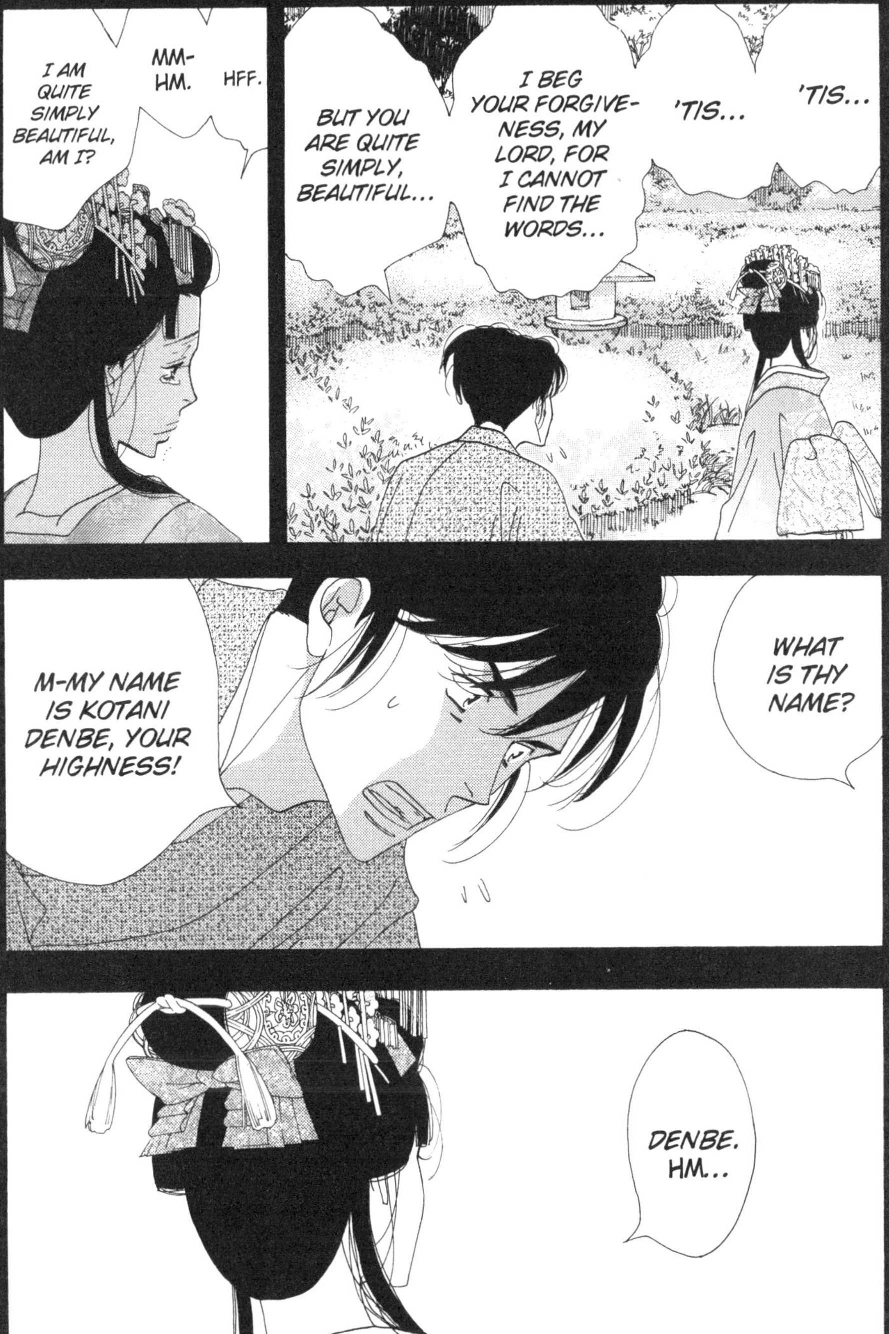
'TIS...
'TIS...
I BEG YOUR FORGIVE-NESS, MY LORD, FOR I CANNOT FIND THE WORDS...
BUT YOU ARE QUITE SIMPLY, BEAUTIFUL...
HFF.
MM-HM.
I AM QUITE SIMPLY BEAUTIFUL, AM I?
WHAT IS THY NAME?
M-MY NAME IS KOTANI DENBE, YOUR HIGHNESS!
DENBE. HM...

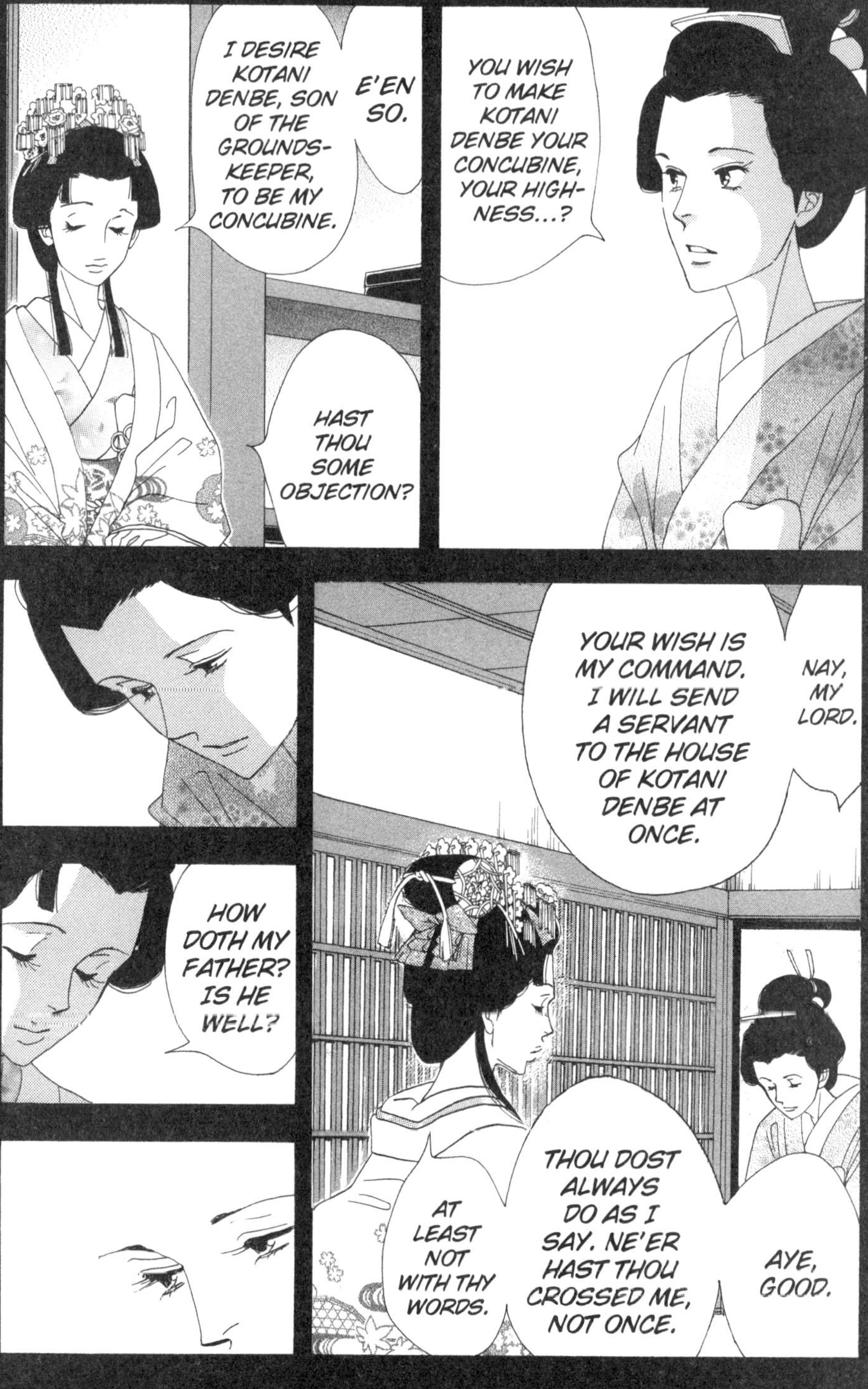
YOU WISH TO MAKE KOTANI DENBE YOUR CONCUBINE, YOUR HIGHNESS...?
E'EN SO.
I DESIRE KOTANI DENBE, SON OF THE GROUNDS-KEEPER, TO BE MY CONCUBINE.
HAST THOU SOME OBJECTION?
NAY, MY LORD.
YOUR WISH IS MY COMMAND. I WILL SEND A SERVANT TO THE HOUSE OF KOTANI DENBE AT ONCE.
AYE, GOOD.
THOU DOST ALWAYS DO AS I SAY. NE'ER HAST THOU CROSSED ME, NOT ONCE.
AT LEAST NOT WITH THY WORDS.
HOW DOTH MY FATHER? IS HE WELL?

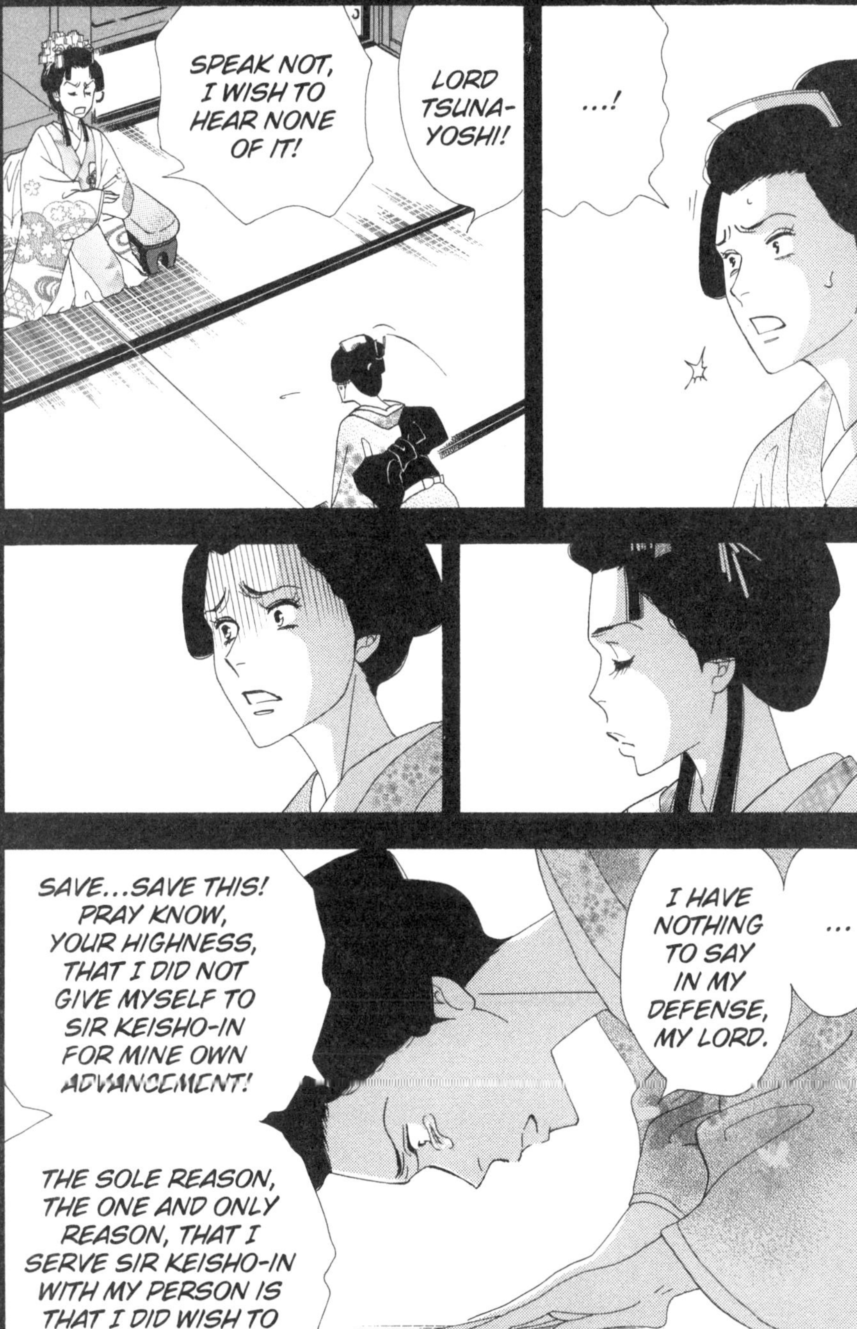
...!
LORD TSUNA-YOSHI!
SPEAK NOT, I WISH TO HEAR NONE OF IT!
...
I HAVE NOTHING TO SAY IN MY DEFENSE, MY LORD.
SAVE...SAVE THIS! PRAY KNOW, YOUR HIGHNESS, THAT I DID NOT GIVE MYSELF TO SIR KEISHO-IN FOR MINE OWN ADVANCEMENT!
THE SOLE REASON, THE ONE AND ONLY REASON, THAT I SERVE SIR KEISHO-IN WITH MY PERSON IS THAT I DID WISH TO REMAIN NEAR YOU!

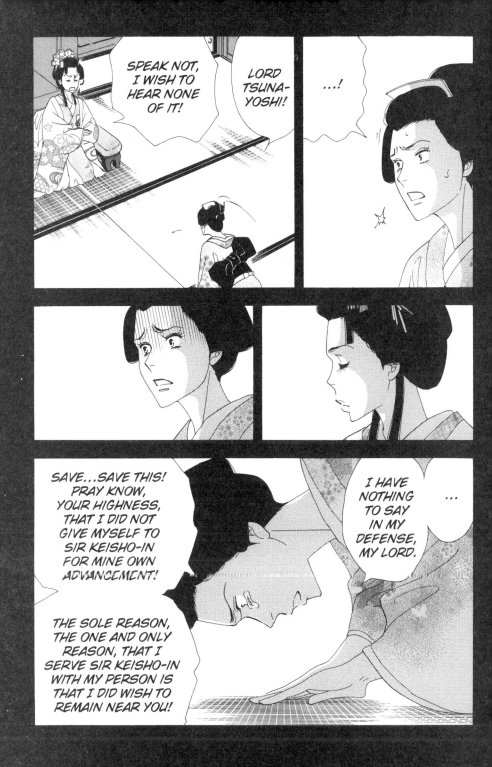

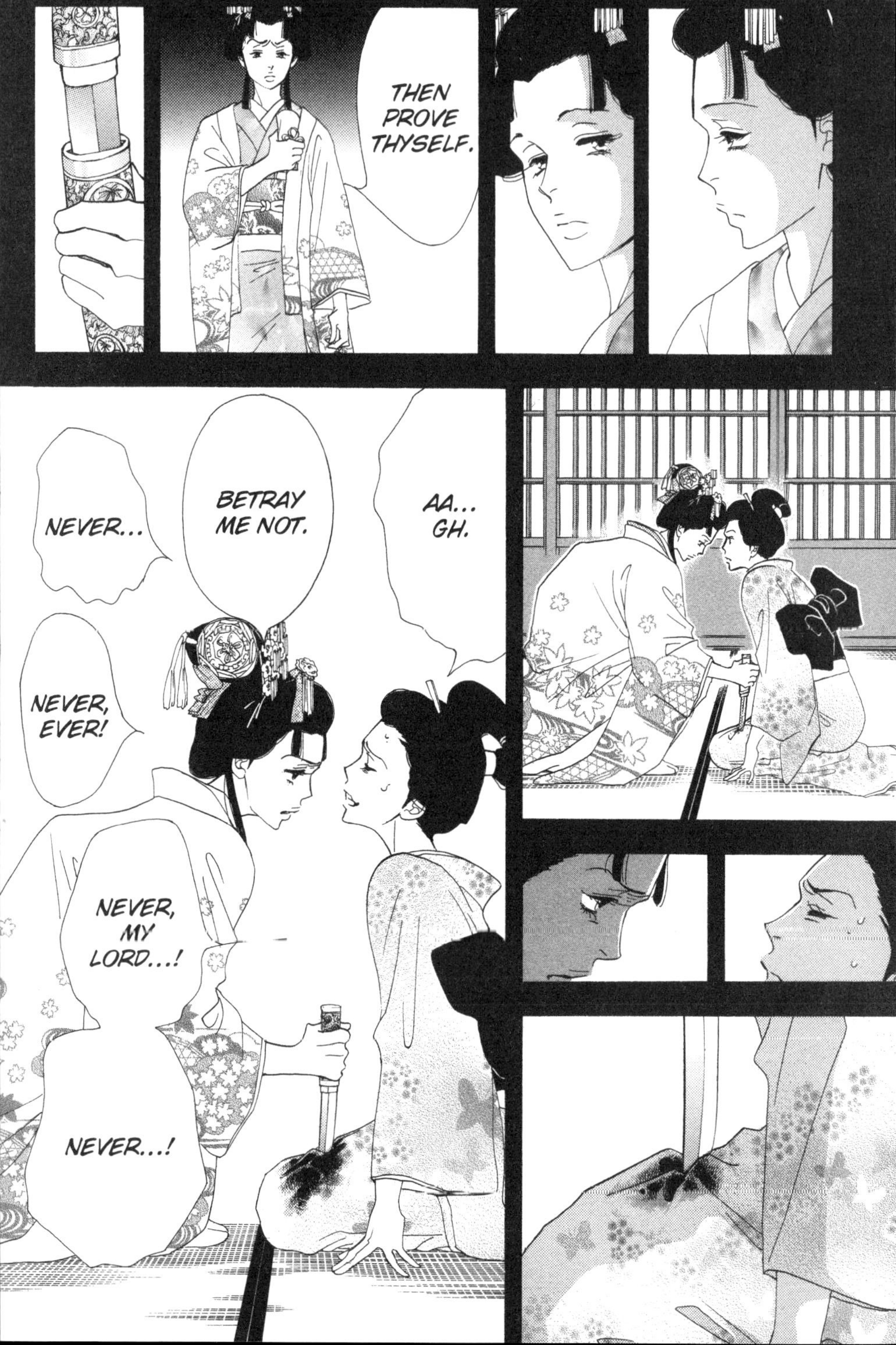
THEN PROVE THYSELF.
AA... GH.
BETRAY ME NOT.
NEVER...
NEVER, EVER!
NEVER, MY LORD...!
NEVER...!

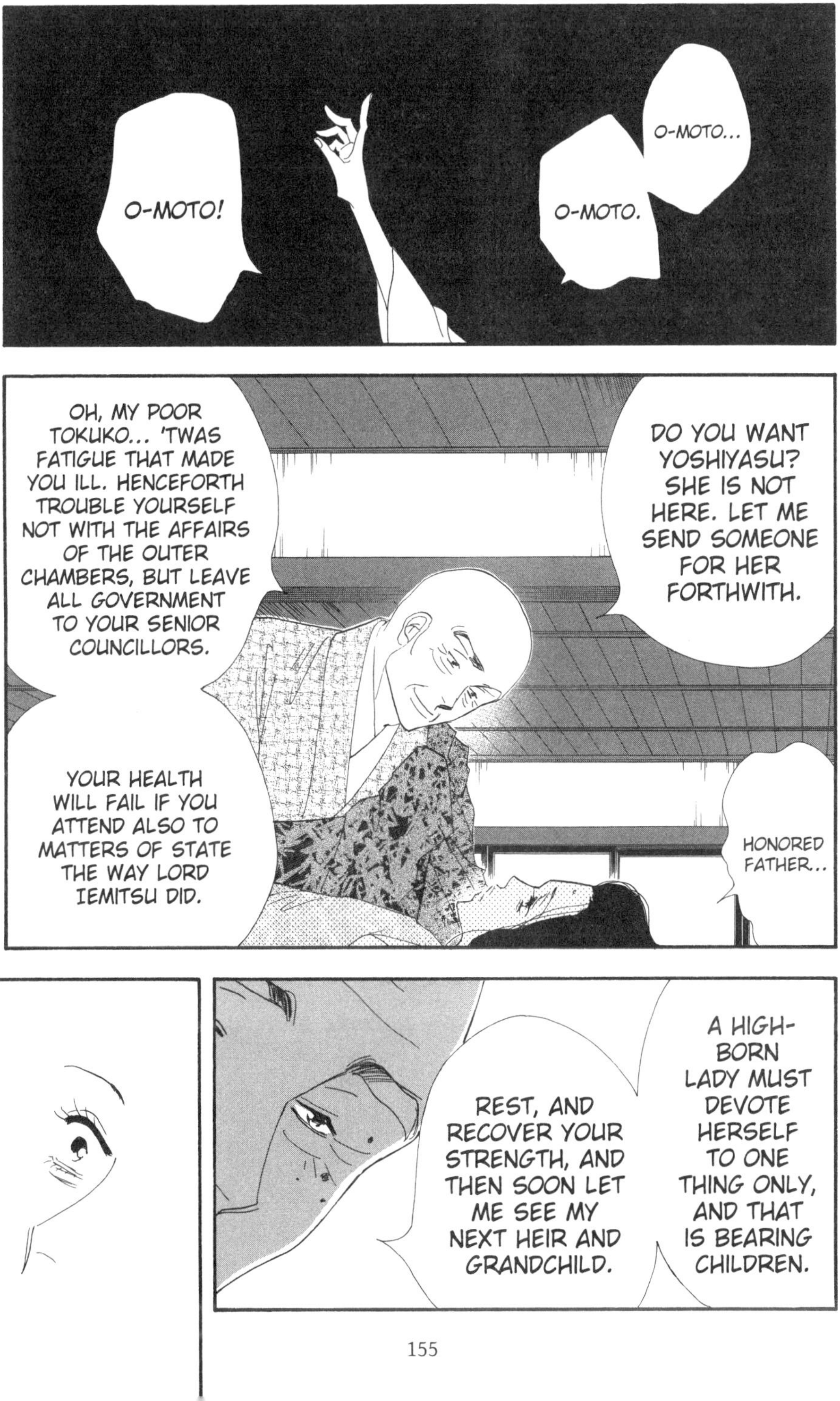
O-MOTO...
O-MOTO.
O-MOTO!
DO YOU WANT YOSHIYASU? SHE IS NOT HERE. LET ME SEND SOMEONE FOR HER FORTHWITH.
OH, MY POOR TOKUKO... 'TWAS FATIGUE THAT MADE YOU ILL. HENCEFORTH TROUBLE YOURSELF NOT WITH THE AFFAIRS OF THE OUTER CHAMBERS, BUT LEAVE ALL GOVERNMENT TO YOUR SENIOR COUNCILLORS.
HONORED FATHER...
YOUR HEALTH WILL FAIL IF YOU ATTEND ALSO TO MATTERS OF STATE THE WAY LORD IEMITSU DID.
A HIGH-BORN LADY MUST DEVOTE HERSELF TO ONE THING ONLY, AND THAT IS BEARING CHILDREN.
REST, AND RECOVER YOUR STRENGTH, AND THEN SOON LET ME SEE MY NEXT HEIR AND GRANDCHILD.

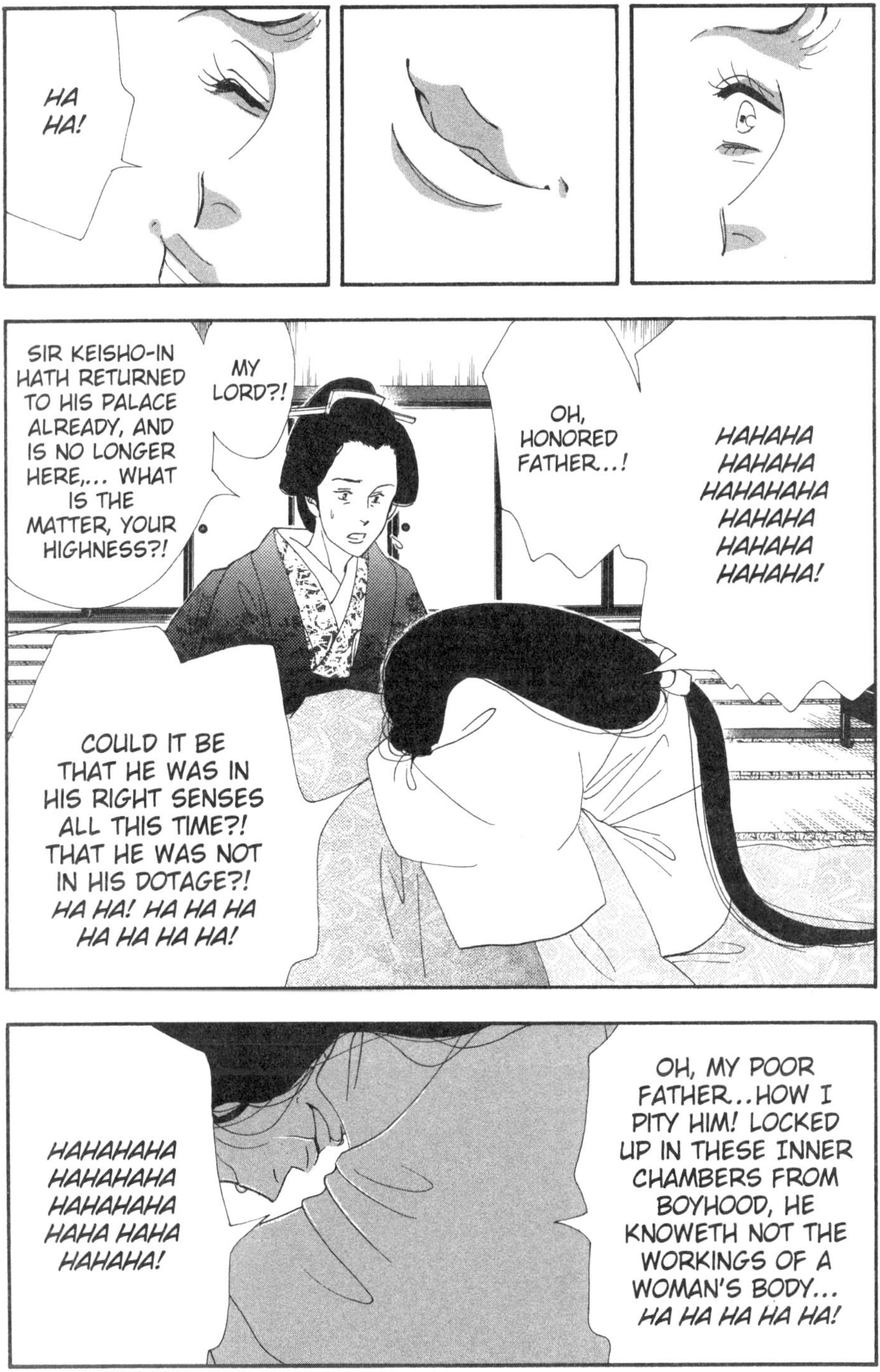
HA HA!
HAHAHA HAHAHA HAHAHAHA HAHAHA HAHAHA HAHAHA!
OH, HONORED FATHER...!
MY LORD?!
SIR KEISHO-IN HATH RETURNED TO HIS PALACE ALREADY, AND IS NO LONGER HERE,... WHAT IS THE MATTER, YOUR HIGHNESS?!
COULD IT BE THAT HE WAS IN HIS RIGHT SENSES ALL THIS TIME?! THAT HE WAS NOT IN HIS DOTAGE?! HA HA! HA HA HA HA HA HA HA!
OH, MY POOR FATHER...HOW I PITY HIM! LOCKED UP IN THESE INNER CHAMBERS FROM BOYHOOD, HE KNOWETH NOT THE WORKINGS OF A WOMAN'S BODY... HA HA HA HA HA!
HAHAHAHA HAHAHAHA HAHAHAHA HAHA HAHA HAHAHA!

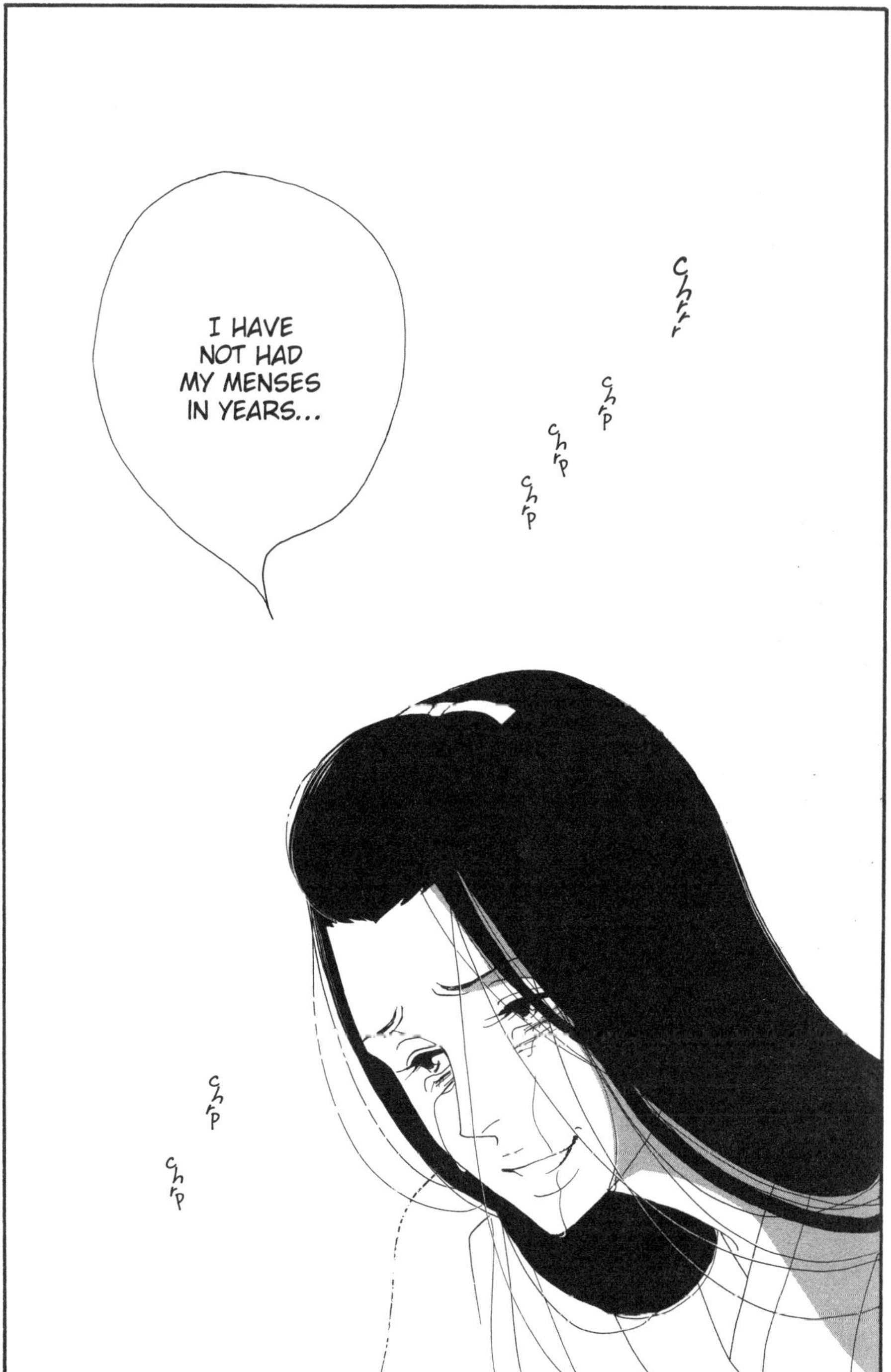
I HAVE NOT HAD MY MENSES IN YEARS...
Chrrr
Chrp
Chrp
Chrp
Chrp
Chrp

Ōoku
THE INNER CHAMBERS

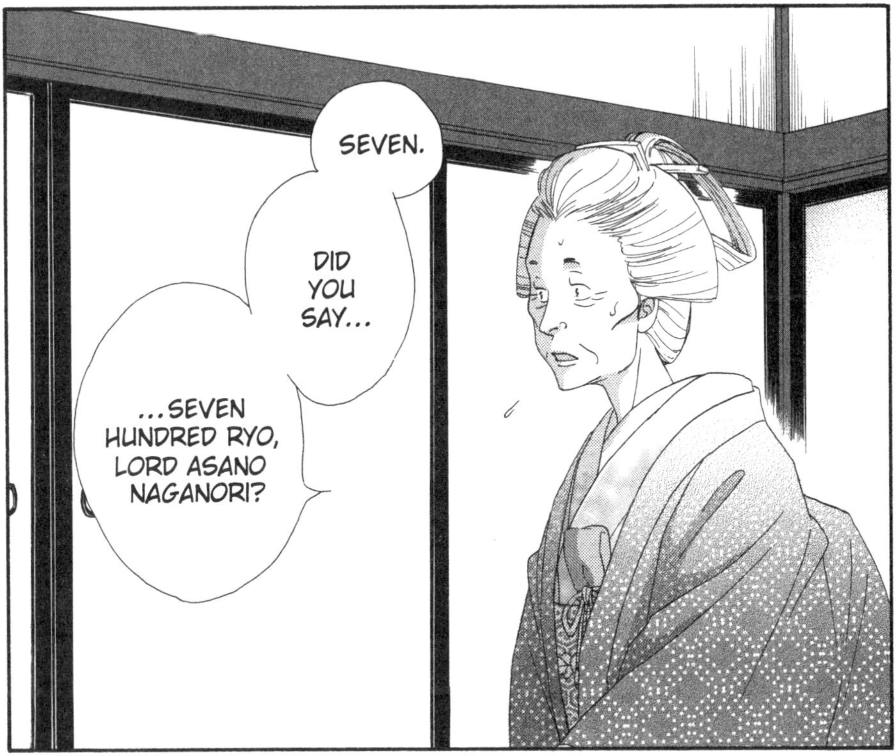
SEVEN.
DID YOU SAY...
...SEVEN HUNDRED RYO, LORD ASANO NAGANORI?

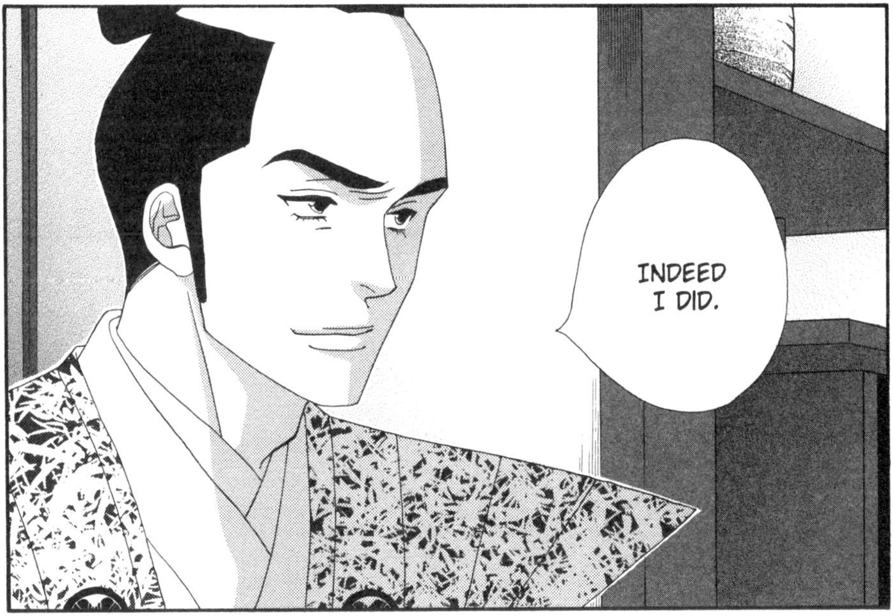
INDEED I DID.

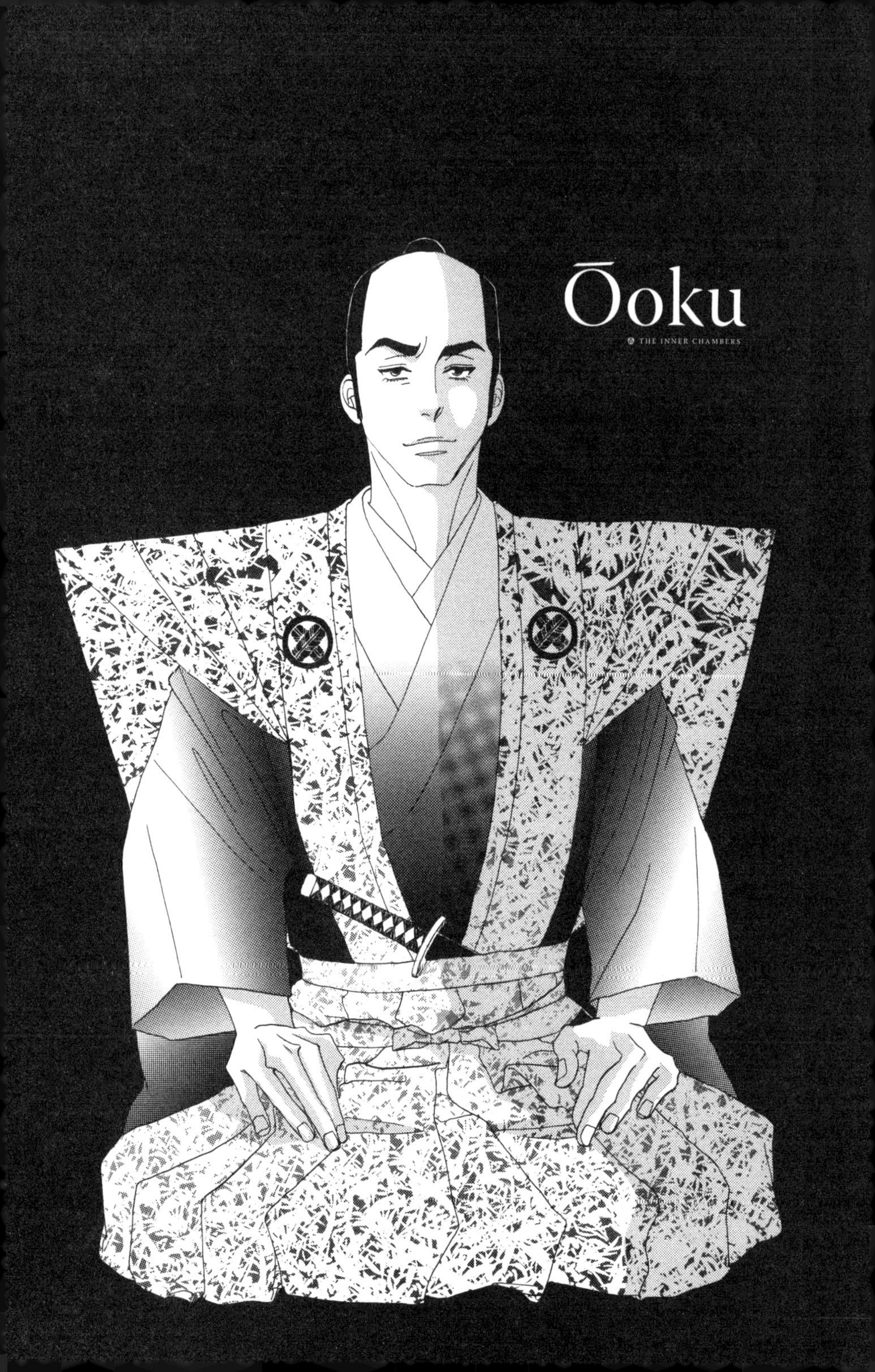

Ōoku
THE INNER CHAMBERS

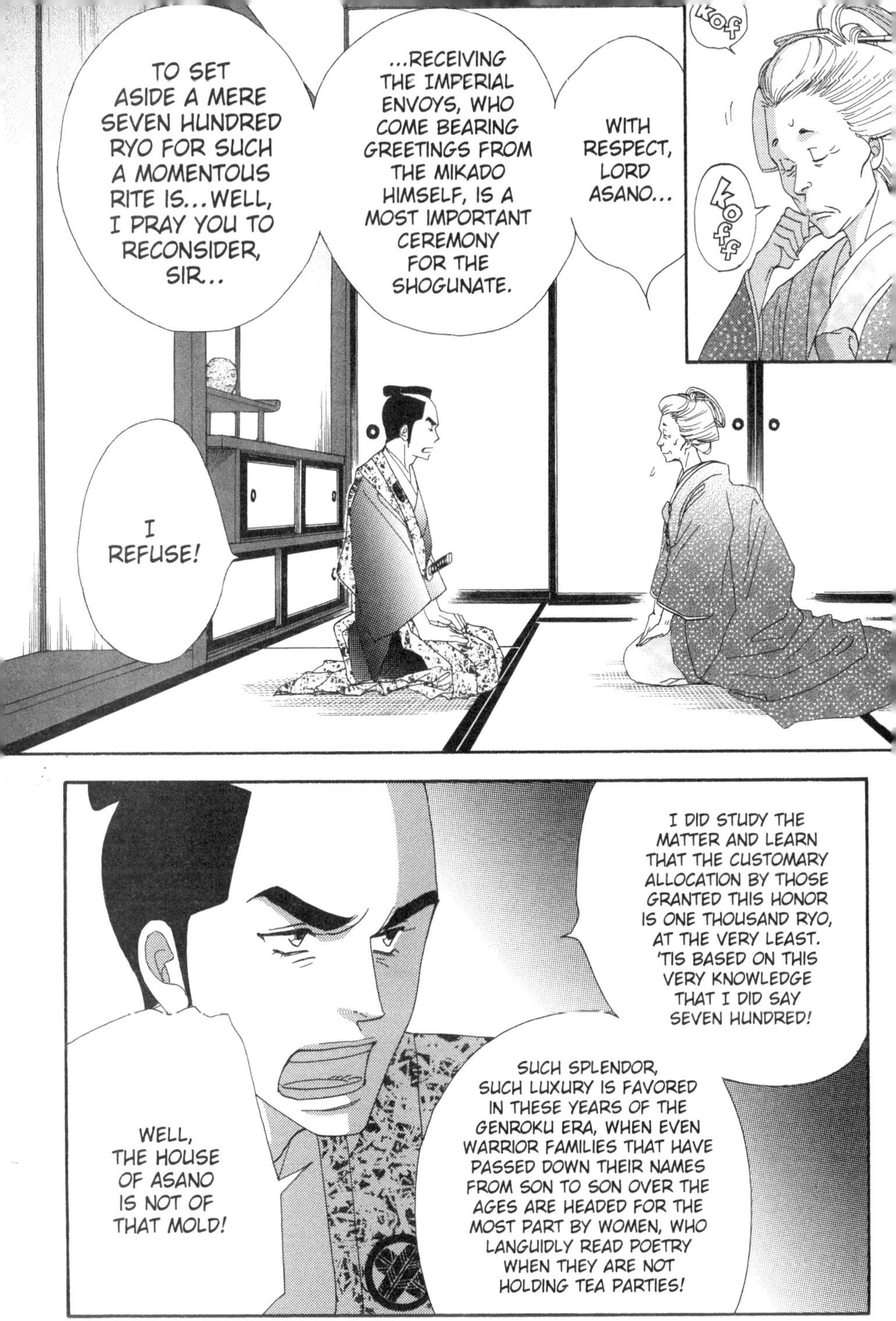
KOF
KOFF
WITH RESPECT, LORD ASANO...
...RECEIVING THE IMPERIAL ENVOYS, WHO COME BEARING GREETINGS FROM THE MIKADO HIMSELF, IS A MOST IMPORTANT CEREMONY FOR THE SHOGUNATE.
TO SET ASIDE A MERE SEVEN HUNDRED RYO FOR SUCH A MOMENTOUS RITE IS...WELL, I PRAY YOU TO RECONSIDER, SIR...
I REFUSE!
I DID STUDY THE MATTER AND LEARN THAT THE CUSTOMARY ALLOCATION BY THOSE GRANTED THIS HONOR IS ONE THOUSAND RYO, AT THE VERY LEAST. 'TIS BASED ON THIS VERY KNOWLEDGE THAT I DID SAY SEVEN HUNDRED!
SUCH SPLENDOR, SUCH LUXURY IS FAVORED IN THESE YEARS OF THE GENROKU ERA, WHEN EVEN WARRIOR FAMILIES THAT HAVE PASSED DOWN THEIR NAMES FROM SON TO SON OVER THE AGES ARE HEADED FOR THE MOST PART BY WOMEN, WHO LANGUIDLY READ POETRY WHEN THEY ARE NOT HOLDING TEA PARTIES!
WELL, THE HOUSE OF ASANO IS NOT OF THAT MOLD!

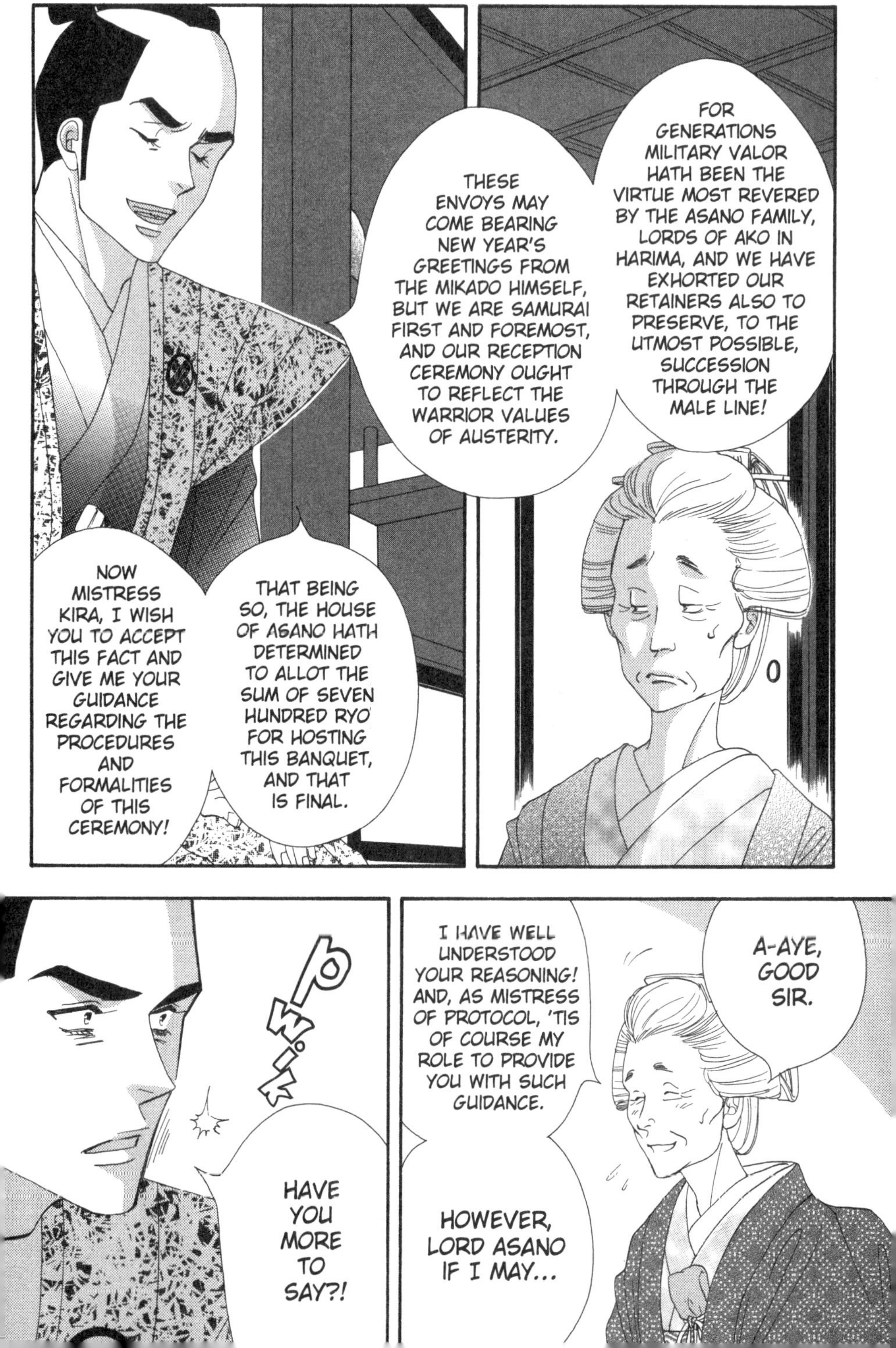
FOR GENERATIONS MILITARY VALOR HATH BEEN THE VIRTUE MOST REVERED BY THE ASANO FAMILY, LORDS OF AKO IN HARIMA, AND WE HAVE EXHORTED OUR RETAINERS ALSO TO PRESERVE, TO THE UTMOST POSSIBLE, SUCCESSION THROUGH THE MALE LINE!
THESE ENVOYS MAY COME BEARING NEW YEAR'S GREETINGS FROM THE MIKADO HIMSELF, BUT WE ARE SAMURAI FIRST AND FOREMOST, AND OUR RECEPTION CEREMONY OUGHT TO REFLECT THE WARRIOR VALUES OF AUSTERITY.
O
THAT BEING SO, THE HOUSE OF ASANO HATH DETERMINED TO ALLOT THE SUM OF SEVEN HUNDRED RYO FOR HOSTING THIS BANQUET, AND THAT IS FINAL.
NOW MISTRESS KIRA, I WISH YOU TO ACCEPT THIS FACT AND GIVE ME YOUR GUIDANCE REGARDING THE PROCEDURES AND FORMALITIES OF THIS CEREMONY!
A-AYE, GOOD SIR.
I HAVE WELL UNDERSTOOD YOUR REASONING! AND, AS MISTRESS OF PROTOCOL, 'TIS OF COURSE MY ROLE TO PROVIDE YOU WITH SUCH GUIDANCE.
HOWEVER, LORD ASANO IF I MAY...
HAVE YOU MORE TO SAY?!

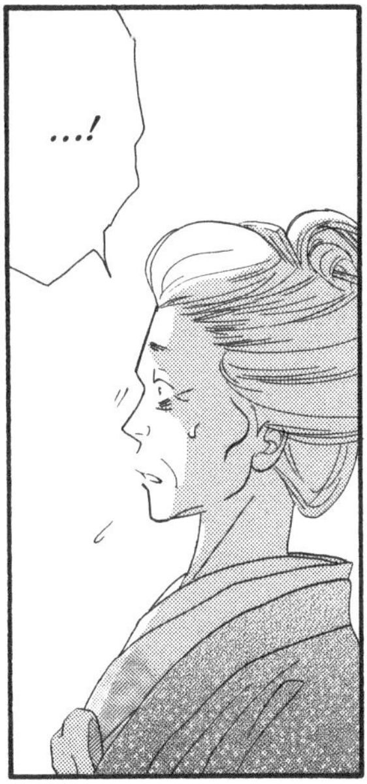
...!

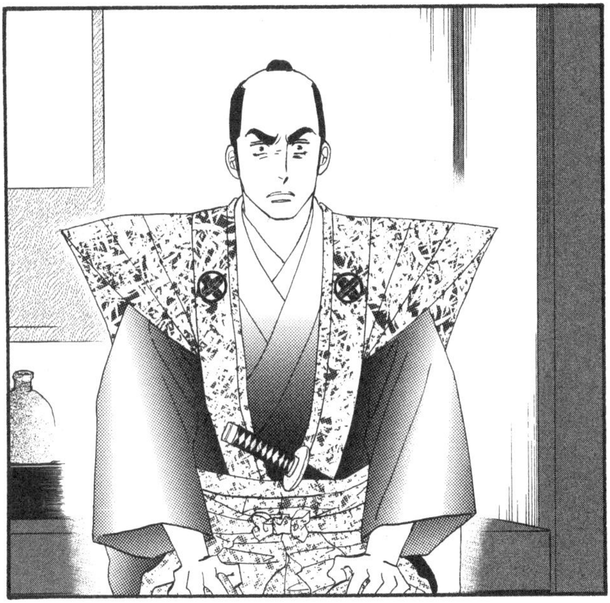

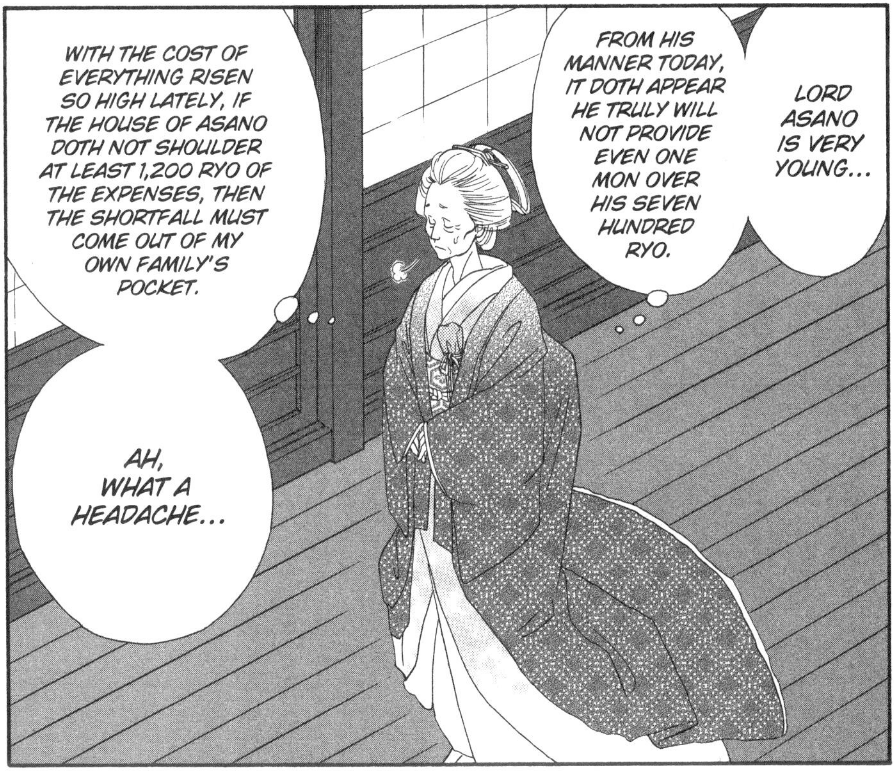
LORD ASANO IS VERY YOUNG...
FROM HIS MANNER TODAY, IT DOTH APPEAR HE TRULY WILL NOT PROVIDE EVEN ONE MON OVER HIS SEVEN HUNDRED RYO.
WITH THE COST OF EVERYTHING RISEN SO HIGH LATELY, IF THE HOUSE OF ASANO DOTH NOT SHOULDER AT LEAST 1,200 RYO OF THE EXPENSES, THEN THE SHORTFALL MUST COME OUT OF MY OWN FAMILY'S POCKET.
AH, WHAT A HEADACHE...

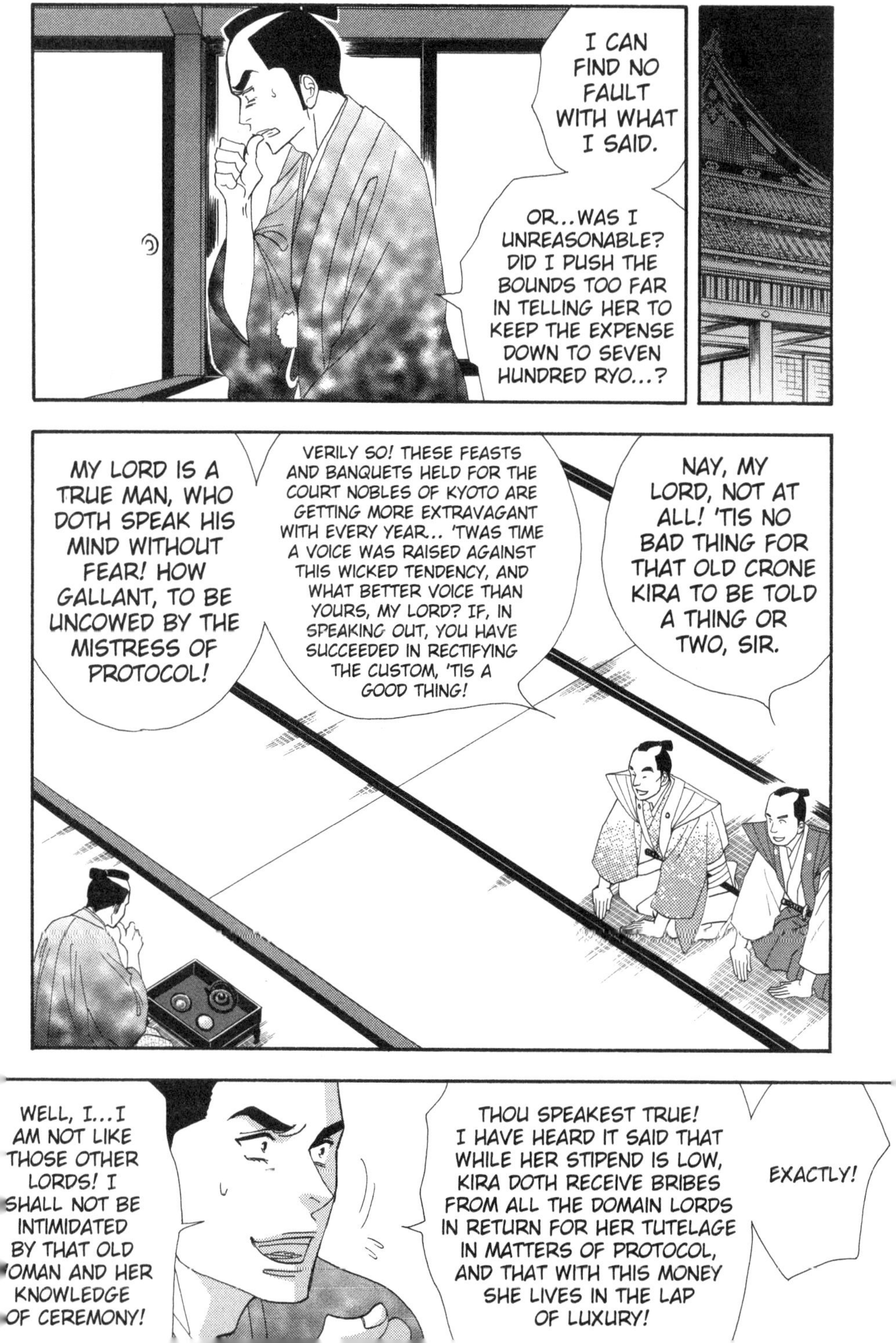
I CAN FIND NO FAULT WITH WHAT I SAID.
OR...WAS I UNREASONABLE? DID I PUSH THE BOUNDS TOO FAR IN TELLING HER TO KEEP THE EXPENSE DOWN TO SEVEN HUNDRED RYO...?
NAY, MY LORD, NOT AT ALL! 'TIS NO BAD THING FOR THAT OLD CRONE KIRA TO BE TOLD A THING OR TWO, SIR.
VERILY SO! THESE FEASTS AND BANQUETS HELD FOR THE COURT NOBLES OF KYOTO ARE GETTING MORE EXTRAVAGANT WITH EVERY YEAR... 'TWAS TIME A VOICE WAS RAISED AGAINST THIS WICKED TENDENCY, AND WHAT BETTER VOICE THAN YOURS, MY LORD? IF, IN SPEAKING OUT, YOU HAVE SUCCEEDED IN RECTIFYING THE CUSTOM, 'TIS A GOOD THING!
MY LORD IS A TRUE MAN, WHO DOTH SPEAK HIS MIND WITHOUT FEAR! HOW GALLANT, TO BE UNCOWED BY THE MISTRESS OF PROTOCOL!
EXACTLY!
THOU SPEAKEST TRUE! I HAVE HEARD IT SAID THAT WHILE HER STIPEND IS LOW, KIRA DOTH RECEIVE BRIBES FROM ALL THE DOMAIN LORDS IN RETURN FOR HER TUTELAGE IN MATTERS OF PROTOCOL, AND THAT WITH THIS MONEY SHE LIVES IN THE LAP OF LUXURY!
WELL, I...I AM NOT LIKE THOSE OTHER LORDS! I SHALL NOT BE INTIMIDATED BY THAT OLD OMAN AND HER KNOWLEDGE OF CEREMONY!

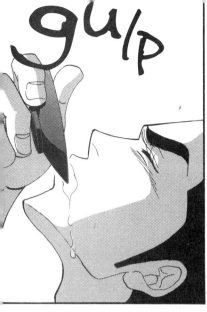

AND IF SHE DOTH BEAR A GRUDGE AGAINST ME FOR'T, AND TRY TO SPITE ME, LET HER DO WHAT SHE WILL—I CARE NOT!

HA HA HA!

A MESSENGER HATH JUST COME FROM THE KIRA MANSE WITH AN URGENT COMMUNICATION FOR MY LORD, AND 'TIS TERRIBLE NEWS!

MY LORD!

But then...

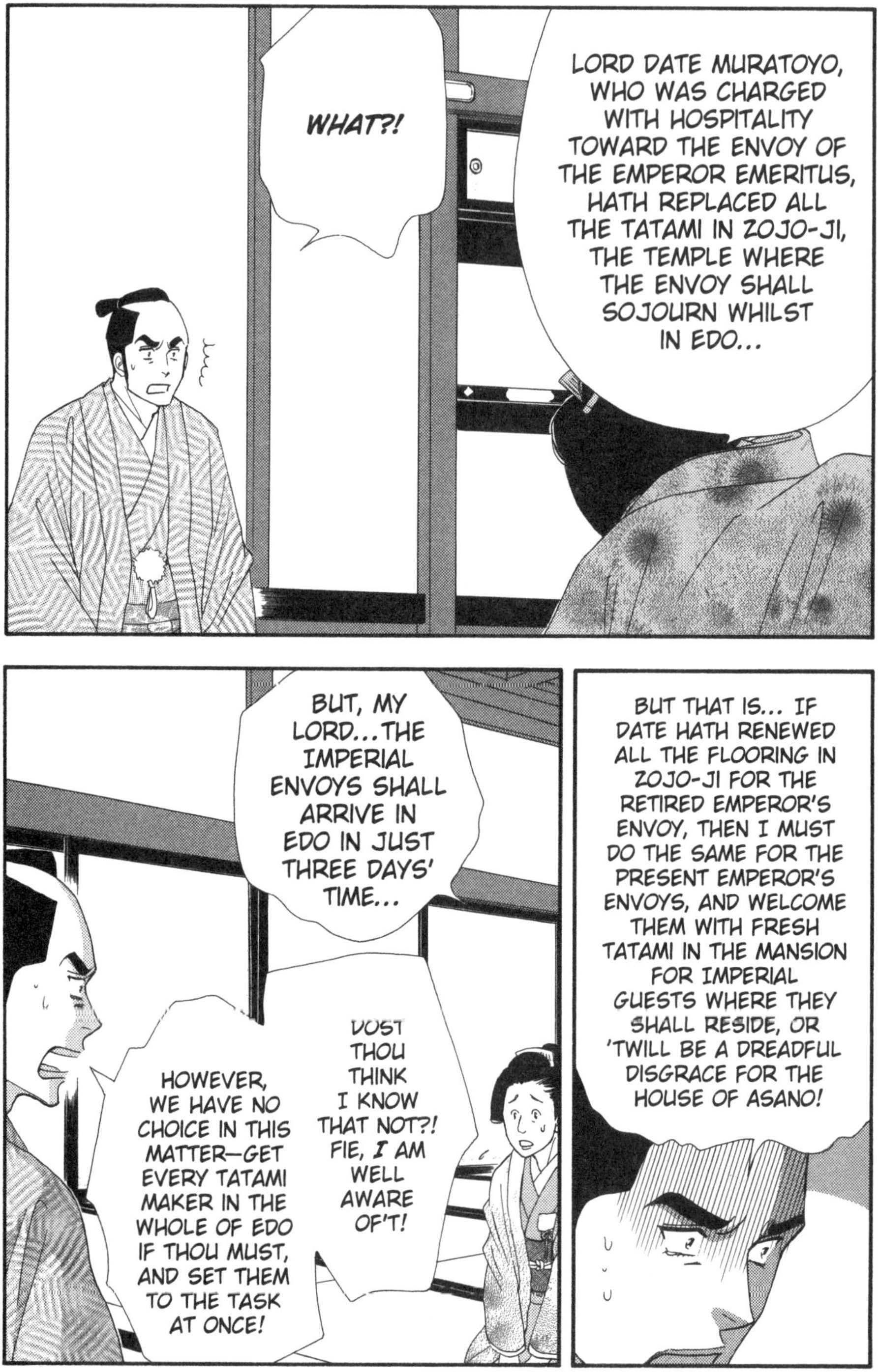
LORD DATE MURATOYO, WHO WAS CHARGED WITH HOSPITALITY TOWARD THE ENVOY OF THE EMPEROR EMERITUS, HATH REPLACED ALL THE TATAMI IN ZOJO-JI, THE TEMPLE WHERE THE ENVOY SHALL SOJOURN WHILST IN EDO...
WHAT?!
BUT THAT IS... IF DATE HATH RENEWED ALL THE FLOORING IN ZOJO-JI FOR THE RETIRED EMPEROR'S ENVOY, THEN I MUST DO THE SAME FOR THE PRESENT EMPEROR'S ENVOYS, AND WELCOME THEM WITH FRESH TATAMI IN THE MANSION FOR IMPERIAL GUESTS WHERE THEY SHALL RESIDE, OR 'TWILL BE A DREADFUL DISGRACE FOR THE HOUSE OF ASANO!
BUT, MY LORD...THE IMPERIAL ENVOYS SHALL ARRIVE IN EDO IN JUST THREE DAYS' TIME...
DOST THOU THINK I KNOW THAT NOT?! FIE, *I* AM WELL AWARE OF'T!
HOWEVER, WE HAVE NO CHOICE IN THIS MATTER—GET EVERY TATAMI MAKER IN THE WHOLE OF EDO IF THOU MUST, AND SET THEM TO THE TASK AT ONCE!

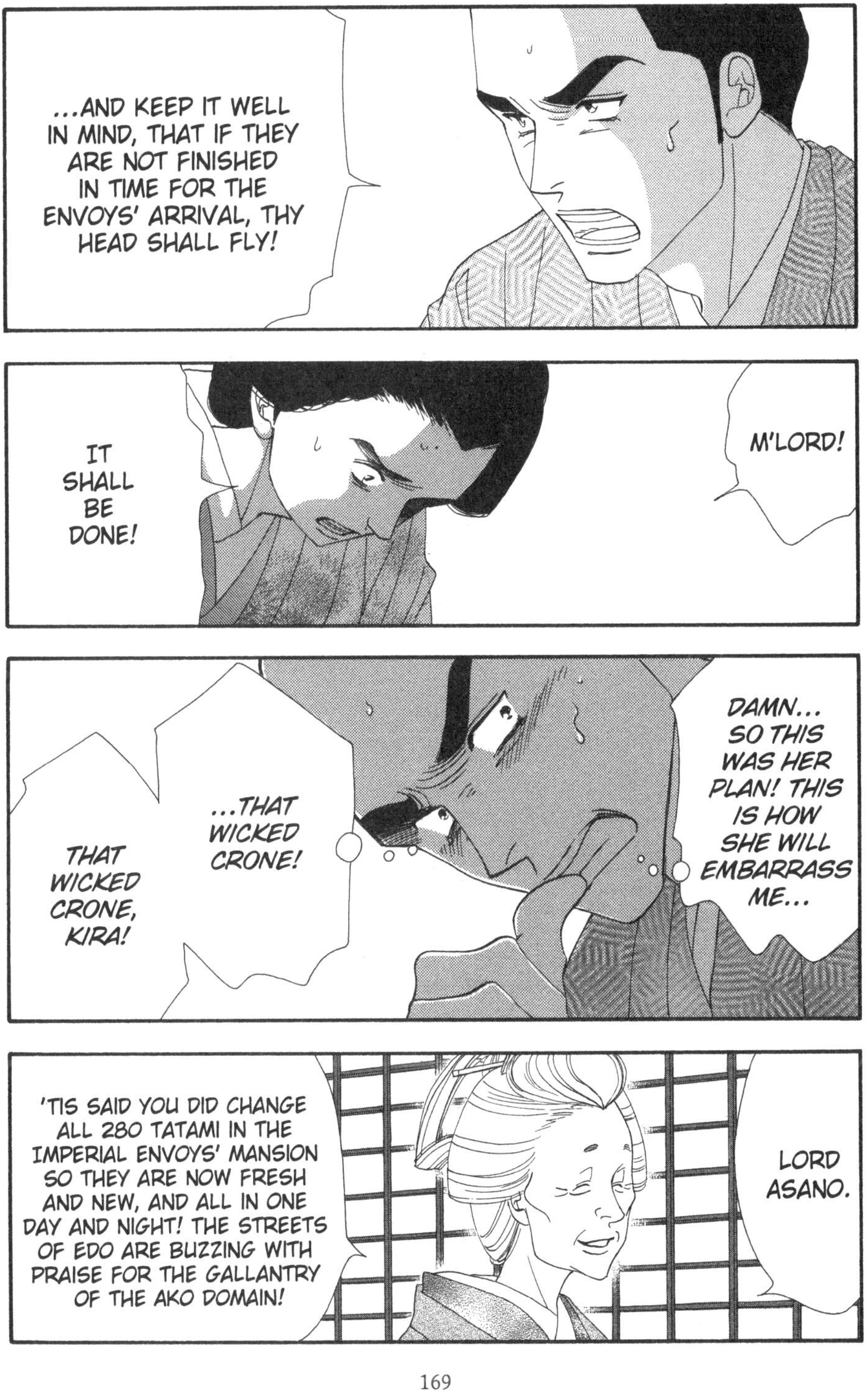
...AND KEEP IT WELL IN MIND, THAT IF THEY ARE NOT FINISHED IN TIME FOR THE ENVOYS' ARRIVAL, THY HEAD SHALL FLY!
M'LORD!
IT SHALL BE DONE!
DAMN... SO THIS WAS HER PLAN! THIS IS HOW SHE WILL EMBARRASS ME...
...THAT WICKED CRONE!
THAT WICKED CRONE, KIRA!
LORD ASANO.
'TIS SAID YOU DID CHANGE ALL 280 TATAMI IN THE IMPERIAL ENVOYS' MANSION SO THEY ARE NOW FRESH AND NEW, AND ALL IN ONE DAY AND NIGHT! THE STREETS OF EDO ARE BUZZING WITH PRAISE FOR THE GALLANTRY OF THE AKO DOMAIN!

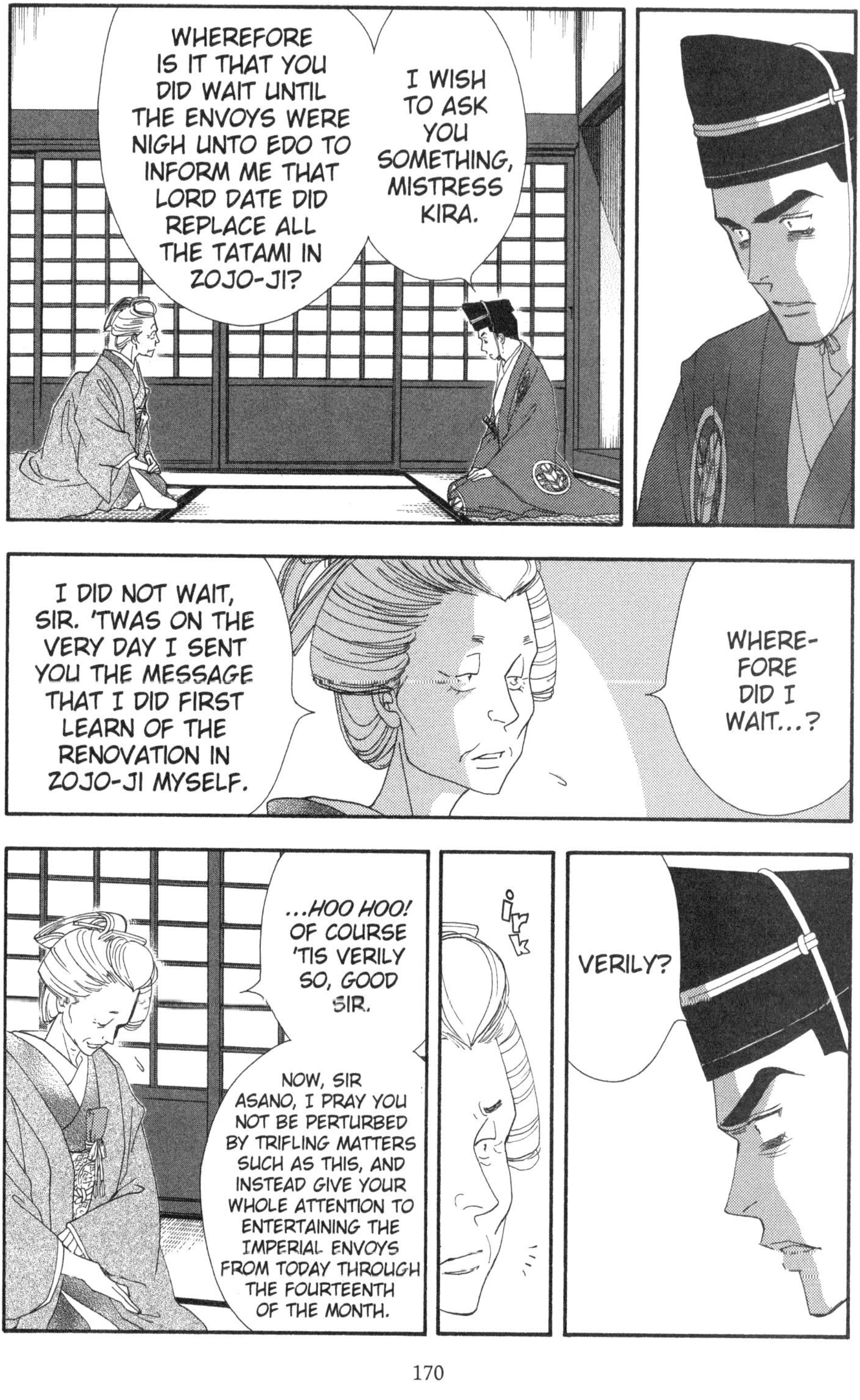
I WISH TO ASK YOU SOMETHING, MISTRESS KIRA.
WHEREFORE IS IT THAT YOU DID WAIT UNTIL THE ENVOYS WERE NIGH UNTO EDO TO INFORM ME THAT LORD DATE DID REPLACE ALL THE TATAMI IN ZOJO-JI?
WHEREFORE DID I WAIT...?
I DID NOT WAIT, SIR. 'TWAS ON THE VERY DAY I SENT YOU THE MESSAGE THAT I DID FIRST LEARN OF THE RENOVATION IN ZOJO-JI MYSELF.
VERILY?
irk
...HOO HOO! OF COURSE 'TIS VERILY SO, GOOD SIR.
NOW, SIR ASANO, I PRAY YOU NOT BE PERTURBED BY TRIFLING MATTERS SUCH AS THIS, AND INSTEAD GIVE YOUR WHOLE ATTENTION TO ENTERTAINING THE IMPERIAL ENVOYS FROM TODAY THROUGH THE FOURTEENTH OF THE MONTH.

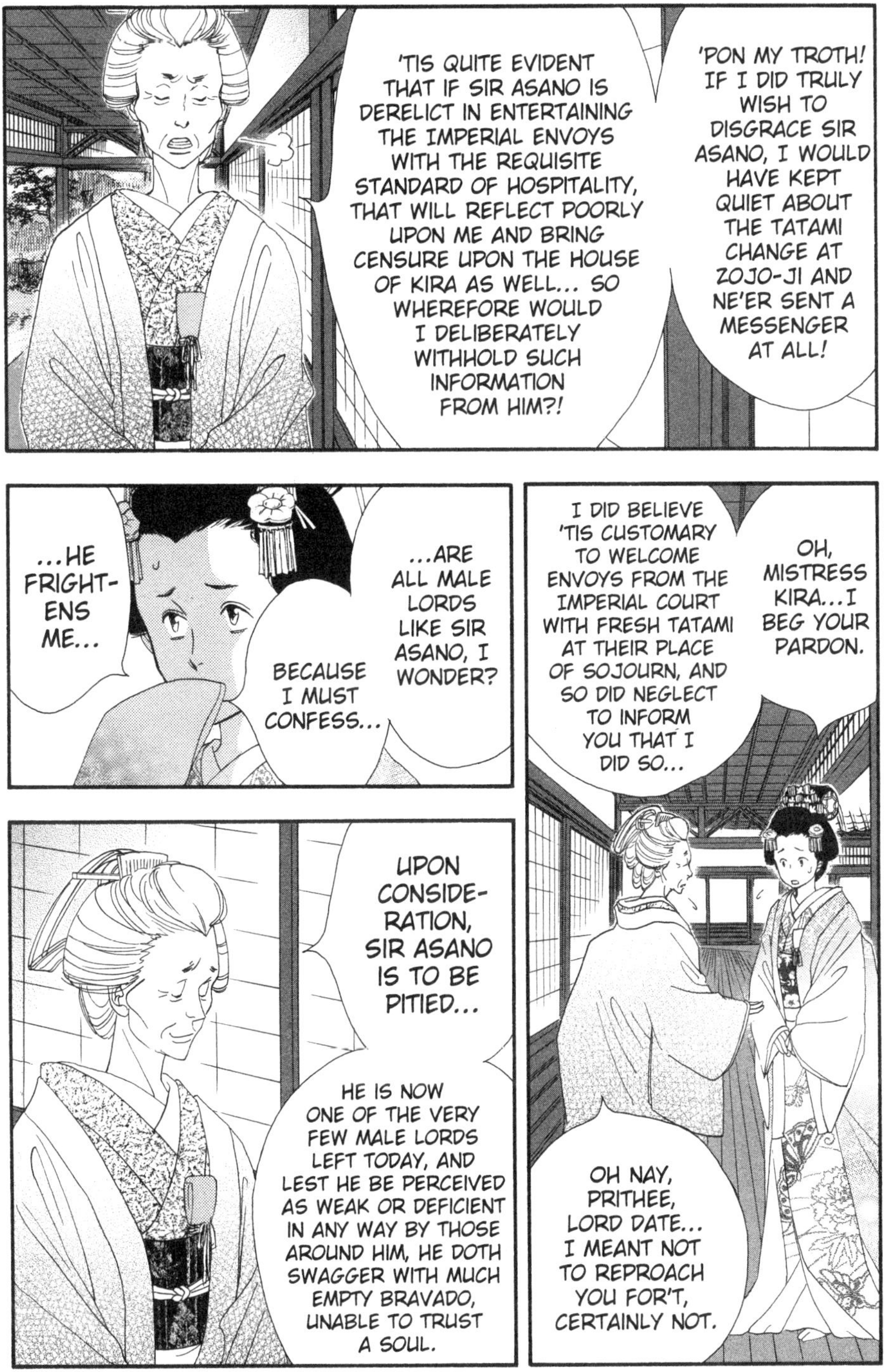
'PON MY TROTH! IF I DID TRULY WISH TO DISGRACE SIR ASANO, I WOULD HAVE KEPT QUIET ABOUT THE TATAMI CHANGE AT ZOJO-JI AND NE'ER SENT A MESSENGER AT ALL!
'TIS QUITE EVIDENT THAT IF SIR ASANO IS DERELICT IN ENTERTAINING THE IMPERIAL ENVOYS WITH THE REQUISITE STANDARD OF HOSPITALITY, THAT WILL REFLECT POORLY UPON ME AND BRING CENSURE UPON THE HOUSE OF KIRA AS WELL... SO WHEREFORE WOULD I DELIBERATELY WITHHOLD SUCH INFORMATION FROM HIM?!
OH, MISTRESS KIRA...I BEG YOUR PARDON.
I DID BELIEVE 'TIS CUSTOMARY TO WELCOME ENVOYS FROM THE IMPERIAL COURT WITH FRESH TATAMI AT THEIR PLACE OF SOJOURN, AND SO DID NEGLECT TO INFORM YOU THAT I DID SO...
OH NAY, PRITHEE, LORD DATE... I MEANT NOT TO REPROACH YOU FOR'T, CERTAINLY NOT.
...ARE ALL MALE LORDS LIKE SIR ASANO, I WONDER?
BECAUSE I MUST CONFESS...
...HE FRIGHT-ENS ME...
UPON CONSIDE-RATION, SIR ASANO IS TO BE PITIED...
HE IS NOW ONE OF THE VERY FEW MALE LORDS LEFT TODAY, AND LEST HE BE PERCEIVED AS WEAK OR DEFICIENT IN ANY WAY BY THOSE AROUND HIM, HE DOTH SWAGGER WITH MUCH EMPTY BRAVADO, UNABLE TO TRUST A SOUL.

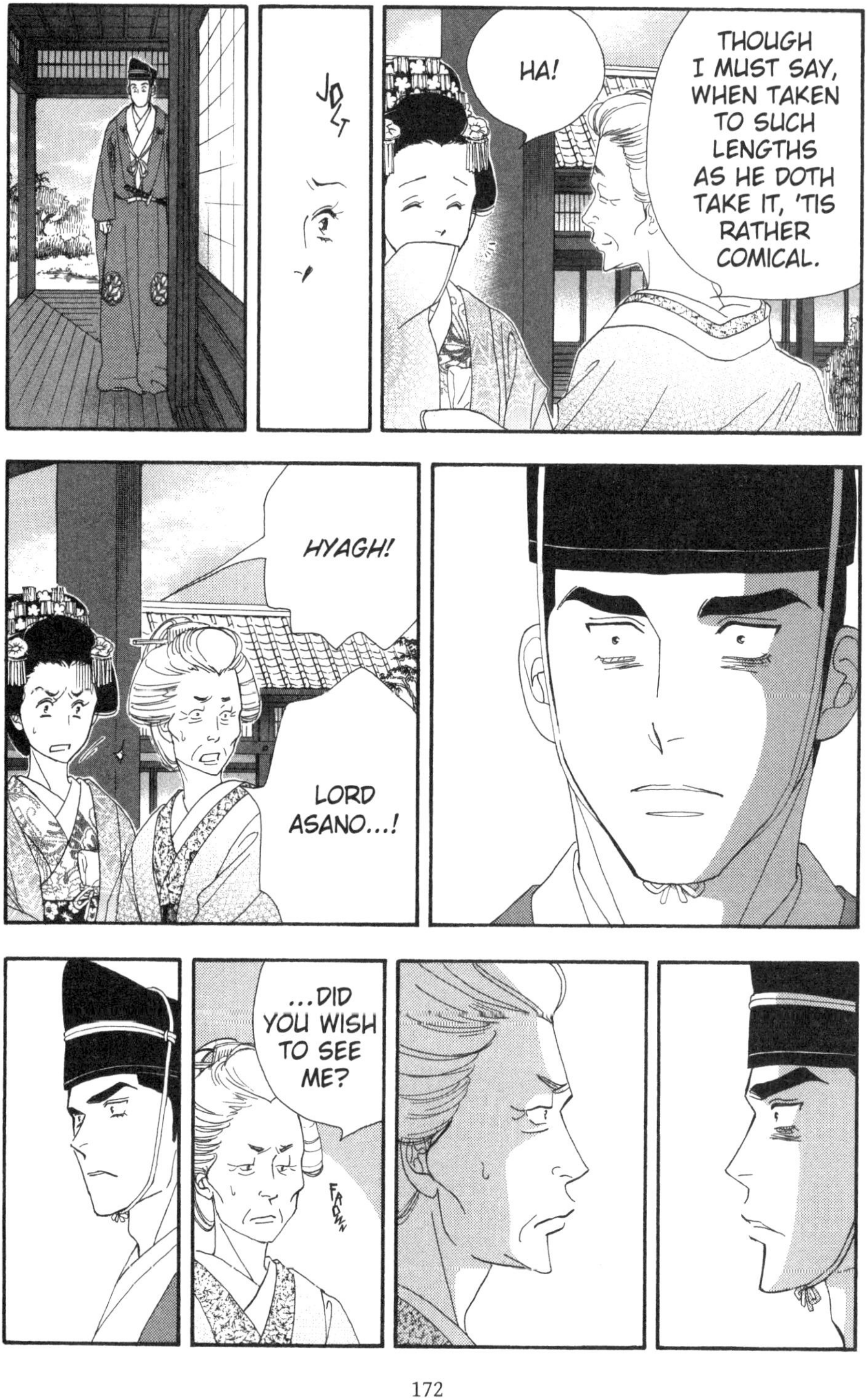
THOUGH I MUST SAY, WHEN TAKEN TO SUCH LENGTHS AS HE DOTH TAKE IT, 'TIS RATHER COMICAL.
HA!
JOLT
HYAGH!
LORD ASANO...!
...DID YOU WISH TO SEE ME?
FROWN

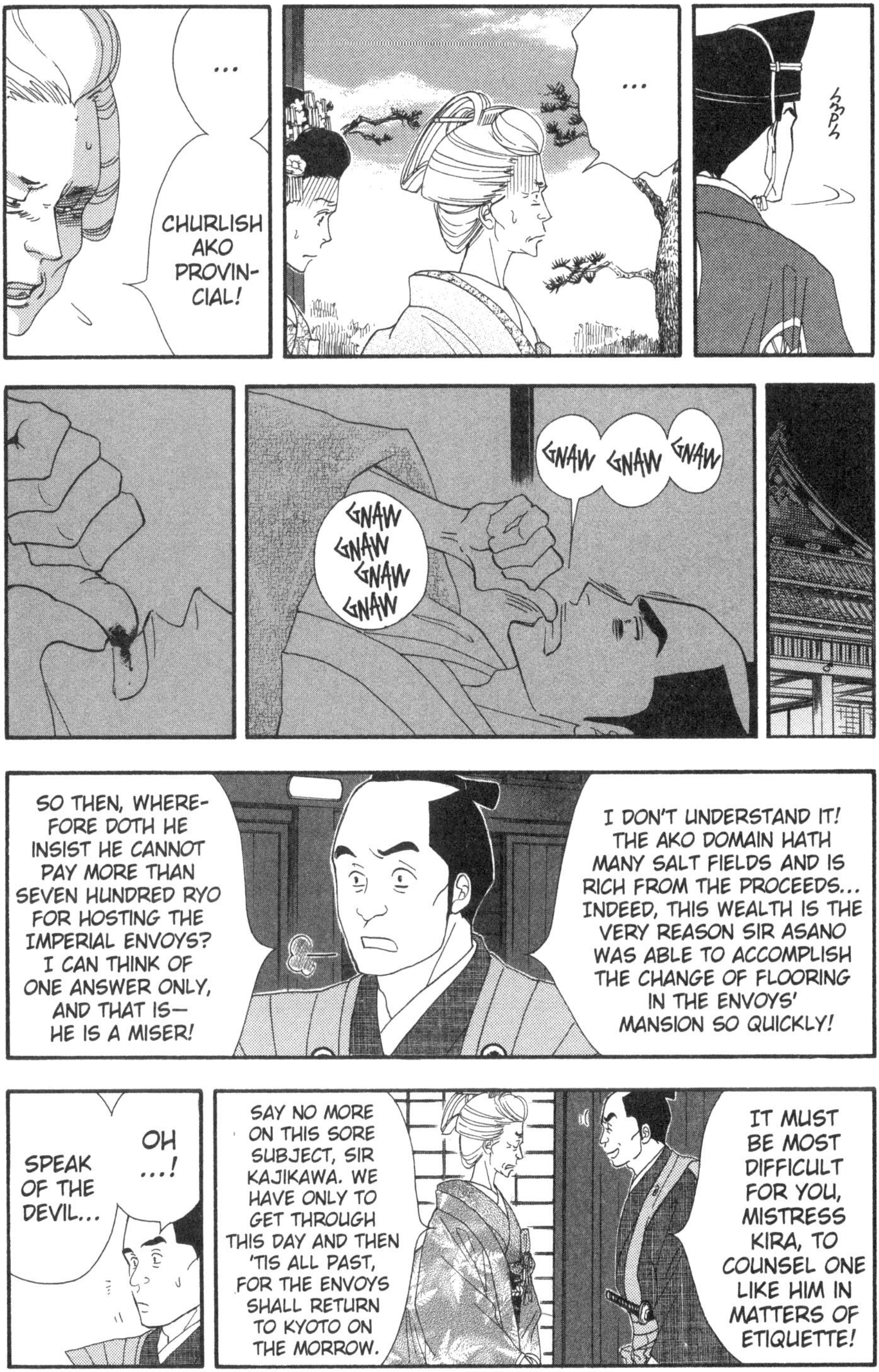
...
...
CHURLISH AKO PROVINCIAL!
GNAW GNAW GNAW
GNAW GNAW GNAW GNAW
I DON'T UNDERSTAND IT! THE AKO DOMAIN HATH MANY SALT FIELDS AND IS RICH FROM THE PROCEEDS... INDEED, THIS WEALTH IS THE VERY REASON SIR ASANO WAS ABLE TO ACCOMPLISH THE CHANGE OF FLOORING IN THE ENVOYS' MANSION SO QUICKLY!
SO THEN, WHEREFORE DOTH HE INSIST HE CANNOT PAY MORE THAN SEVEN HUNDRED RYO FOR HOSTING THE IMPERIAL ENVOYS? I CAN THINK OF ONE ANSWER ONLY, AND THAT IS— HE IS A MISER!
IT MUST BE MOST DIFFICULT FOR YOU, MISTRESS KIRA, TO COUNSEL ONE LIKE HIM IN MATTERS OF ETIQUETTE!
SAY NO MORE ON THIS SORE SUBJECT, SIR KAJIKAWA. WE HAVE ONLY TO GET THROUGH THIS DAY AND THEN 'TIS ALL PAST, FOR THE ENVOYS SHALL RETURN TO KYOTO ON THE MORROW.
OH ...!
SPEAK OF THE DEVIL...

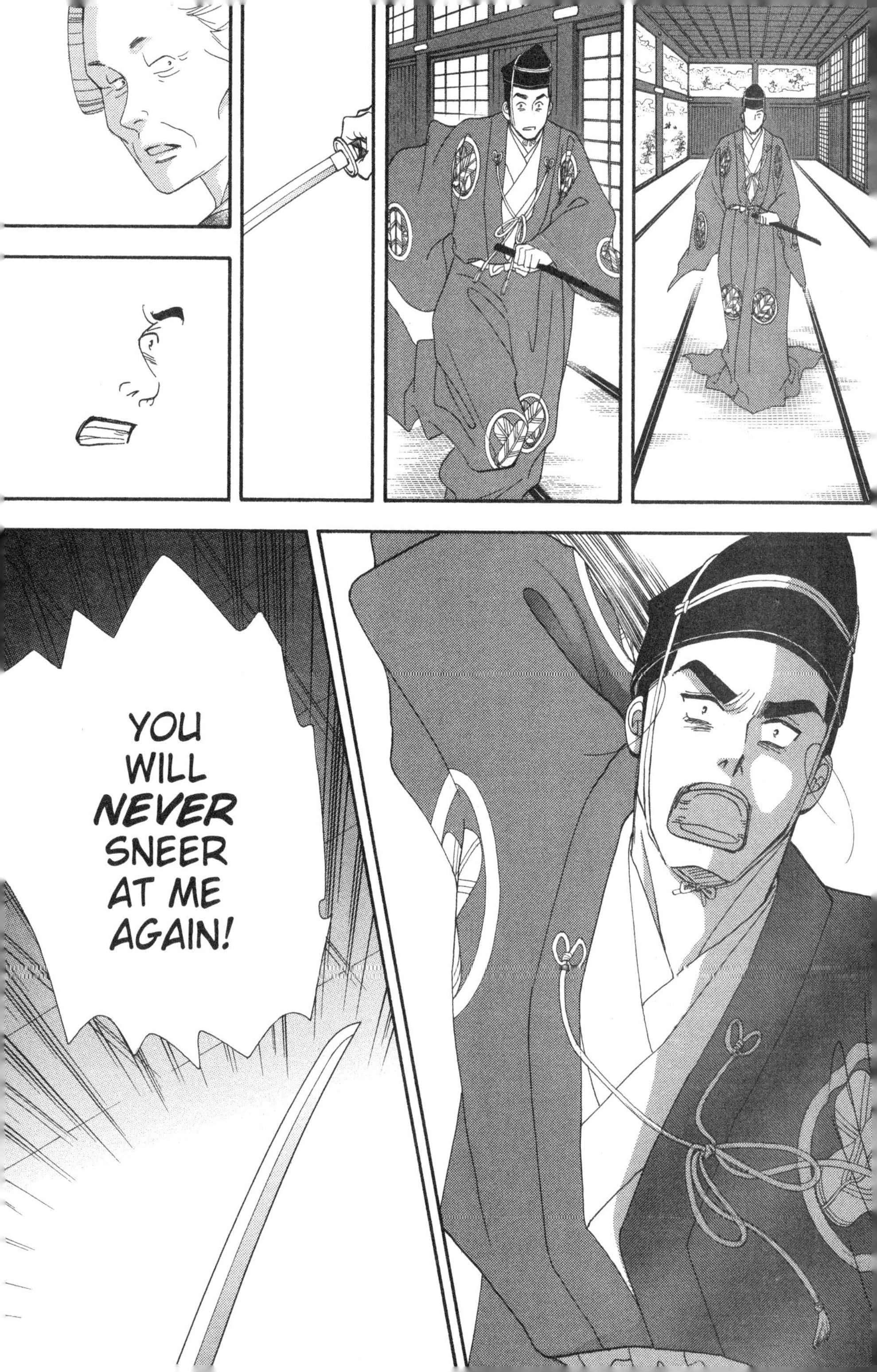
YOU WILL NEVER SNEER AT ME AGAIN!

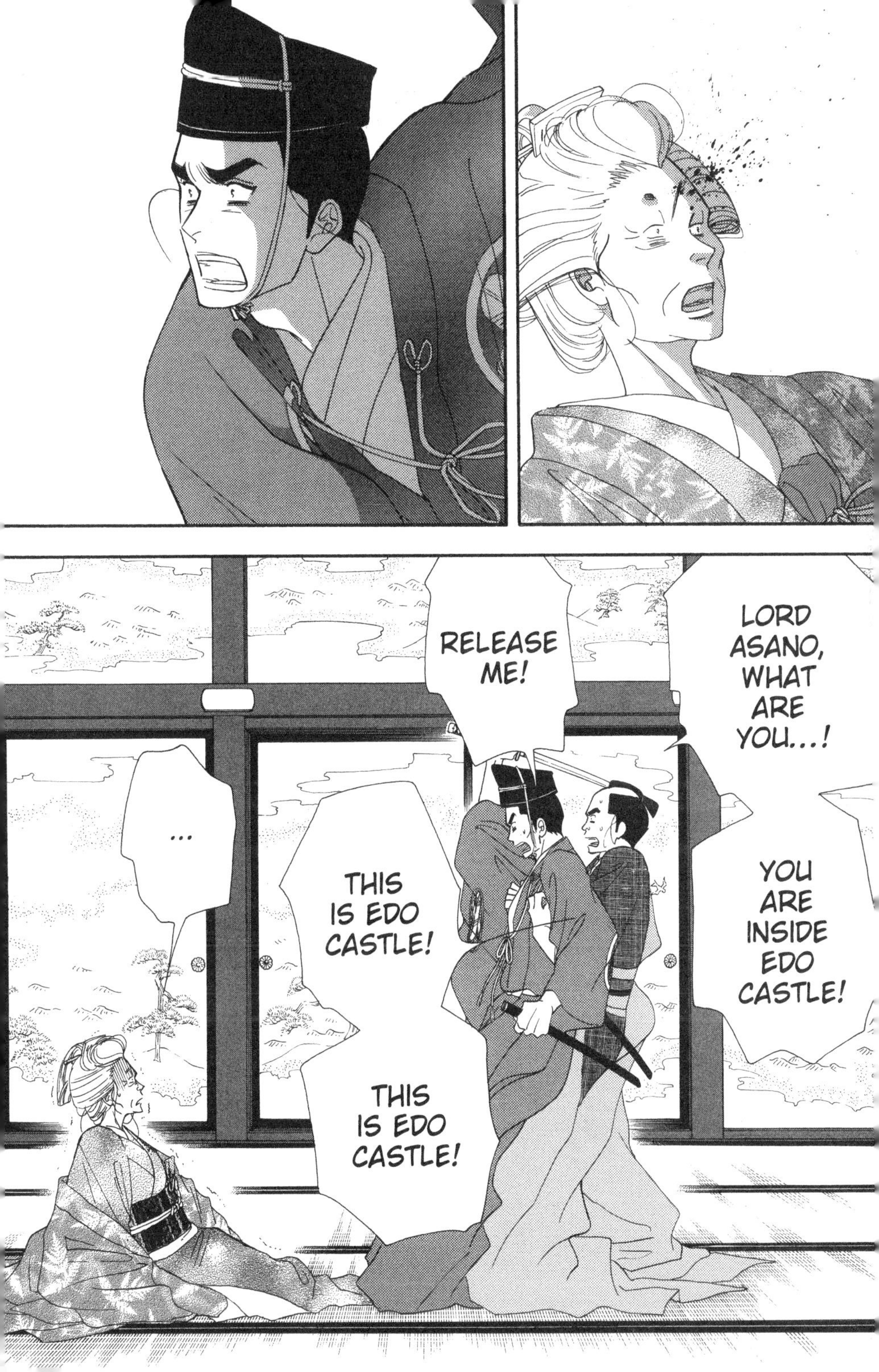
LORD ASANO, WHAT ARE YOU...!
RELEASE ME!
YOU ARE INSIDE EDO CASTLE!
THIS IS EDO CASTLE!
THIS IS EDO CASTLE!
...

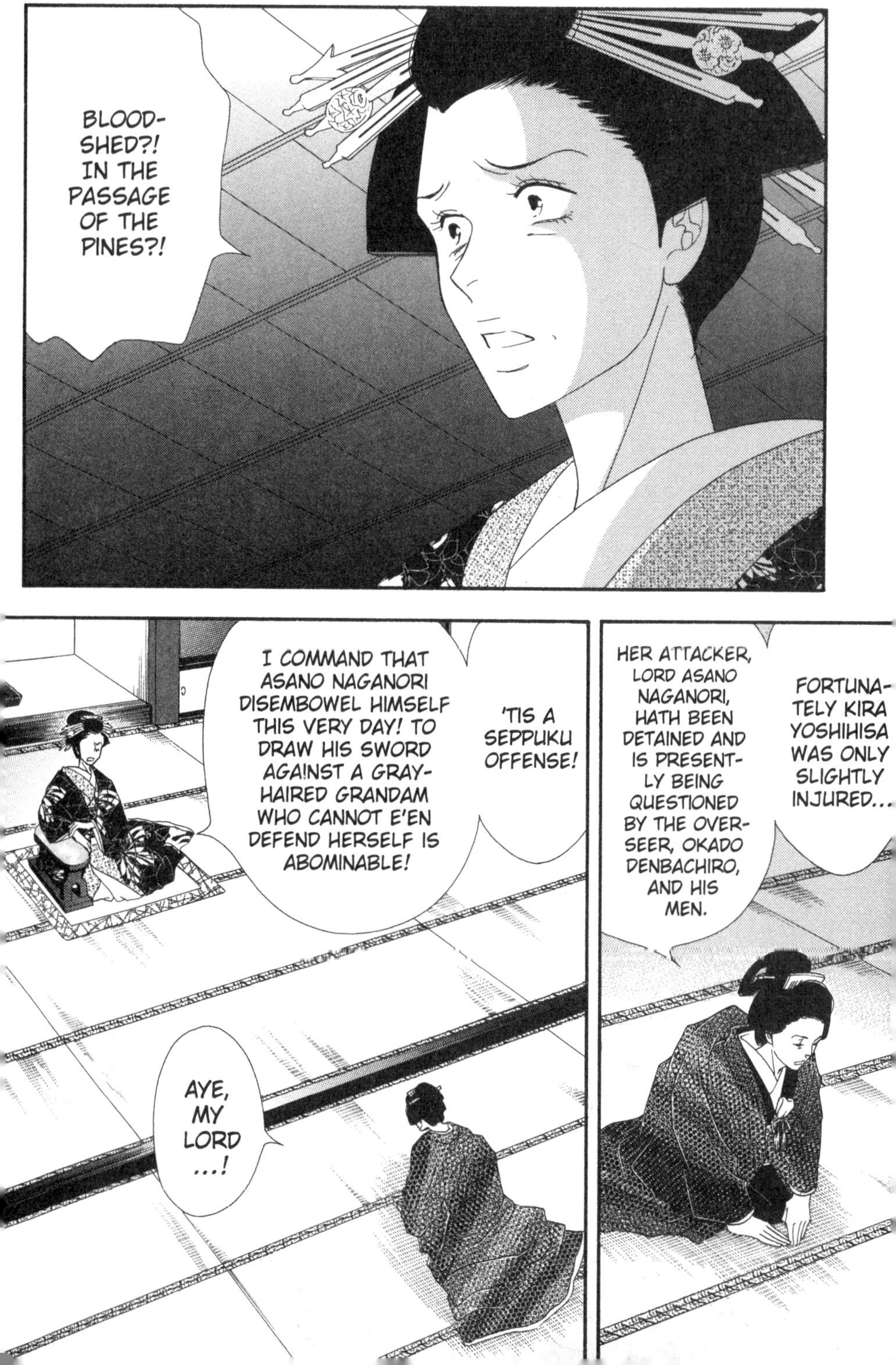
BLOOD-SHED?! IN THE PASSAGE OF THE PINES?!
FORTUNATELY KIRA YOSHIHISA WAS ONLY SLIGHTLY INJURED...
HER ATTACKER, LORD ASANO NAGANORI, HATH BEEN DETAINED AND IS PRESENTLY BEING QUESTIONED BY THE OVERSEER, OKADO DENBACHIRO, AND HIS MEN.
'TIS A SEPPUKU OFFENSE!
I COMMAND THAT ASANO NAGANORI DISEMBOWEL HIMSELF THIS VERY DAY! TO DRAW HIS SWORD AGAINST A GRAY-HAIRED GRANDAM WHO CANNOT E'EN DEFEND HERSELF IS ABOMINABLE!
AYE, MY LORD ...!

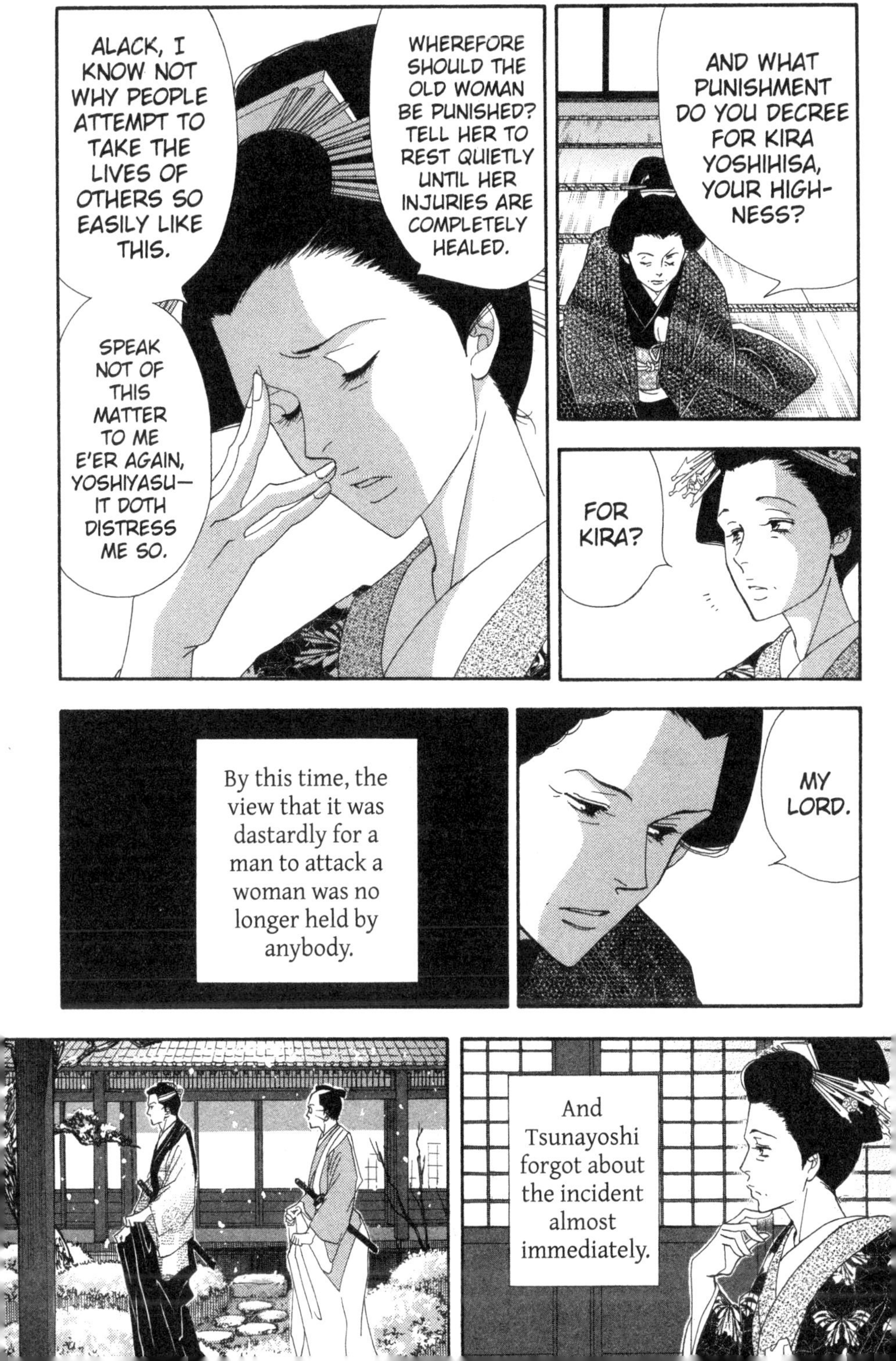
AND WHAT PUNISHMENT DO YOU DECREE FOR KIRA YOSHIHISA, YOUR HIGH-NESS?
FOR KIRA?
WHEREFORE SHOULD THE OLD WOMAN BE PUNISHED? TELL HER TO REST QUIETLY UNTIL HER INJURIES ARE COMPLETELY HEALED.
ALACK, I KNOW NOT WHY PEOPLE ATTEMPT TO TAKE THE LIVES OF OTHERS SO EASILY LIKE THIS.
SPEAK NOT OF THIS MATTER TO ME E'ER AGAIN, YOSHIYASU— IT DOTH DISTRESS ME SO.
MY LORD.
By this time, the view that it was dastardly for a man to attack a woman was no longer held by anybody.
And Tsunayoshi forgot about the incident almost immediately.

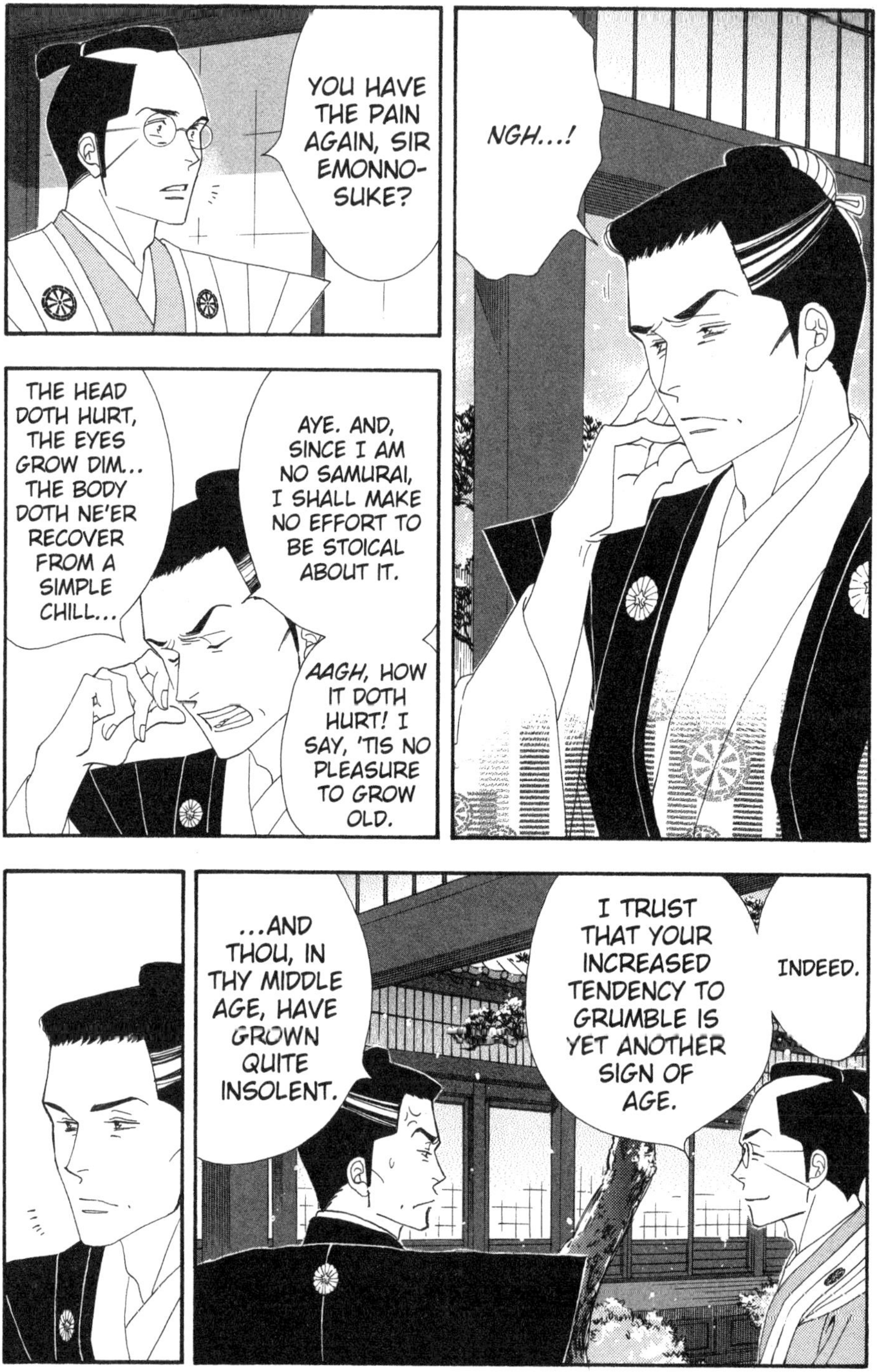
NGH...!
YOU HAVE THE PAIN AGAIN, SIR EMONNO-SUKE?
AYE. AND, SINCE I AM NO SAMURAI, I SHALL MAKE NO EFFORT TO BE STOICAL ABOUT IT.
THE HEAD DOTH HURT, THE EYES GROW DIM... THE BODY DOTH NE'ER RECOVER FROM A SIMPLE CHILL...
AAGH, HOW IT DOTH HURT! I SAY, 'TIS NO PLEASURE TO GROW OLD.
INDEED.
I TRUST THAT YOUR INCREASED TENDENCY TO GRUMBLE IS YET ANOTHER SIGN OF AGE.
...AND THOU, IN THY MIDDLE AGE, HAVE GROWN QUITE INSOLENT.

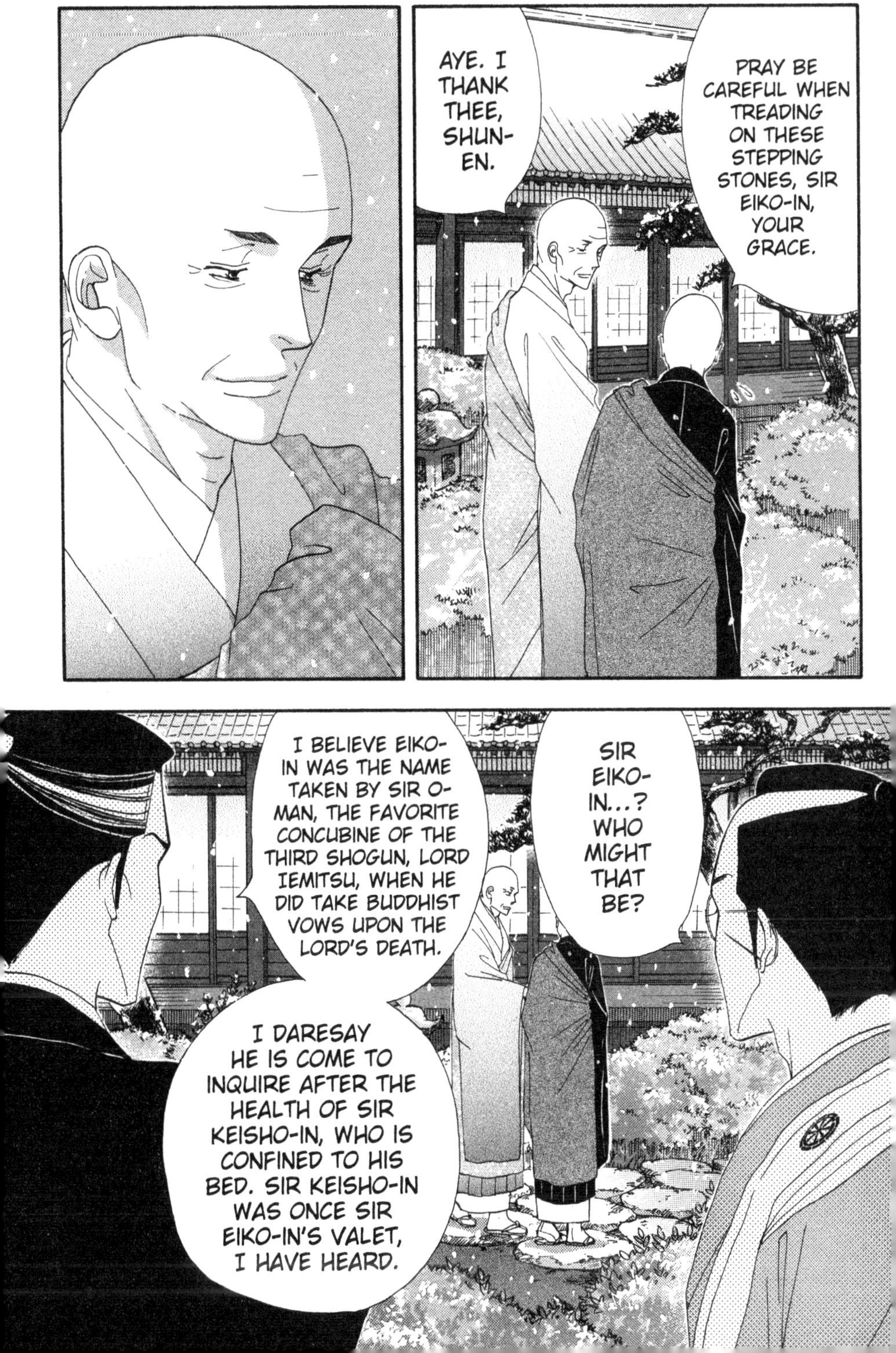
PRAY BE CAREFUL WHEN TREADING ON THESE STEPPING STONES, SIR EIKO-IN, YOUR GRACE.
AYE. I THANK THEE, SHUN-EN.
SIR EIKO-IN...? WHO MIGHT THAT BE?
I BELIEVE EIKO-IN WAS THE NAME TAKEN BY SIR O-MAN, THE FAVORITE CONCUBINE OF THE THIRD SHOGUN, LORD IEMITSU, WHEN HE DID TAKE BUDDHIST VOWS UPON THE LORD'S DEATH.
I DARESAY HE IS COME TO INQUIRE AFTER THE HEALTH OF SIR KEISHO-IN, WHO IS CONFINED TO HIS BED. SIR KEISHO-IN WAS ONCE SIR EIKO-IN'S VALET, I HAVE HEARD.

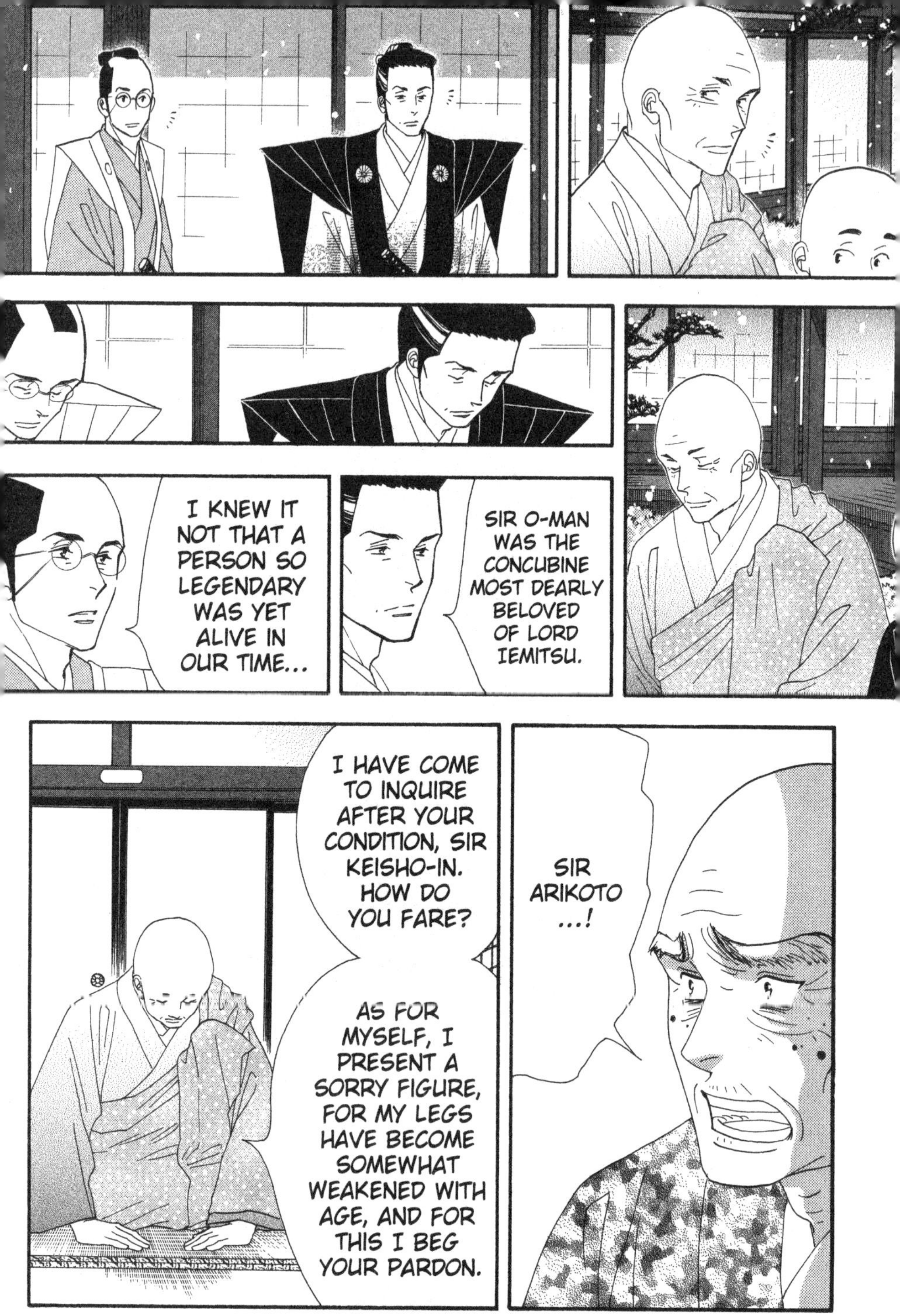
SIR O-MAN WAS THE CONCUBINE MOST DEARLY BELOVED OF LORD IEMITSU.
I KNEW IT NOT THAT A PERSON SO LEGENDARY WAS YET ALIVE IN OUR TIME...
SIR ARIKOTO ...!
I HAVE COME TO INQUIRE AFTER YOUR CONDITION, SIR KEISHO-IN. HOW DO YOU FARE?
AS FOR MYSELF, I PRESENT A SORRY FIGURE, FOR MY LEGS HAVE BECOME SOMEWHAT WEAKENED WITH AGE, AND FOR THIS I BEG YOUR PARDON.

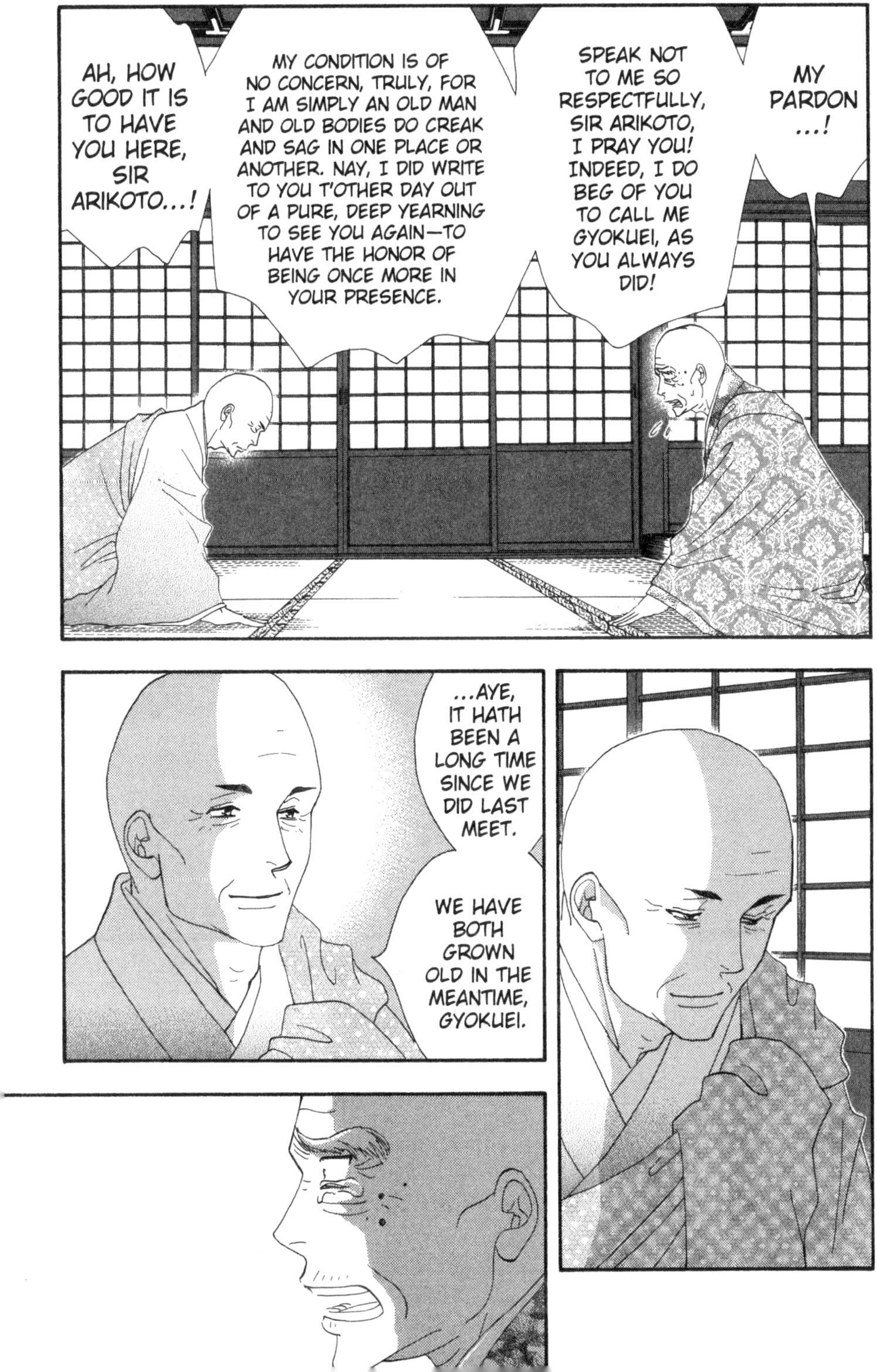
MY PARDON ...!
SPEAK NOT TO ME SO RESPECTFULLY, SIR ARIKOTO, I PRAY YOU! INDEED, I DO BEG OF YOU TO CALL ME GYOKUEI, AS YOU ALWAYS DID!
MY CONDITION IS OF NO CONCERN, TRULY, FOR I AM SIMPLY AN OLD MAN AND OLD BODIES DO CREAK AND SAG IN ONE PLACE OR ANOTHER. NAY, I DID WRITE TO YOU T'OTHER DAY OUT OF A PURE, DEEP YEARNING TO SEE YOU AGAIN—TO HAVE THE HONOR OF BEING ONCE MORE IN YOUR PRESENCE.
AH, HOW GOOD IT IS TO HAVE YOU HERE, SIR ARIKOTO...!
...AYE, IT HATH BEEN A LONG TIME SINCE WE DID LAST MEET.
WE HAVE BOTH GROWN OLD IN THE MEANTIME, GYOKUEI.

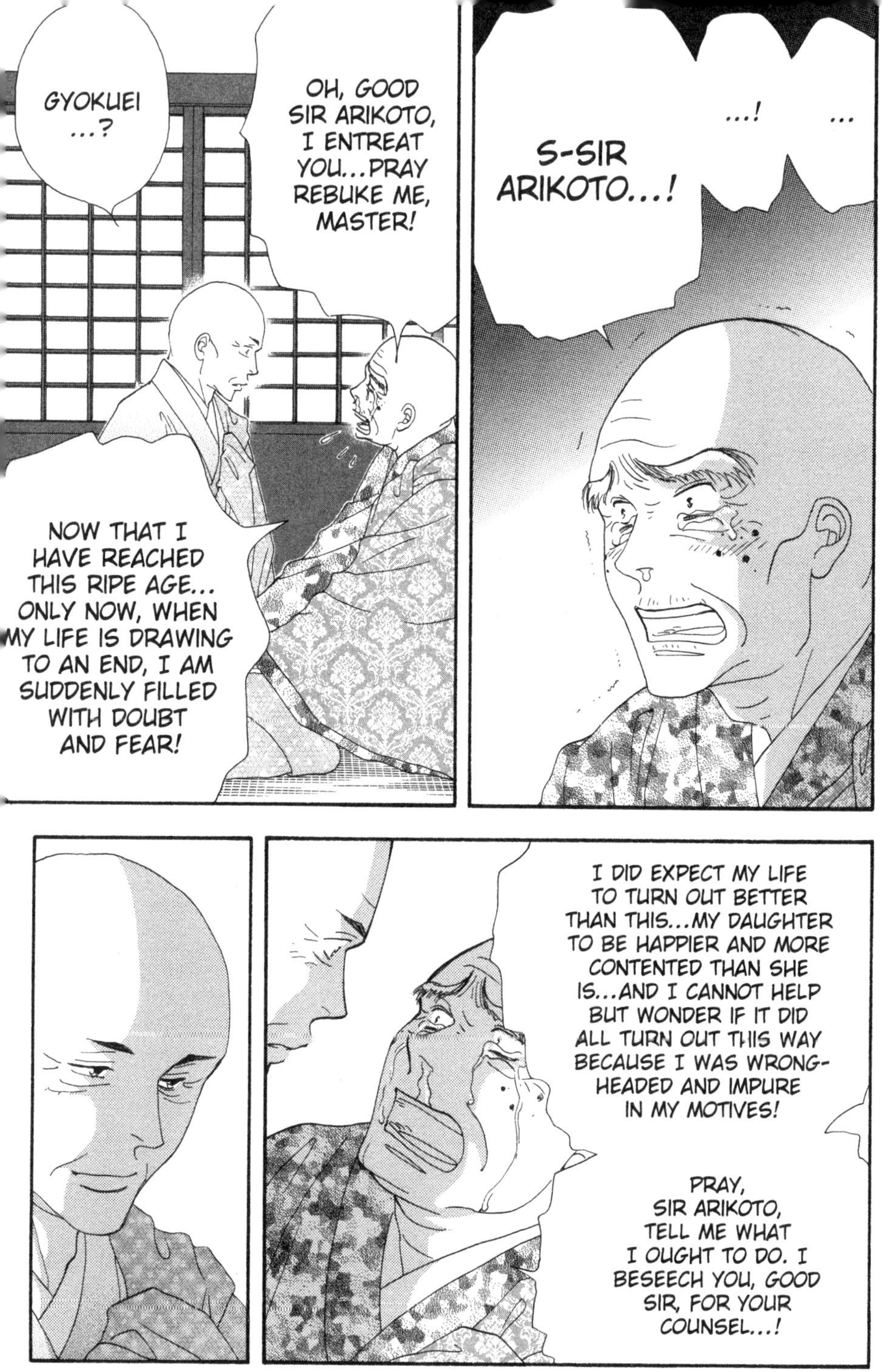
...
...!
S-SIR ARIKOTO...!
OH, GOOD SIR ARIKOTO, I ENTREAT YOU...PRAY REBUKE ME, MASTER!
GYOKUEI ...?
NOW THAT I HAVE REACHED THIS RIPE AGE... ONLY NOW, WHEN MY LIFE IS DRAWING TO AN END, I AM SUDDENLY FILLED WITH DOUBT AND FEAR!
I DID EXPECT MY LIFE TO TURN OUT BETTER THAN THIS...MY DAUGHTER TO BE HAPPIER AND MORE CONTENTED THAN SHE IS...AND I CANNOT HELP BUT WONDER IF IT DID ALL TURN OUT THIS WAY BECAUSE I WAS WRONG-HEADED AND IMPURE IN MY MOTIVES!
PRAY, SIR ARIKOTO, TELL ME WHAT I OUGHT TO DO. I BESEECH YOU, GOOD SIR, FOR YOUR COUNSEL...!

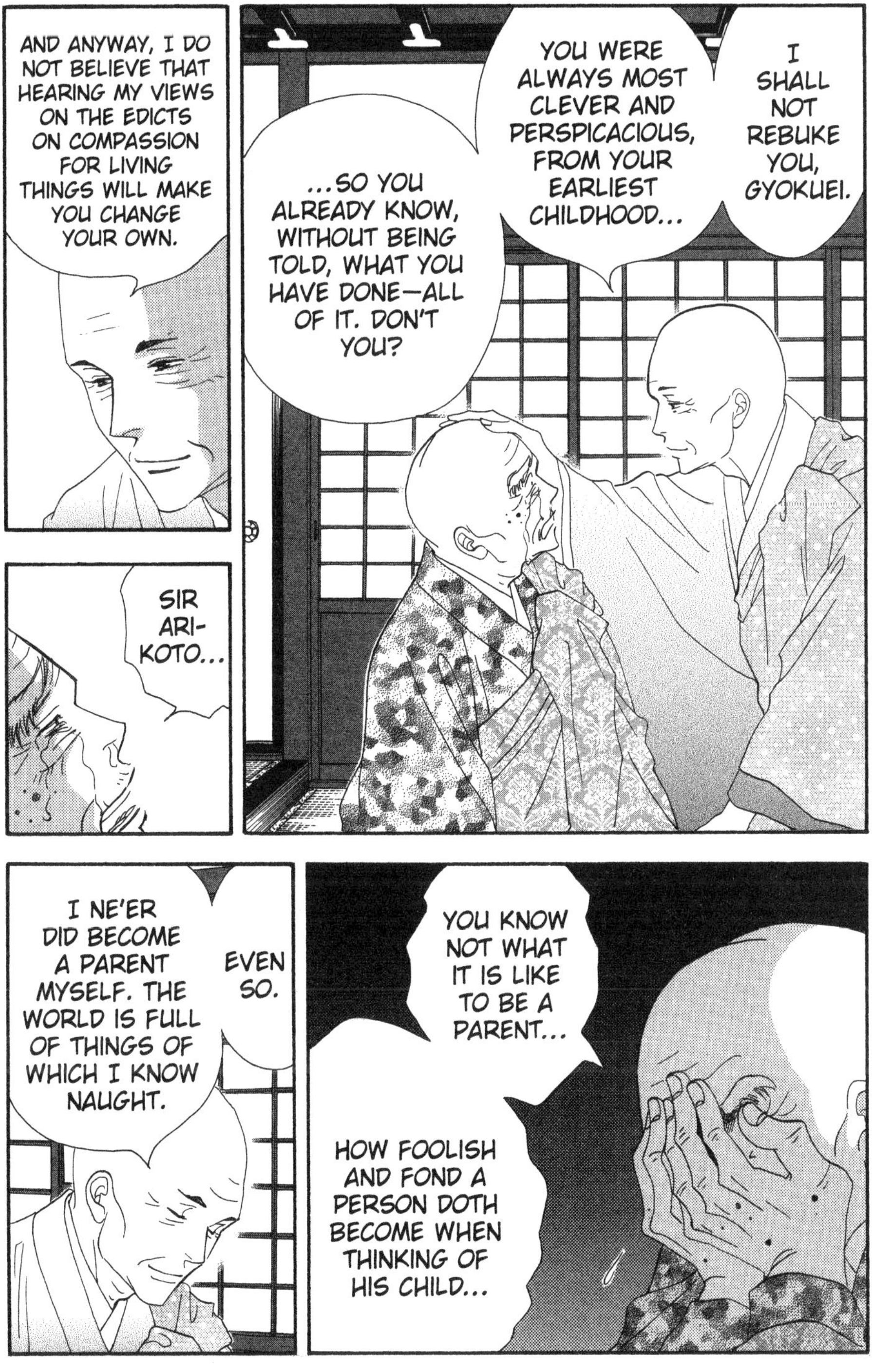
I SHALL NOT REBUKE YOU, GYOKUEI.
YOU WERE ALWAYS MOST CLEVER AND PERSPICACIOUS, FROM YOUR EARLIEST CHILDHOOD...
...SO YOU ALREADY KNOW, WITHOUT BEING TOLD, WHAT YOU HAVE DONE—ALL OF IT. DON'T YOU?
AND ANYWAY, I DO NOT BELIEVE THAT HEARING MY VIEWS ON THE EDICTS ON COMPASSION FOR LIVING THINGS WILL MAKE YOU CHANGE YOUR OWN.
SIR ARI-KOTO...
YOU KNOW NOT WHAT IT IS LIKE TO BE A PARENT...
HOW FOOLISH AND FOND A PERSON DOTH BECOME WHEN THINKING OF HIS CHILD...
EVEN SO.
I NE'ER DID BECOME A PARENT MYSELF. THE WORLD IS FULL OF THINGS OF WHICH I KNOW NAUGHT.

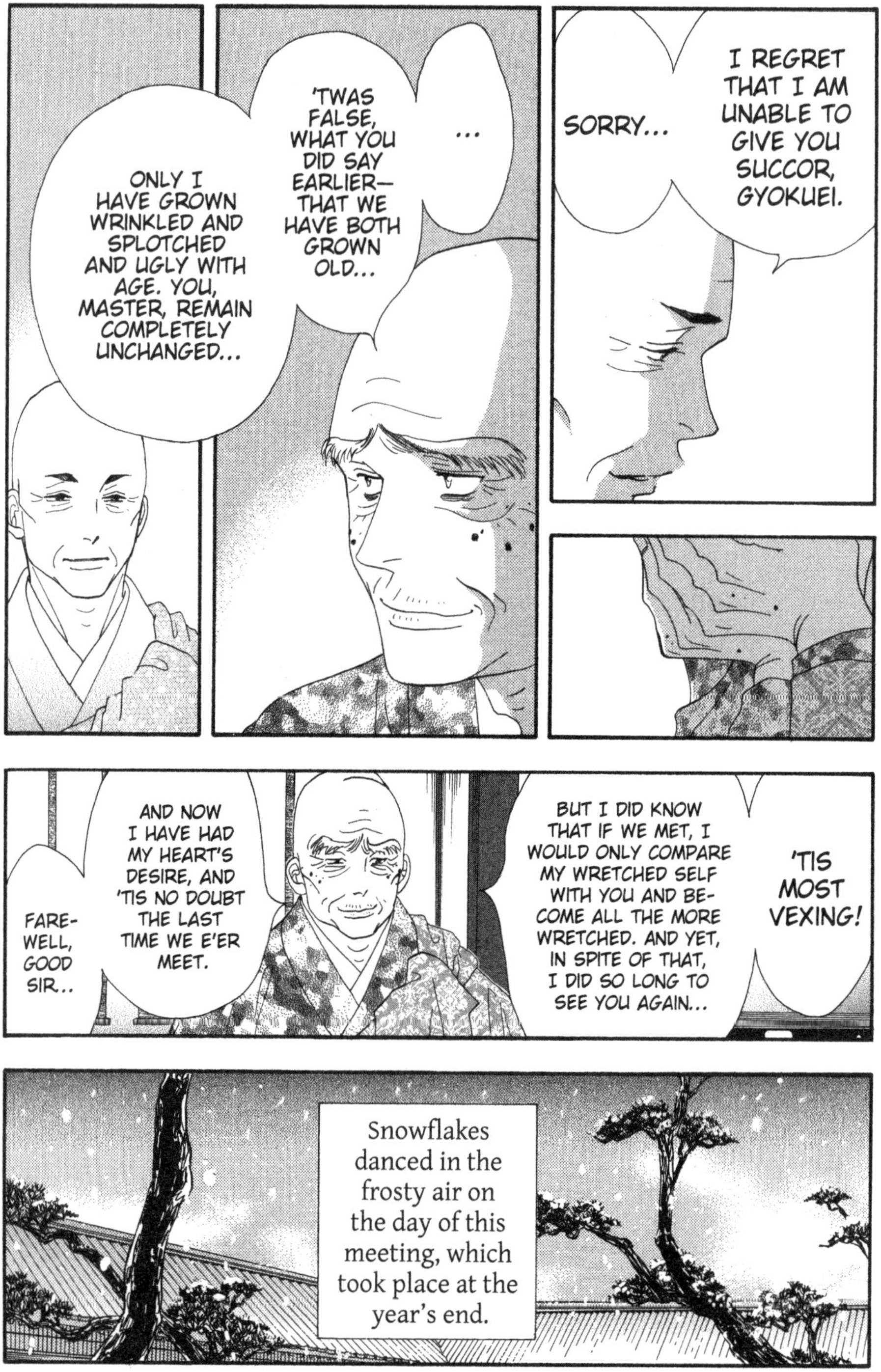
I REGRET THAT I AM UNABLE TO GIVE YOU SUCCOR, GYOKUEI.
SORRY...
...
'TWAS FALSE, WHAT YOU DID SAY EARLIER—THAT WE HAVE BOTH GROWN OLD...
ONLY I HAVE GROWN WRINKLED AND SPLOTCHED AND UGLY WITH AGE. YOU, MASTER, REMAIN COMPLETELY UNCHANGED...
'TIS MOST VEXING!
BUT I DID KNOW THAT IF WE MET, I WOULD ONLY COMPARE MY WRETCHED SELF WITH YOU AND BE-COME ALL THE MORE WRETCHED. AND YET, IN SPITE OF THAT, I DID SO LONG TO SEE YOU AGAIN...
AND NOW I HAVE HAD MY HEART'S DESIRE, AND 'TIS NO DOUBT THE LAST TIME WE E'ER MEET.
FARE-WELL, GOOD SIR...
Snowflakes danced in the frosty air on the day of this meeting, which took place at the year's end.

And then,
one year
later...

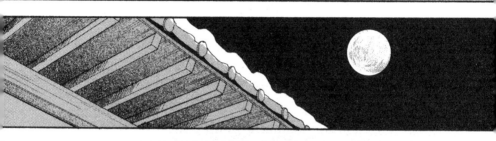

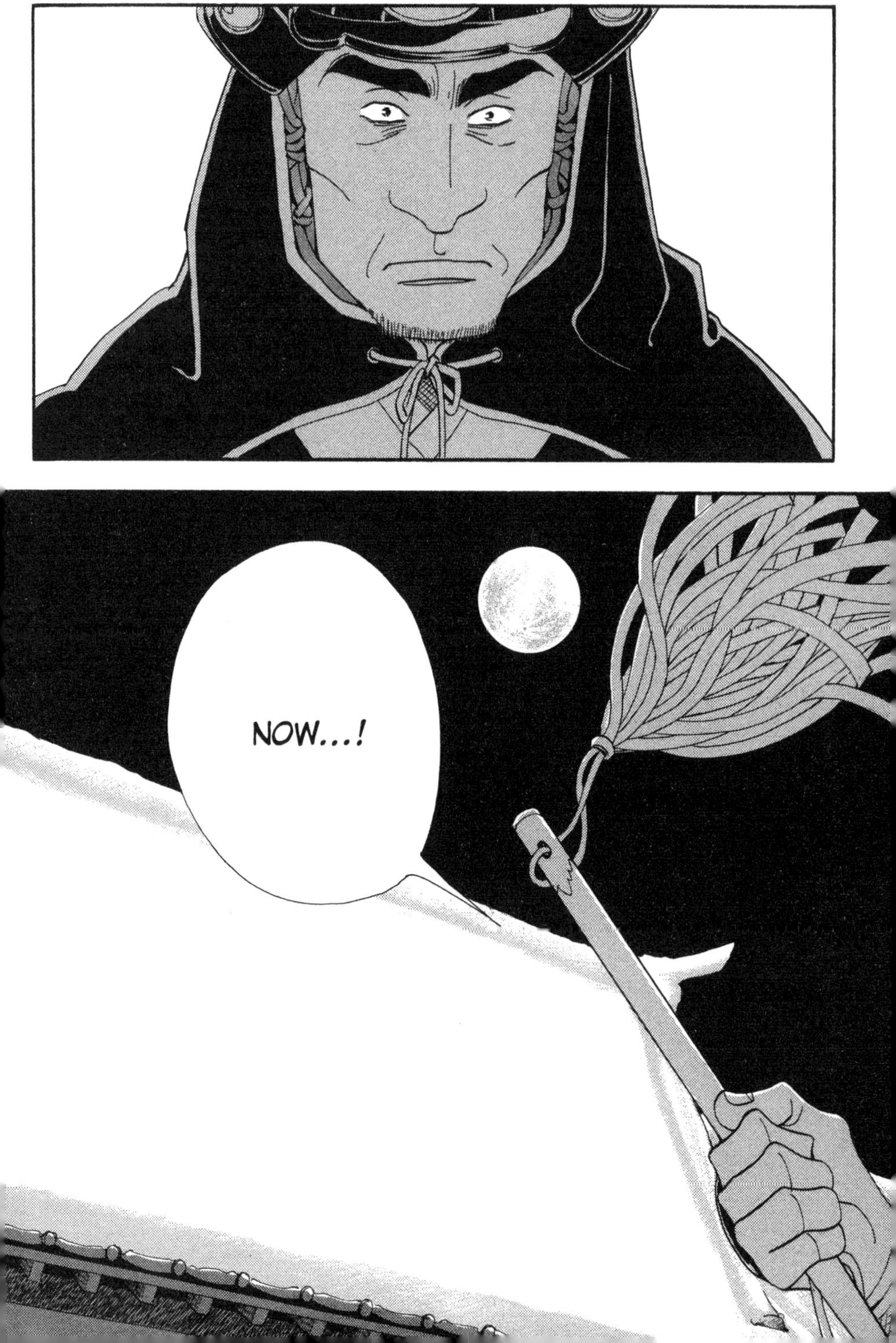
NOW...!

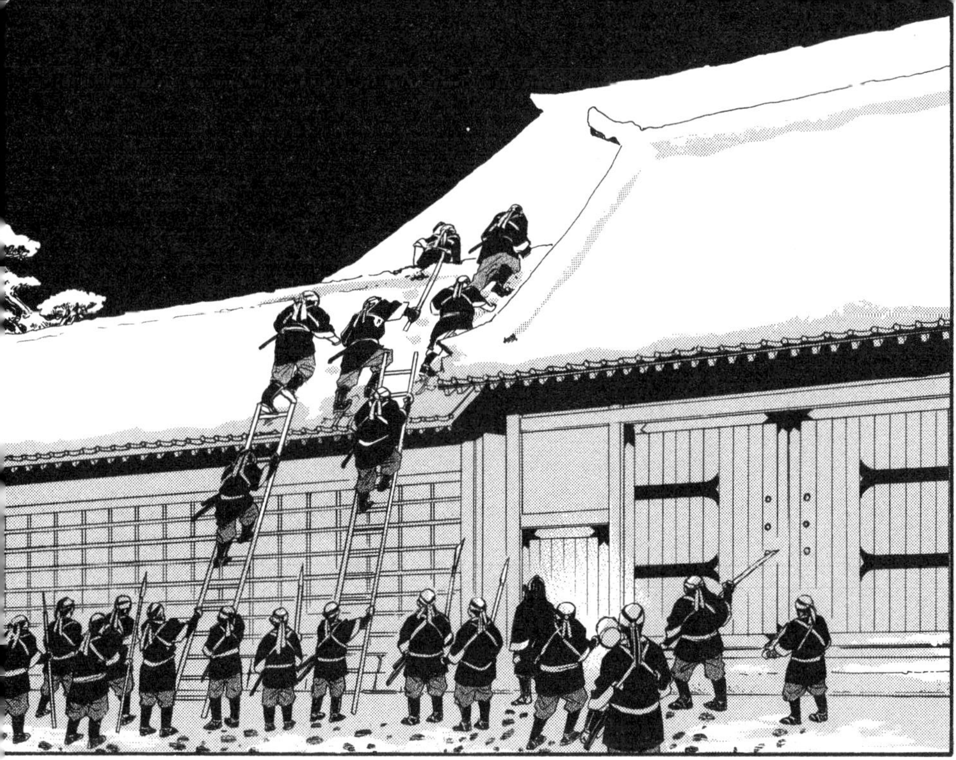

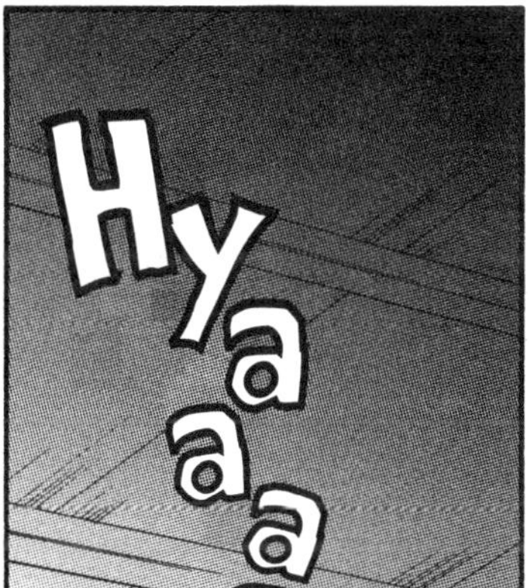
Hyaaaaagh!

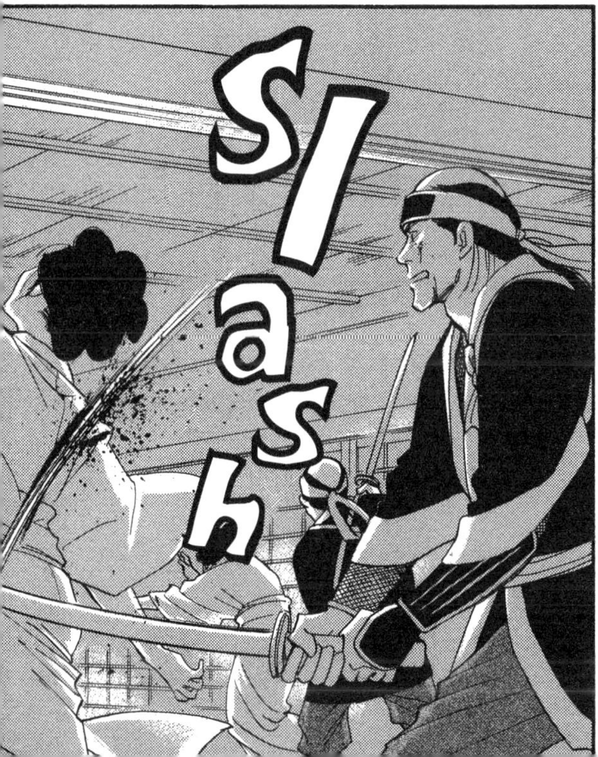
Slash

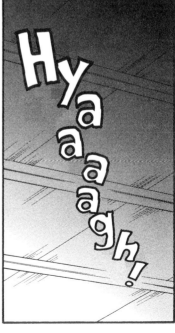

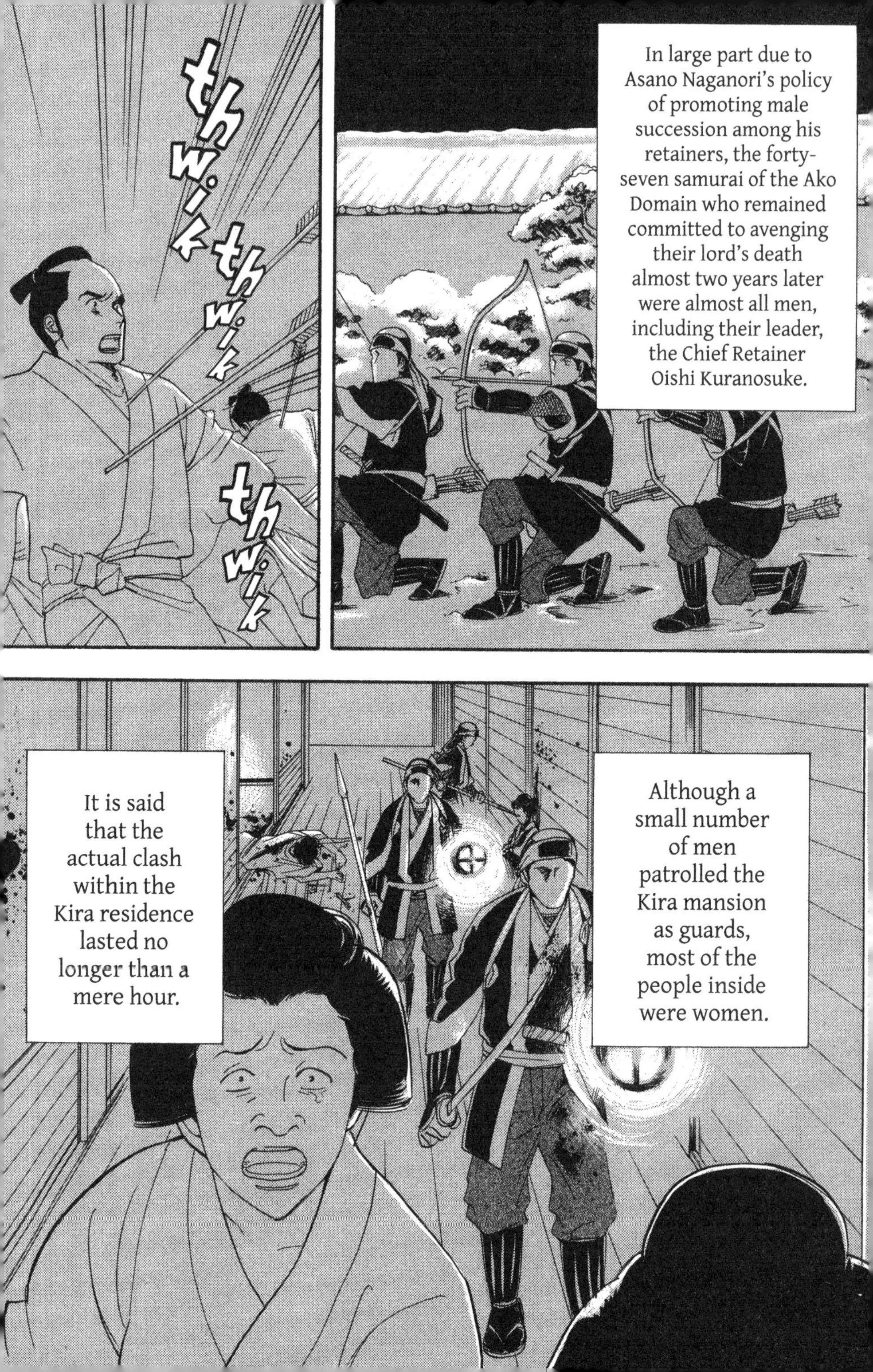
In large part due to Asano Naganori's policy of promoting male succession among his retainers, the forty-seven samurai of the Ako Domain who remained committed to avenging their lord's death almost two years later were almost all men, including their leader, the Chief Retainer Oishi Kuranosuke.
thwik
thwik
thwik
Although a small number of men patrolled the Kira mansion as guards, most of the people inside were women.
It is said that the actual clash within the Kira residence lasted no longer than a mere hour.

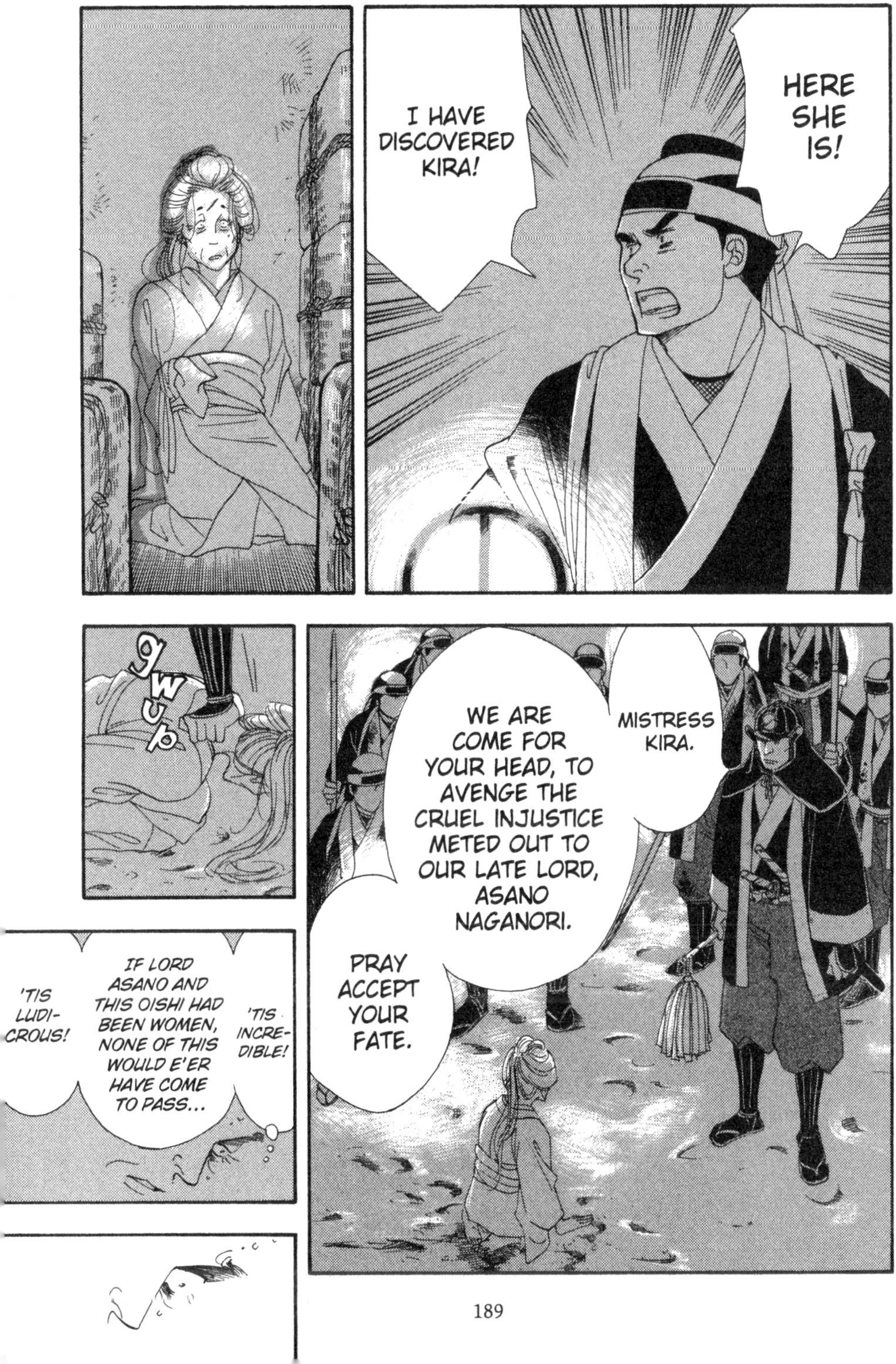
HERE SHE IS!
I HAVE DISCOVERED KIRA!
MISTRESS KIRA.
WE ARE COME FOR YOUR HEAD, TO AVENGE THE CRUEL INJUSTICE METED OUT TO OUR LATE LORD, ASANO NAGANORI.
PRAY ACCEPT YOUR FATE.
gwup
'TIS INCREDIBLE!
IF LORD ASANO AND THIS OISHI HAD BEEN WOMEN, NONE OF THIS WOULD E'ER HAVE COME TO PASS...
'TIS LUDICROUS!

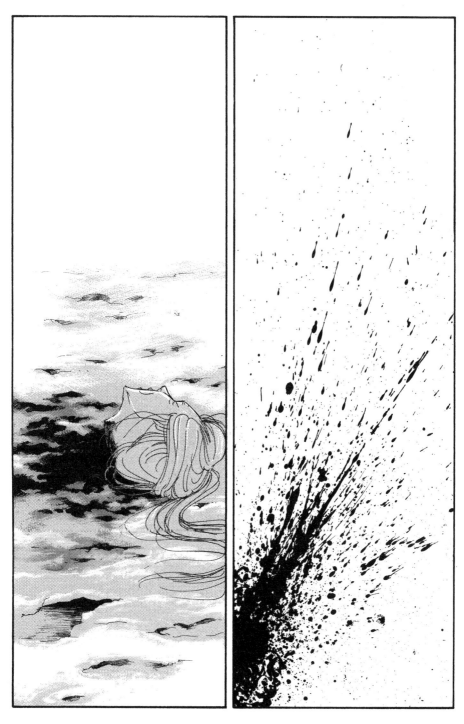

190

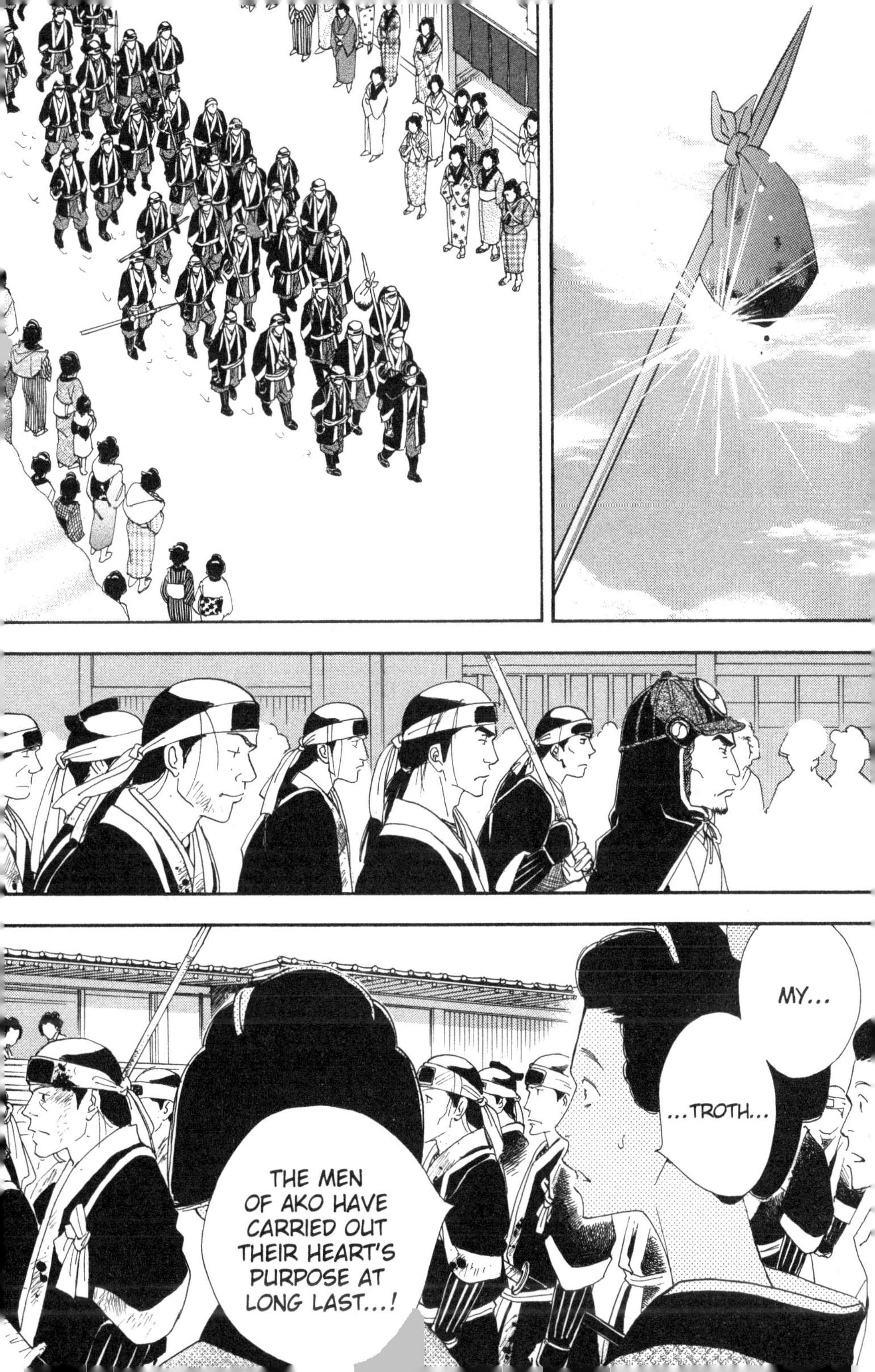
MY...
...TROTH...
THE MEN OF AKO HAVE CARRIED OUT THEIR HEART'S PURPOSE AT LONG LAST...!

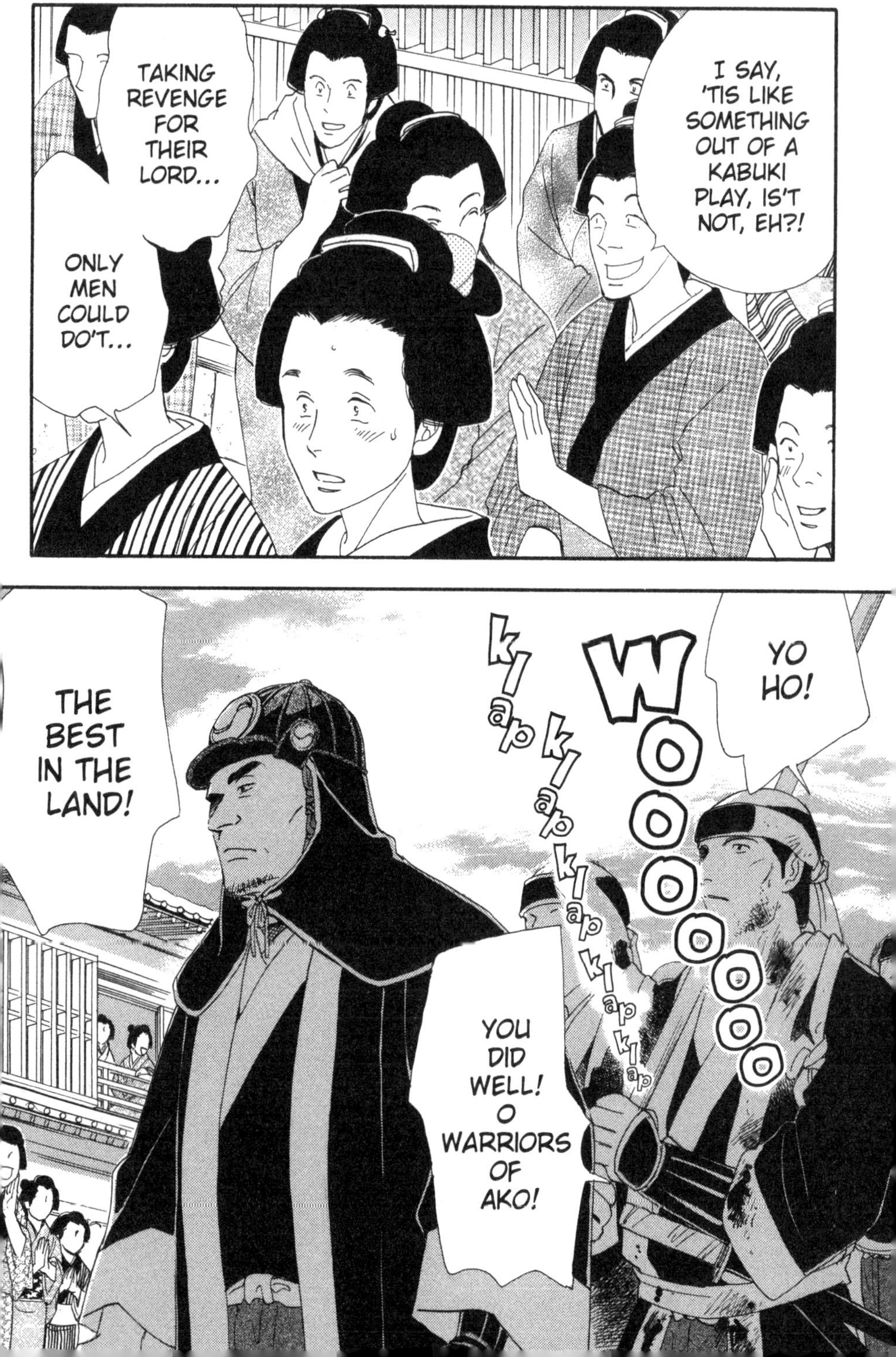
I SAY, 'TIS LIKE SOMETHING OUT OF A KABUKI PLAY, IS'T NOT, EH?!
TAKING REVENGE FOR THEIR LORD...
ONLY MEN COULD DO'T...
YO HO!
WOOOOOOO
klap klap klap klap klap
THE BEST IN THE LAND!
YOU DID WELL! O WARRIORS OF AKO!

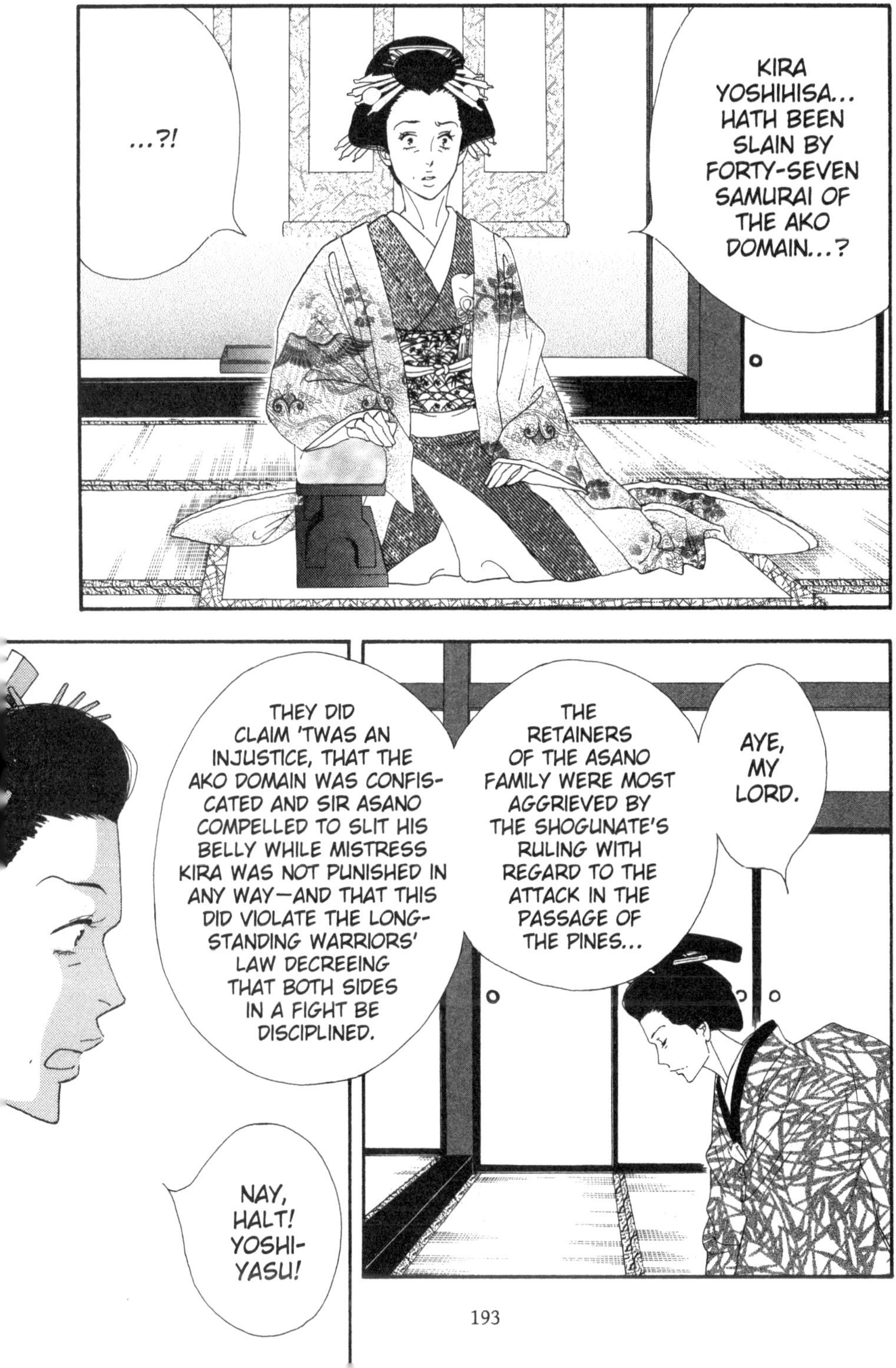
KIRA YOSHIHISA... HATH BEEN SLAIN BY FORTY-SEVEN SAMURAI OF THE AKO DOMAIN...?
...?!
AYE, MY LORD.
THE RETAINERS OF THE ASANO FAMILY WERE MOST AGGRIEVED BY THE SHOGUNATE'S RULING WITH REGARD TO THE ATTACK IN THE PASSAGE OF THE PINES...
THEY DID CLAIM 'TWAS AN INJUSTICE, THAT THE AKO DOMAIN WAS CONFISCATED AND SIR ASANO COMPELLED TO SLIT HIS BELLY WHILE MISTRESS KIRA WAS NOT PUNISHED IN ANY WAY—AND THAT THIS DID VIOLATE THE LONG-STANDING WARRIORS' LAW DECREEING THAT BOTH SIDES IN A FIGHT BE DISCIPLINED.
NAY, HALT! YOSHI-YASU!

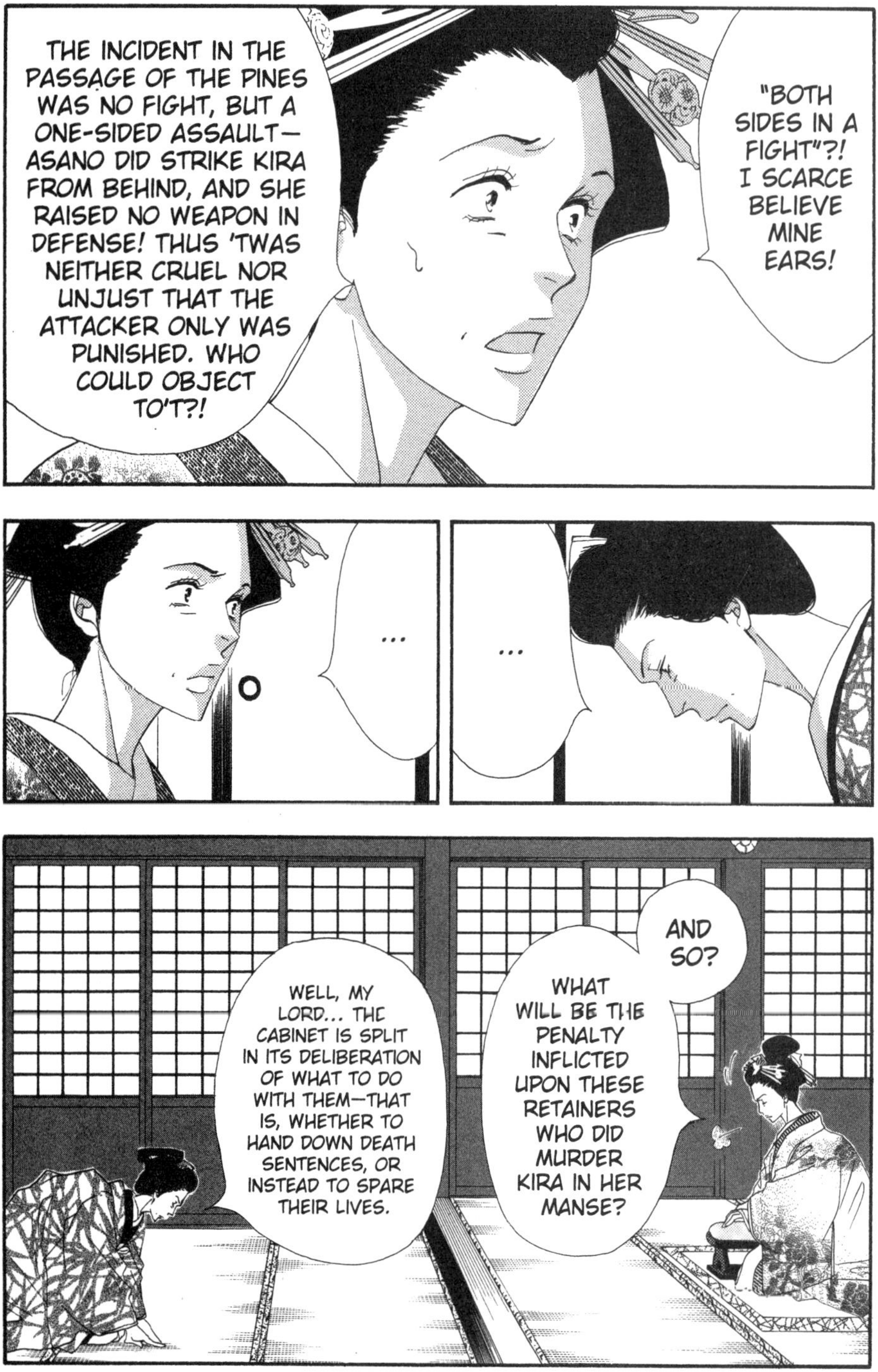
"BOTH SIDES IN A FIGHT"?! I SCARCE BELIEVE MINE EARS!
THE INCIDENT IN THE PASSAGE OF THE PINES WAS NO FIGHT, BUT A ONE-SIDED ASSAULT— ASANO DID STRIKE KIRA FROM BEHIND, AND SHE RAISED NO WEAPON IN DEFENSE! THUS 'TWAS NEITHER CRUEL NOR UNJUST THAT THE ATTACKER ONLY WAS PUNISHED. WHO COULD OBJECT TO'T?!
...
...
AND SO?
WHAT WILL BE THE PENALTY INFLICTED UPON THESE RETAINERS WHO DID MURDER KIRA IN HER MANSE?
WELL, MY LORD... THE CABINET IS SPLIT IN ITS DELIBERATION OF WHAT TO DO WITH THEM—THAT IS, WHETHER TO HAND DOWN DEATH SENTENCES, OR INSTEAD TO SPARE THEIR LIVES.

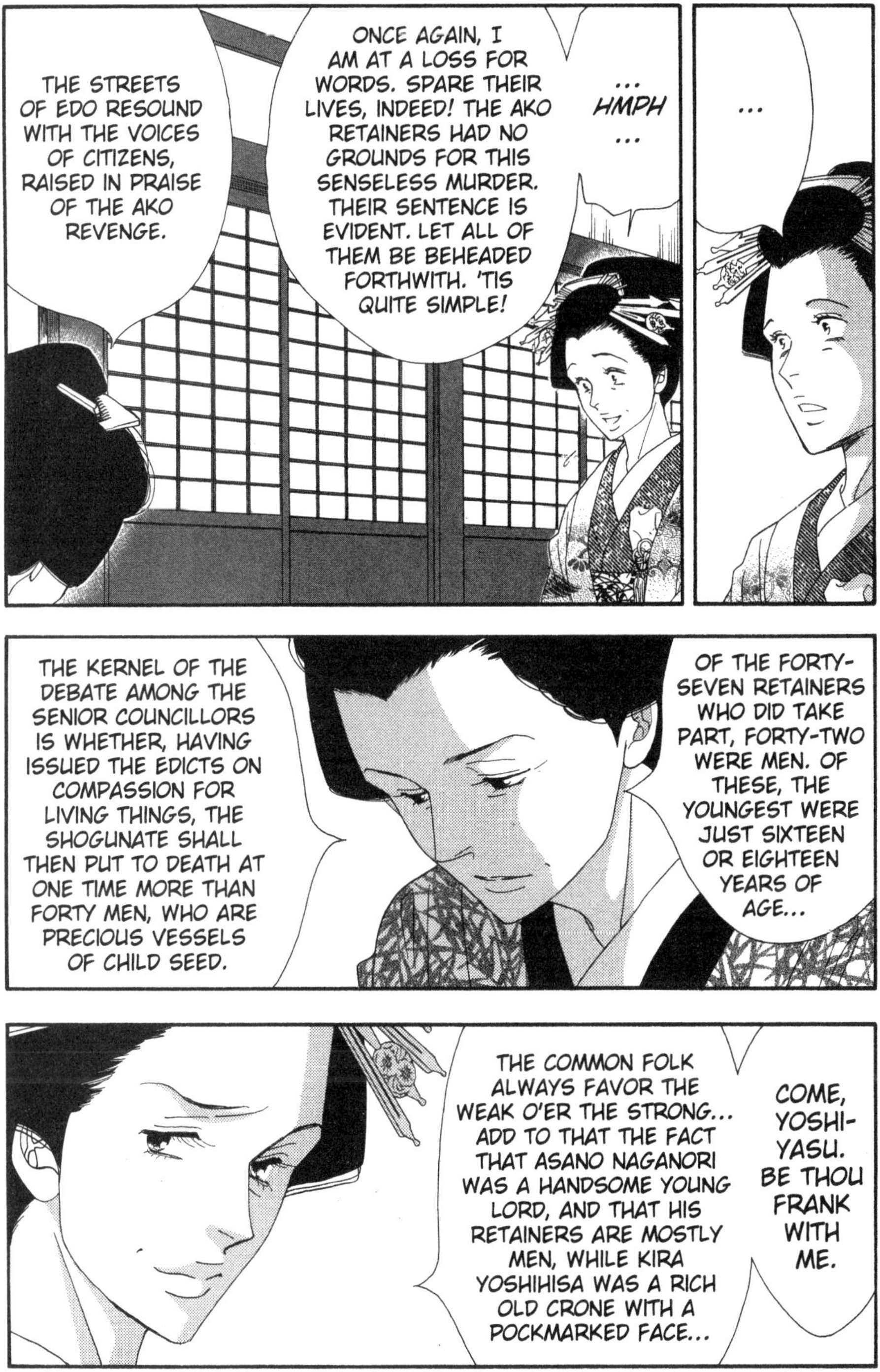
...
... HMPH ...
ONCE AGAIN, I AM AT A LOSS FOR WORDS. SPARE THEIR LIVES, INDEED! THE AKO RETAINERS HAD NO GROUNDS FOR THIS SENSELESS MURDER. THEIR SENTENCE IS EVIDENT. LET ALL OF THEM BE BEHEADED FORTHWITH. 'TIS QUITE SIMPLE!
THE STREETS OF EDO RESOUND WITH THE VOICES OF CITIZENS, RAISED IN PRAISE OF THE AKO REVENGE.
OF THE FORTY-SEVEN RETAINERS WHO DID TAKE PART, FORTY-TWO WERE MEN. OF THESE, THE YOUNGEST WERE JUST SIXTEEN OR EIGHTEEN YEARS OF AGE...
THE KERNEL OF THE DEBATE AMONG THE SENIOR COUNCILLORS IS WHETHER, HAVING ISSUED THE EDICTS ON COMPASSION FOR LIVING THINGS, THE SHOGUNATE SHALL THEN PUT TO DEATH AT ONE TIME MORE THAN FORTY MEN, WHO ARE PRECIOUS VESSELS OF CHILD SEED.
COME, YOSHIYASU. BE THOU FRANK WITH ME.
THE COMMON FOLK ALWAYS FAVOR THE WEAK O'ER THE STRONG... ADD TO THAT THE FACT THAT ASANO NAGANORI WAS A HANDSOME YOUNG LORD, AND THAT HIS RETAINERS ARE MOSTLY MEN, WHILE KIRA YOSHIHISA WAS A RICH OLD CRONE WITH A POCKMARKED FACE...

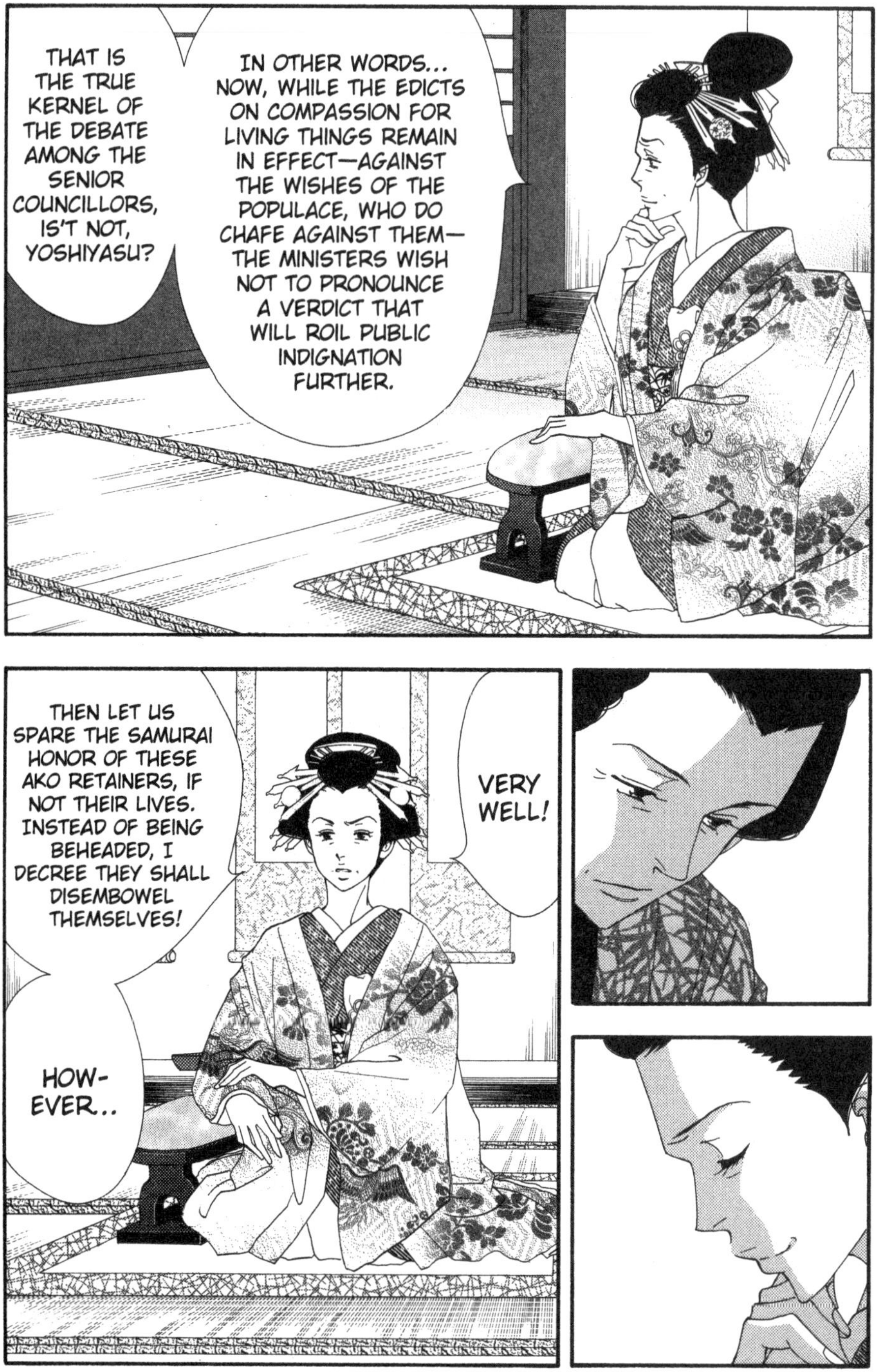
IN OTHER WORDS... NOW, WHILE THE EDICTS ON COMPASSION FOR LIVING THINGS REMAIN IN EFFECT—AGAINST THE WISHES OF THE POPULACE, WHO DO CHAFE AGAINST THEM—THE MINISTERS WISH NOT TO PRONOUNCE A VERDICT THAT WILL ROIL PUBLIC INDIGNATION FURTHER.
THAT IS THE TRUE KERNEL OF THE DEBATE AMONG THE SENIOR COUNCILLORS, IS'T NOT, YOSHIYASU?
VERY WELL!
THEN LET US SPARE THE SAMURAI HONOR OF THESE AKO RETAINERS, IF NOT THEIR LIVES. INSTEAD OF BEING BEHEADED, I DECREE THEY SHALL DISEMBOWEL THEMSELVES!
HOW-EVER..

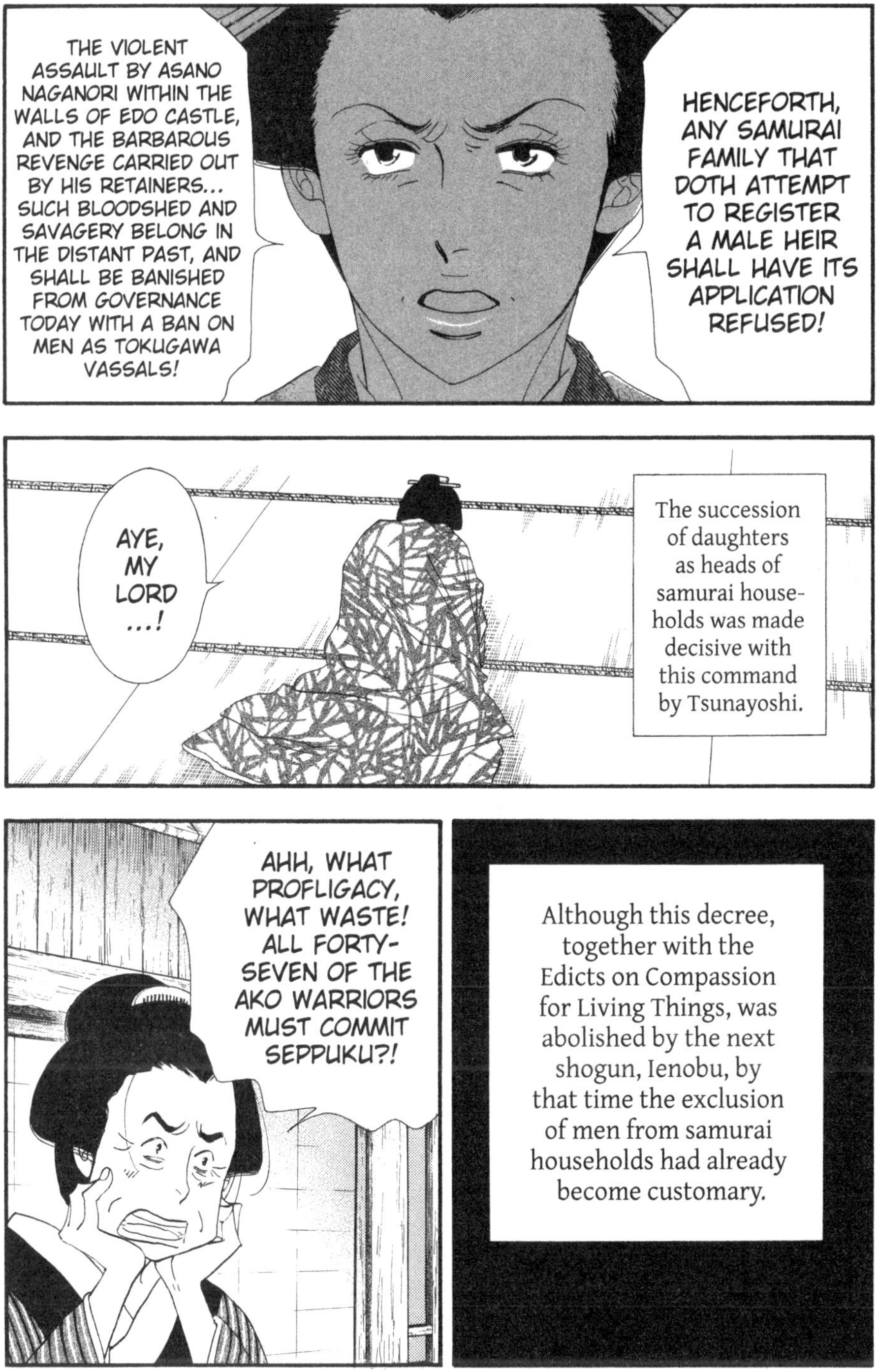
HENCEFORTH, ANY SAMURAI FAMILY THAT DOTH ATTEMPT TO REGISTER A MALE HEIR SHALL HAVE ITS APPLICATION REFUSED!
THE VIOLENT ASSAULT BY ASANO NAGANORI WITHIN THE WALLS OF EDO CASTLE, AND THE BARBAROUS REVENGE CARRIED OUT BY HIS RETAINERS... SUCH BLOODSHED AND SAVAGERY BELONG IN THE DISTANT PAST, AND SHALL BE BANISHED FROM GOVERNANCE TODAY WITH A BAN ON MEN AS TOKUGAWA VASSALS!
The succession of daughters as heads of samurai households was made decisive with this command by Tsunayoshi.
AYE, MY LORD ...!
Although this decree, together with the Edicts on Compassion for Living Things, was abolished by the next shogun, Ienobu, by that time the exclusion of men from samurai households had already become customary.
AHH, WHAT PROFLIGACY, WHAT WASTE! ALL FORTY-SEVEN OF THE AKO WARRIORS MUST COMMIT SEPPUKU?!

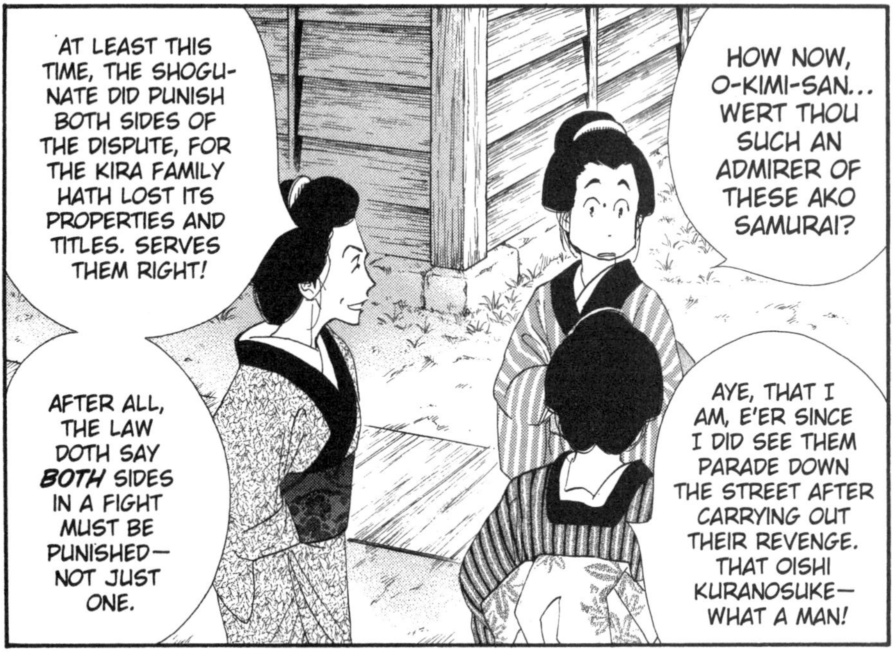
HOW NOW, O-KIMI-SAN... WERT THOU SUCH AN ADMIRER OF THESE AKO SAMURAI?
AYE, THAT I AM, E'ER SINCE I DID SEE THEM PARADE DOWN THE STREET AFTER CARRYING OUT THEIR REVENGE. THAT OISHI KURANOSUKE—WHAT A MAN!
AT LEAST THIS TIME, THE SHOGUNATE DID PUNISH BOTH SIDES OF THE DISPUTE, FOR THE KIRA FAMILY HATH LOST ITS PROPERTIES AND TITLES. SERVES THEM RIGHT!
AFTER ALL, THE LAW DOTH SAY BOTH SIDES IN A FIGHT MUST BE PUNISHED—NOT JUST ONE.
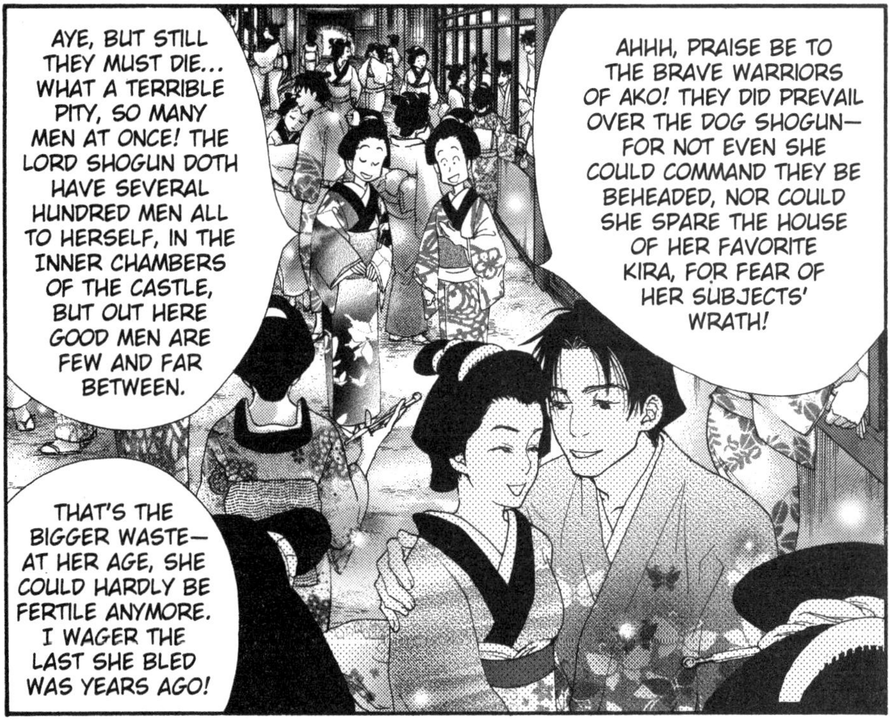
AHHH, PRAISE BE TO THE BRAVE WARRIORS OF AKO! THEY DID PREVAIL OVER THE DOG SHOGUN—FOR NOT EVEN SHE COULD COMMAND THEY BE BEHEADED, NOR COULD SHE SPARE THE HOUSE OF HER FAVORITE KIRA, FOR FEAR OF HER SUBJECTS' WRATH!
AYE, BUT STILL THEY MUST DIE... WHAT A TERRIBLE PITY, SO MANY MEN AT ONCE! THE LORD SHOGUN DOTH HAVE SEVERAL HUNDRED MEN ALL TO HERSELF, IN THE INNER CHAMBERS OF THE CASTLE, BUT OUT HERE GOOD MEN ARE FEW AND FAR BETWEEN.
THAT'S THE BIGGER WASTE—AT HER AGE, SHE COULD HARDLY BE FERTILE ANYMORE. I WAGER THE LAST SHE BLED WAS YEARS AGO!

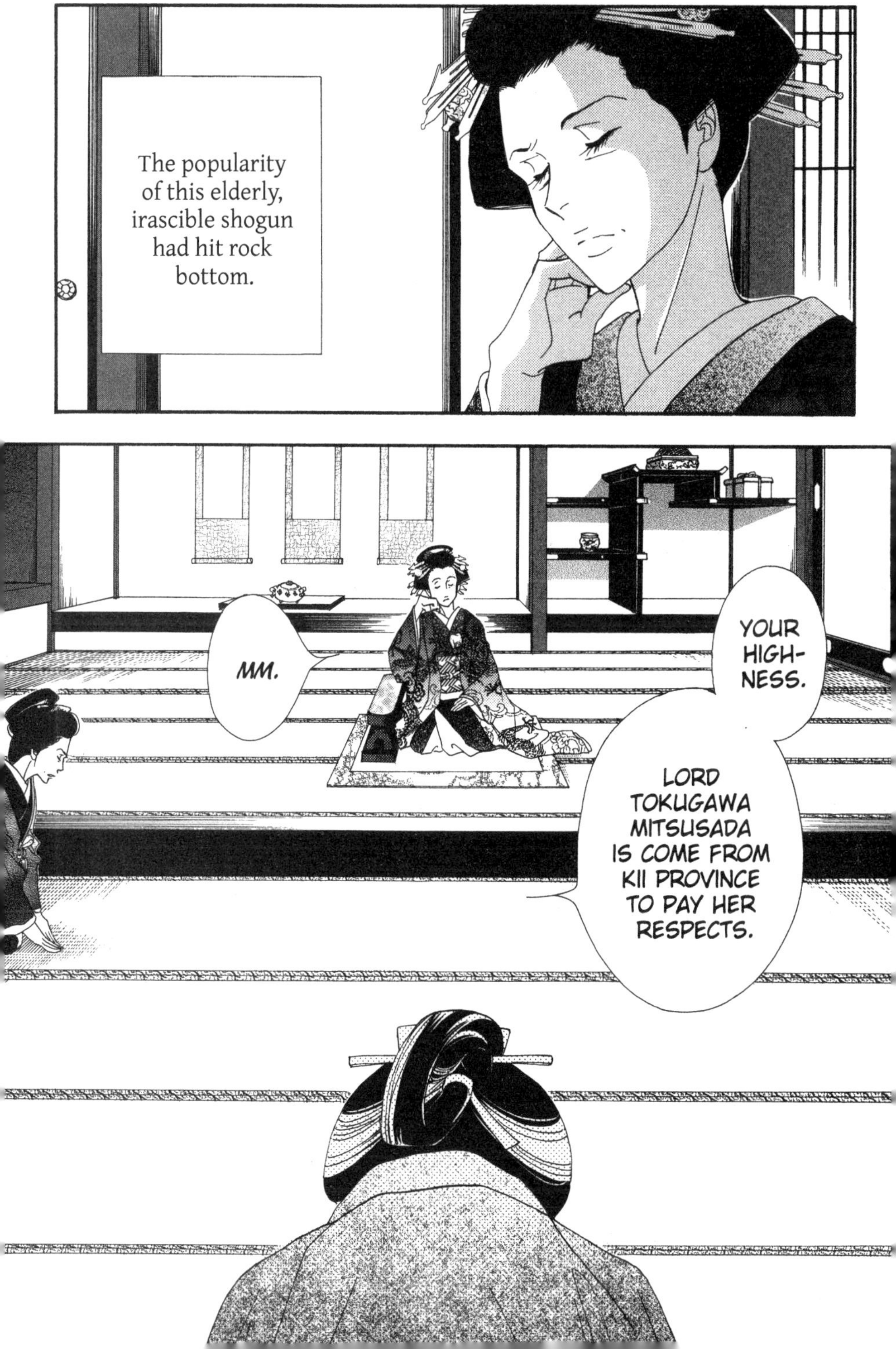
The popularity of this elderly, irascible shogun had hit rock bottom.
YOUR HIGH-NESS.
LORD TOKUGAWA MITSUSADA IS COME FROM KII PROVINCE TO PAY HER RESPECTS.
MM.

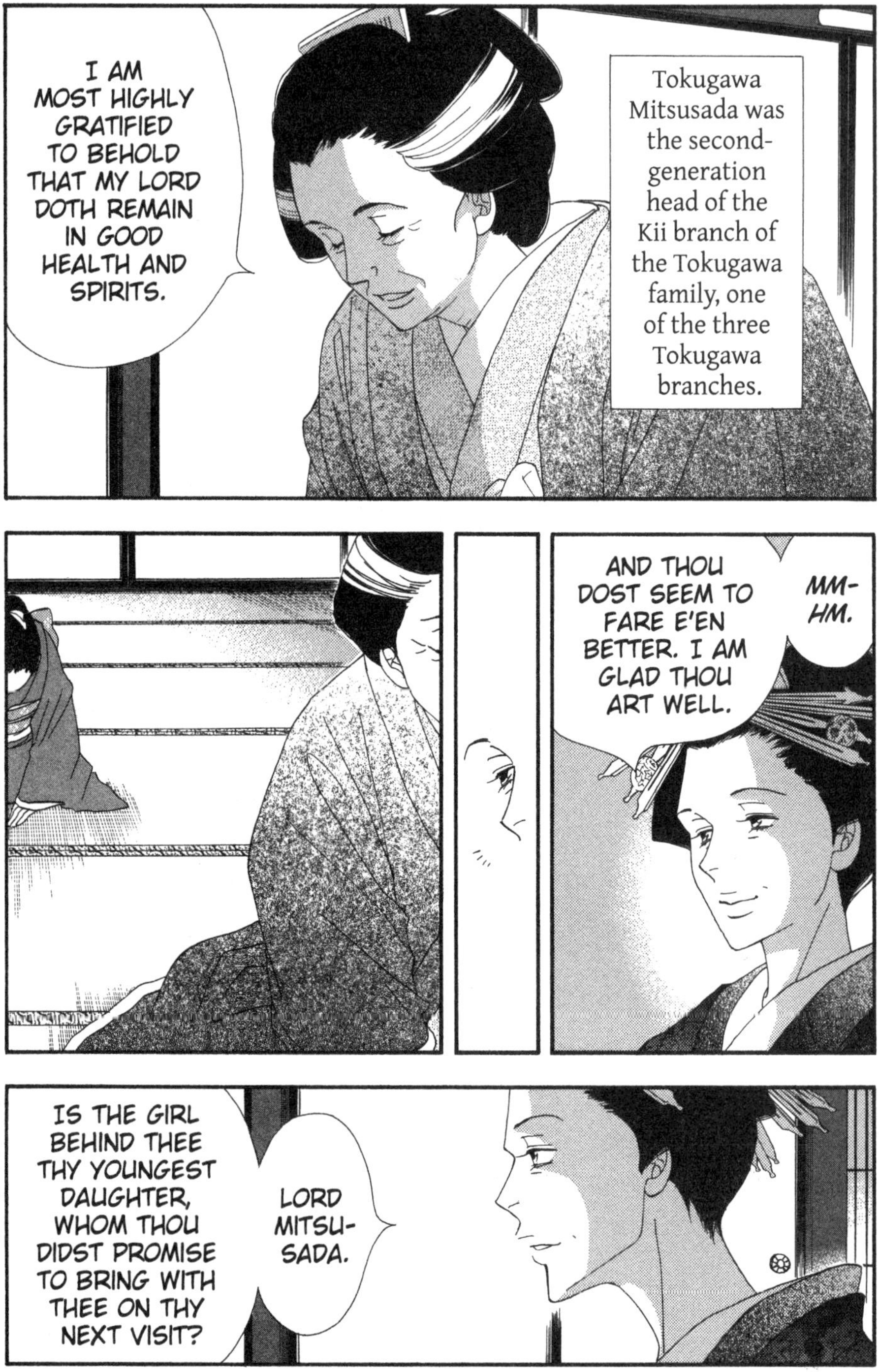
Tokugawa Mitsusada was the second-generation head of the Kii branch of the Tokugawa family, one of the three Tokugawa branches.
I AM MOST HIGHLY GRATIFIED TO BEHOLD THAT MY LORD DOTH REMAIN IN GOOD HEALTH AND SPIRITS.
MM-HM.
AND THOU DOST SEEM TO FARE E'EN BETTER. I AM GLAD THOU ART WELL.
LORD MITSU-SADA.
IS THE GIRL BEHIND THEE THY YOUNGEST DAUGHTER, WHOM THOU DIDST PROMISE TO BRING WITH THEE ON THY NEXT VISIT?

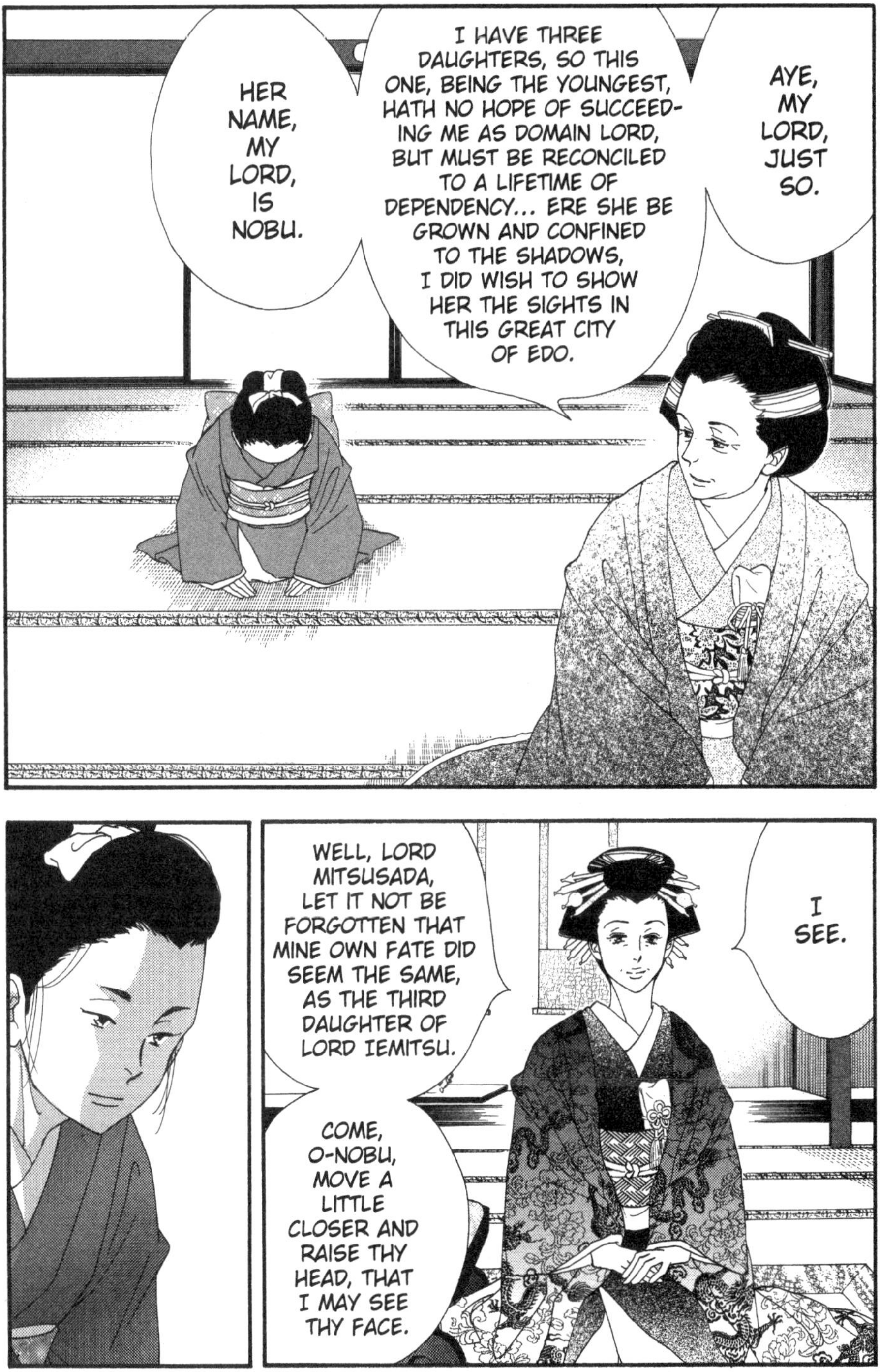
AYE, MY LORD, JUST SO.
I HAVE THREE DAUGHTERS, SO THIS ONE, BEING THE YOUNGEST, HATH NO HOPE OF SUCCEEDING ME AS DOMAIN LORD, BUT MUST BE RECONCILED TO A LIFETIME OF DEPENDENCY... ERE SHE BE GROWN AND CONFINED TO THE SHADOWS, I DID WISH TO SHOW HER THE SIGHTS IN THIS GREAT CITY OF EDO.
HER NAME, MY LORD, IS NOBU.
I SEE.
WELL, LORD MITSUSADA, LET IT NOT BE FORGOTTEN THAT MINE OWN FATE DID SEEM THE SAME, AS THE THIRD DAUGHTER OF LORD IEMITSU.
COME, O-NOBU, MOVE A LITTLE CLOSER AND RAISE THY HEAD, THAT I MAY SEE THY FACE.

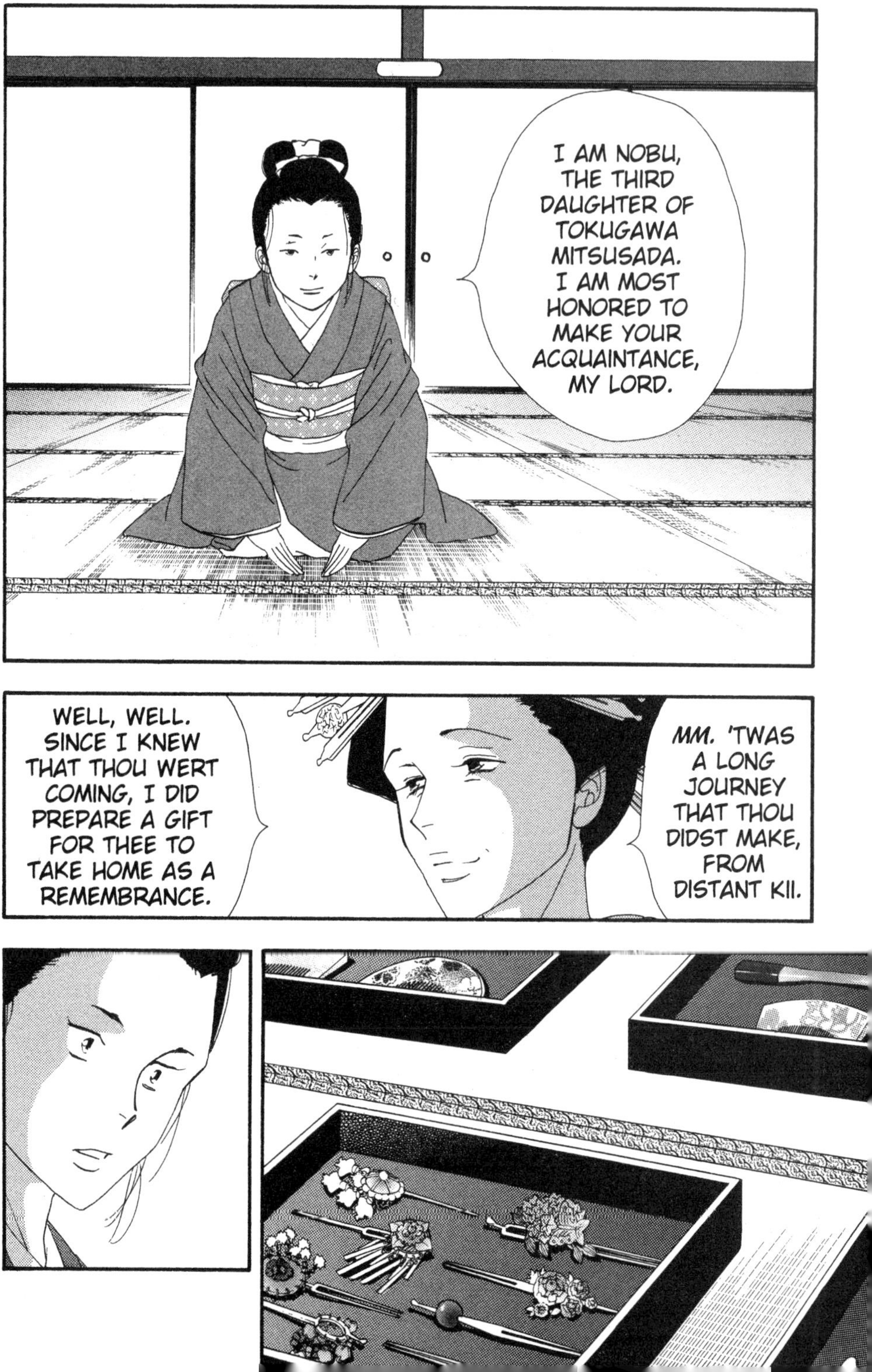
I AM NOBU, THE THIRD DAUGHTER OF TOKUGAWA MITSUSADA. I AM MOST HONORED TO MAKE YOUR ACQUAINTANCE, MY LORD.
MM. 'TWAS A LONG JOURNEY THAT THOU DIDST MAKE, FROM DISTANT KII.
WELL, WELL. SINCE I KNEW THAT THOU WERT COMING, I DID PREPARE A GIFT FOR THEE TO TAKE HOME AS A REMEMBRANCE.

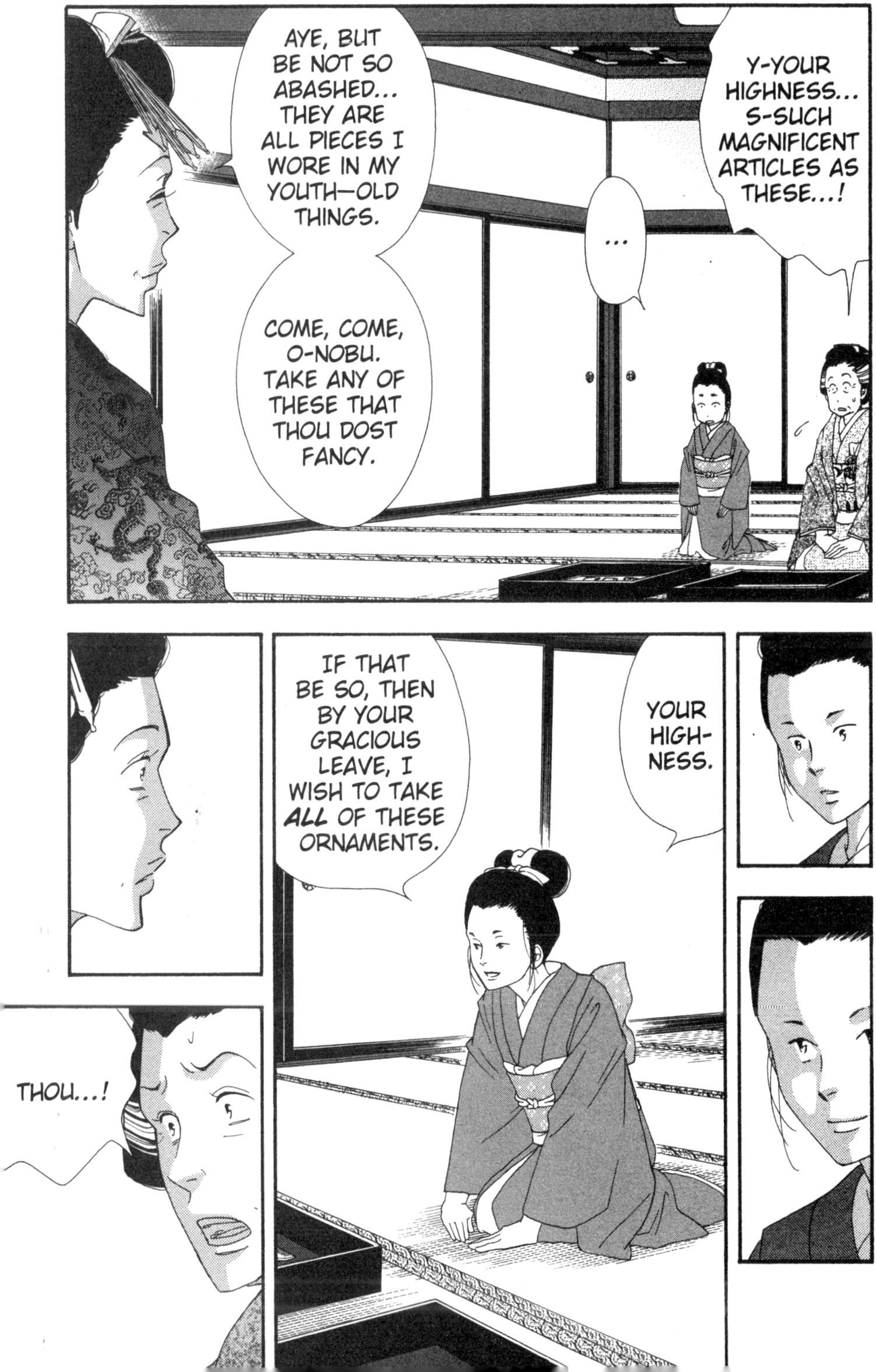
Y-YOUR HIGHNESS... S-SUCH MAGNIFICENT ARTICLES AS THESE...!
...
AYE, BUT BE NOT SO ABASHED... THEY ARE ALL PIECES I WORE IN MY YOUTH—OLD THINGS.
COME, COME, O-NOBU. TAKE ANY OF THESE THAT THOU DOST FANCY.
YOUR HIGH-NESS.
IF THAT BE SO, THEN BY YOUR GRACIOUS LEAVE, I WISH TO TAKE ***ALL*** OF THESE ORNAMENTS.
THOU...!

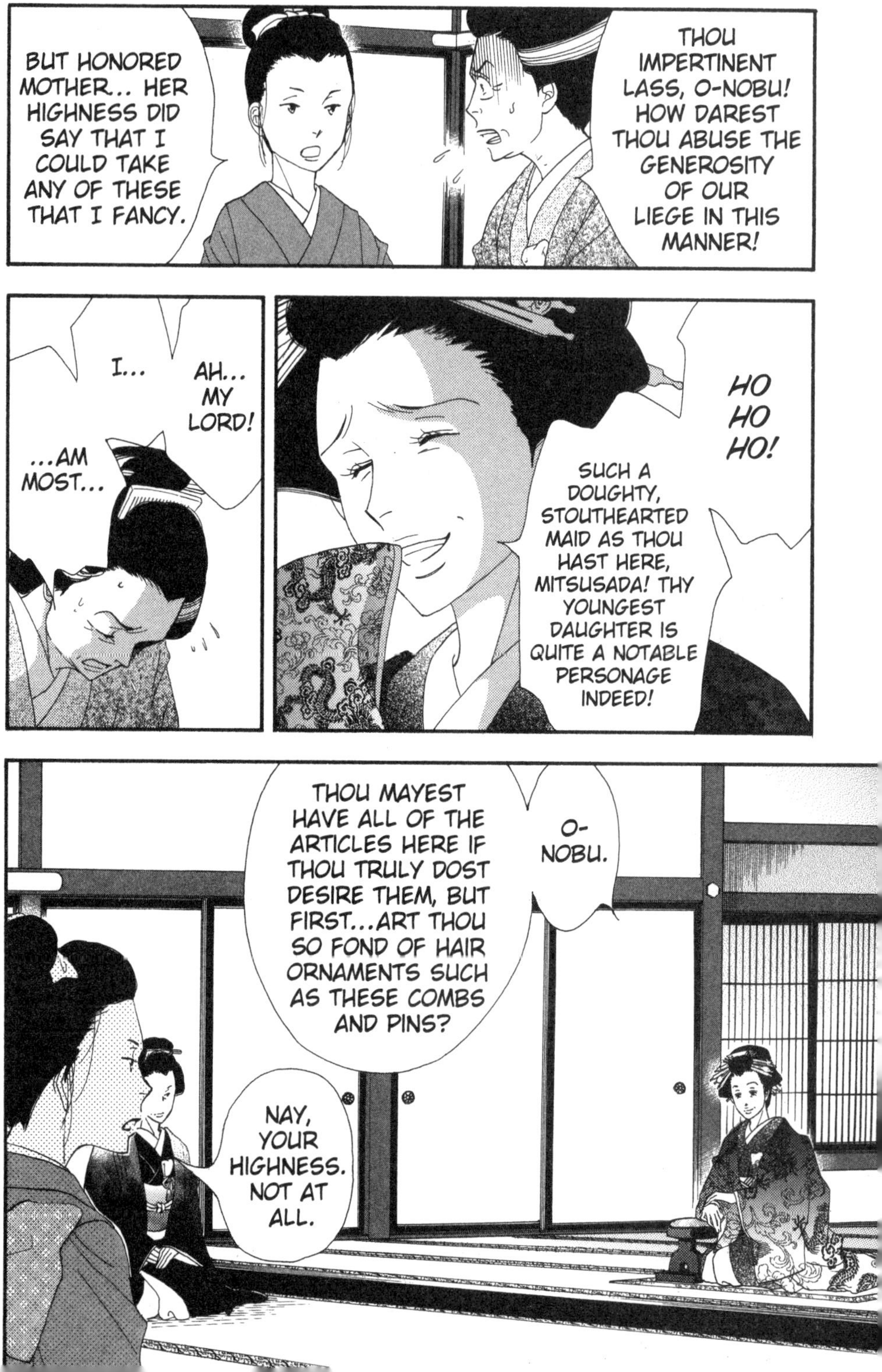
THOU IMPERTINENT LASS, O-NOBU! HOW DAREST THOU ABUSE THE GENEROSITY OF OUR LIEGE IN THIS MANNER!
BUT HONORED MOTHER... HER HIGHNESS DID SAY THAT I COULD TAKE ANY OF THESE THAT I FANCY.
HO HO HO!
SUCH A DOUGHTY, STOUTHEARTED MAID AS THOU HAST HERE, MITSUSADA! THY YOUNGEST DAUGHTER IS QUITE A NOTABLE PERSONAGE INDEED!
AH... MY LORD!
I...
...AM MOST...
O-NOBU.
THOU MAYEST HAVE ALL OF THE ARTICLES HERE IF THOU TRULY DOST DESIRE THEM, BUT FIRST...ART THOU SO FOND OF HAIR ORNAMENTS SUCH AS THESE COMBS AND PINS?
NAY, YOUR HIGHNESS. NOT AT ALL.

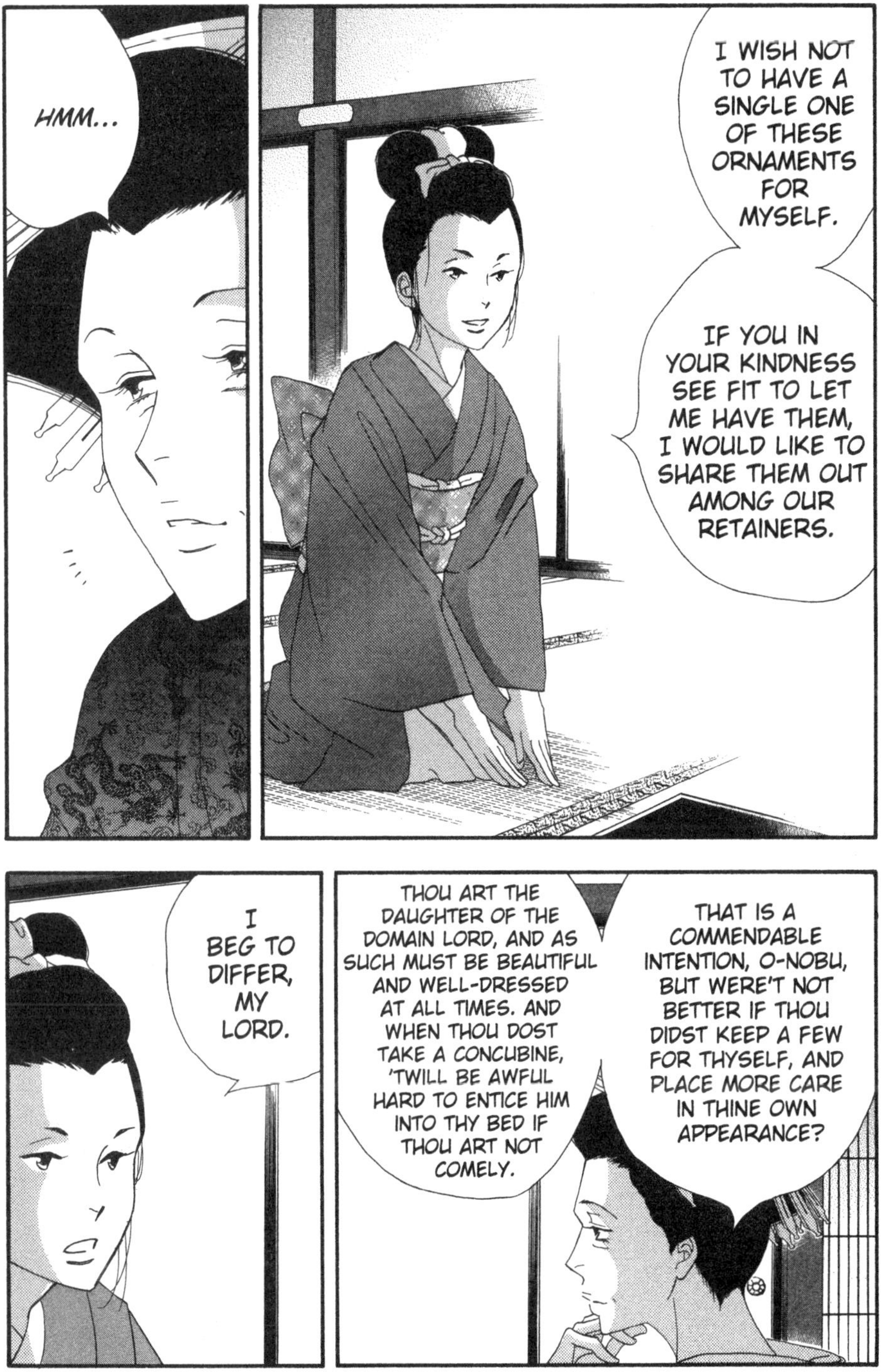
I WISH NOT TO HAVE A SINGLE ONE OF THESE ORNAMENTS FOR MYSELF.
IF YOU IN YOUR KINDNESS SEE FIT TO LET ME HAVE THEM, I WOULD LIKE TO SHARE THEM OUT AMONG OUR RETAINERS.
HMM...
THAT IS A COMMENDABLE INTENTION, O-NOBU, BUT WERE'T NOT BETTER IF THOU DIDST KEEP A FEW FOR THYSELF, AND PLACE MORE CARE IN THINE OWN APPEARANCE?
THOU ART THE DAUGHTER OF THE DOMAIN LORD, AND AS SUCH MUST BE BEAUTIFUL AND WELL-DRESSED AT ALL TIMES. AND WHEN THOU DOST TAKE A CONCUBINE, 'TWILL BE AWFUL HARD TO ENTICE HIM INTO THY BED IF THOU ART NOT COMELY.
I BEG TO DIFFER, MY LORD.

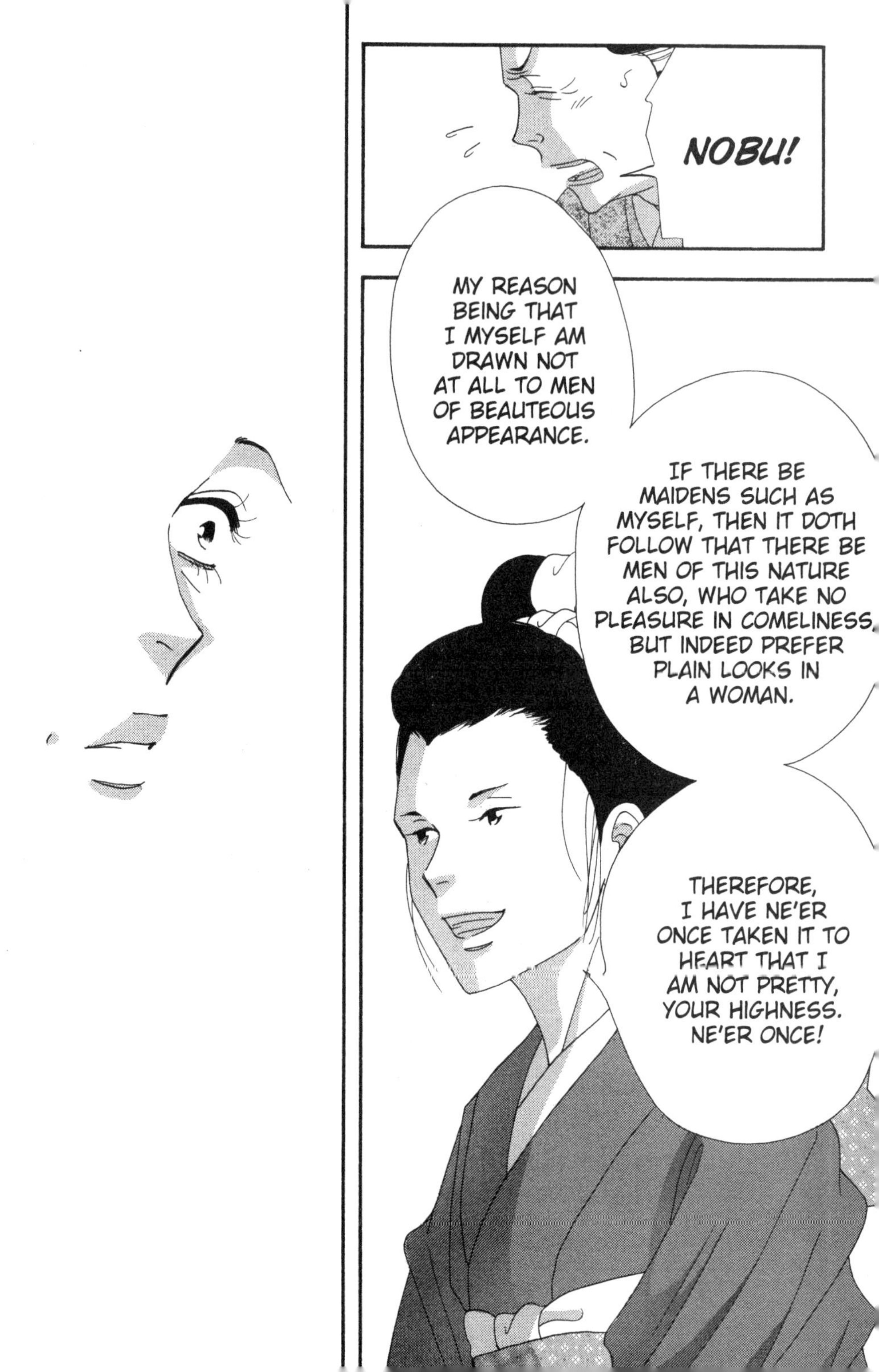
NOBU!
MY REASON BEING THAT I MYSELF AM DRAWN NOT AT ALL TO MEN OF BEAUTEOUS APPEARANCE.
IF THERE BE MAIDENS SUCH AS MYSELF, THEN IT DOTH FOLLOW THAT THERE BE MEN OF THIS NATURE ALSO, WHO TAKE NO PLEASURE IN COMELINESS, BUT INDEED PREFER PLAIN LOOKS IN A WOMAN.
THEREFORE, I HAVE NE'ER ONCE TAKEN IT TO HEART THAT I AM NOT PRETTY, YOUR HIGHNESS. NE'ER ONCE!

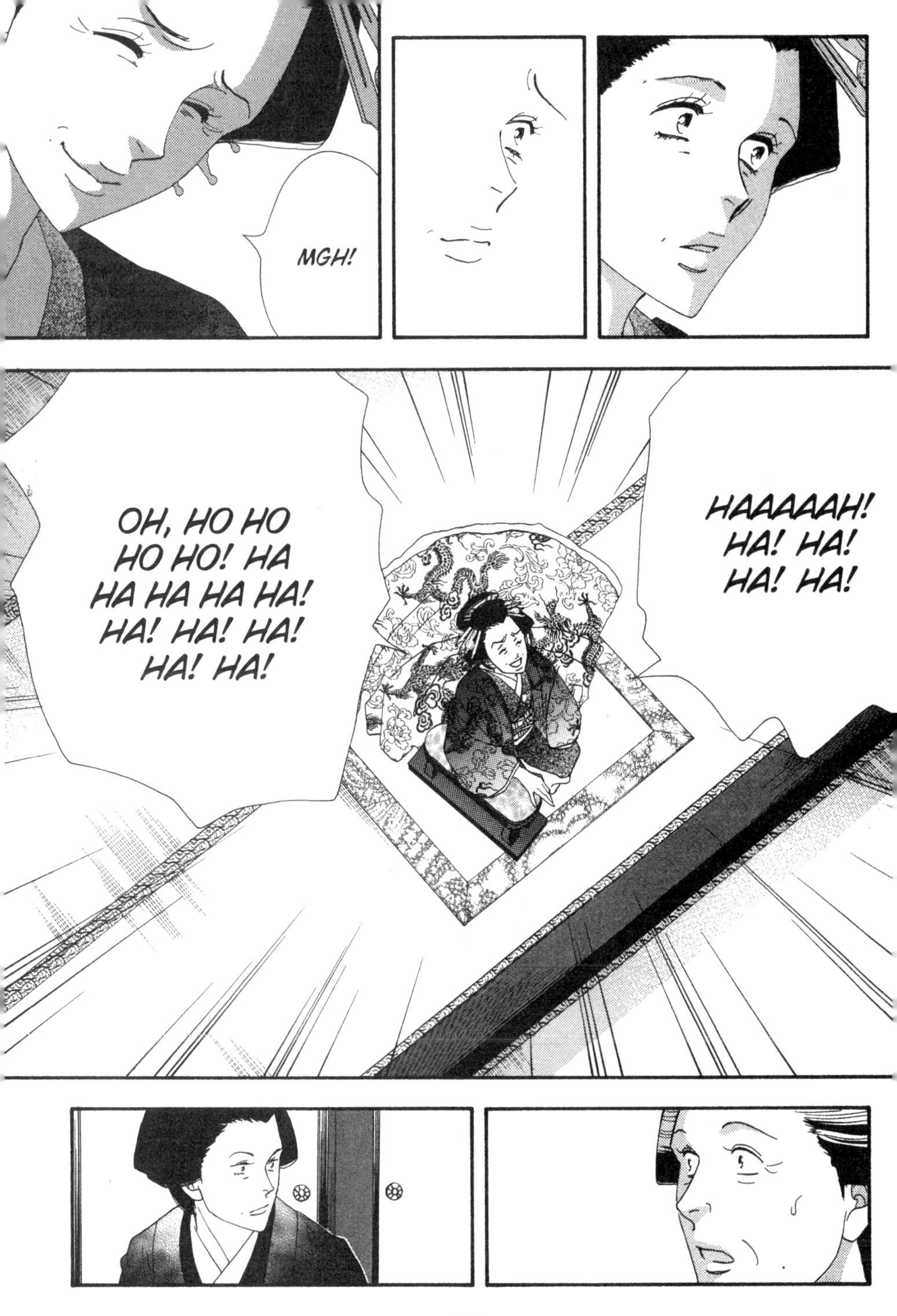
MGH!
HAAAAAH! HA! HA! HA! HA!
OH, HO HO HO HO! HA HA HA HA HA! HA! HA! HA! HA! HA!

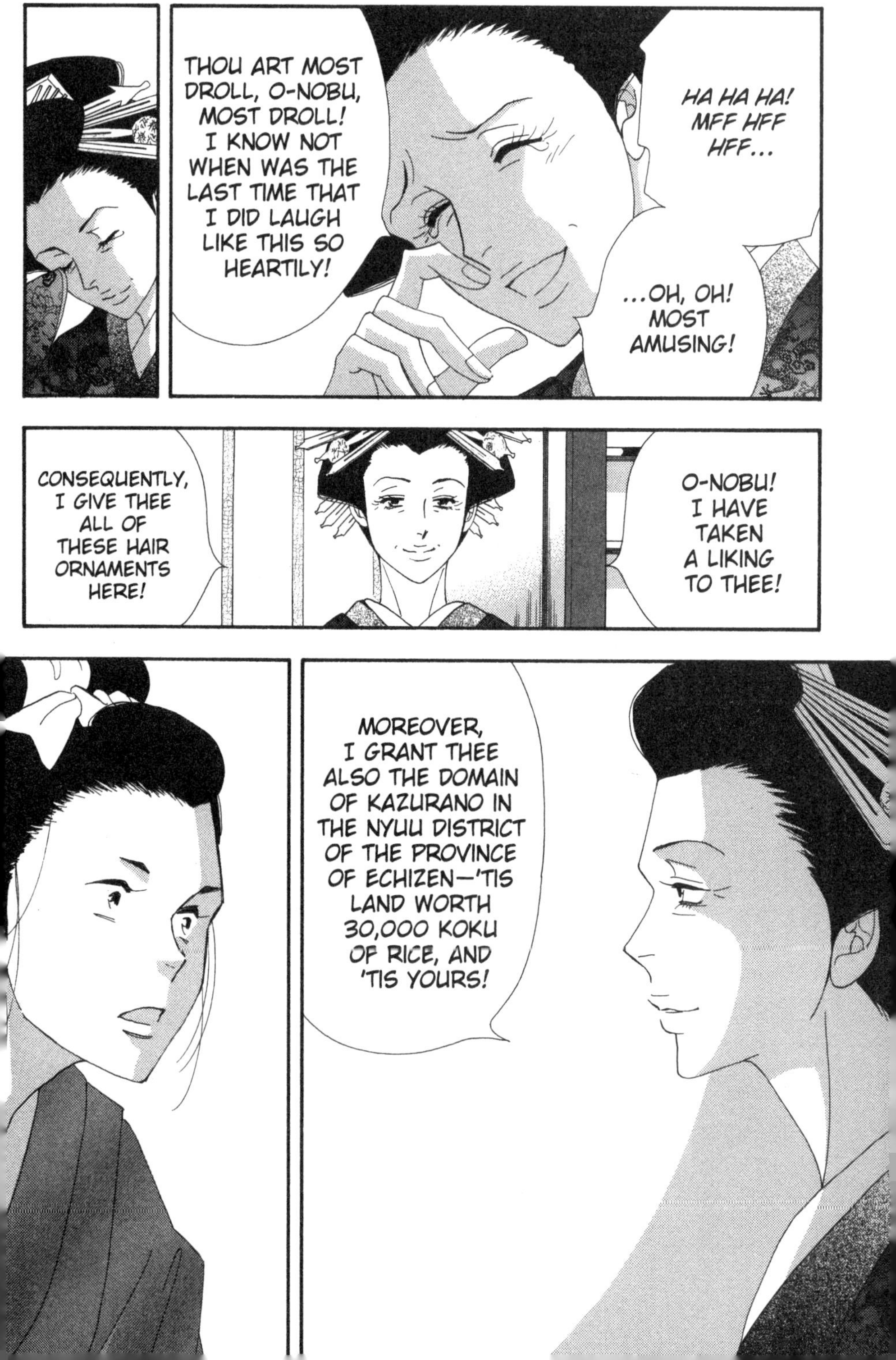
HA HA HA! MFF HFF HFF...
...OH, OH! MOST AMUSING!
THOU ART MOST DROLL, O-NOBU, MOST DROLL! I KNOW NOT WHEN WAS THE LAST TIME THAT I DID LAUGH LIKE THIS SO HEARTILY!
O-NOBU! I HAVE TAKEN A LIKING TO THEE!
CONSEQUENTLY, I GIVE THEE ALL OF THESE HAIR ORNAMENTS HERE!
MOREOVER, I GRANT THEE ALSO THE DOMAIN OF KAZURANO IN THE NYUU DISTRICT OF THE PROVINCE OF ECHIZEN—'TIS LAND WORTH 30,000 KOKU OF RICE, AND 'TIS YOURS!

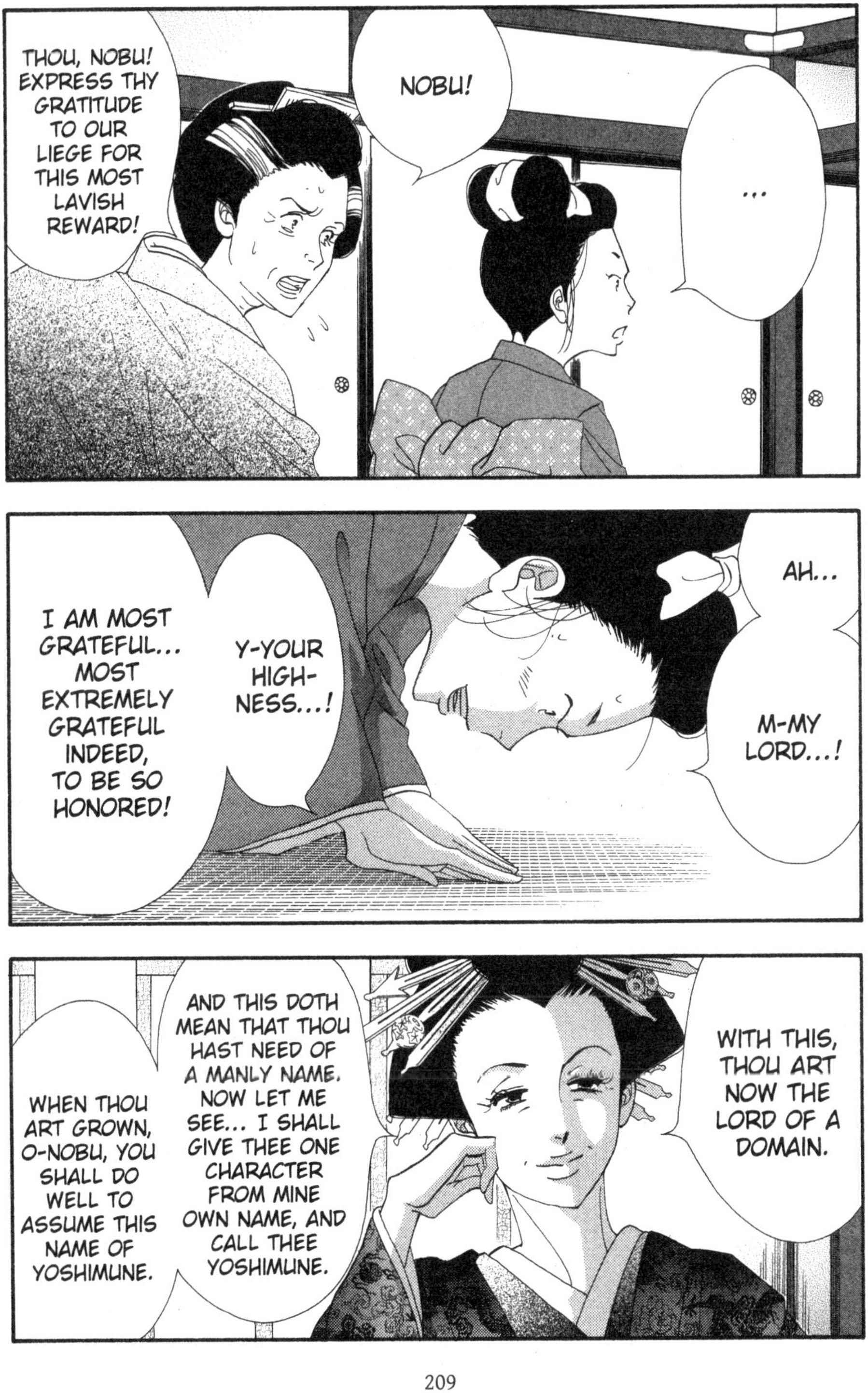
...
NOBU!
THOU, NOBU! EXPRESS THY GRATITUDE TO OUR LIEGE FOR THIS MOST LAVISH REWARD!
AH...
M-MY LORD...!
Y-YOUR HIGHNESS...!
I AM MOST GRATEFUL... MOST EXTREMELY GRATEFUL INDEED, TO BE SO HONORED!
WITH THIS, THOU ART NOW THE LORD OF A DOMAIN.
AND THIS DOTH MEAN THAT THOU HAST NEED OF A MANLY NAME. NOW LET ME SEE... I SHALL GIVE THEE ONE CHARACTER FROM MINE OWN NAME, AND CALL THEE YOSHIMUNE.
WHEN THOU ART GROWN, O-NOBU, YOU SHALL DO WELL TO ASSUME THIS NAME OF YOSHIMUNE.

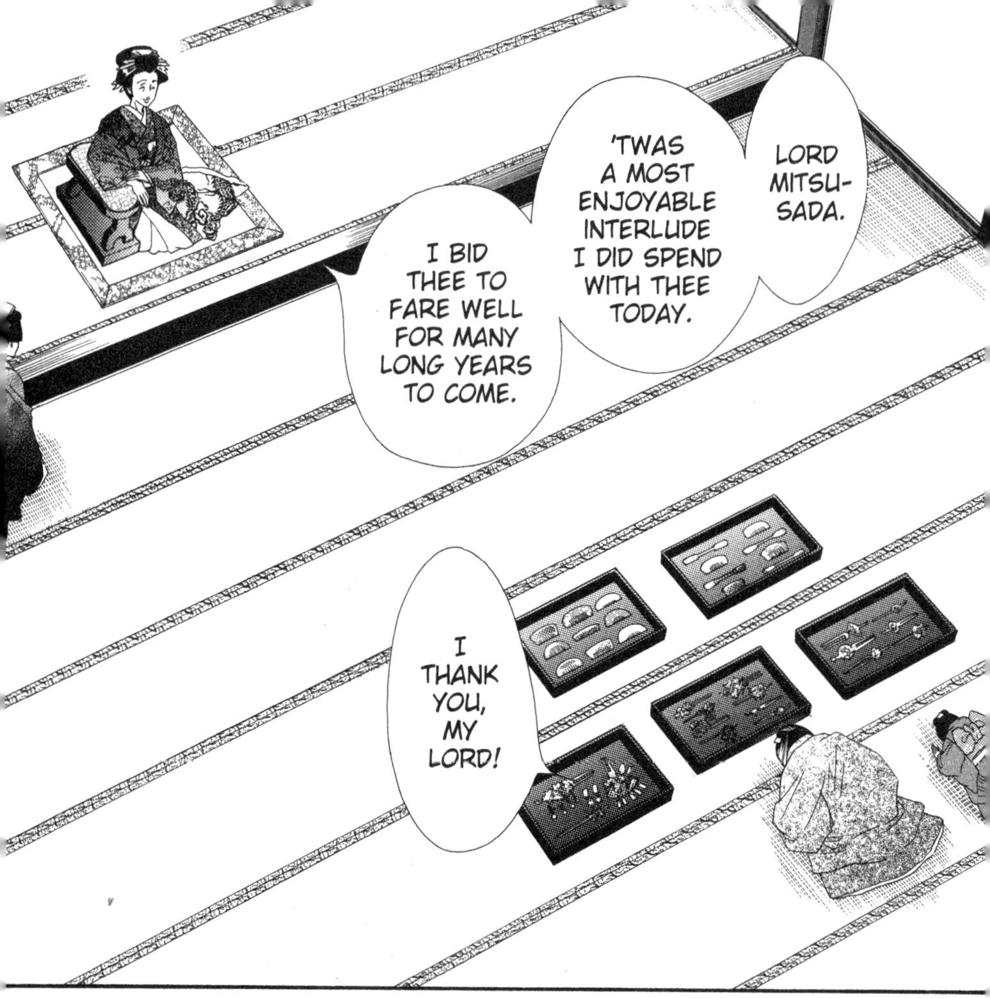
LORD MITSU-SADA.
'TWAS A MOST ENJOYABLE INTERLUDE I DID SPEND WITH THEE TODAY.
I BID THEE TO FARE WELL FOR MANY LONG YEARS TO COME.
I THANK YOU, MY LORD!

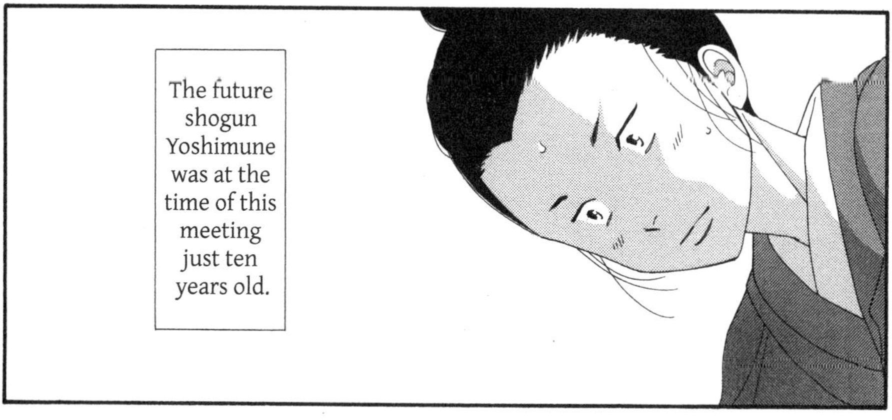
The future shogun Yoshimune was at the time of this meeting just ten years old.

It was the
one and only
time that
Yoshimune
and
Tsunayoshi
came face
to face.

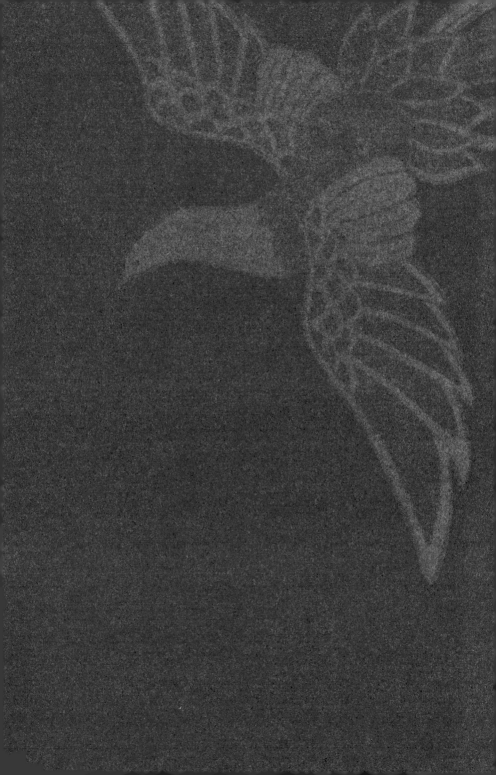

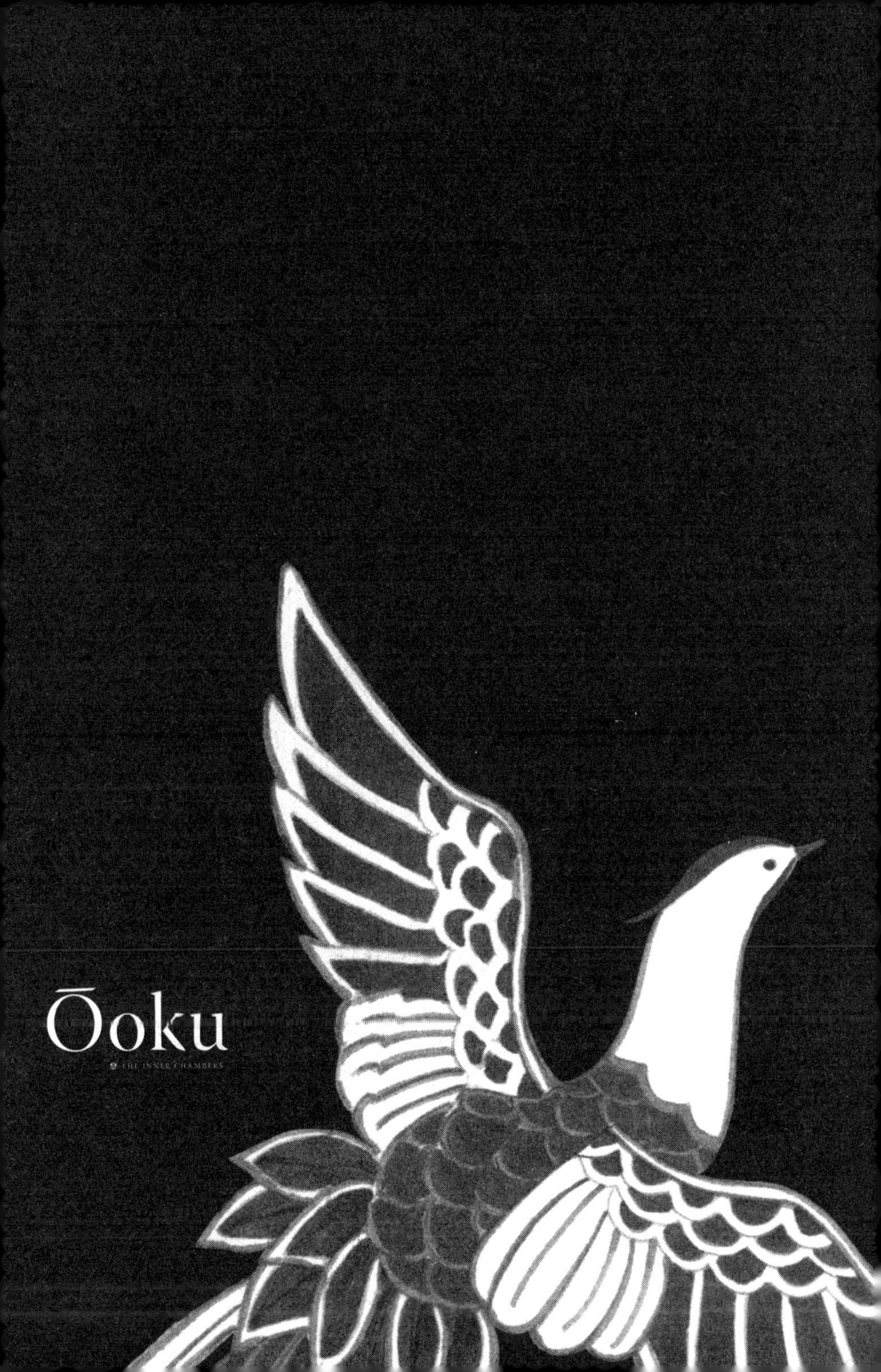
Ōoku
THE INNER CHAMBERS

ŌOKU: THE INNER CHAMBERS

VOLUME 5 · END NOTES

BY AKEMI WEGMÜLLER

Page 13, panel 1 · MIKADO
Another term for the emperor of Japan.

Page 18, panel 2 · SUGOROKU
A Japanese board game.

Page 75, panel 1 · GENROKU ERA
1688–1704. The era marked by the reign of the emperor Higashiyama. It was a time of general prosperity and cultural growth.

Page 81, panel 3 · GOKENIN
Gokenin is the lowest rank of direct vassals to the shogun. They are paid in rice, which is measured in terms of how many people it will feed a year.

Page 98, panel 1 · THE EDICTS ON COMPASSION FOR LIVING THINGS
The historical Tsunayoshi passed these edicts in 1685, which prohibited capturing or killing any animals. Tsunayoshi's astrological sign was the dog, and so dogs were considered especially important.

Page 110, panel 1 · KOJIKI
Literally "Record of Ancient Matters," it is a chronicle from the early eighth century and the oldest known written record in Japan.

Page 113, panel 1 · YOTSUYA, OKUBO AND NAKANO
Suburbs of Edo (Tokyo).

Page 116, panel 1 · HATCHOBORI
A neighborhood in Tokyo.

Page 120, panel 2 · DEN DEN MUSHI MUSHI
The play being performed is a *Kyogen* (a comedic interlude in Noh) called *Kagyu* (The Snail). There are several words for snail in Japanese such as *kagyu*, *katatsumuri*, and *dendenmushi*.

Page 193, panel 1 · FORTY-SEVEN SAMURAI
Based on a historical event that is also called the Ako Incident.

Page 200, panel 1 · KII BRANCH
The three Tokugawa branches (*gosanke*) descended from three of the historical Ieyasu's sons. The branches are the Owari, Mito, and Kii.

Creator Biography

Fumi Yoshinaga

Fumi Yoshinaga is a Tokyo-born manga creator who debuted in 1994 with *Tsuki to Sandaru* (*The Moon and the Sandals*). Yoshinaga has won numerous awards, including the 2009 Osamu Tezuka Cultural Prize for *Ōoku*, the 2002 Kodansha Manga Award for her series *Antique Bakery* and the 2006 Japan Media Arts Festival Excellence Award for *Ōoku*. She was also nominated for the 2008 Eisner Award for Best Writer/Artist.

Ōoku: The Inner Chambers
Vol. 5

VIZ Signature Edition

Story and Art by Fumi Yoshinaga

Translation & Adaptation/Akemi Wegmüller
Touch-up Art & Lettering/Monalisa De Asis
Design/Frances O. Liddell
Editor/Pancha Diaz

Ōoku by Fumi Yoshinaga © Fumi Yoshinaga 2009
All rights reserved. First published in Japan in 2009 by
HAKUSENSHA, Inc., Tokyo. English language translation
rights arranged with HAKUSENSHA, Inc., Tokyo.

The stories, characters and incidents mentioned in this
publication are entirely fictional.

No portion of this book may be reproduced or transmitted
in any form or by any means without written permission
from the copyright holders.

Printed in the U.S.A.

Published by VIZ Media, LLC
P.O. Box 77010
San Francisco, CA 94107

10 9 8 7 6 5 4 3 2 1
First printing, December 2010

www.viz.com   www.vizsignature.com

RATED

PARENTAL ADVISORY
ŌOKU: THE INNER CHAMBERS is rated
M for Mature and is recommended for
ages 18 and up. Contains violence and
sexual situations.
ratings.viz.com

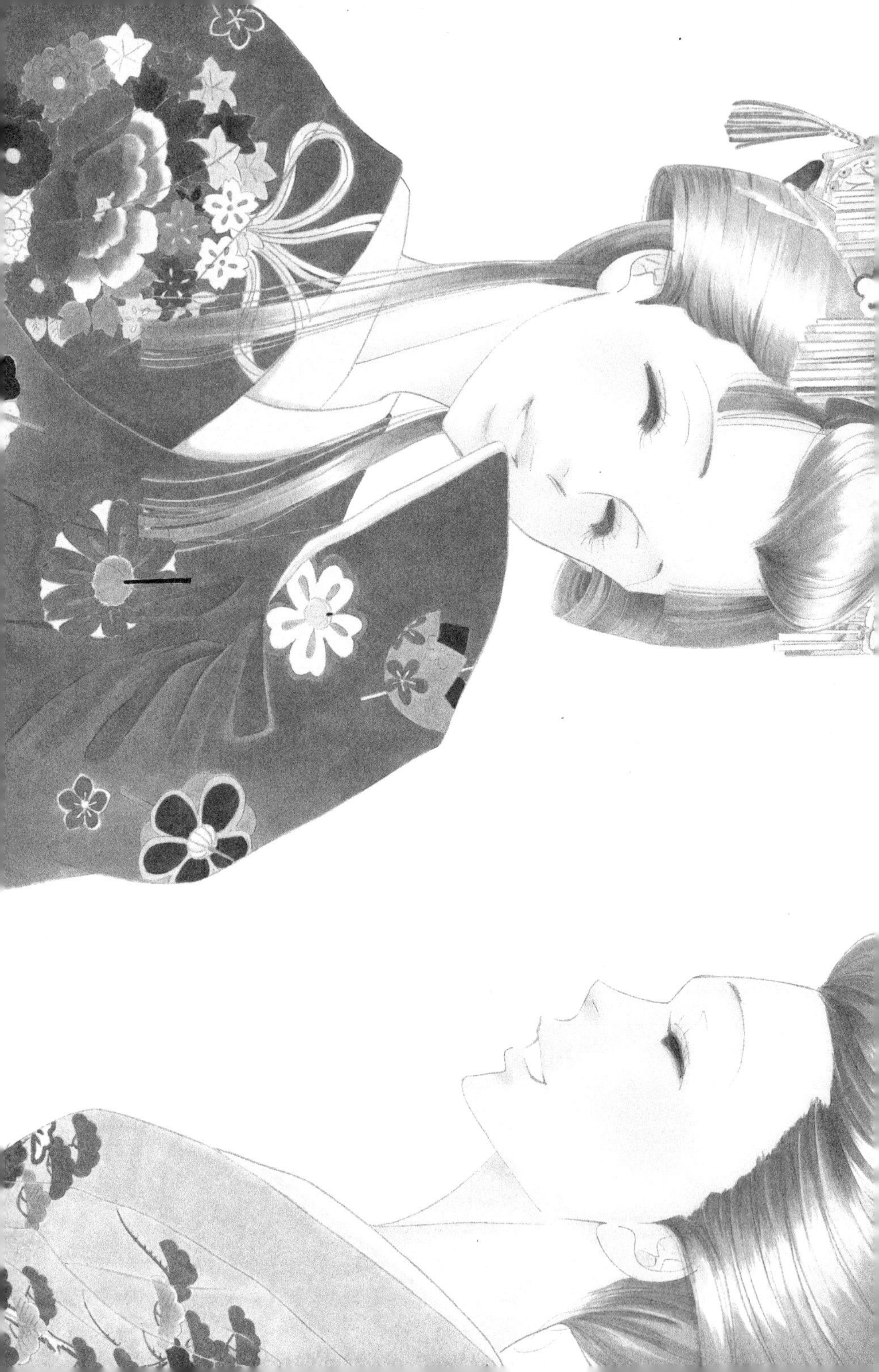

THIS IS THE LAST PAGE.

Ōoku: The Inner Chambers has been printed in
the original Japanese format in order to preserve
the orientation of the original artwork.